Visionary of the Word

Visionary of the Word

Melville and Religion

✦

Edited by Jonathan A. Cook
and Brian Yothers

NORTHWESTERN UNIVERSITY PRESS
EVANSTON, ILLINOIS

Northwestern University Press
www.nupress.northwestern.edu

Printed in the United States of America

10 9 8 7 6 5 4 3 2 1

Library of Congress Cataloging-in-Publication Data

Names: Cook, Jonathan A. (Jonathan Alexander), 1953– editor. | Yothers, Brian, 1975– editor.
Title: Visionary of the word : Melville and religion / edited by Jonathan A. Cook and Brian Yothers.
Description: Evanston, Illinois : Northwestern University Press, 2017. | Includes index.
Identifiers: LCCN 2016031992| ISBN 9780810134256 (pbk. : alk. paper) | ISBN 9780810134263 (cloth : alk. paper) | ISBN 9780810134270 (e-book)
Subjects: LCSH: Melville, Herman, 1819–1891 — Criticism and interpretation. | Melville, Herman, 1819–1891—Religion. | Religion in literature.
Classification: LCC PS2388.R4 V57 2017 | DDC 813.3—dc23
LC record available at https://lccn.loc.gov/2016031992

CONTENTS

Acknowledgments *vii*

Introduction *3*
Jonathan A. Cook and Brian Yothers

Faith, Doubt, Secularization: Transatlantic Contexts

Clarel and the Victorian Crisis of Faith *21*
Jonathan A. Cook

"Change Irreverent": Evolution and Faith in "The Encantadas" and *Clarel* *71*
Eileen McGinnis

Faith among the Weeds: Melville's Religious Wildings beyond These Deserts *97*
Martin Kevorkian

Religious Communities

Melville and the Unitarian Conscience *129*
Dawn Coleman

Melville and the Mormons *159*
Zachary McLeod Hutchins

Melville's Asia, Melville's Missionaries *185*
Brian Yothers

Melville among the Heathens: Religion, Race, and Representation in the South Seas *211*
Richard A. Garner

Free Will and Determinism

Coleridge, Edwards, and the Peculiar Progress of Melville's Free Will Problem *243*
Brad Bannon

"The Apocalypse of Pain": Suffering, Theodicy, and Religious Identity in *Moby-Dick* *265*
Haein Park

Contributors *287*

Index *289*

ACKNOWLEDGMENTS

The editors would first like to thank Steven Olsen-Smith and the Melville Society for the invitation to organize a panel on "Melville and Religion" at the American Literature Association conference in 2010, an invitation that provided the initial impetus for this collection. We are also grateful to Henry L. Carrigan, Gianna Mosser, Anne Gendler, Michael Levine, and Maggie Grossman at Northwestern University Press for their editorial guidance, and to the anonymous readers for the Press for their many useful suggestions. We likewise appreciate the varied work of each of our contributors in opening up new vistas in the study of Melville and religion. Soraya Howard and Maryse Jayasuriya provided encouragement, wisdom, and moral support.

Visionary of the Word

Introduction

Jonathan A. Cook and Brian Yothers

The present volume is designed to address an often neglected subject in contemporary critical approaches to the writings of Herman Melville, namely, the pervasive influence of religion on his fiction and poetry. Throughout his rich and varied literary productions, one finds ample evidence of plots, characterizations, themes, settings, symbolism, imagery, and figurative language principally (but not exclusively) deriving from the Christian Bible and Judeo-Christian tradition, and forming a central part of his essentially syncretic religious imagination. Steeped in the cadences of the King James Bible from his childhood, Melville retained the expressive modes of this influential cultural and linguistic landmark throughout his career, even as he later went on to explore alternative traditions of belief and myth derived from classical Greece and Rome, northern Europe, Polynesia, India, and the Near and Far East. And while he was initially shaped by the severe Calvinistic theology of the Dutch Reformed church of his mother's family, Melville was also keenly interested in the varied forms of contemporary Christianity which included the Unitarianism of his father's and his wife's family (a denomination to which Melville nominally belonged later in his life); the mainline Protestant denominations of Congregationalists, Presbyterians, and Episcopalians; the growing ranks of the Methodists and Baptists; the Catholicism of the nation's swelling immigrant population; and the smaller sects of Quakers, Shakers, Universalists, Adventists, and Mormons, among others.

It is no coincidence in this regard that Melville was born in 1819 into the midst of the country's Second Great Awakening, an era of evangelical revivalism extending from the end of the eighteenth century to the eve of the Civil War, with perhaps its most intensive phase in the 1830s during Melville's teenage years. The era was, in effect, the most Christianized period of the nation's history with respect to church membership and the cultural diffusion of Protestant values. The signs of this evangelical influence extended from the aggressive missionary enterprise that reached around the world—an enterprise that Melville would strongly critique in his first two Polynesian narratives—to the middle-class moral vigilance of the publishing establishment that included the Methodist Harper Brothers who issued most of Melville's books in the United States. Although never apparently experiencing an epochal "conversion" promoted by the many evangelical ministers active at the time, Melville was nevertheless steeped in the various modes of contemporary religious experience and the faith traditions that supported them. Beginning with a youthful immersion in the fearsome rigors of Calvinism and followed by the broadening perspective of global travel as a sailor, Melville moved from adherence to an ecumenical liberal Christianity in his early career to the uneasy religious skepticism of his more mature years—a skepticism that developed a decade before the publication of Darwin's *Origin of Species* in 1859 revolutionized the religious landscape for many of his intellectual contemporaries.

It is thus only by viewing Melville as a product of his intensely religious yet transitional era that we can better understand the prime importance of religious ideas in his writings, notably his obsession with the problem of evil and the formal theological and philosophical issue known as theodicy. By the same token, we may also gain insight into the tenor of Melville's conflicted personal beliefs, as famously recorded in his remarks to Hawthorne in Liverpool in November 1856, when his older friend noted Melville's constant vacillations between the will to believe and a recalcitrant doubt. Such a paradoxical, ambivalent, and skeptical mindset is in fact crucial to understanding his literary oeuvre as a reflection of the conflicted religious trends of his age.

Any study of the subject of Melville and religion must acknowledge the books that shaped his ideas and beliefs on the subject, beginning with the King James Bible. Throughout his life Melville owned multiple copies of this text in various forms, including the capacious 1810 Melville family Bible, the copy of the New Testament and Psalms given to him by his Aunt Jean in 1846, and the Bible and Apocrypha purchased in March 1850 just as he began composition of *Moby-Dick*, likely using John Kitto's popular *Cyclopaedia of Biblical Literature* (1845) as a study aid. (Building on the previous work of Merton M. Sealts Jr., the key resource for Melville's reading and book ownership is the website *Melville's Marginalia Online* created by Steven Olsen-Smith, Peter Norberg, and Dennis C. Marnon.) Melville's limited schooling in New York City, Albany, and Lansingburgh, New York, included the study of classical and Judeo-Christian "antiquities" as well as exposure to the era's pervasive natural theology typified by the writings of the Anglican divine William Paley. To this may be added a likely boyhood reading of Bunyan's *Pilgrim's Progress* as well as some of the various popular juvenile tracts produced by the evangelical publishing establishment at this time. Almost half of American publishing in the first half of the nineteenth century was devoted to sermons, tracts, and other religious matters, and we can assume Melville's familiarity with many now-forgotten aspects of this homiletic tradition.

It is only after taking into account his solid grounding in Protestant religious doctrine and his familiarity with the ambitious goals of the contemporary American missionary enterprise that we can understand the transformative impact of Melville's exposure to the paradisiacal islands of Polynesia which were on the front lines of the Anglo-American missionary effort in the Pacific. This experience showed him the glaring disparity between the ostensibly benevolent goals of the missionary endeavor and the coercive conversion of native peoples, with Christianity spearheading an invasion of lethal diseases and commercial exploitation. Since many of the early chroniclers of Polynesian cultures were missionaries, it was inevitable that Melville relied on them for otherwise unobtainable information; hence he freely drew on the American missionary Charles S. Stewart's *A Visit to the South Seas* (1831) and the English missionary William Ellis's three-volume *Polynesian Researches* (1829–32) as key resources for the composition of *Typee*, *Omoo*, and *Mardi*.

Following his return home from the Pacific in October 1844, Melville began formulating his memorable four weeks in July 1842 as a captive of "cannibals" in the Marquesas Islands into a literary narrative revealing his ambivalent attitude toward the European and American invasion of this pristine, highly sexualized "heathen" culture. From his first work of narrative fiction Melville was thus imbued with a sense of the relativity of cultural and religious values, even as he retained an awareness of the universally valid ethical idealism embodied in the life and mission of Christ. After his assumption of the role of professional author with the publication of *Typee* in 1846, Melville's feast of reading in the later 1840s launched him on a wide-ranging quest for greater knowledge of religious and philosophical traditions, among which the writings of Montaigne and Sir Thomas Browne provided influential examples of the fideist skepticism that pervades *Mardi* and would continue to influence his writing throughout much of his career. Another key influence on his creative development at this time was his reading of Plato, whose persuasive idealism and model of intellectual inquiry in the figure of Socrates helped shape Melville's mental growth beyond the limited realms of Christian dogmatism. During these years Melville also likely read Robert Chambers's *Vestiges of the Natural History of Creation* (1844), a widely known work of popular science setting forth an evolutionary narrative of the origins of the solar system and the earth's varied life forms, with species developing according to the laws of nature—the beginning of Melville's self-education in science, as reflected in several chapters of *Mardi*. It is also during the composition of *Mardi* that Melville read Charles Darwin's *Journal of Researches* (1839), now generally entitled *The Voyage of the Beagle*, with its record of the natural history of many of the South American regions Melville had seen as a whaleman, notably the Galapagos Islands, with their challenge to orthodox Christian ideas of natural theology and divine benevolence.

An epochal new phase of Melville's intellectual development came with his 1849 acquisition of a multivolume edition of Pierre Bayle's *Critical and Historical Dictionary*, which provided a plethora of information on the varied religious traditions, notably Gnosticism and Zoroastrianism, that formed an essential background for the writing of the religiously heterodox *Moby-Dick*.

He likely supplemented his knowledge of Gnosticism and early Christianity at this time through a reading of the retired Harvard Divinity School professor Andrews Norton's *Evidences of the Genuineness of the Gospels* (1837, 1844). Melville thus apparently came to his religious skepticism through the influence of Montaigne and Bayle rather than (as might be expected) through Hume, the leading skeptic of English philosophy, whose *Natural History of Religion* he might have also read. In *Moby-Dick* Melville also left a record of the crucial impact that Shakespearean drama had on his creative life in the late 1840s, particularly the playwright's treatment of the problem of evil in his great tragedies; Shakespeare accordingly became his literary ideal of an impartial, non-doctrinal "truth," as he reported in letters to his close New York friend Evert Duyckinck in 1849, and in his rhapsodic 1850 review of Hawthorne's *Mosses from an Old Manse*. By the same token, Melville's extensive reading (and rereading) of the great poetic epics by Homer, Virgil, Dante, Camões, Tasso, and Milton included an appreciation of their grounding in classical and Christian religious traditions, with *The Divine Comedy* and *Paradise Lost* providing lifelong literary models and influences. Other important literary discoveries at this time were the essays of Emerson and the writings of Goethe, both of whom acted as influential conduits of European romanticism and its liberalized religious agenda. The first part of Goethe's *Faust*, along with Marlowe's *Dr. Faustus*, would offer Melville important prototypes for his anti-Christian overreacher Ahab. Melville's familiarity with the tenets of pantheism and the philosophy of Spinoza, as attested by the chapter on "The Mast-Head" in *Moby-Dick*, was also likely grounded in his reading of Goethe along with information gleaned in Bayle's *Dictionary*, later augmented by a reading of Matthew Arnold's analysis of the Jewish philosopher in the *Essays on Criticism*.

By the early 1850s, Melville was probably one of the most well-informed students of Protestant history and theology in the country, and his fiction amply reflected this fact. In addition to his immersion in a broad array of European classics and leading literary contemporaries, Melville in the later 1840s and early 1850s assimilated the writings of various seventeenth- and eighteenth-century English divines and religious writers such as Robert Burton, Thomas Fuller, Joseph Butler, and Joseph Priestley, as well as the works of prominent colonial and contemporary American theologians, principally Cotton Mather, Jonathan Edwards, and William Ellery Channing. The influential critical and religious writings of Samuel Taylor Coleridge, beginning with the *Biographia Literaria* (1817) and likely including other key works such as the *Aids to Reflection* (1825), also provided Melville with an awareness of contemporary idealist tradition and the revolution in religious thought emanating from the writings of Kant and other Germans such as the liberal romantic-era theologian Friedrich Schleiermacher, with his influential grounding of Christianity in emotional dependency. Melville's reading of Carlyle's *Sartor Resartus* (1833–34) and *On Heroism, Hero-Worship, and the Heroic in History* (1841) similarly broadened his understanding of the contemporary romantic revaluation of religion beyond the narrow dogmatisms of the institutional church. The strong impact of Hawthorne's fiction, beginning with Melville's reading and review of *Mosses from an Old Manse* in the summer of 1850, also contributed to his knowledge of the formative impact of Calvinism on the New England character and culture, which was largely his own inheritance. By the same token, Melville's interest in contemporary American religious sects is indicated by his purchase that same summer of a volume of Shaker theology (which, like his knowledge of Hawthorne's fiction, would be of use in writing *Moby-Dick*), just before he moved with his family to Pittsfield, Massachusetts, in order to finish his whaling novel and be close to his new literary icon Hawthorne.

Like many of his peers, Melville was strongly receptive to classical texts and traditions, some of which helped to shape his evolving religious views. He accordingly assimilated the Roman Stoicism of Seneca, Marcus Aurelius, and Epictetus, and enjoyed the skeptical debunking of the Greek gods in the satirical dialogues of Lucian. As a student of the debate over religious faith in the classical world and its relevance to the nineteenth century, Melville read some of the essays of Plutarch (notably "On Isis and Osiris" and "On the Cessation of the Oracles") and the writings of Cicero on the chief classical philosophical schools and their associated religious beliefs, *On the Nature of the Gods* and the *Tusculan Disputations*. As we know from one of his annotations in Hazlitt, Melville was also acquainted with Lucretius's poetic exposition of the materialist Epicurean philosophy, *On the Nature of Things*, with its promotion of Democritus's atomic theory and its dismissal of the gods from any active role in human destiny. At some point he may have also read the Scottish freethinker Frances Wright's evocation of Epicurus and his school in her popular defense of the philosopher in *A Few Days in Athens* (1822). The lifelong devotion to the Greek and Roman classics that began in Melville's youth continued in his later reading in the 37-volume *Harper's Classical Library* which he acquired in early 1849; henceforth the Greek tragedians, with their disparate ideas of divine justice, would further expand his awareness of Western religious traditions and play a role in his writings beginning with *Moby-Dick* and *Pierre*.

Having moved beyond the rigid Calvinism of his youth to the liberal Unitarianism of his young adulthood, Melville now entered a period of religious disenchantment, fueled by his increasingly disillusioned view of the corruption of institutional Christianity in the Anglo-American world. Melville's *Pierre* and his short fiction of the 1850s, with their pervasive use of Christian symbolism, are largely shaped by his conflicted and disintegrating Protestant faith, as the example of Christ's life and teachings became overshadowed by a growing array of doubts about their relevance to the modern world. This development received its fullest fictional expression in the stringent apocalyptic satire of *The Confidence-Man*, with its encyclopedic range of dialogues on a wide array of contemporary religious, philosophical, and cultural topics. Melville's trip to Europe and the Levant in late 1856 and early 1857 seems to have confirmed his alienation from traditional forms of Christian faith, and his anguish over a lost belief is evident in the disparaging comments in his travel journal on Barthold Georg Niebuhr, author of a well-known demythologizing *History of Rome* (English translations 1827 and 1847–51), and David Strauss, author of a notorious *Life of Jesus* (English translation by George Eliot in 1846) showing the mythic messianic overlay given to the human founder of Christianity. It is thus clear that by the mid-1850s Melville was well aware of the higher criticism of the Bible emanating from Germany, along with the general historical revaluation of the Christian Bible that was taking place at this time. His likely reading of Edward Gibbon's *Decline and Fall of the Roman Empire* sometime in the 1850s would also have given him a skeptical view of the opportunistic spread of Christianity throughout the ancient world. In any case, the journal of his tour of the Holy Land in early 1857 is marked by revulsion at the arid terrain, sectarian discord, endemic poverty, and vulgar commercialization of the sacred sites of Christianity, and the growing signs of its seeming obsolescence in the modern secularized world.

In the early 1860s, Melville's absorption in the tragedy of the American Civil War, together with his experiments with the new medium of poetry that eventuated in the publication of *Battle-Pieces and Aspects of the War*, temporarily placed him in the conservative position of a patriot poet imbued with the spirit of the nation's Christian heritage. But the later 1860s, a time of crisis in Melville's personal life in New York City with his son's suicide and his wife's near-abandonment, also brought a renewal of his interest in a more ecumenical Christianity as well as in non-Western theologies and mythologies. Post-Civil War America was increasingly fascinated by the religious traditions of Asia, as demonstrated by a sharp rise in the number of books and articles devoted to this subject, notably the Unitarian James Freeman Clarke's pioneering comparative study *Ten Great Religions* (1876). Melville probably read Thomas Maurice's seven-volume *Indian Antiquities* (1793–1800) during his extensive reading in the late 1840s, for a basic knowledge of some of the features of Hinduism is evident in *Moby-Dick*. In any case, we have direct testimony to Melville's mysteriously acquired expertise in the subject in an account by Maunsell B. Field, in his *Memories of Many Men and Some Women* (1874), of a conversation between Melville and Oliver Wendell Holmes, likely taking place during the summer of 1854 at the latter's Pittsfield residence and witnessed by Field and the artist Felix Darley: "At length, somehow, the conversation drifted to East India religions and mythologies, and soon there arose a discussion between Holmes and Melville, which was conducted with the most amazing skill and brilliancy on both sides. It lasted for hours, and Darley and I had nothing to do but listen. I never chanced to hear better talking in my life. It was so absorbing that we took no note of time, and the Doctor lost his dinner, as we lost ours."

It is important to recall that the academic discipline of comparative religion was being created in the 1860s and 1870s, a development for which Melville created a contemporaneous literary monument in his multicultural epic poem *Clarel* based on his excursion in early 1857 through the Holy Land. As a preparation for writing this work, with its probing exploration of Jewish, Muslim, and Christian faith traditions—the latter subsuming the dominant Protestant, Catholic, and Orthodox variants—Melville's reading included a number of contemporary British travel narratives and area studies, including William H. Bartlett's *Forty Days in the Desert* (1840), *Walks about the City and Environs of Jerusalem* (1844), and *The Nile Boat; or, Glimpses of the Land of Egypt* (1849); Eliot Warburton's *The Crescent and the Cross* (1844); Arthur P. Stanley's *Sinai and Palestine* (1856); John Macgregor's *The Rob Roy on the Jordan, Nile, Red Sea, and Gennesareth* (1869); and Edward H. Palmer's *The Desert of the Exodus* (1871). These titles were being added to a likely earlier acquaintance with the American explorer John Lloyd Stephens's *Incidents of Travel in Egypt, Arabia Petraea, and the Holy Land* (1837), and the American Protestant missionary William McClure Thomson's best-selling *The Land and the Book* (1859), as well as the French skeptic Constantine de Volney's *Travels through Syria and Egypt* (1787) and the French romantic poet and politician Alphonse de Lamartine's *Pilgrimage to the Holy Land* (1835).

The poetry and prose of Matthew Arnold, with their complementary reassessments of the contemporary crisis of Christianity, also became an important influence on Melville at this time. Melville attentively read Arnold's poetry, whose melancholy mood at the modern retreat of Christian faith would match his own, as dramatized in *Clarel*. He also read Arnold's *Essays in Criticism* in the 1860s, and *Literature and Dogma*, *Culture and Anarchy*, and *Mixed Essays* in the early 1880s, all of which would attempt to purge Christianity of its obsolete dogmas and superstitions, in keeping with Arnold's modernizing liberal perspective. We do not know when Melville read Darwin's *Origin of Species* (1859), but he was clearly aware of the revolutionary implications of this work for the future of Christianity, as is evident in the polyphonic religious debates of *Clarel*.

During the last decade of his life, in the late poetry and the unfinished *Billy Budd*, Melville also produced his final literary explorations of the religious obsessions that had shaped his creative life, balancing skepticism about Christianity with nostalgia for a lost ethical ideal in the person of Christ. At the same time, the philosophical writings of Arthur Schopenhauer, with their positive depiction of the central tenets of Hinduism and Buddhism and their emphasis on the universality of human suffering, became a major source of interest for him. Melville's knowledge of Buddhism had earlier been expanded by his reading of William Rounseville Alger's *The Solitudes of Nature and of Man* (1867) and Sir Edwin Arnold's popular long poem on the Buddha's life and thought, *The Light of Asia* (1879). On the other hand,

Melville's familiarity with the spiritual traditions of medieval Islamic Persia, another important influence on his late meditative poetry, can be linked to his concurrent reading of Sa'di's *Gulistan, or Rose Garden*, as well as Edward Fitzgerald's popular translation of a selection of Omar Khayyam's mystical quatrains, the *Rubaiyat*. These influences would be added to an earlier acquaintance with the popular fourteenth-century poet and mystic Hafiz, with his lyrics on love, wine, and faith, and attacks on religious hypocrisy.

The obscurity into which Melville had fallen as a man of letters in the years leading up to his death in 1891 is confirmed by the fact that he had to publish the poems in *John Marr and Other Sailors* and *Timoleon* himself, while leaving a collection of *Weeds and Wildings* in manuscript along with the nearly completed *Billy Budd*. In this late poetry, ecumenical spiritual currents drawn from historical Christianity, medieval Islam, Buddhism, and classical Greece and Rome (among others) freely mix in a nondogmatic meditative manner, with the Epicurean model of a tranquil mind, undistorted by pain or fear, likely acting as his ruling ideal. In *Billy Budd*, however, Melville revisited the central Christian myth of the Fall in a final exploration of the problem of evil that shaped many of his earlier writings. Not surprisingly, at his death Melville's library in his New York City residence contained a large number of texts on religion and theology, which his wife turned over to a Brooklyn bookseller, A. F. Farnell, and being of no current value, they were subsequently scrapped for wastepaper, with no surviving record of their identity.

This final fact should remind us that our knowledge of Melville's reading on religious subjects and the evolution of his religious beliefs are necessarily limited and schematic. The former is dependent on the miscellaneous and incomplete record of book purchases and gifts, borrowings from his friend Evert Duyckinck, the New York Society Library, and other libraries in New York and Boston, and the evidence presented in his published writings and surviving correspondence. There is relatively limited data on Melville's reading in the Anglo-American periodical literature of his day, starting with the journals in which he was published or otherwise interested, notably the *Literary World*, *Harper's Monthly*, *Putnam's*, and *The Democratic Review*; he also occasionally consulted the great British quarterlies of the era such as *Blackwood's*, the *Edinburgh*, the *Quarterly*, and the *Westminster Review*. What is certain is that Melville was one of the best-informed students of religion of his generation and had a profound knowledge of the Christian Bible on a level with that of the professional clergy. In addition, the conflicted evolution of his beliefs was representative of many English and European intellectuals and literary figures of the era, revealing the ecumenical range of his thought in comparison with the relative provincialism of his own native culture.

If Calvinism was the formative influence on his early intellectual and emotional development, skepticism characterized Melville's mature attitude toward religion, while his manifest awareness of the varied religious traditions of the modern global community provided him with an appreciation of religion as a universal human construct and concern. For this reason, Melville's conflicted religious development and its influence on his writing commands attention as an anticipation of contemporary debates on multiculturalism and the controversial role of religion in the twenty-first-century world, particularly in relation to conflicts between Christianity and Islam. With the rapid growth of new scholarly work on American religion, biblical studies, the history of religion, and comparative religion, critics are likely to gain new insights into Melville's fiction and poetry should they familiarize themselves with these developments. By the same token, the central influence of religion on Melville's writing potentially confirms modern psychological research on the existence of an evolutionarily rooted "faith instinct," and the paradoxical nature—both redemptive and destructive—of its tenacious hold on human consciousness. But most important of all, recognizing the protean role of religion in Melville's writing restores an essential feature to a literary artist whose full recognition has always been an evolving process of readerly education.

The early critical response to Melville's writings highlighted his engagement with religious questions. During his own lifetime, Melville received a number of harsh reviews in the missionary press and religious press more broadly, with both groups correctly identifying Melville as a critic of many aspects of nineteenth-century Christianity. Even Melville's friend and sometime literary advisor Evert Duyckinck, an orthodox Episcopalian, could express discomfort with the frequent heterodoxy of Melville's religious imagination, warning him privately and, later, in print that he might go too far in his religious speculations, as expressed in Duyckinck's *Literary World* review of *Moby-Dick*.

The "Melville Revival" of the 1920s was likewise marked by religious resonances. Raymond Weaver routinely described Melville in terms usually reserved for a prophet in *Herman Melville, Mariner and Mystic*, and D. H. Lawrence both ridiculed what he saw as Melville's American moralism and praised Melville's psychological and spiritual insights. As the Melville Revival progressed beyond the initial rediscovery of *Moby-Dick*, the newly published *Billy Budd* presented Melville scholars with a significant new text to assimilate, and one way in which numerous scholars attempted to understand Melville's great posthumous novella was viewing it as a kind of spiritual final "testament." For E. L. Grant Watson, who coined the term "testament of acceptance" to describe Melville's presumed message in *Billy Budd*, the novella represented Melville's turn toward faith in his last days. For others, however, Melville's concluding masterpiece revealed irony, skepticism, and a subversive critique of religious, social, and political institutions.

The first attempt to speak authoritatively about Melville's religious ideas throughout his career appeared in 1943 with the publication of William Braswell's *Melville's Religious Thought*, which sorted through the varied religious perspectives that Braswell found in Melville's fiction. Braswell mainly was concerned with Melville's relationship to Protestant Christianity, but later in the decade Geoffrey Stone would address Melville's religious development from a Catholic standpoint, and William Ellery Sedgwick and Ronald Mason both wrote more broadly philosophical and religious studies of Melville's work in the 1940s as well. Nathalia Wright's *Melville's Use of the Bible* (1949) demonstrated beyond any doubt that Melville's language was suffused with biblical rhetoric and allusion, and it remains the foundational study of the biblical roots of Melville's prose. One of Wright's important contributions was to show Melville's particular interest in the Hebrew Bible (known to Christians as the Old Testament) and thus expand the discussion of Melville's religious thought and allusions beyond Christianity.

As part of the surge in published Melville scholarship in the 1950s surrounding the centennial of the publication of *Moby-Dick*, Lawrance Thompson expressed a renewed and intensified acknowledgment of the skeptical elements of Melville's approach to Christianity in his *Melville's Quarrel with God* (1952), which argued that Melville was throughout his career an outspoken critic of Christianity and the Christian God but had to mask his rebellion in layers of irony and indirection. In an influential article, Millicent Bell in 1950 identified Pierre Bayle's *Dictionary* as a major source for Melville's philosophical and religious pluralism and skepticism, particularly in relation to *Moby-Dick*. In a different vein, James Baird's *Ishmael* (1956) provided a probing survey of Melville's Pacific writings and *Moby-Dick* (along with a host of other American and European authors) in the context of Jungian archetypes and the modern history of primitivism. Toward the end of the decade, Milton R. Stern's *The Fine Hammered Steel of Herman Melville* (1957) identified a formal movement toward naturalism in Melville's fiction that also had implications for religious readings of his work.

The 1960s witnessed the development of a more complex approach to Melville's treatment of religious issues. An important foundational piece of scholarship from this era was Dorothee Metlitsky Finkelstein's *Melville's Orienda* (1961), which collated Melville's numerous references to the Middle East, North Africa, and Asia, making plain how widely Melville had read both in the history of Judaism and Christianity and in such faiths as Islam, Hinduism, Buddhism, and Zoroastrianism. H. Bruce Franklin's *The Wake of the Gods* (1963) traced Melville's use of a wide range of European, Near Eastern, and Asian mythologies across his most artistically ambitious novels, while Edgar Dryden's *Melville's Thematics of Form* (1968) sought broadly to identify how Melville dealt with questions of truth, knowledge, and values throughout his career and thus inevitably engaged the religious dimensions of Melville's work. Dryden's study forecast a tendency in the 1970s, 1980s, and 1990s to deal with Melville's treatment of religion in the context of intellectual and cultural history more broadly construed, often with a theoretical inflection in keeping with the ebb and flow of post-structuralism, New Historicism, and cultural studies across the period. The studies most explicitly concerned with religious or philosophic themes in Melville's fiction from the period were T. Walter Herbert's *"Moby-Dick" and Calvinism: A World Dismantled* (1977), Rowland Sherrill's *The Prophetic Melville* (1979), Bainard Cowan's *Exiled Waters: "Moby-Dick" and the Crisis of Allegory* (1981), James Duban's *Melville's Major Fiction: Politics, Theology, and Imagination* (1983), John Wenke's *Melville's Muse* (1993), and Christopher Sten's *The Weaver God, He Weaves* (1996). A concurrent development was the increased attention to Melville's poetry, with its plethora of religious themes, by Vincent Kenny, Joseph Knapp, William Shurr, and William Bysshe Stein in the late 1960s and early 1970s.

The past two or three decades of scholarship on Melville and religion have been marked by the same eclecticism that has characterized literary studies more broadly, even as it has continued the expansion of both topics and texts that have been deemed worthy of inquiry in Melville criticism. Melville's last full-length novel, *The Confidence-Man*, provides an example of the dazzlingly syncretic possibilities of Melville's religious imagination, as Jonathan A. Cook's *Satirical Apocalypse* (1996) demonstrates through its identification of Menippean satire and Christian apocalyptic as central formal and thematic sources for the narrative. The growth of studies devoted to *Clarel* provides another case in point. Stan Goldman's *Melville's Protest Theism* (1993) uses Melville's long poem *Clarel* to suggest a Jewish theological paradigm rooted in the Hebrew Bible for Melville's mature artistic and religious imagination. Hilton Obenzinger's *American Palestine* (1999) finds a stringent critique of the covenantal dimensions of American civic and religious culture in *Clarel*. William Potter's *Melville's "Clarel" and the Intersympathy of Creeds* (2005) proposes the pioneering discipline of comparative religion as a major source for Melville's longest and most ambitious poem. Brian Yothers's *The Romance of the Holy Land* (2007) finds a cultural and religious pluralism in the poem reflecting strands of American culture resistant to being absorbed into a single covenant tradition. Finally, in a selective examination of Melville's fiction, Jamie Lorentzen's *Sober Cannibals, Drunken Christians: Melville, Kierkegaard, and Tragic Optimism in Polarized Worlds* (2010) lays the groundwork for a comparative analysis of the writings of Kierkegaard and Melville as masters of social criticism and ironic indirection in their dissenting views of nineteenth-century Christianity.

The presence of the Bible and other faith traditions in Melville's literary imagination has likewise been the subject of several recent studies. Robert Milder's *Exiled Royalties: Melville and the World We Imagine* (2005) gives a wider scope to the question of belief and secularization in Melville's work throughout his career than had previously been attempted. Robert Alter's *Pen of Iron* (2010), Ilana Pardes's *Melville's Bibles* (2008), and Jonathan A. Cook's *Inscrutable Malice* (2012) all consider Melville's treatment of the Hebrew and Christian scriptures in *Moby-Dick*. Alter gives a characteristically lucid exposition of Melville's creative adaptation of biblical rhetoric, while Pardes explores the nineteenth-century exegetical traditions relating to five key Old Testament figures in *Moby-Dick*. Cook, on the other hand, provides a comprehensive exposition of the mythological and theological origins of Melville's pervasive use of the Christian Bible in the novel, focusing in particular on Melville's thematic paradigms of theodicy, as exemplified by the book of Job, and eschatology, as found in various parts of both testaments, chiefly the books of Daniel and Revelation.

Melville's use of religion in his writings also plays an important role in recent books by contributors to the present volume. Dawn Coleman's *Preaching and the Rise of the American Novel* (2013) analyzes Father Mapple's sermon and other sermonic forms and influences in *Moby-Dick*, while Martin Kevorkian's *Writing Beyond Prophecy: Emerson, Hawthorne, and Melville after the American Renaissance* (2013) examines *Clarel* in the context of the author's investment of religious authority in his late poetry. Finally, Brian Yothers's *Sacred Uncertainty: Religious Difference and the Shape of Melville's Career* (2015) provides a comprehensive survey of Melville's awareness in his writings of a religiously pluralistic universe, paying particular attention to his annotations of his readings on religious subjects. Melville thus continues to loom large for scholars devoted to broad questions of religion and literature in America and provides fertile ground for investigations of his complex, idiosyncratic religious representations.

The essays in the present volume, then, arrive at an opportune moment in the century-long arc of Melville scholarship and criticism. As a man and writer Melville was inescapably engaged with the varied aspects of Christian tradition in nineteenth-century America, and several of the essays here accordingly examine Melville's relationship to his native religious culture. Others consider Melville's thought in relation to transatlantic currents in literature, philosophy, and theology. All track Melville's development as a thinker and writer informed by diverse religious themes and ideas throughout his long career. Part 1 accordingly concerns Melville's treatment of religious doubt and secularization in the context of nineteenth-century transatlantic intellectual and literary history; part 2 deals with Melville's interactions with distinctive religious traditions within nineteenth-century American culture; and part 3 deals with Melville's treatment of the specific theological issues of determinism and free will.

In the opening essay of part 1, Jonathan A. Cook demonstrates that Melville's later religious interests encompass transatlantic manifestations of faith and doubt. Using a broad variety of Victorian literary texts and writings on religion to situate *Clarel* in the contemporary debate over the legitimacy of Christian faith, Cook sheds new light on the characters of Clarel, Rolfe, Derwent, and Ungar in relation to comparable British authors and ideas during the middle decades of the nineteenth century. Cook situates *Clarel* in an Anglophone literary and religious context that supports the critical claim for the poem as the most representative literary product of the so-called Victorian Crisis of Faith. Scholars have long noted that Melville was influenced by a number of leading Victorian writers, notably Carlyle, Ruskin, and Arnold, but this essay is the first to map Melville's extensive engagement with transatlantic dialogues on faith and doubt.

Melville's engagement with Darwinian scientific thought has likewise formed the basis for several efforts by scholars considering Melville's relationship to secularization, faith, and doubt, but the subject has remained relatively underexplored. In the second essay in this section, Eileen McGinnis treats Melville's dialogue with Darwin (pre-*Origin of the Species*) in "The Encantadas" and (post-*Origin of the Species*) in *Clarel*. McGinnis finds that "The Encantadas" constitutes a dialogue with Darwin's *Journal of Researches* that alternately satirizes and adapts Darwin's developing understanding of evolutionary biology. Drawing on the work of historians of science, McGinnis finds as much continuity as rupture between Melville's pre- and post- *Origin of the Species* engagement with Darwinian thought.

Perhaps no portion of Melville's body of work has suffered more relative neglect than the poetry of his late years. Several modern interpreters—notably John Bryant, William B. Dillingham, Robert Milder, and Douglas Robillard—have found the unpublished *Weeds and Wildings Chiefly, with a Rose or Two* to be an important terminal instance of Melville's lifelong engagement with religious and philosophical questions. Martin Kevorkian reads this collection of late poetry in relation to Hawthorne's private commentary on Melville's religious beliefs and tracks the concurrent influence of Dante's *The Divine Comedy*, and especially the *Paradiso*, which provides a necessary intertext for understanding these poems.

The essays in part 2 concern Melville's engagement with various American religious communities. As with the transatlantic faith-doubt crisis, Melville's engagement with these communities (as opposed merely to bodies of doctrine) has been often invoked in passing but rarely analyzed in depth. Perhaps no American religious group has a more evident claim to Melville than the Unitarians, and perhaps no claim has been more neglected with the exception of Walter D. Kring's brief study *Herman Melville's Religious Journey* (1997) building on his discovery of Melville's membership in the Church of All Souls in New York City after the Civil War. Dawn Coleman works to remedy this neglect in her essay on Melville and the Unitarian conscience. Through a careful reading of both Unitarian beliefs and Melville's literary works, Coleman challenges the conventional view that Melville's relationship to the faith of his father and his wife was largely oppositional. In addition to adding substantially to Melville's intellectual biography, Coleman provides illuminating readings of several of Melville's works, notably *Pierre* and *Billy Budd*, in light of questions of conscience.

If Melville's connection with Unitarianism forms part of his family history, his connection with the Church of Jesus Christ of Latter-day Saints consists of an extended pattern of awareness and allusion. Zachary Hutchins takes up the matter of Melville's interest in the contentious history and alternative scriptures of this homegrown religious group throughout his career. Hutchins pays particular attention to possible connections with the Book of Mormon in *Mardi*, a novel that has long been recognized as a vital part of Melville's development as a religious and philosophical thinker, and his antithetical evaluations of Mormonism in *Pierre* and *Clarel*, which postdate the emergence of polygamy as the focus of national attention on Mormonism.

Drawing on Melville's early novels and later poetry, Brian Yothers regards Melville's representations of missionaries as more complex and ambivalent than has previously been recognized; moreover, Melville's treatment of missionaries cannot be fully understood without considering the many allusions to Asia and Asian religious traditions in Melville's body of work. To that end, Yothers begins with the depiction of Nehemiah, the millenarian Protestant missionary in *Clarel*. Yothers suggests that reading Melville's engagement with missionaries backwards across his career, and forward to his later poetry, through the lens provided by the character of Nehemiah reveals much about the nuances of Melville's engagement with a variety of literary cultures and communities, including missionaries and sailors. The intersecting strands of the missionary encounter and the cross-cultural encounter with Asia are never absent over the course of Melville's career.

Melville's vexed relationship to Christian missions also forms an important backdrop for the last essay in this section in which Richard A. Garner considers Melville's treatment of the relationship between Christian and non-Christian religious traditions primarily in his early Polynesian narratives. Garner accordingly addresses the confrontation between Christianity and indigenous religious faiths in *Typee* and *Omoo* while demonstrating the significance of this opposition for an understanding of *Moby-Dick* that does justice to the tensions in Melville's treatment of religion, race, and politics.

The essays in part 3 are dedicated to the religious and philosophical issue of free will and determinism. Perhaps no doctrinal tradition in Christianity has been more frequently invoked in considering the religious dimensions of Melville's work than Calvinism, especially since T. Walter Herbert's study on Calvinism and *Moby-Dick*. At the heart of these explorations is the fascination with questions of determinism and free will that spanned Melville's career. In the opening essay of this section, Brad Bannon points out that through the romantic poet and religious thinker Samuel Taylor Coleridge, Melville found a resource providing a counterpoint to the Calvinist theology of Jonathan Edwards in addressing the perennially beguiling issue of determinism. By considering Melville in relation to both Edwards and Coleridge, Bannon shows how Melville could be engaged by religious impulses that run counter to each other, adding to our understanding of how Calvinism and romanticism interact in Melville's body of work, particularly in "Bartleby, the Scrivener" and *Billy Budd*.

In the final essay of the collection, Haein Park confronts Melville's ambivalent relation to Calvinism, suffering, and theodicy in *Moby-Dick*. A long-standing tradition in Melville scholarship has associated *Moby-Dick* with the biblical book of Job, and recent works by Ilana Pardes and Jonathan A. Cook have provided distinctive views of how this association plays out. Park extends this work while drawing on Charles Taylor's widely influential study *A Secular Age* (2007). Park takes issue with readings of *Moby-Dick* that see Melville moving in a direct line from theocentric belief to anthropocentrism and instead seeks to account for the pressures placed on theodicy by contemporary revisions to Edwardsian Calvinism, thus revising our understanding of Melville's perceptions of the problem of suffering within the nineteenth-century American religious scene.

In one of the most evocative moments in *Moby-Dick*, Ishmael reflects upon the "fountain" that proceeds from the whale's blowhole. Considering the whale's spray as a visible corollary to the invisible truths of the spiritual world, Ishmael reflects that the light shining through the mist of the whale's fountain is suggestive of his own mind: "Doubts of all things earthly, and intuitions of some things heavenly; this combination makes neither believer nor infidel, but makes a man who regards them both with equal eye" (374). Ishmael's reflection indicates something important about Melville's treatment of religion. The critique of religious dogmatism that informs much of Melville's work is a critique of the limits of human knowledge more generally; hence Ishmael's "doubts of all things earthly." The impulses toward transcendence that also run through his writings are qualified equally: his "intuitions of some things heavenly" are necessarily incomplete and uncertain. Taken as a whole, the essays in this collection offer a selection of innovative approaches while offering the potential to suggest wide-ranging new directions in Melville scholarship. As such, these essays balance doubt and intuition, varieties of belief and taxonomies of unbelief, in a manner reminiscent of Ishmael's luminous observations and apprehensions.

Visionary of the Word takes its name from a passage in part 1 of *Clarel*, in a scene describing the obscure dwelling place of the elderly American missionary and millenarian Nehemiah, who has become Clarel's guide around the holy sites of Jerusalem:

> With these be hearts in each degree
> Of craze, whereto some creed is key;
> Which, mastered by the awful myth,
> Find here, on native soil, the pith;
> And leaving a shrewd world behind—
> To trances open-eyed resigned—
> As visionaries of the Word
> Walk like somnambulists abroad. (1.21.40–47)

Unlike the "crazed" and "tranced" captives of various forms of modern belief described here, Melville's view of religion, evoked in his fiction and poetry, was an "open-eyed" evaluation of the role of religious faith in human affairs, as transformed by his imagination; the sublime logos of Christianity was thus transmuted into the compelling words and ideas of his literary creations. And while Melville may have been "mastered" by the "awful myth" of Calvinism in his youth, his subsequent intellectual development allowed him freely to move both inside and outside the belief systems of Christianity in order to grasp the essential ideas of other systems of faith. It is from this unique vantage point that Melville proved to be a masterful literary visionary of the word.

Faith, Doubt, Secularization: Transatlantic Contexts

Clarel and the Victorian Crisis of Faith

Jonathan A. Cook

In November 1856 while on his way to tour the Holy Land—an experience that would ultimately lead to the composition and publication of *Clarel* two decades later—Melville stopped in Liverpool, England, to visit his sometime literary friend Nathaniel Hawthorne, whom he had not seen in almost four years. As many commentators have noted, Hawthorne's account of Melville's visit provides us with the best historical account of Melville's unsettled religious beliefs, or more precisely, his habitual skepticism punctuated by a compulsive desire for faith. The most important part of Hawthorne's journal entries on Melville's visit was based on a conversation the two had while sitting on the sand hills outside Liverpool where Hawthorne was the United States consul:

> Melville, as he always does, began to reason of Providence and futurity, and of everything that lies beyond human ken, and informed me that he had "pretty much made up his mind to be annihilated"; but still he does not seem to rest in that anticipation; and, I think, will never rest until he gets hold of a definite belief. It is strange how he persists—and has persisted ever since I knew him, and probably long before—in wandering to-and fro over these deserts, as dismal and monotonous as the sand hills amid which we were sitting. He can neither believe, nor be comfortable in his unbelief; and he is too honest and courageous not to try to do one or the other. If he were a religious man, he would be one of the most truly religious and reverential; he has a very high and noble nature, and better worth immortality than most of us.[1]

Despite their frequent appearance in discussions of Melville and religion, the full implications of Hawthorne's comments here have still not been adequately evaluated or explored. The most generally overlooked fact about Hawthorne's candid evocation of Melville's religious doubts is that the encounter is taking place in England, a country where, unlike the United States, the confession of such doubts was an increasingly frequent occurrence in the 1840s and 1850s, as the lives and writings of such eminent Victorians as Carlyle, Tennyson, Ruskin, Eliot, Arnold, Clough, and Froude, among others, all attest. Indeed, such confessions of doubt or unbelief would not be heard in America until a decade or two later, and they would never attain the prominence or critical mass that they did in England. In addition, Melville's quasi-Calvinistic speculations on the influence of "Providence and futurity" on human destiny, as Hawthorne noted, concluding with the statement that Melville had "pretty much made up his mind to be annihilated," indicate that Melville had given up on the idea of a Christian afterlife and hence on a formal doctrinal adherence to Christianity. Such a confession was in fact not uncommon in an age and nation that, in the words of one intellectual historian of Victorian England, was "morbidly preoccupied with personal immortality."[2]

On the other hand, Hawthorne's reference to Melville's penchant for metaphysical speculation, all geared toward the identification of "a definite belief" but involving chronic and depressive "wandering to-and fro over deserts" of such speculation, was in fact symptomatic of the younger writer's skeptical mindset while also being uncannily anticipative of the book-length poem Melville would compose based on his forthcoming visit to the Holy Land—a poem in which Hawthorne himself would figure as the model for an outwardly alluring but psychologically troubled artist figure, Vine.[3] Thus, while Hawthorne was providing posterity with a succinct portrait of Melville as a neurotic Victorian doubter who was nevertheless worthy of immortality, Melville himself would eventually produce a more extensive and ambivalent portrait of his older friend wandering the Holy Land under the shadow of a comparable spiritual malaise. Finally, Hawthorne's paradoxical assertion that Melville could "neither believe, nor be comfortable in his unbelief"—that Melville was, in short, torn between the classic Victorian antinomies of head and heart, reason and emotion—was adduced as a sign that Melville was intellectually "honest and courageous," whereas in the immediately preceding sentence in his account, Hawthorne considered his Berkshire friend's obsession with religious metaphysics as "dismal and monotonous as the sand hills amid which we were sitting." Clearly, a philosophically and theologically conservative Hawthorne might have felt as potentially ambivalent about the problem of modern Christian faith as Melville, had Hawthorne given himself the intellectual latitude of his younger friend.[4]

These remarks are offered by way of introduction to a discussion of the religious thematics of *Clarel* in the context of the so-called Victorian Crisis of Faith, a cultural phenomenon for which Melville created perhaps the single most cogent Anglo-American literary formulation, and he paradoxically did so as an American writer who shared many of his Victorian peers' religious preoccupations. So while later nineteenth-century American literary figures such as James Russell Lowell, Henry Adams, Charles Eliot Norton, Ambrose Bierce, Stephen Crane, and Mark Twain all might share some of Melville's doubts about the benevolence of the Judeo-Christian deity, the divinity of Christ, or the moral value of contemporary Protestant Christianity, and all might visit or live in England for extended periods and so share Melville's transatlantic perspective; nevertheless, for the depth and sophistication of Melville's literary explorations of faith and doubt in *Clarel* we must turn to his English peers for anything comparable. Hence despite the fact that there is only one Englishman, the Anglican clergyman Derwent, among the characters in the poem, as compared to the sizable group of Americans (Clarel, Nehemiah, Nathan, Agar, Ruth, Rolfe, Vine, and Ungar); nevertheless, the central theological and philosophical dilemmas of the poem are more closely allied to historical developments in mid-Victorian England than to related trends in postbellum America.[5]

As is generally recognized, Melville likely assimilated the melancholy tone and religious concerns of some of Arnold's poetry for the creation of *Clarel*; but it is less clear which other Victorian literary figures shared or contributed to the broad cultural, philosophical, and theological subject matter evident in his long narrative poem set in the Holy Land, about which scores of travel narratives had been written but little in the way of poetry or fiction in England or America.[6] For this reason we must turn to a broad range of representative expressions of religious doubt in the varied writings—poetry, fiction, and literary prose—of the mid-Victorian period in order to gain a fuller idea of *Clarel*'s transatlantic contexts. It is ironic that Melville made the most cheerful, optimistic, and progressive-minded figure in the poem an Englishman since these were the traits often given to nineteenth-century Americans, while he represented the major American characters—Clarel, Rolfe, Vine, and Ungar—as skeptical or deeply troubled by the spectacle of religious decline in the manner of many contemporary English writers and intellectuals. While identifying the Broad Church affiliation of the poem's representative English clergyman, Derwent, and the recognizable shape that this gives his characterization, this essay will also analyze how the characterization of Clarel expresses the religious melancholy of such poets as Tennyson, Arnold, and Clough; how the figure of Rolfe evokes the ideas of such Victorian freethinkers as Leslie Stephen and John Stuart Mill as well as the religious nostalgia of Arnold; and how the portrait of the Confederate veteran Ungar recalls the reactionary conservatism of Carlyle. By examining these and other parallels, we will discover how extensively *Clarel* reflects many of the larger religious and intellectual currents of his age emanating from England.[7]

Victorian Religion and the Crisis of Faith

It is a central paradox of the era that the development of religious skepticism and agnosticism in nineteenth-century Britain occurred in the midst of a larger long-term Protestant revival that attained a pervasive influence in Victorian culture. As in America, an upsurge of evangelicalism led to unprecedented levels of church affiliation, and for many of the same historical reasons. Thus, the alarming example of an atheistic Revolutionary France in the 1790s and the ensuing Napoleonic Wars provided a strong political catalyst for the renewed embrace of traditional Christian faith at the start of the nineteenth century. In addition, the retreat of an Anglican monopoly on faith through such parliamentary actions as the repeal of the Test and Corporation Acts in 1828 (ending the requirement that all government officials take Anglican communion), Catholic emancipation in 1829, Jewish emancipation in 1845 and 1858, and the disestablishment of the Anglican Church in Ireland in 1871 led to a more competitive environment in which the Nonconformist denominations—notably Methodists (in many varied forms), Baptists, Presbyterians, Congregationalists, Unitarians, Quakers, and Roman Catholics—vied for worshippers with the state-sponsored church. Anglicanism itself was divided into the parties of Low Church evangelicals, Broad Church liberals, and High Church conservatives, all of whom at mid-century composed a little over half the churchgoing population. Facilitating the spread of evangelical faith in both nation and empire were the revolutions in transportation and print technology promoting the unprecedented spread of religious literature and missionary outreach at the same time that the movement for social and moral reform advanced, eventually leading to the Reform Bill of 1832, the Slavery Abolition Act of 1833, and a host of later reforms in the voting franchise, social welfare, education, and trade. Many members of the aristocracy and leading figures of government—notably the Seventh Earl of Shaftesbury, Robert Peel, William Gladstone, and Queen Victoria—were ardent believers and set influential examples of philanthropy and devotion.[8]

As in America, too, the Victorian evangelical revival led to an intensified interest in the Holy Land as well as in the fate of the Jews and their possible restoration to Ottoman-controlled Palestine, in keeping with New Testament prophecy. Faced with a newly resurgent Anglo-Catholicism and the threat of domination from Rome, British Protestants promoted the emergence of a Christian Zionism and philo-Semitism focused on the Holy Land, while British imperial interests sought to ensure a measure of control over affairs in Ottoman Palestine in competition with the other Great Powers of France, Prussia, Austria, and especially Russia, against whom England, France, and the Ottoman Turks fought the Crimean War in 1854–56. The first British consul was sent to Jerusalem in 1838 to facilitate diplomatic communications and service the rise of religious tourism, and over the next decade Prussia, France, the United States, and Austria all followed suit, while the first Protestant bishopric in Jerusalem in 1842 was a joint British and Prussian undertaking, with the appointment of a Jewish convert to Anglicanism, Michael Solomon Alexander. One notable indication of England's growing religious and political interests in the region was the young Prince of Wales's four-month tour of Egypt and the Holy Land in early 1862, accompanied by the celebrated Broad Church clergyman Arthur P. Stanley, an expert on the region. The mystique of the Holy Land in British Protestantism and the traditional Puritan and evangelical identification with ancient Israel and the lands of the Bible led to a steady increase in English visitors in the second half of the nineteenth century. The leading commercial agency providing tours of the Holy Land, Thomas Cook, accordingly conducted 5,000 tourists a year around Palestine between the years 1869 and 1882, and a decade later the number had risen to 12,000. Among well-known writers who toured and wrote about the region in the first half of the century were Benjamin Disraeli, Harriet Martineau, and William Thackeray, while a growing roster of clerical and lay authors—but no other major literary figures—published accounts of their tours in the second half of the century.[9]

Concurrent with the spread of evangelical faith in Victorian England and its rediscovery of the Holy Land, the Victorian Crisis of Faith derived from intellectually destabilizing developments in the fields of science and history.[10] The newly developed science of geology, as documented in Charles Lyell's *Principles of Geology* in the early 1830s, undermined the Mosaic creation and chronology of the Old Testament, while Robert Chambers's anonymously published *Vestiges of the Natural Creation* in 1844 provided a complete narrative of the Lamarckian evolution of life on earth beginning with the origins of the solar system, all according to the known laws of the physical universe, thereby creating a sensation in British cultural life and facilitating the acceptance of Darwin's more accurate theory of evolution over a decade later.[11] In the field of biblical studies, the publication of the German theologian David Strauss's *Life of Jesus* in 1837, translated into English by George Eliot in 1846, undermined the supernaturalism of the New Testament and identified a mythical messianic Jewish overlay on the historical figure of Christ. In 1854 Eliot published her translation of Ludwig Feuerbach's *The Essence of Christianity*, which argued that Christianity was a strategic projection of the human personality into divine form. The official arrival of the destabilizing higher criticism of the Bible within the Victorian church eventually came with the 1860 publication of *Essays and Reviews*, written by a variety of liberal churchmen headed by the Oxford scholar Benjamin Jowett. The contemporary sense of the slow breakup of the traditional view of God and the creation was also intensified with the appearance in 1859 of Darwin's *Origin of Species*, an epoch-making text which would exert a steadily increasing influence on Anglo-American culture, philosophy, and theology for the rest of the century and beyond.[12]

The tangible signs of religious crisis in England were just emerging at the time of the coronation of the new queen in 1837, and they continued over the ensuing decades with gathering force. Here we may briefly examine some of the evidence of this crisis in the fields of poetry, fiction, and literary nonfiction in the early and mid-Victorian eras. Thus, a few years before her premature death in 1849 from the tuberculosis that killed most of her family, Anne

Brontë published "The Doubter's Prayer," the lament of a Christian praying for a restoration of religious faith. In the middle of the poem, the speaker describes the simultaneous psychological necessity and seeming impossibility of maintaining her Christian faith:

> While Faith is with me, I am blest;
> It turns my darkest night to day;
> But while I clasp it to my breast,
> I often feel it slide away.
>
> Then, cold and dark, my spirit sinks,
> To see my light of life depart;
> And every field of Hell, methinks,
> Enjoys the anguish of my heart.
>
> What shall I do, if all my love,
> My hopes, my toil, are cast away,
> And if there be no God above,
> To hear and bless me when I pray?
>
> If this be vain delusion all,
> If death be an eternal sleep,
> And none can hear my secret call,
> Or see the silent tears I weep! (ll. 17–32)

The speaker then prays to God to banish doubt so that a faith in Christ's life and mission can be restored and the "Sorrow, Sin, and Pride" associated with unbelief can be replaced with "Peace, and Hope, and Love." In a pattern found in many of her doubting contemporaries, Christian faith is seen by the poet as the key to psychological health.[13]

In his widely popular *In Memoriam* (1850), which Melville read soon after its appearance, Alfred Lord Tennyson (1809–1892) chronicled his grief over the loss of his close friend Arthur Hallam in 1833, together with the shattering psychological impact of contemporary scientific thought, chiefly Lyell's geology and Chambers's evolutionism, with their shared accounts of eons of time in which a seemingly amoral nature evolved amid the extinction of innumerable species. The speaker of the poem thus goes through several stages of grief, despair, depression, and ultimate reconciliation as he recovers from the psychic trauma of his loss, and reintegration with his family and friends. The death of the beloved friend thus becomes a symptom of the potential loss of religious faith, as demonstrated by the horrors of geological time famously depicted in canto LVI, when the personification of a predatory nature undermines the poet's consolatory idea that if individuals randomly perished, then at least species (or "types") remained:

"Thou makest thine appeal to me:
  I bring to life, I bring to death:
  The spirit does but mean the breath:
I know no more." And he, shall he,

Man, her last work, who seem'd so fair,
  Such splendid purpose in his eyes,
  Who roll'd the psalm to wintry skies,
Who built him fanes of fruitless prayer,

Who trusted God was love indeed
  And love Creation's final law—
  Tho' Nature, red in tooth and claw
With ravine, shriek'd against his creed–

Who loved, who suffer'd countless ills,
  Who battled for the True, the Just,
  Be blown about the desert dust,
Or seal'd within the iron hills?

No more? A monster then, a dream,
  A discord. Dragons of the prime
  That tare each other in their slime,
Were mellow music match'd with him.

O life as futile, then, as frail!
  O for thy voice to soothe and bless!
  What hope of answer, or redress?
Behind the veil, behind the veil.[14]

It is this idea of ultimate cosmic futility and unjust divine abandonment that the poet must overcome in order to heal his grief and accept the death of his friend, with a partial restoration of faith.[15]

In the poetry of Arthur Hugh Clough (1819–1861) and Matthew Arnold (1822–1888) we find other important expressions of religious doubt and despair. After leaving his Oxford fellowship at Oriel College in early 1849 because of his inability to endorse the Thirty-Nine Articles, Clough was in Rome during the siege of the city by French troops in the late spring of 1849, then briefly worked at University College in London before visiting Cambridge, Massachusetts, in 1852 to lecture and develop a friendship with Emerson. Clough spent the rest of the decade working in the Education Office in London, punctuated by professional foreign travel, and left a record of his tormented doubts in his private diaries at his premature death in Italy in 1861. Of his poetry, "Through a Glass Darkly" reveals the poet's bewilderment over the ultimate cosmic purpose of human life, while "Easter Day: Naples, 1849" best expressed his skepticism of Christian dogma in a poem casting doubt on the Resurrection.

Like his older friend Clough, for whom he wrote the elegy "Thyrsis," Matthew Arnold suffered through a period of religious doubts as a young man while a student of contemporary European literature and thought, notably Goethe's writings, and as self-conscious heir of his famous father's dedication to a liberalized Anglican Church. As perhaps the era's best-known elegist of the loss of traditional faith, Arnold's poems of the 1850s and 1860s articulated the collective sense of melancholy of his mid-Victorian generation. In his "Stanzas from the Grande Chartreuse," for example, Arnold presented an influential image of the poet

> Wandering between two worlds, one dead,
> The other powerless to be born,
> With nowhere yet to rest my head,
> Like these, on earth I wait forlorn.
> Their faith, my tears, the world deride—
> I come to shed them at their side.
>
> Oh, hide me in your gloom profound,
> Ye solemn seats of holy pain!
> Take me, cowl'd forms, and fence me round,
> Till I possess my soul again;
> Till free my thoughts before me roll,
> Not chafed by hourly false control! (ll. 85–96)[16]

In "Memorial Verses April 1850," Arnold called his age "this iron time / Of doubts, disputes, distractions, fears" (ll.43–44), and in "The Scholar Gypsy," he similarly complained of "this strange disease of modern life, / With its sick hurry, its divided aims, / Its heads o'ertaxed, its palsied hearts" (ll. 203–5). Finally, in "Dover Beach" Arnold wrote the signature poem of Victorian doubt as he dramatized a night scene overlooking the English Channel, where the roar of the waves on the beach evokes the idea of a "Sea of Faith" now "Retreating, to the breath / Of the night-wind, down the vast edges drear / And naked shingles of the world" (ll. 21, 27–28). The poet must find consolation in his beloved because the world outside is ultimately bereft of joy, love, light, certitude, peace, and "help for pain" (l. 34). Thereafter, images of the retreat of a "sea of faith" became a familiar shorthand reference to the era's growing religious doubts.[17]

In the realm of early Victorian fiction, one finds a number of novels dedicated to a dramatization of the painful loss—and occasional regaining—of religious faith. The earliest and most influential of these was Carlyle's *Sartor Resartus* (1833–34), a semiautobiographical account of a fictional German professor's loss of faith and reconversion to a belief in a transcendent quasi-Calvinist God divested of all traditional theological identity. Blending strains of romantic orientalism and ironic bildungsroman, Benjamin Disraeli's *Tancred* (1845) depicted an upper-class English hero who feels impelled to revisit the Holy Land like his crusading ancestors in order to regain a troubled faith; falling in love with a local Jewish maiden, Tancred has a religious vision on Mount Sinai that addresses the issue of Christian doubt by a modern restatement of the Mosaic precepts suitable for the author's Jewish heritage. In his seriocomic novel *Loss and Gain* (1848), the well-known Catholic convert John Henry Newman dramatized the stages of his transformation from High Church Anglican to Roman Catholic, in contrast to his younger brother Francis's spiritual autobiography, *Phases of Faith* (1850), which recounted a deconversion from Calvinist Christianity to a liberal Unitarianism. In *The Nemesis of Faith* (1849), which reenacted his own painful loss of faith and resignation from an Oxford fellowship, the historian and journalist James Anthony Froude, younger brother of the Oxford Movement's prematurely deceased Richard Hurrell Froude, depicted the fictionalized plight of a young Anglican clergyman, Markham Sutherland, whose doubts on some aspects of his Christian faith eventuate in alienation from his narrow-minded parish and resignation from his priestly office. A deracinated Sutherland later has an adulterous affair with an Englishwoman while traveling in Switzerland; and when the woman's child dies during one of their trysts, she enters a convent while he attempts suicide—the influence of Goethe's Werther is patent here—as the author enacts a displaced punishment on his alter ego for his own religious derelictions.[18]

The two greatest novelists of the mid-Victorian era, Charles Dickens (1812–1870) and George Eliot (1819–1880), were both heavily influenced by the evangelical culture of the age, and both unsparingly critiqued it. In his recurrent fictionalized engagements with contemporary social reform, Dickens frequently exposed religious hypocrisy and obtuseness—one thinks of Mrs. Jellyby and Mr. Chadband in *Bleak House*—while drawing on biblical themes to show his society's endemic corruption and injustice, concurrently relying on a series of New Testament parables and other biblical texts as moral benchmarks for much of his major fiction.[19] As the translator of both Strauss and Feuerbach, George Eliot in the later 1840s and early 1850s gradually freed herself from her early evangelical identity as she developed a career in journalism with the liberal *Westminster Review* and aligned herself with the Comtean ideal of a Religion of Humanity promoted by her longtime companion George Henry Lewes—an ideology that shaped her fiction beginning with *Scenes from Clerical Life* (1857). Positing a three-stage scheme of historical development that included theological, metaphysical, and positivist phases, the French social theorist Auguste Comte created a secular substitute for Christianity that included the doctrines of solidarity with humanity, resignation to the unalterable facts of life, openness to public opinion, the channeling of egotism into "altruism" (a word he invented, via Lewes's translation), and the idea of subjective immorality for the dead. In much of her fiction, Eliot both embraced and critiqued positivist ideals while adapting her early evangelical beliefs to a more secular format, even as Christian ideals of goodness, sacrifice, and love regularly appeared in her fiction, as in the Christlike role of the charismatic young Jewish hero of her last novel, *Daniel Deronda* (1876).[20]

In the realm of literary nonfiction, the writings of Thomas Carlyle (1795–1881) and John Ruskin (1819–1900) present two different influential models of belief and nonbelief. As mentioned above, the writings of Carlyle had a decisive influence on the evolution of Victorian intellectual life, with this modern prophet berating his country for its embrace of moral utilitarianism, laissez-faire capitalism, and feckless parliamentary democracy. In *Past and Present* (1844) Carlyle contrasted the workings of a thirteenth-century monastery ruled by the Abbot Samson with modern English society, with its pervasive industrial poverty and greedy materialistic values. In his withering diagnosis of the ills of the present, Carlyle pointed to the rise of materialism and loss of genuine religious faith as a key to England's social conflicts, and the source of the endemic misery and moral corruptions of the new industrial economy, with its utilitarian ethics and laissez-faire ideology:

> There is no longer any God for us! God's Laws are become a Greatest-Happiness Principle, a Parliamentary Expediency: the Heavens overarch us only as an Astronomical Time-keeper; a butt for Hershel-telescopes to shoot science at, to shoot sentimentalities at;—in our and old Jonson's dialect, man has lost the *soul* out of him; and now, after the due period—begins to find the want of it! This is verily the plague-spot; centre of the universal Social Gangrene, threatening all modern things with frightful death. To him that will consider it, here is the stem, with its roots and taproot, with its world-wide upas-boughs and accursed poison-exudations, under which the world lies writhing in atrophy and agony. You touch the focal-centre of all our disease, of our frightful nosology of diseases, when you lay your hand on this. There is no religion; there is no God; man has lost his soul, and vainly seeks antiseptic salt.[21]

In Carlyle's vision, then, loss of faith was a prime reason for the alleged decline of English civilization amidst the splendors of empire and rapid industrial development.

Raised in an evangelical household in which he memorized vast portions of the Bible, the art and social critic John Ruskin gradually weaned himself from doctrinal Christianity in the 1850s, writing in May 1851 to a friend, Henry Ackland, about how the science of geology was literally undermining his biblical faith:

> You speak of the Flimsiness of your own faith. Mine, which was never strong, is being beaten into mere gold leaf, and flutters in weak rags from the letter of its old forms; but the only letters it can hold by at all are the old Evangelical formulae. If only the Geologists would let me alone, I could do very well, but those dreadful Hammers! I hear the clink of them at the end of every cadence of the Bible verses—

As he later chronicled in his autobiographical *Praeterita* (1885–89), Ruskin eventually felt the painless disappearance of his remaining Christian faith after a visit to a Waldensian church in Turin, Italy, in 1858, near his completion of the series of volumes on *Modern Painters* that established his reputation. Still shaped by his evangelical upbringing, Ruskin went on to become a fierce social critic of industrial blight and economic inequality by embracing the role of modern prophet in the tradition of Carlyle, while acting as a purveyor of Solomonic wisdom and Christian socialism to his society.[22]

It should be noted that the later 1860s and early 1870s was a time of increasing retreat for traditional faith among many English Protestants. As A. N. Wilson has written, "By the 1870s it had begun to seem, even to believers, that the English people were about to abandon faith; that the story which began in the pages of the Venerable Bede was to end in the high-brow periodicals."[23] The advent of a liberal government under Gladstone in 1868 eliminated religious tests for admission to universities, nullified church rates, and disestablished the Anglican Church in Ireland; and along with such liberalizations, a host of books and essays critical of Christianity also appeared. Among these were Winwood Reade's *The Martyrdom of Man* (1872), the Duke of Somerset's *Christian Theology and Modern Skepticism* (1872), John Stuart Mill's *Three Essays on Religion* (1874), and Walter Richard Cassels's *Supernatural Religion: An Inquiry into the Reality of Divine Revelation* (1874–77). Important essay collections and treatises by leading self-identified agnostics also appeared, for example, T. H. Huxley's *Lay Sermons, Addresses, and Reviews* (1870), Leslie Stephen's *Essays in Freethinking and Plainspeaking* (1873), John Morley's *On Compromise* (1874), John Tyndall's *Belfast Address* (1874), George L. Romanes's *A Candid Examination of Theism* (1874), and W. K. Clifford's *Ethics of Belief* (1877). Satirizing the decline of religious belief was the Anglo-Catholic W. H. Mallock in his novel *The New Republic; or, Culture, Faith, and Philosophy in an English Country House* (1877), in which astute fictional caricatures of Arnold, Pater, Ruskin, Pusey, Jowett, Tyndall, Clifford, and Huxley (among others) highlighted the religious and moral confusions of the age. Finally, the poetry of Algernon Swinburne, which began to appear in the volumes *Poems and Ballads* (1866) and *Songs before Sunrise* (1871), was notoriously subversive of Christian belief and favorable toward a reversion to paganism, adding to the era's sense of lost religious moorings.[24]

Representative of the unsettled state of Christian belief was the formation of the Metaphysical Society in 1869, whose forty members, meeting nine times a year in London, were dedicated to debating the conflict of science and religion, based on papers read—and often later published—by members, until the society disbanded in 1880. (About a dozen members usually attended each session, while the total membership over the decade amounted to about sixty.) In this informal debating society founded by the architect and man of letters James Knowles, who became editor of *The Contemporary Review* in 1870 and later founded *The Nineteenth Century* in 1877, many of the leading lights of the Victorian church and political and cultural establishments—notably Arthur P. Stanley, W. E. Gladstone, Arthur Russell, Archbishop Manning, W. G. Ward, R. H. Hutton, James Martineau, John Lubbock, Walter Bagehot, Tennyson, and Ruskin—met with some of the leading contemporary religious skeptics and agnostics such as T. H. Huxley, John Tyndall, W. K. Clifford, Henry Sidgwick, James Anthony Froude, Mark Pattison, Frederic Harrison, John Morley, and Fitzjames and Leslie Stephen. It was in response to these meetings that Huxley coined the word "agnostic" to describe someone who believed God to be unknowable, in accordance with St. Paul's reference to an "Unknown God" of the Athenians (Acts 17:23), and the principles of Kantian philosophy promoted at the time by the Oxford professor of metaphysics, Henry Mansel.[25]

One of the leading agnostics of the 1870s was the educational reformer, journalist, editor, and man of letters Leslie Stephen (1832–1904), who was raised in a prominent evangelical household but who lost his faith while a fellow at Oxford in the late 1850s and early 1860s. Following his reading of Mill, Comte, and others, Stephen developed doubts about the truth of his Christian faith, notably the historicity of the biblical Flood, and felt he could no longer conduct services at his college, ultimately leaving Cambridge in 1864 for a career as a journalist. The latter began with his visit to America in 1863 to report on the Civil War, during which time he befriended Holmes, Lowell, and Norton in Cambridge, Massachusetts. Beginning his journalistic career as English correspondent for the newly founded American magazine *The Nation*, Stephen established himself as a leading agnostic intellectual when he assumed editorship of *The Cornhill Magazine* in 1871 and helped popularize the word "agnostic" following T. H. Huxley's initial coinage. As an educational reformer, Stephen worked to end the Anglican restrictions on admissions and fellowships at Oxford and Cambridge, which forced him to leave academia after his own loss of faith. Believing that the dogmatic constraints of the Anglican Church posed a pervasive threat to the progress of reform in England, Stephen composed a series of essays in *Fraser's*, *The Fortnightly Review*, and *The Saturday Review* on the condition of Christianity in England, reprinting some of these in his *Essays on Freethinking and Plainspeaking* (1873). Stephen made his name as a man of letters by producing *The History of English Thought in the Eighteenth Century* (1876) and editing the multivolume *Dictionary of National Biography*. Throughout his career he was concerned with the development of a rationalist system of ethics to replace the obsolete dogmas of Christianity, as in *The Science of Ethics* (1882) as well as the occasional writings collected in *An Agnostic's Apology and Other Essays* (1893).[26]

A key influence on Stephen and other Victorian intellectuals and agnostics was John Stuart Mill (1806–1873). As England's leading nineteenth-century philosopher and the author of many works on politics, logic, political economy, and current affairs, John Stuart Mill was an intellectual prodigy brought up by his Benthamite father to promote the contemporary philosophical school of utilitarianism. Mill famously suffered a nervous breakdown at the age of twenty, which he overcame by his immersion in Wordsworth's poetry, as described in his *Autobiography* (1873). Having been raised without religious beliefs, Mill was a de facto atheist who refused to subscribe to the Thirty-Nine Articles required for admission to Oxford or Cambridge and spent most of his life working outside academia at the East India Company; he eventually assumed the position of lord rector of the University of St. Andrews in 1865–68 while also serving as a Liberal member of Parliament for the City and Westminster. A friend and disciple of Comte in the 1840s, Mill followed the founder of positivism in advocating a new Religion of Humanity to replace the increasingly obsolete Christianity of the nineteenth century. Written independently in the 1850s and late 1860s but published together as a single volume a year after Mill's death in 1873, his *Three Essays on Religion* undermined the claims of deism and natural theology promoting the idea of a beneficent nature ("Nature"); argued against the social utility of traditional Christian faith ("Utility of Religion"); and critiqued the logical proofs of God's existence, arguing that a divine agent cannot be proven as either false or true, all while advocating Mill's own belief in a Religion of Humanity ("Theism"). Yet to the dismay of some of his followers, in his last essay Mill postulated the existence of a finite creator god of limited power and endorsed the imaginative hope in a personal immortality.[27]

Finally, it should be noted that in the 1870s after he stopped writing poetry, Matthew Arnold produced a related series of books—*St. Paul and Protestantism* (1870), *Literature and Dogma* (1872), *God and the Bible* (1875), and *Last Essays on Church and Religion* (1877)—that attempted to separate the enduring ethical core of Christianity from an added supernatural element that must be identified and superseded in order to ensure the church's survival.[28] Believing that human beings needed religious faith but that Christianity in its present form was being destroyed by its obsolete dogmas, Arnold claimed that contemporary Christianity failed to acknowledge the essentially poetic nature of biblical language and style. Whereas the faith of the Old Testament might be reduced to the idea of the pursuit of a divine form of righteousness, the Christian faith relied on an array of *Aberglaube*, or "after-beliefs" such as Christ's incarnation, miracles, and resurrection, based on the human need for such fables. Defining religious belief as "morality touched with emotion," Arnold advocated the recognition of Christianity's supernatural element as possessing a poetic but not a literal truth, offering a means of appeal to the believer that ethical truth alone could not effectuate. Christianity's rich store of mythology and symbolism must therefore be released from the rigid confines of dogma and be interpreted as literary elements making appeal to the imagination and emotions; the key to Christian moral teaching was Christ's dying to the world, which the faithful must imitate.

The preceding discussion of the varied commentators chronicling the declining state of Protestant Christianity in England is intended to provide an introduction to the intellectual milieu and dominant mood of Melville's *Clarel*, and of its title character in particular. The latter is a young divinity student who, suffering from a crisis of Christian faith, has come to Jerusalem in the early 1870s and joins an expedition of modern pilgrims—a kind of ambulatory Metaphysical Society—to explore the major sites in the vicinity of Jerusalem, reproducing a journey that Melville himself took in January 1857. As we have seen, in the late 1860s and early 1870s, the era when Melville composed his long narrative poem, there was a widespread feeling in England that the Christian faith was in permanent decline, a feeling that was much more pervasive in England than in an America still recovering from the traumas of the Civil War. Thus, in addition to the recognized sources of the poem in Anglo-American Holy Land travel narratives and area studies, and his documented reading in the works of Carlyle, Ruskin, Tennyson, Arnold, and Swinburne, Melville's composition of *Clarel* also likely included undocumented reading of other British authors and periodicals related to some of the issues raised by the poem. By whatever means obtained, it is clear from *Clarel* that Melville was conversant with many developments in the religious, philosophical, and scientific thought of the era emanating from England.[29]

The only major English member of the modern pilgrimage evoked in *Clarel* is, of course, the Anglican clergyman Derwent, whose role in the poem is to provide a voice of liberal moderation in many of the religious and philosophical disputes between the characters. Derwent is in fact a self-identified adherent of the Broad Church party within the Anglican Church, a semi-official group situated between Low Church evangelicals and High Church conservatives first officially named in the 1850s. The basic principle of the Broad Church movement was to accommodate as many disparate believers as possible under the shelter of the national church. Believing the Bible to be a fallible human document, Broad Churchmen encouraged latitude in interpreting the Thirty-Nine Articles of the Anglican faith in order to include as many adherents as possible. Well-known Broad Church clergymen and educators included Thomas Arnold, Charles Kingsley, Benjamin Jowett, Baden Powell, Henry Milman, John William Colenso, and—most notably for our purposes—Arthur P. Stanley.[30]

A professor of ecclesiastical history at Oxford from 1856 to 1863 and then dean of Westminster Cathedral from 1864 to 1881, Arthur Penryn Stanley (1815–1881) had been a student of Thomas Arnold at Rugby and had written the influential 1844 biography of this honorary founding father of the Broad Church movement. Stanley was also one of the key figures promoting the idea of a Broad Church through his extensive writings, as in such volumes as his *Essays Chiefly on the Question of Church and State from 1850 to 1870* (1870). Based on his trip through the Holy Land in 1852–53, Stanley produced a learned travelogue, *Sinai and Palestine, in Connection with Their History* (1856)—an important source for *Clarel*—and he subsequently accompanied the Prince of Wales on the latter's tour of Egypt and the Holy Land in 1862, preaching to the future Edward VII a series of sermons during their tour. In a history of the mid-nineteenth-century Broad Church movement, Tod E. Jones calls Stanley "the greatest spokesman for the Broad Church among the clergy." The figure of Derwent in *Clarel* appears to owe much to Stanley's famously liberal-minded personality as expressed in his writings, as well as his close identification for contemporary Anglo-American readers with accounts of the Holy Land.[31]

"Derwent" is also highly appropriate for the name of *Clarel*'s Broad Church clergyman, given that the foundation for Broad Church doctrines was first set forth by Samuel Taylor Coleridge, who advocated a liberal, tolerant, and inclusive form of Anglicanism in such works as *Aids to Reflection* (1825) and *On the Constitution of Church and State* (1830). Coleridge's home in Keswick, Cumberland, in the Lake District near his friend William Wordsworth in 1800–1804 was situated near Derwentwater Lake, fed and drained by the Derwent River; the name was accordingly given to Coleridge's third son, Derwent (1800–1883), a noted educator, linguist, and Anglican clergyman. As Melville would have known, the Derwent River was given special mention in book 1 of Wordsworth's *Prelude* as a beautiful soothing presence in the poet's childhood:

> O Derwent! Traveling over the green Plains
> Near my "sweet Birthplace," didst thou, beauteous Stream,
> Make ceaseless music through the night and day
> Which with its steady cadence, tempering
> Our human waywardness, compos'd my thoughts
> To more than infant softness, giving me,
> Among the fretful dwellings of mankind,
> A knowledge, a dim earnest, of the calm
> Which Nature breathes among the hills and groves. (I, 277–85)

It is thus no coincidence that the clergyman Derwent in Melville's poem is depicted as a temperate, soothing presence to the other pilgrims, although his efforts to assuage the painful religious and philosophical conflicts of

Mortmain, Ungar, and Clarel lead to their pointed criticisms of his liberal faith, or outright rejection of his company.[32]

Clarel

In Melville's *Clarel*, the eponymous hero is a young man who has trained for the ministry but who has been overwhelmed by crippling religious doubts, partly stemming from reservations about the sacrament of Communion. As such, Clarel bears an identity like that found in numerous Victorian lives in poetry, fiction, and fact. As in the mid-Victorian poems expressing crippling doubt or fading faith by Anne Brontë, Tennyson, Clough, and Arnold, Melville's Clarel is deeply conflicted, feeling the loss of faith with poignant regret while lamenting the moral vacuum created by the apparent decline of Christianity like one "wandering between two worlds, one dead, / The other powerless to be born." Like the hero of Disraeli's *Tancred*, Clarel has journeyed to the Holy Land in order to deal with a personal religious crisis, and during his tour of the region falls in love with a young Jewess, like his English aristocratic predecessor. Clarel also embodies the familiar Victorian figure of the doubting cleric who has resigned from the ministry, a type depicted in the career of Markham Sutherland in James Anthony Froude's *The Nemesis of Faith*. Other leading Victorian figures whose religious doubts led to resignation from a clerical career included Arthur Hugh Clough, Francis Newman, Leslie Stephen, John Morley, W. K. Clifford, and George John Romanes. One of the most distressing consequences of the Victorian doubter's loss of faith was the feeling of radical alienation from more devout family members, friends, and society in general, and this sense of crippling loneliness is an integral part of Clarel's identity in Melville's poem.

Like these Victorians whose loss of faith was akin to the experience of mourning, expressed as feelings of depression, guilt, self-torment, and ambivalence over giving up their religious commitments, a melancholy Clarel is visiting the Holy Land to explore the religious landscape in search of an answer to his spiritual troubles. Visiting the Church of the Holy Sepulcher, for example, with its host of international pilgrims, Clarel imagines himself targeted as an unbeliever: "O heart profane, / O pilgrim-infidel, begone! / Nor here the sites of Faith pollute, / Thou who misgivest we enthrone / A God untrue, in myth absurd" (1.6.18–22).[33] Self-consciously unchurched, Clarel bears the imagined social stigma felt by such youthful doubters as Clough and Froude, who were forced to abandon promising academic careers following their loss of faith (a copy of Froude's *Nemesis of Faith* was burned by a fellow of Exeter College at Oxford). Befriending the elderly American millenarian Nehemiah, Clarel is quick to identify himself as a mere "traveler" rather than a "pilgrim" in the Holy Land (1.9.20–28); yet he goes on to visit the Christian antiquities in and around Jerusalem with Nehemiah as his guide, like any Protestant pilgrim looking to confirm his faith.[34]

Deeply lonely in his painful state of alienation and doubt, Clarel envisages a possible kindred spirit in the appealing figure of Celio, a crippled Italian and lapsed Catholic occasionally seen during Clarel's tours around the city; but the two ultimately fail to meet before the young Italian dies of a tubercular "gasping ill distressed" (1.19.12). In the representation of Clarel's lost confidant, we see a similar poignant despair over lost faith including a reminder, as Celio stands at the Ecce Homo Arch in Jerusalem, of the classic Victorian antinomy of disbelieving head and believing heart ("The head rejects; so much the more / The heart embraces—what? the love?" [1.13.68–69]) as well as a bitter reproach to Christ himself for promising a seemingly false ideal of spiritual immortality and letting "the heart / Of heavenly love, so sweet, so good, / Corrupt into creeds malign" (1.13.87–89). For Celio, as for Clarel, the ultimate fate of Christ's mission is grotesquely ironic in that his crucifixion has led to nearly two millennia of conflict in the West: "Tortured, shalt prove a torturer" (1.13.99). The intensity of Celio's perception of the suffering that Christ's mission has inflicted on the course of history is comparable to some of the notorious contemporaneous poems of Algernon Swinburne, whose "Hymn to Proserpine" (from *Poems and Ballads*) famously declared, "Thou has conquered, O pale Galilean; the world has grown gray from thy breath"; while "Before a Crucifix" (from *Songs before Sunrise*) expressed the ironic results of the consolations of Christianity to the poor:

It was for this then, that thy speech
   Was blown about the world in flame
And men's souls shot up out of reach
   Of fear or lust or thwarting shame—
That thy faith over souls should pass
As sea-winds burning the grey grass?

It was for this, that prayers like these
   Should spend themselves about thy feet,
And with hard overlaboured knees
   Kneeling, these slaves of men should beat
Bosoms too lean to suckle sons
And fruitless as their orisons?

It was for this, that men should make
   Thy name a fetter on men's necks,
Poor men's made poorer for thy sake,
   And women's withered out of sex?
It was for this, that slaves should be,
Thy word was passed to set men free?

The nineteenth wave of the ages rolls
  Now deathward since thy death and birth.
Hast thou fed full men's starved-out souls?
  Hast thou brought freedom upon earth?
Or are there less oppressions done
In this wild world under the sun? (ll. 19–43)[35]

In Swinburne's poem, the suffering of Christ has been coopted by agents of power in church and state, leaving the poor with only an exploited faith—a corruption of Christianity comparable to the Italian Celio's complaints about tormented modern Christians like himself "by a myth abused" (1.14.83).[36]

Having failed to meet his alter ego in Celio, Clarel under the auspices of Nehemiah befriends the American Jewish family of Nathan, Agar, and Ruth, who have moved to Jerusalem because of Nathan's quixotic scheme to reclaim the Holy Land for modern Jewry following his conversion to the older faith. Falling in love with Nathan's daughter Ruth ("She looked a legate to insure / That Paradise is possible / Now as hereafter" [1.17.161–63]), the two soon become engaged, thereby forestalling any problems Clarel might face with a traditionally devout Christian spouse. Having grown up without mother or sister ("bereft while still but young, / Mother or sister had not known" [1.39.17–18]), Clarel now quickly finds in Ruth and her mother this missing domestic affection; moreover, "both for freedom yearned" (1.27.26) and they accordingly welcome the young American divinity student as a reminder of their homeland. But following the unexpected murder of Nathan by Bedouins and Ruth's enforced seclusion for a period of mourning, Clarel decides to join a band of modern secular pilgrims in their ten-day excursion to the Jordan River, Dead Sea, Mara Saba monastery, and Bethlehem, even though he has last-minute doubts about leaving Ruth when seeing the Armenian funeral procession of a young bride, "her groom that Blue-Beard, cruel Death" (1.43.22)—an ominous sign that will haunt him throughout his excursion. Clarel is now put into the company of two older Americans, Rolfe and Vine, whom he has met during his rambles around Jerusalem, and an Englishman, Derwent—three modern "wise men" suitable for the pilgrims' ultimate destination of Bethlehem, who offer him different perspectives on the sights of the biblical landscape and on the status of Christianity in the modern world.[37]

Like all four parts of the poem, the end of part 1 is marked by an aura of death, an indication of the many life-threatening diseases and hazards that characterized the region; for in addition to the news of Nathan's murder, in canto 40 ("The Mounds") Clarel makes a visit to the grave of Celio, who was allegedly forced to reaffirm his ancestral Catholic faith before his death ("Life's flickering hour they made command / Faith's candle in Doubt's dying hand" [1.40.17–18]), and subsequently encounters Rolfe meditating over the grave of an acquaintance in Jerusalem's Protestant burial ground, both grave sites evoking the region's divisive religious sectarianism as well as the integral relationship of death and religious affiliation. When Clarel returns to his Jerusalem inn again while pondering his loss of faith, he dutifully tries reading the early church fathers and then the gospels before he notices some writing on the wall under a disintegrating coat of lime, a mysterious message hinting at the well-known motif of the divine "writing on the wall" in chapter 5 of the book of Daniel. The lines appear to set forth a spontaneous testament of faith written after a visit to the Church of the Holy Sepulcher by one "B.L.," a student at St. Mary's Hall, Oxford, a small college later merged with Oriel.[38] The mysterious anonymous writer seems to present primitive Christianity as a sanctuary from the threat of contemporary religious and political radicalism: "If Atheists and Vitriolists of doom / Faith's glimmering night with rockets red illume— / So much the more in pathos I adore / The low lamps flicking in Syria's Tomb [i.e., the Church of the Holy Sepulcher]" (1.41.112–15).

When Clarel asks the innkeeper Abdon who might have written these lines, the latter gives Clarel two of the unknown pilgrim's books. The first book "treated of high church Anglican, / Confession, fast, saint-day—deplored / That rubric old was not restored" (1.41.127–29), apparently a product of the Oxford Movement of the 1830s and 1840s—a movement that the book's owner criticized in a note to the volume. The second book is a skeptical tome that "started from Strauss, disdained Renan— / By striding paces up to Pan" (1.41.133–34) and that also embraced the political radicalism of the French socialist Pierre-Joseph Proudhon (1809–1865) and the communists—a work that, based on its markings, also inspired vigorous dissent in the reader. Offering a riddling tripartite testament of faith, as seen in the writing on the wall and the annotations to the two antithetical volumes showing the vast divide between conservative and radical beliefs of the era, the unknown English pilgrim is yet another kindred spirit whom Clarel fails to meet, and whose documented awareness of some of the contradictory religious and philosophical currents of the age acts as yet another reminder of the transatlantic context of Clarel's conflict of faith and doubt.

Throughout much of the second part of Melville's poem, Clarel is allured by Vine's mysterious reticence, personal beauty, and seemingly sympathetic nature in his quest for a spiritual confidant—an attraction partly based on the young divinity student's intense loneliness and thwarted emotional development, having been deprived of a mother's or sister's love as a youth and now lacking faith in a caring paternal god. But Vine ultimately rejects Clarel's desire for more emotional and intellectual intimacy while the pilgrims are resting by the Jordan River, the legendary scene of Christ's transformative encounter with John the Baptist. The sacred setting where Vine and Clarel's conversation takes place there is designed to make Vine look like a quasi-divine being: "So pure, so virginal in shrine / Of true unworldliness looked Vine" (2.27.63–64). But when Clarel begins to talk of his spiritual troubles,

Vine implicitly dismisses the young man's difficulties, as Clarel quickly perceives Vine's unreceptiveness to the young man's needs:

> Why, on this vernal bank to-day,
> Why bring oblations of thy pain
> To one who hath his share? here fain
> Would lap him in a chance reprieve?
> Lives none can help ye; that believe.
> Art thou the first soul tried by doubt?
> Shalt prove the last? Go, live it out. (2.27.217–23)

Frigidly unsympathetic to Clarel's plight, Vine would seem to sense moral weakness in the young man's doubts; yet this is partly because they remind him of some unspecified past pain of his own that won't bear repeating. Vine's attributed use of the word "oblation"—an offering to a deity, as in the bread and wine of the Communion—underlines Vine's perception that Clarel is seeking some kind of substitute for Christian ritual in his desired friendship, an idea recalling Clarel's rejection of a clerical vocation based on his doubts about the sacrament of Communion. In a larger sense, Vine's rejection of Clarel's spiritual travails also ironically demonstrates Vine's failure to live up to the New Testament symbolism of his name; for in the gospel of John, Jesus is represented as the "vine" ensuring the transmission of Christian faith to his disciples: "I am the vine, ye are the branches: He that abideth in me, and I in him, the same bringeth forth much fruit: for without me ye can do nothing. / If a man abide not in me, he is cast forth as a branch, and is withered" (John 15:5–6). Reclining next to Vine like the disciples at the Communion meal evoked in the fourth gospel, Clarel nevertheless fails to produce any "fruit" or attain the status of a "beloved disciple" to the charismatic Vine and is even told by the older American that—contrary to the universal love Christ gave as "new commandment" (John 13:34)—such love between men in Vine's view was impossible: "The negatives of flesh should prove / Analogies of non-cordialness / In spirit" (2.27.126–28). Critics who focus on the homoerotic hints found in the scene of Vine's rejection of Clarel generally overlook the biblical ironies of the encounter as well as its reminder of the self-protective emotional inhibitions of Vine's biographical model, Nathaniel Hawthorne.[39]

Denied any intellectual or emotional intimacy with Vine, Clarel later turns to Derwent for consolation, again failing to gain any solace for his theological troubles when the party is lodged at the Greek Orthodox monastery of Mar Saba (see below). When the pilgrims move on to their visit to Bethlehem, the Confederate veteran Ungar joins the party as the voice of an outspoken religious and political conservatism with little appeal to the other pilgrims; Clarel thus tells Rolfe that Ungar is "most strange; / Wild, too, adventurous in range; / And suffers" (4.17.49–51). But the young American eventually finds a more appealing figure in his sociable roommate for the night before his return to Jerusalem, a young Lyonese Jewish commercial agent, the "Prodigal," who encourages Clarel to stop torturing himself ("Put up, put up your monkish thong!" [4.26.285]) and embrace the pleasures of the flesh in the skeptical tradition of the biblical book of Ecclesiastes. Clarel's conversation with the Prodigal touches on their divergent interpretations of the biblical Song of Songs, the Prodigal reading it literally as a frankly sensual celebration of sexuality, while Clarel naively cleaves to the older Christian interpretation of the poem as an allegory of divine love, a demonstration of the repressive Puritan heritage from which Clarel has emerged.[40]

Not surprisingly, the Prodigal is full of praise for the seductive allure of Jewish women, priming Clarel for his imminent return to his waiting Jewish bride Ruth. Contemplating a new appreciation of the enjoyments of the flesh in accordance with the example of the Prodigal, Clarel now fatefully imagines himself another Adam eating from the tree of life: "Yea, now his hand would boldly reach / And pluck the nodding fruit to him, / Fruit of the tree of life" (4.29.55–57). With this tempting thought in mind, Clarel hastily proceeds back to Jerusalem on a night ride with the other pilgrims at the beginning of Lent, when he accidentally discovers that his fiancée Ruth and her mother Agar have both recently died from one of the region's many fatal diseases and are being privately buried according to Jewish ritual; the onset of Ash Wednesday the next day is thus suited to Clarel's tragic reminder of human mortality. Such a shocking and ironic end to Clarel's philosophical pilgrimage plunges him into a renewed state of religious melancholy, now over the existential fact of death and the inexplicable tragedies of the human condition that have again left him an orphan.

Having given up his vocation as a clergyman at the start of the poem and then failed to create a new life in marriage to a non-Christian by the end, Clarel is faced with a personal grief for which only the consolations of Christ as the embodiment of human suffering would seem at all adequate. In the penultimate stanza of the poem set on Whitsunday or Pentecost, Clarel thus walks down the crowded Via Crucis of Jerusalem where Jesus allegedly went from his trial to his crucifixion: "In varied forms of fate they wend— / Or man or animal, 'tis one: / Cross-bearers all, alike they tend / And follow, slowly follow on" (4.34.41–44). Without Christian faith, however, Clarel has no compelling religious myth to give meaning to his loss. The final irony of the poem, then, is that while traditional Christian belief is apparently fading from the modern Western world, the need for some form of faith to justify the otherwise inexplicable evils of the human condition remains unchanged.

Among the potential prototypes in mid-Victorian literature for the tragic outcome of Clarel's religious quest, the works of Tennyson, Clough, and Arnold stand out. Like Tennyson's *In Memoriam*, Melville's *Clarel* ends up as an epic-length elegy for troubled faith and lost love in its eponymous hero. Thus Clarel during the Easter celebrations in Jerusalem painfully witnesses the ritual commemoration of Christ's resurrection while thinking of Ruth: "The cheer, so human, might not call / The maiden up; *Christ is arisen*: / But Ruth, may Ruth so burst the prison?" (4.33.64–66). Seven weeks later on Whitsunday, Clarel again laments the fact that despite the material progress of the world illustrated by the spread of undersea telegraph lines, the dead Ruth cannot communicate with him, thereby negating the Pentecostal access of the Holy Spirit on this day: "They wire the world—far under sea / They talk; but never comes to me / A message from beneath the stone" (4.34.51–53). A similar despairing view of the impossibility of the resurrection of the dead is expressed in Clough's "Easter Day: Naples, 1849," which describes the poet's wandering the streets of the crowded southern Italian city saying to himself in haunting refrain "Christ is not risen":

> Is He not risen, and shall we not rise?
> Oh, we unwise!
> What did we dream, what wake we to discover?
> Ye hills, fall on us, and ye mountains, cover!
> In darkness and great gloom
> Come ere we thought it is *our* day of doom,
> From the cursed world which is one tomb,
> Christ is not risen!
>
> Eat drink, and die, for we are men deceived,
> Of all the creatures under heaven's wide cope
> We are most hopeless who had once most hope
> We are most wretched that had most believed.
> Christ is not risen.
>
> Eat, drink, and play, and think that this is bliss!
> There is no heaven but this!
> There is no Hell;—
> Save Earth, which serves the purpose doubly well,
> Seeing it visits still
> With equallest apportionment of ill
> Both good and bad alike, and brings to one same dust
> The unjust and the just
> With Christ, who is not risen. (ll. 64–85)[41]

In a series of despairing stanzas Clough's poem proclaims a counter-gospel to the "good news" of the Resurrection, the belief which St. Paul had made a touchstone for Christian faith (1 Cor. 15:12–19).

So, too, in the poetry of Matthew Arnold one finds Clarel's same mix of grief, regret, melancholy, loneliness, and despair over waning faith or lost love, as poignantly expressed in such lyric, elegiac, and dramatic poems as "Resignation," "Switzerland," "Faded Leaves," "Despondency," "Self-Deception," "Dover Beach," "Thyrsis," "Stanzas from the Grand Chartreuse," "Stanzas to the Author of 'Obermann,' " and "Empedocles on Aetna." At the beginning of "To Marguerite-Continued" in the sequence "Switzerland," for example, the poet meditates on the existential fact of human isolation decreed by some unknown god:

> Yes! in the sea of life enisled,
> With echoing straits between us thrown,
> Dotting the shoreless watery wild,
> We mortal millions live alone.
> The islands feel the enclasping flow,
> And then their endless bounds they know. (ll. 1–6)

In "Too Late," the second in the five-poem series "Faded Leaves," the speaker in the first stanza notes the permanent separation of lovers in life or death: "Each on his own strict line we move, / And some find death ere they find love; / So far apart their lives are thrown / From the twin soul which halves their own." And in "Separation," the next poem in the series, the speaker in the first stanza seeks to blot out the pain of a remembered lost love:

> Stop!—not to me, at this bitter departing,
>   Speak of the sure consolations of Time!
> Fresh be the wound, still-renew'd be its smarting,
>   So but thy image endure in its prime. (ll. 1–4)

It is in such a state of lonely isolation that we last see Clarel in the poem, walking down the streets of Jerusalem on Whitsunday, the day when Christ allegedly appeared to his disciples following the Resurrection; yet no such sacred companionship or assurance of spiritual immortality is given to the desolate Clarel except for the narrator's final exhortation in the "Epilogue" to keep up his spiritual search (see below).

Rolfe

The character of Rolfe is introduced late in part 1 as an American traveler who has come to the Holy Land to seek "some lurking thing" from behind the conventional "parrot-lore" of the modern tourist's Palestine (1.31.36–38). The name Rolfe may represent Melville's nominal homage to America's greatest transcendentalist philosopher, Ralph Waldo Emerson, even though Rolfe is an independent thinker of no discernible philosophical school. A figure of "genial heart" with a "brain austere," who "supplemented Plato's theme" of philosophical investigation with "daedal life in boats and tents"

(1.31.14–20), Rolfe combines intellectual inquiry with wide travel and worldly experience and is often assumed to be a partial portrait of Melville himself. As a religious seeker and freethinking philosophical commentator, however, Rolfe's opinions often bear a resemblance to those of English skeptics and freethinkers of the 1860s and 1870s, notably Leslie Stephen and John Stuart Mill; yet Rolfe is also nostalgic for the ethical core of Christianity, in the manner of Matthew Arnold, as well as for recognition of Christianity as embodying an enduring sacred myth, in keeping with the new Victorian discipline of comparative religion.[42]

Rolfe has a richly informed mind and so regularly provides the pilgrims with larger historical contexts for debate. Rolfe's first remark in the poem is ironically to note that a Moslem minaret stands higher than the dome of the Church of the Holy Sepulcher in the skyline of Jerusalem; and he goes on to recite the early history of Jerusalem while noting the tendency of Christian churches in Jerusalem and Peru to survive disasters of war and earthquake, respectively. This leads Rolfe to posit the existence of a religious instinct that guarantees the continued survival of Christian priest and church:

> Not less religion's ancient port,
> Till the crack of doom, shall be resort
> In stress of weather for mankind.
> Yea, long as children feel affright
> In darkness, men shall fear a God;
> And long as daisies yield delight
> Shall see His footprints in the sod.
> Is't ignorance? This ignorant state
> Science doth but elucidate— (1.31.184–92)

Rolfe's supposition of a permanent religious instinct in humanity, which echoes the thought of Schleiermacher and Coleridge earlier in the century, also matches the contemporaneous skeptical claims of Leslie Stephen in his *Essays in Freethinking and Plainspeaking*: "Whatever happens, the religious instincts of mankind will survive and will find some mode of expression. Whether they take such a form as is expected by the followers of Comte, or return to the ancient modes of thought, they have a vitality independent of any existing organization."[43]

According to Rolfe, even if it were demonstrable that God didn't exist, the "ghost" of the deity would still haunt humanity. Confirming the apparent continuity of a religious instinct in the human psyche, the Egyptian myth of Osiris as a dying and rising god, in Rolfe's view, suggests the story of Christ's rising from the tomb, as does the text from the Old Testament prophet Hosea linking Egypt with the calling of God's divine "son," just as Christ came back from Egypt following his family's escape from Jerusalem to avoid Herod's slaughter of the innocents (Matt. 2:12–23). Such speculation was well suited to the time of the poem's setting, when the field of comparative religion was first being developed in England in the work of Herbert Spencer, Max Müller, and Edward B. Tylor, to be continued later in the century by W. Robertson Smith, Andrew Lang, and James G. Frazer.[44] Pursuing the same comparative theme, Rolfe praises the religious dialogues of Cicero, chiefly *The Nature of the Gods*, while noting the similarity of the religious doubts current in late republican Rome and nineteenth-century England: "the gods were gone. / Tully scarce dreamed they could be won / Back into credence" (1.31.255–57). Such a comparison of the weakening faith in Roman intellectuals just before the advent of Christianity with an increasingly de-Christianized modern British intelligentsia was not uncommon and could be found, for example, in Leslie Stephen's contemporaneous essay on "The Religion of All Sensible Men": "We should perhaps find the best guidance in any attempt at prophesying the future of religion, from studying the history of the last great revolution in faith. The analogy between the present age and that which witnessed the introduction of Christianity is too striking to have been missed by many observers. The most superficial acquaintance with the general facts shows how close a parallel might be drawn by a competent historian."[45]

In a subsequent canto in which Rolfe, Clarel, and Vine sit on the hill outside Jerusalem from which Christ allegedly made his prediction of the destruction of the city, Rolfe notes the pervasive influence of religious doubt suggested by the condition of Jerusalem, due to the spread of scientific rationalism: "Then tell, tell then, what charm may save / Thy marvel, Palestine, from grave / Whereto winds many a bier and pall / Of old Illusion?" (1.34.32–35). Rolfe then questions the ultimate reality of change since the "germs" of all things are allegedly the same, as described in the book of Ecclesiastes to which Rolfe makes implicit reference: "what novel thing may be, / No germ being new? By Fate's decree / Have not earth's vitals heaved in change / Repeated?" (1.34.48–50). Amid all the upheavals chronicled by the new science of geology, the present, like the past, still remains a persistent contest of good and evil; for the "rudiments persistent flow, / From age to age transmitting, own, / The evil with the good—the taint / Deplored by Solomon's complaint [i.e., Ecclesiastes]" (1.34.56–59).

In his essay on "Dreams and Realities," in which he claimed that Ecclesiastes and Job were "the most impressive books in the Hebrew canon," Leslie Stephen likewise noted the inextricable mix of good and evil in the world: "It is as impossible to separate light from darkness, height from depth, object from subject, as to conceive of good without evil."[46] John Stuart Mill similarly wrote in his essay on "Nature" on the ineluctable role of evil in the world undermining traditional belief in a benign creator: "Not even on the most distorted and contracted theory of good which ever was framed by religious or philosophical fanaticism, can the government of Nature be made to resemble the work of a being at once good and omnipotent." He went on to remark:

> The only admissible moral theory of Creation is that the Principle of Good *cannot* at once and altogether subdue the powers of evil, either physical or moral; could not place mankind in a world free from the necessity of an incessant struggle with maleficent powers, or make them always victorious in that struggle, but could and did make them capable of carrying on the fight with vigour and with progressively increasing success. Of all the religious explanations of the order of nature, this alone is neither contradictory to itself, nor to the facts for which it attempts to account.[47]

It should be noted that unlike the agnostic Stephen or the atheist Mill, Rolfe is not a proponent of a scientific rationalism but rather an ambivalent skeptic who regrets the relentless advance of the scientific spirit in making the world a more prosaic place, a position more like that of Stephen's contemporary Matthew Arnold. In subsequent conversations between Rolfe and Derwent in part 2, as the pilgrims travel from Jerusalem to the Dead Sea, we thus find a recurrent opposition between Rolfe's regrets concerning modernity and Derwent's progressive faith. In part 2, canto 21, after the pilgrims encounter the German Jewish geologist Margoth, Derwent is eager to assert the claims of scientific progress, while Rolfe claims that modern physics, for example, "but drudges after Plato's theme; / Or supplements—but little more—/ Some Hindoo's speculative dream / Of thousand years ago" (2.21.20–23). Such a critique of modern science is in keeping with the romantic era's insistence on the limits of scientific truth, anticipating the argument of Matthew Arnold's essay "Literature and Science" (1882), written in response to T. H. Huxley's outspoken campaign for science education in England. Rolfe persists in noting the limits of recent scientific advances, even as he nostalgically looks back to the life of Christ as embodying an ideal innocent world when "a god with peasants went abreast: / Man clasped a deity's offered hand" (2.21.68–69). Borrowing the nostalgic tones of Arnold's pastorals "The Scholar Gypsy" and "Thyrsis," Rolfe hails the "gypsy" life of Christ and his disciples: "What dream they knew, that primal band / Of gypsy Christians! But it died; / Back rolled the world's effacing tide" (2.21.76–78). In the modern world, faith is in retreat and, in another Arnoldian image of separation and spiritual alienation, Rolfe complains: "Where stretched an isthmus, rolls a strait: / Cut off, cut off!" (2.21.91–92). Rolfe thus questions how Derwent can feel elated "while all the depths of Being moan" (2.21.93) from the seeming death of God.

In part 3, canto 3, after the accidental death of Nehemiah, we witness Rolfe meditating on different ideas of the afterlife in different religious cultures. Thus, he remarks that before the onset of Christianity it was rare "to pledge indemnifying good / In worlds not known" (3.3.15–16). The promise of posthumous justice and redemption so eloquently preached by Christ may, however, only be a means of betraying the believer, as Rolfe now seems to revert to his earlier skeptical manner: "So winning in enthusiast plea, /

Here may the Gospel but the more / Operate like a perfidy?" (3.3.30–32). In Rolfe's paradoxical formulation, Christ's idealism could all too easily betray believers who expected a spiritual afterlife as the ultimate reward for virtue. The issue is implicitly relevant to the recent death of the elderly millenarian Nehemiah, whose delusive dreams of a New Jerusalem caused him to sleepwalk into the Dead Sea and drown; the vision of the holy city here thus acts as a symbol of death, not eternal life, as in the concluding chapters of the book of Revelation. Such an ironic event confirms the contemporary assessment of the Christian afterlife as a dream in Leslie Stephen's essay on "Dreams and Realities": "the so-called belief in a future life—whether in hell or in heaven—has always been in reality a dream, and not strictly speaking a belief at all. Occasionally this dream, like others, passes into hallucination; as a rule it is as flimsy in its texture as other dreams, and really supplies new symbols for the emotions instead of suggesting genuine motives for action."[48]

One of the most important discussions of the general decline of faith in the modern world occurs in part 3, canto 5 ("The High Desert"), as the pilgrims travel from the shores of the Dead Sea, where they have just buried Nehemiah, up to the Greek Orthodox monastery of Mar Saba. The conversation here develops between Clarel, Rolfe, Vine, and Mortmain as Derwent goes off to talk to the Muslim guard Belex. The narrator, assuming a speculative tone suggestive of the voice of Rolfe, now summarizes the direction of their conversation while they look down on the wastes of the Dead Sea shore of Siddim and contrast this with memories of the agricultural richness of their "vernal homes" in America. The contrast expresses the ambiguous universal intermingling of good and evil in nature, as first set forth in the early revealed religion of Zoroastrianism:

> The spleen of nature and her love:
> At variance, yet entangled too—
> Like wrestlers. Here in review
> They call to mind Abel and Cain—
> Ormuzd involved with Ahriman
> In deadly lock. Were those Gods gone?
> Or under other names lived on? (3.5.32–38)[49]

The discussion then turns to the early Christian Gnostic heresy of a good Christ and evil Jehovah, which had recently reappeared in modern form in the attacks on the tyrannical evils of the Calvinist Old Testament god in Unitarianism and other liberal Protestant faiths, in contrast to the superlative morality of Christ. The question arises whether the shadow of doubt cast over Christian belief anticipates its "complete eclipse" (3.5.63), as was discussed in the British periodical literature of the later 1860s and 1870s. In its current form of "Protestant repose" (3.5.73), is Christianity dying, the narrator asks, or will it reappear in another form?

—is faith dead *now*,
A petrifaction? Grant it so,
Then what's in store? What shapeless birth?
Reveal the doom reserved for the earth?
How far may seas retiring go?
But, to redeem us, shall we say
That faith, undying, does but range,
Casting the skin—the creed. In change
Dead always does some creed delay. (3.5.79–87)

Combining the classical symbolism of a portentous misshapen fetus as a divine warning with the Arnoldian image of a receding "sea of faith," the narrator raises the idea of religious creeds transforming themselves through time like long-lived reptiles shedding their "skin"; the imagery of birth and monstrosity here anticipates W. B. Yeats's well-known poetic prophecy in "The Second Coming" of a "rough beast" that is "slouching towards Bethlehem." A similar curiosity and apprehension about the possible future forms of religious faith is expressed in Leslie Stephen's "The Religion of All Sensible Men": "How will men satisfy the needs hitherto met by the various forms of worship? What will be the heaven and hell of the future? Will men pray at all, and, if so, to whom? How will they express what have been called the supernatural dictates of the conscience? What will be the precise meaning given to such words as holy, spiritual, and divine, which have hitherto expressed some of the profoundest moods of which we are conscious?" Stephen goes on to note the resemblances between the current age of religious transition and the era that saw the birth of Christianity: "Now, as then, we can find mystical philosophers trying to evolve a satisfactory creed by some process of logical legerdemain out of theosophical moonshine; and amiable and intelligent persons labouring hard to prove that the old mythology could be forced to accept a rationalistic interpretation." In the midst of this disintegration of traditional Christian faith one finds "beneath all, a vague disquiet, a breaking-up of ancient social and natural bonds, and a blind groping toward some more cosmopolitan creed and some deeper satisfaction for the emotional needs of mankind."[50]

The pilgrims in *Clarel* similarly ponder the enigma of the future and its beliefs: "Shall endless time no more unfold / Of truth at core?" (3.5.104–5). For the American pilgrims, the question of whether their current material progress can be endless is particularly relevant, or whether a surfeit of prosperity will lead to corruption and decline; in fact, the current nominally Christian age is really a "league avowed / Of Mammon and Democracy" (3.5.153–54), while the question remains whether a triumphant science may merely "new doors to superstition ope?" (3.5.158). While Rolfe and others are earnestly engaged with such ideas, a bored Vine throws bits of porous stone down the valley, tired of the abstract discussion:

how ill he brooked
That weary length of arguing—
Like tale interminable told
In Hades by some gossip old
To while the never-ending night. (3.5.191–95)

Vine's impatient characterization here is consonant with his exclusive interest in the past, as he later states at the Mar Saba monastery:

For my part, I but love the past—
The further back the better; yes,
In the past is the true blessedness;
The future's ever overcast—
The present aye plebian. (3.26.14–18)

Vine's impatience with the discussion in "The High Desert" evokes Melville's conversations with Hawthorne in Liverpool in November 1856, which showed the latter's strong aversion to abstract philosophical and theological discussion, and which had subsequently appeared in the redacted version of Hawthorne's *Passages from the English Note-Books* (1870) prepared by his wife Sophia. The portrait of Vine thus reflects Melville's sense of Hawthorne's emotional and intellectual limitations, as confirmed by his posthumously published notebooks and fiction, in contrast to Rolfe's eager embrace of contemporary religious and cultural controversies as an indication of his restlessly inquiring mind—the mirror of Melville's own lifelong intellectual curiosity.[51]

Derwent

After his introduction in the first canto of part 2 as a worldly cleric in the mode of Chaucer's Monk ("A priest he was—though but in part" [2.1.29]), Derwent assumes the role of the pilgrim group's resident optimist: "Cordial he turned his aspect clear / On all that passed; man, yea, and brute / Enheartening by a blithe salute, / Chirrup, or pat, or random cheer" (2.1.21–24). An up-to-date votary of modern thought as found in "each bright optimistic mind" (2.1.37), Derwent as a proponent of the Broad Church is in the vanguard with his forward-looking transatlantic fellow clerics like Henry Ward Beecher; for he keeps "abreast with whistling Jonathan" (2.1.41). Thus, when passing the Garden of Gethsemane on their way to Jericho and the Jordan River, Derwent debates with the dour Swede Mortmain over the betrayal of Christ at this site, glibly claiming that "rightly considered, they [i.e., the precincts] give / A hope to man, a cheerful hope" (2.3.125–26). Later on, Derwent and Rolfe discuss the merits of modern science following the pilgrims' encounter with the geologist Margoth, and not surprisingly Derwent applauds recent progress in this field. They go on to give their opinions on modern Catholicism following the encounter with the Dominican by the Jordan River. Like any good Anglican, Derwent anticipates the decline of an increasingly reactionary Catholic Church but still finds reason to praise its older poetic legends: "In brief, since Rome must still decay; / Less care I to disown or hide / Aught that she has of merit rare: / Her legends—some are sweet as May" (2.26.83–86). Yet if Derwent thinks that "the world is now too civilized / For Rome" (2.28.118–19), a more skeptical Rolfe sees the recent revolutions and political turmoil in Europe as leading to an eventual conflict of Catholicism and atheism, with Protestantism merely "being retained / For base of operations sly / By Atheism" (2.26.142–44).

Such an insinuation is in keeping with contemporary English criticism of the Anglican Broad Church party as being eventually subverted by its liberal embrace of modern science and rationalism. The shortcomings of Derwent's faith are especially apparent as he talks to Clarel in part 3, canto 21 ("In Confidence"), a counterpart to Clarel's earlier attempt get closer to Vine. As they watch the dawn from the Mar Saba monastery, Clarel and Derwent discuss the nature of Christian faith available in their time, the latter figure revealing his liberal and tolerant Broad Church affiliation to an unreceptive Clarel. As Derwent early notes in their conversation: "We broader clergy think it good / No more to use censorious tone: / License to all" (3.21.94–96). Clarel, on the other hand, is eager to point out the clash of faiths so evident in Palestine, especially in the Jerusalem Church of the Holy Sepulcher, with its jealous zones of Catholic, Orthodox, Armenian, and Protestant stewardship and worship: "The very pews are each a sect; / No one opinion's steadfast sway: / A wide, an elemental fray" (3.21.109–11). Faltering at first in reaction to Clarel's charge, Derwent tells the young divinity student to throw his burden on Christ, while also confessing that many individuals like him are tortured by the seeming absence of a higher divine power: "No umpirage! they cry—we dote / To dream heaven drops a casting vote, / In these perplexities takes part!" (3.21.167–69). Now fully opening up to Clarel, Derwent identifies them both as Christian "clerics" and insists that even the "myth" of Christianity contains a valid measure of truth: "Have Faith, which, even from the myth, / Draws something to be useful with: / In any form some truths will hold; / Employ the present-sanctioned mold" (3.21.184–87).

Derwent's representation of Christian faith divested of dogma and reduced to a mere "myth" highlights the risks of its gradual irrelevance, as liberal-minded clergy like him seek to create a more inclusive church. Derwent accordingly presents the case of a creed like Christianity which is in apparent decay but which radiates out into various cultural forms, belying its apparent decline by becoming a ubiquitous spiritual presence:

> Suppose an instituted creed
> (Or truth or fable) should indeed
> To ashes fall; the spirit exhales,
> But reinfunds in active forms:
> Verse, popular verse, it charms or warms—
> Bellies Philosophy's flattened sails—
> Tinctures the very book, perchance,
> Which claims arrest of its advance.
> Why, the true import, deeper use
> Shows first when Reason quite slips noose,
> And Faith's long dead. (3.21.191–200)

Derwent's hypothesis of how faith infuses cultural forms even as it dwindles in potency again evokes the generally skeptical English religious climate of the 1870s while suggesting an expertise in ecclesiastical history associated with Derwent's apparent historical model, Arthur P. Stanley. In keeping with the Arnoldian redefinition of religious faith as grounded in moral conduct and made more appealing with a poetic mythology, moreover, Derwent adduces the comparable case of the priests of Greek religion after the advent of Christ who have no choice but to "temporize," being "stranded upon an interim / Between the ebb and flood" (3.21.215–16). In reply, Clarel invokes the controverted sacrament of Christian Communion, and whether the bread and wine are "mystic flesh and blood" or "conjurer's balsam" (3.21.223, 226); for against what he believes is Derwent's moral trimming, he claims an earnest concern for religious truth. Derwent then retreats to the Arnoldian position that the moral conduct of doing good is the ultimate task of religion, and no man can doubt the utility of good "done any way, / In any name, by any brotherhood" (3.21.234–35). Furthermore, Derwent advocates a reliance on the emotions over the intellect according to the needs of all humanity:

> Less light
> Than warmth needs earthly wight.
> Christ built a hearth: The flame is dead
> We'll say, extinct; but lingers yet,
> Enlodged in stone, the hoarded heat.
> Why not nurse that? Would rive the door
> And let the sleet in? (3.21.243–47)

Derwent confesses that he, too, went through a phase of early doubts, but he learned to imitate the example of Christ and he advises Clarel to adhere to a rationalistic golden mean: "But, for the rest, / Be not extreme. Midway is best" (3.21.277–78). In reaction to Derwent's consolatory rationalizations of the decline of contemporary faith, Clarel violently reacts to the Anglican priest's evasions by telling Derwent to "Forbear!" (3.21.300) while presenting the figure of Job as an example of the emotional pain of doubting: "Own, own with me, and spare to feign / Doubt bleeds, nor Faith is free from pain!" (3.21.303–4). But Derwent's closing advice to Clarel is still to keep to the surface and not explore the dangerous depths of thought that promise only despair: "This shaft you sink shall strike no bloom: / The surface, ah, heaven keeps *that* green; / Green, sunny: nature's active scene, / For man appointed, man's true home" (3.21.309–12).

Throughout this discussion, then, Derwent plays the role of a representative Broad Church clergyman, seeking to accommodate Clarel within the expansive realm of contemporary Protestant faith, where many may harbor doubts but all still hold to the moral mission of Christianity to do good in the world. The debate between Clarel and Derwent accordingly evokes the penetrating criticisms of the Broad Church party by Leslie Stephen in his contemporaneous essay on this group, which Stephen saluted as containing some of the best minds of the country and praised for being open to debate. "The great merit of Broad Churchmen is that they try to meet argument fairly, and admit in theory the importance of searching, fair, and unfettered inquiry." But the problem was that the Broad Churchmen inevitably held onto their faith by willfully or inadvertently overlooking the logical contradictions of their arguments. "They protest, and I doubt not with perfect sincerity, that they throw aside all considerations except the simple desire of discovering the truth. And yet their investigations always end in opinions which are at least capable of expression in the words of the most antiquated formulae." Such a species of intellectual trimming is typical of how the Broad Church clergy watered down Christian doctrine until it was virtually meaningless: "The Atonement is spiritualized till it becomes difficult to attach any definite meaning to it whatever. The authority of the Bible becomes more difficult to define and to distinguish from the authority of any other good book. Everlasting punishment is put out of the way by the aid of judicious metaphysical distinctions. The sharp edges of old-fashioned doctrine are rounded off till the whole outline of the creed is materially altered." In short, members of the Broad Church party liberalize and transform the essential biblical and dogmatic tenets of Christianity into something so reasonable and insipid that it utterly fails to appeal to those like Clarel, Mortmain, and Ungar who look to faith to justify the universal sins and sufferings of the world.[52]

Ungar

The figure of Ungar in part 4 is the last major character added to the group of pilgrims and shows up while they are on their way to Bethlehem from Mar Saba. A disillusioned part Native American Confederate veteran whose family originated in Catholic Maryland, Ungar has apparently worked to train the Egyptian army in a program initiated by the ambitious Egyptian khedive

Ismail in the late 1860s in an attempt to modernize his country's armed forces and expand his power into the Upper Nile using former Union and Confederate officers; a total of forty-eight American veterans served in various capacities until the program ended in 1878, after which many of them gave lectures and published books and articles on their Egyptian adventures.[53] Thus, in canto 4 ("An Intruder"), in answer to a query from Rolfe about the new stranger's identity, the Druze reports that he had previously seen the displaced American veteran "drilling some tawny infantry / In shadow of a Memphian wall, / White-robed young conscripts up the Nile" (4.5.28–30); and accordingly to the Druze, Ungar has more recently been seen in the role of arms dealer "on Jaffa beach, / With Turkish captains holding speech / Over some cannon in pile / Late landed" (4.5.31–34). Rolfe inwardly speculates on the potential reason for Ungar's self-exile to a Muslim country and culture, whether because of the devastation of the South in the Civil War, or scorn of the dishonor of Reconstruction; but as the narrator goes on to note, Ungar's bitter temper stems from the sense of multiple disinheritance he has experienced as a descendant of Maryland Catholics in a Protestant land; as a white man with Indian blood (Ungar, the narrator notes, is his "forest name" [4.5.142]); and as a Southern opponent of slavery within the defeated South. Refusing to resign himself to humiliation and defeat, Ungar upholds his loyalty to his vanquished section by framing it in terms of the Old Testament story of Rizpah standing guard, like Antigone, over the bodies of Saul's seven dead sons, killed by his enemy David; for "true is one / Unto death" (4.6.178–79).

The close resemblance between Ungar's reactionary conservatism and the influential thought of Thomas Carlyle becomes evident as Ungar enters into debate with the other pilgrims. The first night in Bethlehem, Ungar thus lingers on the terrace stairs of the convent where the pilgrims are staying in order to look at the stars: "Look up: the age, the age forget— / There's something to look up at yet!" (4.7.99–100). Ungar's reverence for the stars here may remind us of a central tenet of Carlyle's thought in the human duty to reverence a higher authority. Diogenes Teufelsdröckh memorably makes such claims in the chapter on "Organic Filaments" near the end of the editor's account of his spiritual evolution in *Sartor Resartus*:

> "True it is that, in these days, man can do almost all things, only not obey. True likewise that whoso cannot obey cannot be free, still less bear rule; he that is the inferior of nothing, can be the superior of nothing, the equal of nothing. Nevertheless, believe not that man has lost his faculty of Reverence; that if it slumber in him, it has gone dead. Painful for man is that same rebellious Independence, when it has become inevitable; only in loving companionship with his fellows does he feel safe; only in reverently bowing down before the Higher does he feel himself exalted."[54]

When the pilgrims go exploring the so-called Valley of the Shepherds after their first night in Bethlehem, a heated debate springs up between Derwent and Ungar. Chafing at Rolfe's avoidance of Ungar's allusion to the act of Southern secession as akin to the story of Lot and Abraham's peaceful agreement to occupy different territories (4.9.65–81), Ungar turns his ire on Derwent in a tirade against the Anglo-Saxon races of England and America who combine evangelical Christianity with free trade to dominate the globe with their imperialistic greed:

> The Anglo-Saxons—lacking grace
> To win the love of any race;
> Hated by myriads dispossessed
> Of rights—the Indians East and West.
> These pirates of the sphere! grave looters—
> Grave, canting, Mammonite freebooters,
> Who in the name of Christ and Trade
> (Oh, bucklered forehead of the brass!)
> Deflower the world's last sylvan glade!" (4.9.117–25)

Ungar's bitter critique of modern Anglo-American materialism and hypocrisy is worthy of Carlyle in his most outspoken prophetic mode, especially when the Confederate veteran attacks the misery of the child laborer and industrial worker in the mills and factories of England: "How may Hughs of Lincoln, say / Does Mammon in his mills, to-day / Crook, if he do not crucify?" (4.9.133–35). Mimicking the indignant accents of book 3 ("The Modern Worker") of Carlyle's *Past and Present* (1843), Ungar, like the Victorian social critic, excoriates the economic and social injustices of industrial England in the manner of Carlyle's attacks on the "Gospel of Mammonism": "In brief, all this Mammon-Gospel, of Supply-and-demand, Competition, Laissez-faire, and Devil take the hindmost, begins to be one of the shabbiest Gospels ever preached on Earth; or altogether the shabbiest. . . . The haggard despair of Cotton-factory, Coal-mine operatives, Chandos Farm-labourers, in these days, is painful to behold; but not so painful, hideous to the inner sense, as that brutish godforgetting Profit-and-Loss Philosophy, and Life-theory, which we hear jangled on all hands of us." The misery of England's laboring classes is relentlessly put on display as Carlyle accuses the aristocracy of crimes against humanity: "Two million shirtless or ill-shirted workers sit enchanted in Workhouse Bastilles, five million more (according to some) in Ugolino Hunger-cellars; and for remedy, you say,—what say you?—'Raise *our* rents!' "[55]

Ungar's complaints against the modern Anglo-American world of commercial dominance continues in the pilgrim's ensuing visits to sites around Bethlehem. In canto 10 ("A Monument"), when the pilgrims are exploring the hills around the city of Christ's birth, Ungar begins a speech praising the sanctity of religion in the Middle Ages. Again sounding like a latter-day Carlyle in *Past and Present*, Ungar notes the vital role of religion in medieval society: "Religion then was the good guest, / First served, and last, in every gate" (4.10.89–90). By contrast, the present people of England and America, with their superficial education, are allegedly more ignorant and more easily misled than their forbears. In a previous era, "the Church was like a bonfire warm; / All ranks were gathered round the charm" (4.10.124–25). Ungar's nostalgia for the inherent moral authority and sanctity of medieval Christianity leads Derwent to label Ungar's nostalgia a "*bric-a-brac-ish* style (outgrown / Almost, where first it gave the tone) / Of lauding the quaint ages old" (4.10.130–33), an apt description of his Carlylean rhetoric. Derwent answers Ungar's outspoken Carlylean charges with a reminder that such medieval times were well named "Dark Ages" (4.10.137). Ungar rebuts this claim by now turning to the argument that the grand cathedrals of the Middle Ages show a superlative religious excellence, thereby anticipating the Carlyle- and Ruskin-inspired arguments of Charles Eliot Norton's *Historical Study of Church-Building in the Middle Ages: Venice, Siena, Florence* (1880) and Henry Adams's *Mont-Saint-Michel and Chartres* (1904). Thus, "the grand minsters" of the time "do intimate, if not declare / A magnanimity which our time / Would envy, were it great enough / To comprehend" (4.10.145–49). Despite the ex-Confederate's insults to Protestant England and its culture, which has allegedly become "lukewarm" and sect-riven, Derwent concludes that Ungar is not worth debating in his "maddest tide" (4.10.158). The reason for Ungar's bitterness is presumed to be a conservative Catholic heritage which, despite his own personal lack of adherence to "any one elected creed" (4.10.182), makes him outspoken. Like Carlyle, Ungar defends the vital role of religion for Western civilization without identifying himself with any particular sect or theological tradition.[56]

Later, on another expedition after visiting the Church of the Nativity in Bethlehem, the pilgrims discuss the credibility of Luke's account of the birth of Christ. To Derwent's soothing claim that the Holy Land shrines keep alive the "spell of the transmitted story" (4.18.69) of Christ's life, Rolfe replies that the Christian sites strain credulity just as in ancient Greece various fabulous sites associated with heroes like Jason and Agamemnon were shown to visitors. To this Derwent replies that even if "Madonna's but a dream, / The Manger and the Crib" (4.18.94–95), human beings will still maintain their faith despite "what sages say" (4.18.97) about scientific laws undercutting such illusions; he goes on to argue that the utility and sentiment of Christianity will keep it vital in the midst of contemporary decline:

> Though Faith no doubt
> Seems insubstantial as a sigh,
> Never ween that 'tis a water-spout
> Dissolving, dropping into dew

At pistol-shot. Besides, review
That comprehensive Christian scheme;
It catches man at each extreme:
Simple—august; strange as a dream,
Yet practical as plodding life:
Not use and sentiment at strife." (4.18.103–12)

According to Derwent, Christianity will not collapse in a scientific age because it is both practical and idealistic. Ungar, on the other hand, adduces the "callousness in clay" (4.18.121) that makes people unable to appreciate "Christ's pastoral parables divine" (4.18.122); and when Derwent argues that the power of Christianity is proven by the historical conversion of the Western world to this creed in the first millennium, Ungar counters that the conversion did not affect humanity's cynical worldliness; indeed, the essential nature of contemporary Protestant Christianity is, as Carlyle might have agreed, more worldly than devout: "So far as working practice goes, / More minds with shrewd Voltaire have part / Than now own Jesus in the heart" (4.18.143–45).

In Ungar's mind, the decline of faith in the modern world is an incontrovertible fact, and Derwent to him represents a smoothly rationalizing opponent who refuses to recognize the dire moral condition of the modern world. Ungar again denounces in Carlylean terms the fate of workers trapped by England's modern industrial economy: "Pauperism's unhappy sons / In cloud so blackly ominous, / Grimy in Mammon's English pen— / Collaterals of his overplus" (4.20.85–88). For Ungar, a more authoritarian Christianity would be the guarantor of moral order to match the evils of the modern day, as seen in the recent "new uprising of the Red" (4.21.126) in the Paris Commune of 1870, whose participants "made a clothes-stand of the Cross" (4.20.128). When in an ensuing canto Rolfe debates with Ungar and questions him concerning the fate of America, which is presumably immune to European moral decline, Ungar harshly rejects such optimism, coming out with a scathing Carlylean judgment on modern America in response to an imagined conversation between the voices of Progress and God: "How profits it? And who are thou / That we should serve Thee? Of Thy ways / No knowledge we desire; *new* ways / We have found out, and better. Go—" (4.21.31–35). When Rolfe adduces the theory that the New World's "vast reserves—the untried fields" (4.21.90) will delay any imminent class war such as one finds in Europe, preserving America from the evils of materialism, Ungar has a ready answer to such exceptionalist views. He thus believes that political and cultural developments in the New World are so rapid that de-Christianized "rival sharp communities" (4.22.115) will eventually be in conflict in another devastating Thirty Years War. For the illiberal Ungar, the absence of Christian faith will allegedly lead America to an atheistic, materialistic, and barbaric future:

"Know,
Whatever happen in the end,
Be sure 'twill yield to one and all
New confirmation of the fall
Of Adam. Sequel may ensue,
Indeed, whose germs one now may view:
Myriads playing pygmy parts—
Debased into equality:
In glut of all material arts
A civic barbarism may be:
Man disennobled—brutalized
By popular science—Atheized
Into a smatterer—" (4.21.21–33)

For Ungar, there is no hope in America for a morally healthy civilization. Indeed, the "pygmy parts" seemingly mandated by democracy evoke the description of the "Pigmean Race" of devils found in Satan's "infernal Court" at the end of book I of *Paradise Lost*, where "Earth's Giant Sons / Now less than smallest Dwarfs, in narrow room / Throng numberless" (I, 778–80). The rest of Ungar's description leaves no doubt of a hellish future in America. In Ungar's hatred of the soullessness and decadence of American democracy, he sounds especially like Carlyle in his later reactionary phase in the 1850s and 1860s as a social prophet, as expressed in his cantankerous attacks on democracy, populism, laissez-faire capitalism, and abolitionism in *Latter-Day Pamphlets* (1850), or in his multivolume hero-worshiping biography of Frederick the Great, *History of Frederick II of Prussia* (1858–65). So, too, in 1867 Carlyle published a scathing attack on the advent of full participatory democracy in England with the passage of an extended franchise that year. Entitled *Shooting Niagara: And After?* and now best known as having provided the catalyst for Whitman's *Democratic Vistas* (1871), Carlyle's long magazine article, subsequently published as a pamphlet, warned England that it was following the lead of America in its reckless plunge into democratic equality and the deluded empowerment of the servile masses. Carlyle therefore appeals to various segments of the aristocracy to assume their rightful role as national leaders. Early in his essay Carlyle envisages the disintegration of Christianity into a series of liberal panaceas such as liberty of conscience, progress of intellect, and general philanthropy; and continuing his relentless attack, he adduced a connection between religious and political corruption through the rising popular tide of democracy, leading to a hellish future:

> Singular, in the case of human swarms, with what perfection of unanimity and quasi-religious conviction the stupidest absurdities can be received as axioms of Euclid, nay as articles of faith, which you are not only to believe, unless malignantly insane, but are (if you have any

> honour or morality) to put into practice, and without delay see done, if your soul would live! Divine commandment to vote ("Manhood Suffrage,"—Horsehood, Doghood ditto not yet treated of); universal "glorious Liberty" (to Sons of the Devil in overwhelming majority, as would appear); count of heads the God-appointed way in this Universe; all other ways Devil-appointed; in one brief word, which includes whatever of palpable incredibility and delirious absurdity, universally believed, can be uttered or imagined on these points, "the equality of men," or any man equal to any other; Quashee Nigger to Socrates or Shakespeare; Judas Iscariot to Jesus Christ;—and Bedlam and Gehenna equal to New Jerusalem, shall we say?[57]

At one point in *Shooting Niagara*, Carlyle advocated military service for all English youth, and he wrote at the end of his diatribe, in a passage reflecting his admiration for Frederick the Great: "I often say, The One Official Person, royal, sacerdotal, scholastic, governmental, of our times, who is still thoroughly a truth and a reality, and *not* in great part a hypothesis, and worn-out humbug, proposing and attempting a duty which he fails to do,—is the Drill-Sergeant who is master of his work, and who will perform it."[58] It would seem that the exiled Confederate veteran Ungar in Melville's poem is just such a Carlylean drill sergeant, with an outspoken contempt for his fellow Americans' democratic dogmas, and a profession of drilling troops for Egyptian and Ottoman despots. The American pilgrims' reaction to Ungar's diatribes is to think of him as overly embittered by exile even as they recognize some possible factual basis for his remarks.

The Epilogue

Following Clarel's disappearance into the obscurities of the Jerusalem streets on the day of Whitsunday or Pentecost, Melville's narrative poem ends with an epilogue that seems to reverse the somber denial of spiritual immortality dramatized in the previous canto; for we now find the assertion that in the natural flux of human emotions, an instinctive Faith will always overcome a cynical Despair by inscribing "on her shards of broken urns / The sign o' of the cross—*the spirit above the dust*!" (4.35.10–11). The debate between humanity's lower and higher natures, its animal and spiritual identities, will in fact continue to run on forever, despite the findings of Darwinian evolutionism and despite the absence of a providential God: "The running battle of the star and clod / Shall run forever—if there be no God" (4.35.16–17). With this in mind, the narrator in his final apostrophe urges Clarel, like Derwent in their previous exchanges, to stay true to his emotions ("Then keep thy heart, though yet but ill resigned— / Clarel, thy heart, the issues there but mind"), for he may eventually find his Christian hopes confirmed in an irrepressible natural process like a "crocus budding through the snow" or "a swimmer rising from the deep" (4.35.29, 30). In the end, Clarel may unexpectedly discover a form of immortality now described in terms similar to St. Paul's well-known interrogation of death at the end of his discussion of the soul as a "seed" that will inevitably emerge with a spiritual body: "O death, where is thy sting? O grave, where is thy victory?" (1 Cor. 15:55). Addressing his heartbroken protagonist, the narrator notes that the apparent spiritual annihilation of death may still bring eternal life: "Emerge thou mayst from the last whelming sea, / And prove that death but routs life into victory" (4.35.33–34). The narrator's final representation of the possibility of personal immortality thus falls back on what modern psychological research has named humanity's "implicit theism," based on the apparent naturalness of religious belief, as opposed to the more unnatural mindset of scientific rationalism.[59]

Commentators have discussed the dramatic, philosophical, and theological dimensions of the "Epilogue" to Melville's poem, and whether it detracts from, or adds to, the development of its themes; in short, whether it is an unearned attempt at an optimistic conclusion, or a hard-won finale to the poem's theological debates.[60] Viewed within the context of the Victorian Crisis of Faith, we can see that the narrator's last-ditch assertion of the possibility of spiritual immortality addresses a much-debated issue underlying the prolonged theological disputes of the era, and one that upheld many contemporary Christians' tenuous religious faith, in accordance with St. Paul's grounding of Christian belief in Christ's resurrection. The hopeful tenor of the "Epilogue" to *Clarel* thus resembles the ultimate message of Clough's "Through a Glass Darkly," which explores the baffling moral mystery of human life, including the enigmatic possibilities for an afterlife. Unlike a number of his poems expressing religious doubt, the speaker here answers his own relentless questions on ultimate spiritual truth with the assurance that human hope for personal immortality will find fulfillment:

> And yet, when all is thought and said,
> The heart still overrules the head;
> Still what we hope we must believe,
> And what is given us receive;
>
> Must still believe, for still we hope
> That in a world of larger scope,
> What here is faithfully begun
> Will be completed, not undone.
>
> My child, we still must think, when we
> That ampler life together see,
> Some true result will yet appear
> Of what we are, together, here. (ll. 21–32)

The insistence in the "Epilogue" to *Clarel* that the young American should trust the conclusions of his heart and may be surprised into the discovery of a heavenly afterlife are thus similar to Clough's uncharacteristically hopeful assertions.

In Tennyson's *In Memoriam* as well, the speaker gradually works toward a sense of faith and hope comparable to that found in the "Epilogue" to *Clarel*, following the speaker's prolonged religious despair and mourning for his lost friend. Thus in section CXXIV late in the poem, the speaker notes that his faith reawakened when his heart asserted the right of the emotions to be heard and felt, with their tenacious belief in a divine father and creator:

> If e'er when faith had fall'n asleep,
> I heard a voice "believe no more"
> And heard an ever-breaking shore
> That tumbled in the Godless deep;
>
> A warmth within the breast would melt
> The freezing reason's colder part,
> And like a man in wrath the heart
> Stood up and answer'd "I have felt." (ll. 9–16)

So, too, in the ensuing section, the speaker moves toward a climactic hymn to love embodied in the person of Christ as he perceives his hope reviving of joining his friend in a future spiritual world:

> Whatever I have said or sung,
> Some bitter notes my harp would give,
> Yea, tho' there often seem'd to live
> A contradiction on the tongue,
>
> Yet Hope had never lost her youth;
> She did but look through dimmer eyes;
> Or Love but play'd with gracious lies,
> Because he felt so fix'd in truth:
>
> And if the song were full of care,
> He breathed the spirit of the song;
> And if the words were sweet and strong
> He set his royal signet there;
>
> Abiding with me till I sail
> To seek thee on the mystic deeps,
> And this electric force, that keeps
> A thousand pulses dancing, fail.

Tennyson's elegy accordingly ends in hope, with the marriage of the poet's sister and the prolonged celebration of Christ as a god of love whose mission and message redeem the evils of the world.

Finally, the hopeful tenor of Melville's "Epilogue" is comparable to John Stuart Mill's unexpected defense of the idea of personal immortality at the end of his essay on "Theism," based on the psychologically beneficial effects of such hope. Here Mill argued that if truth requires the rigorous use of reason, the imagination also needs liberal cultivation; and "in the regulation of the imagination literal truth of facts is not the only thing to be considered."

> On these principles it appears to me that the indulgence of hope with regard to the government of the universe and the destiny of man after death, while we recognize as a clear truth that we have no ground for more than a hope, is legitimate and philosophically defensible. The beneficial effect of such a hope is far from trifling. It makes life and human nature a far greater thing to the feelings, and gives greater strength as well as greater solemnity to all the sentiments which are awakened in us by our fellow-creatures and by mankind at large. . . . The truth that life is short and art is long is from of old one of the most discouraging parts of our condition; this hope admits the possibility that the art employed in improving and beautifying the soul itself may avail for good in some other life, even when seemingly useless for this.[61]

In the "Epilogue" to *Clarel*, the narrator evokes the figure of Despair writing its "bitter pasquinade" (4.35.7) on the ancient Sphinx, a symbol of the mystery of human identity and destiny, thereby implying just such an irony as Mill evokes above in the futility of developing a full human character in the face of human extinction. Maintaining the hope for a spiritual immortality is thus a means to promote good character development and human welfare generally. Moreover, just as Mill himself had recovered from a crippling depression and spiritual crisis in his youth by reading Wordsworth's poetry, so at the end of his largely skeptical discussion of Christian theism, Mill admits the psychological utility of its chief doctrinal tenet.

At the end of his prolonged exploration in *Clarel* of the Anglo-American crisis of modern Christian faith, then, Melville had apparently reversed himself from his earlier resigned decision, while in conversation with Hawthorne in 1856, to be "annihilated" at death; such an apparent retreat of an earlier persistent skepticism is comparable to that found in the poetry of the older Emily Dickinson who, becoming more conscious of her own extinction, became more open to the doctrine of personal immortality. Yet the "Epilogue" to *Clarel* also illustrates the fact that religious faith in the modern world will be a constant battle between the cumulative findings of science and the residual instinct for faith, or between the demands of the critical intellect and the needs of the believing heart. From our review of the background to the poem in Victorian culture, it is also apparent that *Clarel* is a representative creation of the 1870s, a decade when the decline of traditional Protestant faith was reaching a critical index among the educated classes, and many writers were speculating on the shape of a post-Christian society in England, with Catholic and Orthodox faiths elsewhere in Europe assumed to be maintaining their hold on believers only through dogmatism and obscurantism. *Clarel* thus captures the tectonic shift in Western religious consciousness resulting from the simultaneous rise of modern skepticism and evolutionary science, creating "that vast eclipse, if slow / Whose passage yet we undergo / Emerging on an age untried" (4.8.12–14). As the most comprehensive literary expression of the Victorian Crisis of Faith, *Clarel* thus melds English intellectual history with a group of pilgrims largely of American composition to create a hybrid, cosmopolitan depiction of a cultural crisis from which we have still not emerged almost a century and a half later.

Notes

1. Herman Melville, *Journals*, ed. Howard C. Horsford with Lynn Horth (Evanston and Chicago: Northwestern University Press and the Newberry Library, 1989), 628–29; for a full record of Hawthorne's comments, see 624–33.

2. William Levine, *Apes, Angels, and Victorians* (Cleveland: World Publishing, 1959), 13.

3. On Vine as a negative portrait of Hawthorne's personal and artistic weaknesses, see Hershel Parker, "The Character of Vine in Melville's *Clarel*," *Essays in Arts and Sciences* 15 (June 1986): 91–113. See also Beverly R. Voloshin, "Parables of Creation: Hawthorne, Melville, and Plato's *Banquet*," *Leviathan* 13 (October 2011): 18–29.

4. The closest Hawthorne came to a confession of faith in spiritual immortality was a notebook entry made on July 29, 1849 in connection with his mother's impending death in which he claimed that human life would be a "mockery" without an afterlife: "But God would not have made the close so dark and wretched, if there were nothing beyond; for then it would have been a fiend that created us, and measured out our existence, and not God. It would be something beyond wrong—it would be an insult—to be thrust out of life into annihilation in this miserable way. So, out of the very bitterness of death, I gather the sweet assurance of a better state of being" (*American Notebooks*, ed. Claude M. Simpson [Columbus: Ohio State University Press, 1972], 429). Hawthorne, unlike Melville, believed that an alternative to conventional Christian faith was simply unthinkable. For a useful review of Hawthorne's religious beliefs, see Joseph Schwartz, "Nathanial Hawthorne and the Natural Desire for God," *The Nathaniel Hawthorne Review 1972*, ed. C. E. Frazer Clark (Washington, D.C.: NCR/ Microcard Editions, 1973), 159–71.

5. On the problem of doubt in later nineteenth-century American culture, see Paul A. Carter, *The Spiritual Crisis of the Gilded Age* (DeKalb: Northern Illinois University Press, 1971); D. H. Meyer, "American Intellectuals and the Victorian Crisis of Faith," *American Quarterly* 27 (1975): 585–603; James Turner, *Without God, Without Creed: The Origins of Unbelief in America* (Baltimore: Johns Hopkins University Press, 1986). On related themes in later nineteenth-century American fiction, see Leo F. O'Connor, *Religion in the American Novel: The Search for Belief, 1860–1920* (Lanham, Md.: University Press of America, 1984).

6. On Melville's knowledge of Arnold's poetry, see Walter E. Bezanson, "Melville's Reading of Arnold's Poetry," *PMLA* 69 (1954): 365–91; Bezanson suggests that "Stanzas from the Grande Chartreuse" had the greatest influence on *Clarel*, followed by "Empedocles on Etna." On the Arnoldian aesthetics of *Clarel*, see Shirley M. Dettlaff, "Ionian Form and Esau's Waste: Melville's View of Art in *Clarel*," *American Literature* 54 (1982): 212–28.

7. A number of critics have examined the religious thematics and the problem of faith in Melville's poem, but none so far have interpreted it specifically in the context of the Victorian Crisis of Faith. See, for example, Richard Harter Fogle, "Melville's *Clarel*: Doubt and Belief," *Tulane Studies in English* 100 (1960): 301–16; Joseph G. Knapp, *Tortured Synthesis: The Meaning of Melville's "Clarel"* (New York: Philosophical Library, 1971); Stanley Brodwin, "Herman Melville's *Clarel*: An Existential Gospel," *PMLA* 86 (May 1971): 375–87; William H. Shurr, *The Mystery of Iniquity: Melville as Poet, 1857–1891* (Lexington: University Press of Kentucky, 1972); chaps. 2–3; Vincent S. Kenny, *Herman Melville's "Clarel": A Spiritual Autobiography* (Hamden, Conn.: Shoe String, 1973); Bernard Rosenthal, "Herman Melville's Wandering Jews," in *Puritan Influences in American Literature*, ed. Emory Elliott (Urbana: University of Illinois Press, 1979), 167–92; Joseph Flibbert, "The Dream of Religious Faith in Herman Melville's *Clarel*," *American Transcendental Quarterly* 50 (Spring 1980): 129–37; Wyn Kelley, "Haunted Stone: Nature and City in *Clarel*," *Essays in Arts and Science* 15 (June 1986): 15–29; Zephyra Porat, "Towards the Promethean Ledge: Varieties of Skeptical Experience in Melville's *Clarel*," *Literature and Theology* 8 (March 1994): 30–46; Shirley M. Dettlaff, "'Counter Natures in Mankind': Hebraism and Hellenism in *Clarel*," in *Melville's Evermoving Dawn: Centennial Essays*, ed. John Bryant and Robert Milder (Kent, Ohio: Kent State University Press, 1997), 192–221; John T. Shawcross, "'Too Intellectual a Poet Ever to Be Popular': Herman Melville and the Miltonic Dimension to *Clarel*," *Leviathan* 4 (March and October 2002): 71–90; William Potter, *Melville's "Clarel" and the Intersympathy of Creeds* (Kent, Ohio: Kent State University Press, 2004); Samuel Otter, "How *Clarel* Works," in *A Companion to Melville*, ed. Wyn Kelley (London: Blackwell, 2006), 467–81; Robert Milder, *Exiled Royalties: Melville and the Life We Imagine* (New York: Oxford University Press, 2009), chap. 9; the essays on *Clarel* in the special issue "Melville and the Mediterranean," *Leviathan* 13 (October 2011); Martin Kevorkian, *Writing Beyond Prophecy: Emerson, Hawthorne, and Melville after the American Renaissance* (Baton Rouge: Louisiana State University Press, 2013), chap. 4. On the influence of the Bible in Melville's poem, see Nathalia Wright, *Melville's Use of the Bible* (Durham, N.C.: Duke University Press, 1949); Stan Goldman, *Melville's Protest Theism: The Hidden and Silent God in "Clarel"* (DeKalb: Northern Illinois University Press, 1993); Edgar

A. Dryden, *Monumental Melville: The Formation of a Literary Career* (Stanford, Calif.: Stanford University Press, 2004), chap. 3; Ilana Pardes, "Melville's Song of Songs: *Clarel* as Aesthetic Pilgrimage," in *Melville and Aesthetics*, ed. Samuel Otter and Geoffrey Sanborn (New York: Palgrave, 2012), chap. 12; and Robert K. Wallace, "Melville's Biblical Prints and *Clarel*," in *Melville as Poet: The Art of "Pulsed Life*," ed. Sanford E. Marowitz (Kent, Ohio: Kent State University Press, 2013). On *Clarel* in relation to nineteenth-century American religious tourism in the Holy Land, see Franklin Walker, *Irreverent Pilgrims: Melville, Browne, and Mark Twain in the Holy Land* (Seattle: University of Washington Press, 1974), chaps. 5–6; Hilton Obenzinger, *American Palestine: Melville, Twain, and the Holy Land Mania* (Princeton, N.J.: Princeton University Press, 1999), chaps. 5–8; Malini Johar Schueller, *U.S. Orientalisms: Race, Nationality, and Gender in Literature, 1790–1890* (Ann Arbor: University of Michigan Press, 2001), 26–40; Bruce A. Harvey, *American Geographics: U.S. National Narratives and the Representation of the Non-European World, 1830–1865* (Stanford, Calif.: Stanford University Press, 2002), chap. 3; Brian Yothers, *The Romance of the Holy Land in American Travel Writing* (Aldershot, Eng.: Ashgate, 2007), chap. 6; Yothers, *Sacred Uncertainty: Religious Difference and the Shape of Melville's Career* (Evanston, Ill.: Northwestern University Press, 2015), chap. 5.

8. On religion in Victorian Britain, see Owen Chadwick, *The Victorian Church*, 2 vols. (1966; London: SCM, 1987); Ian Bradley, *The Call to Seriousness: The Evangelical Impact on the Victorians* (New York: Macmillan, 1976); Hugh McLeod, *Religion and Society in England, 1850–1914* (New York: St. Martin's, 1996); Herbert Schlossberg, *The Silent Revolution and the Making of Victorian England* (Columbus: Ohio State University Press, 2002); Julie Melnyk, *Victorian Religion: Faith and Life in Britain* (Westport, Conn.: Praeger, 2008); Herbert Schlossberg, *Conflict and Crisis in the Religious Life of Late Victorian England* (New Brunswick, N.J.: Transaction, 2009).

9. On the larger history of England's relationship with the Holy Land, see Barbara W. Tuchman: *Bible and Sword: England and Palestine from the Bronze Age to Balfour* (1956; New York: Ballantine Books, 1981). On the rise of Christian Zionism in nineteenth-century England, see Donald M. Lewis, *The Origins of Christian Zionism: Lord Shaftesbury and Evangelical Support for a Jewish Homeland* (New York: Oxford University Press, 2009). On the "vernacular orientalism" uniting England to the Holy Land at this time, see Eitan Bar-Yosef, *The Holy Land in English Culture 1799–1917: Palestine and the Question of Orientalism* (Oxford: Clarendon, 2005); on Thomas Cook and the Holy Land, see 64–65.

10. On the Victorian Crisis of Faith as a general cultural phenomenon, see Basil Willey, *Nineteenth-Century Studies: Coleridge to Matthew Arnold* (New York: Columbia University Press, 1949); Basil Willey, *More Nineteenth-Century Studies: A Group of Honest Doubters* (New York: Columbia University Press, 1956); A. O. J. Cockshut, *The Unbelievers: English Agnostic Thought, 1840–1890* (New York: New York University Press, 1966); Bernard M. G. Reardon, *From Coleridge to Gore: A Century of Religious Thought in Britain* (New York: Longman, 1971); Elizabeth Jay, *Faith and Doubt in Victorian Britain* (Basingstoke, Eng.: Macmillan, 1986); Richard Helmstadter and Bernard Lightman, eds., *Victorian Faith in Crisis: Essays on Continuity and Change in Nineteenth-Century Religious Belief*

(Stanford, Calif.: Stanford University Press, 1991); Frank M. Turner, *Contesting Cultural Authority: Essays in Victorian Intellectual Life* (New York: Cambridge University Press, 1993); A. N. Wilson, *God's Funeral: A Biography of Faith and Doubt in Western Civilization* (New York: Ballantine, 1999); James C. Livingston, *Religious Thought in the Victorian Age: Challenges and Reconceptions* (New York: Continuum, 2006); Giles St. Aubyn, *Souls in Torment: Victorian Faith in Crisis* (London: Sinclair-Stevenson, 2011); Christopher Lane, *The Age of Doubt: Tracing the Roots of Our Religious Uncertainty* (New Haven, Conn.: Yale University Press, 2011). On the expression of faith and doubt in Victorian literature, see Robert Lee Wolff, *Gains and Losses: Novels of Faith and Doubt in Victorian England* (New York: Garland, 1977); David Jasper and T. R. Wright, eds., *The Critical Spirit and the Will to Believe: Essays in Nineteenth-Century Literature and Religion* (Basingstoke, Eng.: Macmillan, 1989); Lance St. John Butler, *Victorian Doubt: Literary and Cultural Discourses* (Lanham, Md.: Rowman and Littlefield, 1991); J. M. I. Klaver, *Geology and Religious Sentiment: The Effect of Geological Discovery on English Society and Literature between 1829 and 1859* (Leiden: Brill, 1997); Norman Vance, *Bible and Novel: Narrative Authority and the Death of God* (New York: Oxford University Press, 2013).

11. On Charles Lyell and geological theory in early nineteenth-century England, see Klaver, *Geology and Religious Sentiment*, chaps. 2–6; Lane, *Age of Doubt*, chap. 2. On Robert Chambers's *Vestiges* and its remarkable impact, see James A. Second, *Victorian Sensation: The Extraordinary Publication, Reception, and Secret Authorship of "Vestiges of the Natural History of Creation"* (Chicago: University of Chicago Press, 2000); Lane, *Age of Doubt*, chap. 4.

12. On George Eliot, Strauss, and Feuerbach, see Willey, *Nineteenth Century Studies*, chap. 8. On Essays and Reviews, see Willey, *More Nineteenth-Century Studies*, chap. 4; Reardon, *From Coleridge to Gore*, chap. 10; Victor Shea and William Whitla, eds., *Essays and Reviews: The 1860 Text and Its Reading* (Charlottesville: University Press of Virginia, 2000). On the relationship of Darwinian science and Protestant faith in England and America in the later nineteenth century, see Levine, *Apes, Angels, and Victorians*; James R. Moore, *The Post-Darwinian Controversies: A Study of the Protestant Struggle to Come to Terms with Darwin in Great Britain and America 1870–1900* (New York: Cambridge University Press, 1979); Jon H. Roberts, *Darwinism and the Divine in America: Protestant Intellectuals and Organic Evolution, 1859–1900* (Madison: University of Wisconsin Press, 1988); Livingston, *Religious Thought in the Victorian Age*, chaps. 5–6.

13. On Anne Brontë and religious doubt, see Lane, *Age of Doubt*, 75–91.

14. Alfred Tennyson, *In Memoriam*, ed. Erik Gray (New York: Norton, 2004), 41. Subsequent quotations from Tennyson's poetry will be from this edition.

15. On the influence of Lyell and Chambers on Tennyson's *In Memoriam*, see Graham Hough, "The Natural Theology of *In Memoriam*," *Review of English Studies* 23 (1947): 244–56; Willey, *More Nineteenth-Century Studies*, chap. 2.

16. Matthew Arnold, *The Poems of Matthew Arnold*, ed. Kenneth Allott (London: Longmans, 1965), 288–899. Subsequent quotations from Arnold's poetry will be from this edition.

17. On Arnold's religious ideas and development, see Willey, *Nineteenth-Century Studies*, chap. 10; Ruth apRoberts, *Arnold and God* (Berkeley: University

of California Press, 1983); James C. Livingston, *Matthew Arnold and Christianity: His Religious Prose Writings* (Columbia: University of South Carolina Press, 1986).

18. On Carlyle's religion and *Sartor Resartus*, see Willey, *Nineteenth-Century Studies*, chap. 4. On Disraeli's *Tancred* as ironic bildungsroman, see Nils Clausson, "'Picturesque Emotion' or 'Great Asian Mystery'? Disraeli's *Tancred* as an Ironic Bildungsroman," *Critical Survey* 16 (January 2004): 1–19. On Newman's *Gain and Loss*, see Wolff, *Gains and Losses*, 41–50. On Francis Newman, see Willey, *More Nineteenth-Century Studies*, chap. 1. On Froude, see Willey, *More Nineteenth-Century Studies*, chap. 3. On Froude's *Nemesis of Faith*, see Wolff, *Gains and Losses*, 394–402; Rosemarie Ashton, "Doubting Clerics: From James Anthony Froude to Robert Elsmere via George Eliot," in Jasper and Wright, *Critical Spirit*, 69–87.

19. See Linda M. Lewis, *Dickens, His Parables, and His Reader* (Columbia: University of Missouri Press, 2012); see also Dennis Walder, *Dickens and Religion* (London: Allen and Unwin, 1981); Janet L. Larsen, *Dickens and the Broken Scripture* (Athens: University of Georgia Press, 2008).

20. On George Eliot's religious development and the influence of Comte, see Willey, *Nineteenth-Century Studies*, chaps. 8–9; T. R Wright, *The Religion of Humanity: The Impact of Comtean Positivism on Victorian Britain* (New York: Cambridge University Press, 1986), chap. 5. On the Christian symbolism of *Daniel Deronda*, see Butler, *Victorian Doubt*, chap. 7; and on Christian themes in Eliot's fiction generally, see Vance, *Bible and Novel*, chap. 4.

21. Thomas Carlyle, *Past and Present*, ed. Richard Altick (1843; Boston: Houghton, Mifflin, 1965), 139–40.

22. John Ruskin, *The Works of John Ruskin*, ed. E. T. Cook and Alexander Wedderburn, 39 vols. (London: George Allen and Longmans, Green, 1903–1912), 36:115. On the development of Ruskin's religious ideas and sense of vocation, see Michael Wheeler, *Ruskin's God* (New York: Cambridge University Press, 2006).

23. Wilson, *God's Funeral*, 164.

24. As the Duke of Somerset noted, "So far from any approach to certainty, the opinions of educated society upon the most important questions which can occupy the human mind, appear at the present time to be more unsettled than at any previous period of European history (*Christian Theology and Modern Skepticism* [New York: Appleton, 1871], 9). On Swinburne's embrace of paganism, see Margot K. Louis, *Swinburne and His Gods: The Roots and Growth of an Agnostic Poetry* (Montreal: McGill-Queens University Press, 1990).

25. See Alan Willard Brown, *The Metaphysical Society: Victorian Minds in Crisis, 1896–1880* (New York: Columbia University Press, 1947). On the background to Huxley's use of the term "agnostic," see Bernard Lightman, *On the Origins of Agnosticism: Victorian Unbelief and the Limits of Knowledge* (Baltimore: Johns Hopkins University Press, 1987).

26. See Noel Annan, *Leslie Stephen: The Godless Victorian* (New York: Knopf, 1984).

27. On Mill's *Three Essays* and his views on religion generally, see Linda C. Raeder, *John Stuart Mill and the Religion of Humanity* (Columbia: University of Missouri Press, 2002).

28. For an extended discussion of Arnold's essays on religion, see apRoberts, *Arnold and God*, chaps. 8–12; Livingston, *Matthew Arnold*.

29. For the record of Melville's reading, see the catalogue at melvillesmarginalia.org. For Melville's personal journal of his trip to Palestine on which he based *Clarel*, see Melville, *Journals*, 73–95. For a survey of the most important Holy Land travelogues that contributed to the poem, see Dorothee Metlitsky Finkelstein, *Melville's Orienda* (New Haven, Conn.: Yale University Press, 1961), 59–91. For an overview of the composition of the poem, see Walter E. Bezanson, "Historical and Critical Note," in Herman Melville, *Clarel: A Poem and Pilgrimage in the Holy Land*, ed. Harrison Hayford, Alma A. MacDougall, Hershel Parker, and G. Thomas Tanselle (Evanston and Chicago: Northwestern University Press and the Newberry Library, 1991), 24–42. For a complete account of Melville's life in New York City while composing *Clarel*, see Hershel Parker, *Herman Melville: A Biography*, vol. 2, *1851–1891* (Baltimore: Johns Hopkins University Press, 2002), chaps. 31–36.

30. For a full account of some of the key figures in the Broad Church movement, see Tod E. Jones, *The Broad Church: A Biography of a Movement* (Latham, Md.: Lexington Books, 2003); see also Wolff, *Gains and Losses*, chap. 4; Jay, *Faith and Doubt*, chap. 3.

31. Jones, *Broad Church*, 296. On Stanley's *Sinai and Palestine* as a source for *Clarel*, see Nathalia Wright, "A Source for Melville's *Clarel*: Dean Stanley's *Sinai and Palestine*," *Modern Language Notes* 62 (1947): 110–16. On Stanley's 1862 Holy Land tour, see Arthur P. Stanley, *Sermons Preached before His Royal Highness The Prince of Wales during His Tour of the East in the Spring of 1862, with Notices of Some of the Localities Visited* (1863). For an insightful critique of the shortcomings of Derwent's optimistic faith, see Knapp, *Tortured Synthesis*, 45–52.

32. William Wordsworth, *The Prelude, or Growth of a Poet's Mind*, ed. Ernest de Selincourt (New York: Oxford University Press, 1970), 8. On Coleridge as the ultimate source of Broad Church ideas, see Charles Richard Sanders, *Coleridge and the Broad Church Movement: Studies in S.T. Coleridge, Dr. Arnold of Rugby, J. C. Hare, Thomas Carlyle, and F. D. Maurice* (Durham, NC: Duke University Press, 1942).

33. All quotations from *Clarel* cited in the text will be from Melville, *Clarel*, ed. Hayford, MacDougall, Parker, and Tanselle.

34. Shirley M. Dettlaff interprets Clarel's spiritual journey as poised between the antithetical religious and philosophical ideas of Hebraism and Hellenism, terms that Matthew Arnold popularized in the later 1860s in the essays that made up his *Culture and Anarchy* (1869). As she notes, "The question for Clarel at the beginning of the poem is whether or not he will become a true Hebraic pilgrim, opening his imagination to all the uncertainties that a sincere search for religious truth in the nineteenth century entails, or a Hellenic tourist, preferring merely a superficial, conventional tour of the Holy Land in which he merely exercises his fancy. The tests involve a dialectical process in which Clarel encounters Hellenic or Hebraic alternatives, not just in the intellectual discussions he hears but in his own personal life" (Dettlaff, "'Counter Natures,'" 206).

35. Algernon Swinburne, *The Works of Algernon Charles Swinburne* (Philadelphia: David McKay, n.d.), 166–67.

36. For a discussion of Swinburne's poem, see Louis, *Swinburne and His Gods*, 91–99.

37. On Rolfe, Vine, and Derwent as modern magi, see Brodwin, "Herman Melville's *Clarel*." On the larger significance of Clarel's relationship with Ruth, see Nina Baym, "The Erotic Motif of Melville's *Clarel*," *Texas Studies in Literature and Language* 16 (Summer 1974): 315–28. On the symbolism of death in the poem, see Basem L. Ra'ad, "The Death Plot in Melville's *Clarel*," *ESQ* 27 (First Quarter, 1981): 14–27.

38. Melville had admiringly visited the Oxford colleges in early May 1857 just before his return to New York following his prolonged tour of Europe and the Holy Land. See the entry for May 2, 1857, in *Journals*, 128–29.

39. See the evocation of Hawthorne's habitual emotional resistance to genuine intimacy with his male companions, as described by his son; Julian Hawthorne, *Nathaniel Hawthorne and His Wife*, 2 vols. (Boston: James R. Osgood, 1884), 1:88–90.

40. For a discussion of the Song of Songs here, see Pardes, "Melville's Song of Songs."

41. Arthur Hugh Clough, *Poetical Works*, ed. A. L. P. Norrington (New York: Oxford University Press, 1968), 56–60. Subsequent quotations from Clough's poetry will be from this edition.

42. For a study of the emergence of comparative religion in England, see Livingston, *Religious Thought in the Victorian Age*, chap. 7; Marjorie Wheeler-Barclay, *The Science of Religion in Britain, 1860–1915* (Charlottesville: University of Virginia Press, 2010). For the emergence of comparative religion in America with some attention to English developments in the work of F. D. Maurice and Max Müller, see Potter, *Melville's "Clarel,"* chaps. 1–6. For an excellent appraisal of some of the religious and philosophical dynamics of Rolfe's character, see Knapp, *Tortured Synthesis*, 84–98.

43. Leslie Stephen, "The Broad Church," in *Essays on Freethinking and Plainspeaking* (London: Longmans, Green, 1873), 7. In keeping with his Comtean perspective, John Stuart Mill noted the developmental nature of religious faith in his essay on "Theism": "the science of human nature and history is considered to show that the creeds of the past are natural growths of the human mind, in particular stages of its career, destined to disappear and give place to other convictions in a more advanced stage" (Mill, *Three Essays on Religion* [1874; Amherst, N.Y.: Prometheus Books, 1998], 126). William Potter (*Melville's "Clarel,"* 17) associates Rolfe's speech here with the teachings of the Roman poet Lucretius on the material and psychological sources of religion.

44. As the Duke of Somerset wrote of modern skepticism, "Some ingenious writers have endeavored to trace the source of Christianity to the schools and synagogues of Alexandria. They would even interpret the prophecy, 'Out of Egypt have I called my son,' in a mystic sense" (*Christian Theology and Modern Skepticism*, 70).

45. Leslie Stephen, *An Agnostic's Apology and Other Essays* (1893; London: Smith, Elder, 1903), 340.

46. Stephen, *Agnostic's Apology*, 91, 115.

47. Mill, *Three Essays*, 38–39.

48. Stephen, *Agnostic's Apology*, 106. John Stuart Mill similarly noted: "To imagine that a miracle will be wrought at death by the act of God making perfect

every one whom it is his will to include among his elect, might be justified by an express revelation duly authenticated, but it is utterly opposed to every presumption that can be deduced from the light of nature" (*Three Essays*, 211).

49. The Duke of Somerset similarly noted one of the forms that contemporary skepticism was taking: "The antiquarian skeptic explores records of undated antiquity, pursues the shadowy forms of Mithra and Zoroaster, and gropes among the oriental relics until he half believes he can descry the cradle of Christianity hidden amid the myths and cosmogonies of the remote East" (*Christian Theology and Modern Skepticism*, 14–15).

50. Stephen, *Agnostic's Apology*, 338–39, 340–41. See also Stephen's essay on "The Broad Church": "It is only a few who have the iconoclastic temperament and desire to break down the convenient old creeds, because they may be rotten at the core; but a large minority, or possibly a large majority, believe they are rotten, and that by a sudden crash or a slower process of decay, they will disappear or undergo some profound transformation" (*Essays on Freethinking and Plainspeaking*, 10). The Duke of Somerset similarly noted: "It is impossible to predict what will be the Protestantism of the future; but there are many indications that none of the existing denominations will resist the mental wear and tear of the next fifty years" (*Christian Theology and Modern Skepticism*, 179).

51. See Parker, "Character of Vine"; Milder, *Exiled Royalties*, 202–6.

52. Stephen, *Essays in Freethinking and Plainspeaking*, 14, 18, 31. For another discussion of Derwent and "In Confidence" highlighting the canto's Arnoldian aspects, see Milder, *Exiled Royalties*, 209–13. For a sympathetic portrayal of Derwent that presents him as espousing liberal "heterodox" beliefs, see Potter, *Melville's "Clarel,"* 55–60.

53. See William B. Hesseltine and Hazel C. Wolf, *The Blue and the Gray on the Nile* (Chicago: University of Chicago Press, 1961); Michael B. Oren, *Power, Faith, and Fantasy: America in the Middle East 1776 to the Present* (New York: Norton, 2007), chap. 9. For a thorough review of Ungar's historical and symbolic significance in relation to American ideas of the Holy Land, see Obenzinger, *American Palestine*, chap. 8.

54. Thomas Carlyle, *Sartor Resartus*, ed. Peter Sabor and Kerry McSweeney (New York: Oxford University Press, 1987), 189–90.

55. Carlyle, *Past and Present*, 185, 188, 173.

56. Basil Willey has noted that Carlyle's "divinity is a sort of amalgam of Jehovah, Odin, Calvin's predestinating God and the Soul of the World; his faith a blend of Old Testament monotheism, pantheism and philosophical necessitarianism" (*Nineteenth-Century Studies*, 113). Bernard Reardon has similarly called Carlyle's religion "a brew of strange ingredients: Old Testament prophecy, Norse mythology, Scotch Calvinism, German metaphysics" (*From Coleridge to Gore*, 378).

57. Thomas Carlyle, *Shooting Niagara: And After?* (London: Chapman and Hall, 1867), 4–5.

58. Carlyle, *Shooting Niagara*, 46.

59. The concept of "implicit theism" is based on three tenets: the intuitive recognition of others' mental states, leading to a "theory of mind"; the instinctive assumption of a mind-body dualism and its associated sense of psychological immortality; and the related teleological inference of a divine being. See Jesse

Bering, *The Belief Instinct: The Psychology of Souls, Destiny, and the Meaning of Life* (New York: Norton, 2011); Robert N. McCauley, *Why Religion Is Natural and Science Is Not* (New York: Oxford University Press, 2011).

60. See, for example, Shurr, *Mystery of Iniquity*, 120–23; James Duban, "From Bethlehem to Tahiti: Transcultural 'Hope' in *Clarel*," *Philosophical Quarterly* 70 (1991): 475–83; Pardes, "Melville's Song of Songs," 229–32. For biblical allusions in the "Epilogue," see Goldman, *Melville's Protest Theism*, 163–65.

61. Mill, *Three Essays*, 248, 249–50.

“Change Irreverent”

Evolution and Faith in “The Encantadas” and *Clarel*

Eileen McGinnis

> None can reply—all seems eternal now.
> The wilderness has a mysterious tongue,
> Which teaches awful doubt.
>
> —P. B. Shelley, “Lines on Mont Blanc,” qtd. in Charles Darwin, *Journal of Researches*

In his 1993 study *Melville’s Protest Theism*, Stan Goldman argues persuasively for reading *Clarel* as both a struggle with, and a search for, a hidden and unknowable deity. Less convincingly, Melville scholars have tended to locate the source of this divine eclipse (a common motif in the poem) in the ascendancy of Darwinian evolution, pointing out that Melville was writing *Clarel* “in the shadow of Darwin, whose theory of evolution had destroyed the idea of superintending providence.”[1] Walter Bezanson, the poem’s pioneering critic, reads *Clarel* as a testimony to “the apparent smash-up of revealed religion in the age of Darwin.”[2] James Corey even frames the poem, published seventeen years after the first edition of *Origin of Species*, as “a direct confrontation of Melville and Darwin.”[3] To complicate matters, Melville sets us up for this premise—faith in crisis during an age of science—in the opening lines. We first encounter Clarel, a young American theology student undergoing a crisis of faith, in his rented lodgings in Jerusalem. Bewildered and alone, he is disturbed in his musings by a “naturalistic knell” (1.1.23).[4] The alliterative adjective seems a red flag for science as antagonist, presiding over the demise of religious belief.

In this essay, I will argue that the easy and recurring opposition of faith and science in *Clarel* is yet another instance of Melville’s penchant for ironic indirection. It masks instead a deep and abiding interest in geological processes and evolutionary hypotheses, particularly as heuristics for thinking through the function and value of literary craft. Rather than reading *Clarel* as a reaction to a set of ideas put forth in 1859 with the publication of Darwin’s *Origin of Species*, I suggest that the poem continues a line of inquiry about the intersection of science, faith, and truth-telling that predates *Origin* by at least several years. To make the case, I will pair *Clarel*, which was published in 1876, with "The Encantadas, or the Enchanted Isles," first published in *Putnam's Monthly* in 1853. "The Encantadas" is a series of sketches that engage Darwin not as the originator of the theory of natural selection but as the naturalist author of the best-selling *Journal of Researches*, an account of his five years aboard the *H.M.S. Beagle*.[5] Although Melville scholars have often read "Encantadas" in isolation, it has a compelling link to *Clarel* in that the Galápagos Islands—the setting of both the sketches and Darwin's *Journal*—haunt Melville's descriptions of the Holy Land decades later. In both *Clarel* and "The Encantadas," moreover, the language of natural science becomes a vehicle for exploring aesthetic, ethical, and theological questions beyond its ken; these questions, Melville argues, can best be examined, if not answered, through literary experiments.

Connecting *Clarel* to the pre-Darwinian "Encantadas" also shows that Melville's preoccupation with evolution was ongoing rather than catalyzed by the publication of Darwin's *Origin*. As modern readers, we have tended to view the poem through a Darwinian lens. As a writer in the 1840s and 1850s, however, Melville was engaged with an earlier and more variegated world of Victorian geology and evolutionary discourse.[6] At the time, the most prominent evolutionary theories in the American popular press and on the lecture circuit were those of French naturalist Jean-Baptiste Lamarck and "Mr. Vestiges," the anonymous author of *Vestiges of the Natural History of Creation* (1844), posthumously confirmed as the Scottish journalist Robert Chambers. Readers would have encountered an extended (albeit critical) synopsis of Lamarckian evolution in the second volume of Charles Lyell's *Principles of Geology* (1832).[7] Although Lamarck is best known today for the concept of inheritance of acquired traits, he also subscribed, as did Chambers, to a widespread if unorthodox alternative to creationism known as *progressive evolution* or *the development hypothesis*. In contrast to Darwin's theory of natural selection, which emphasizes contingency and non-directed change, progressive evolution traces a movement from simplicity to ever-greater complexity, based on the unfolding of natural law. As such, it is considerably more expansive than species evolution, also incorporating hypotheses about cosmic change, embryonic development, and even political and social reform.

Moreover, while Charles Darwin would quickly become a scientific celebrity and figurehead for evolutionary theory in the 1860s and 1870s, the ideas expressed in Darwin's *Origin* were often not perceived as radically new, and the developmental theories that preceded natural selection continued to have currency long after 1859.[8] For instance, Harvard professor Francis Bowen framed Darwin's *Origin* as "the latest form of the development theory," while American botanist Asa Gray, a Darwin supporter, wrote in the *Atlantic Monthly* that Darwin's innovation was a "revival" of the "derivative hypothesis in a more winning shape."[9] Similarly, in one of three references to Darwin in *Clarel*, Melville claims that "Darwin is but his grandsire's son" (2.21.24).

By invoking Charles Darwin's proto-evolutionist grandfather Erasmus Darwin, Melville reveals both his own and others' sense of continuity between late-eighteenth-century and contemporary evolutionary ideas.

In calling attention to this continuity, I don't mean to suggest that the Darwinian context is irrelevant for our understanding of the poem. In fact, I will argue that there is an increased distance and abstraction in Melville's relationship to geological discourse in his late career, and that *Clarel* articulates problems of evolution, origins, and belief in a more overt way than would have made sense or would have been possible before 1859. But by casting *Clarel* as merely a response to the publication of *Origin* and its ideological aftermath, we risk losing sight of Melville's long-standing engagement with both questions of faith and evolution, not as necessary antagonists but as ongoing factors in Melville's attempts to craft an experimental American literature that bravely pursues the visible truth.[10]

Melville's Traveling Theory

Conceptually, the present essay has a close kinship with the fruitful contributions on Melville and religion in the last few decades that have defined themselves against Lawrance Thompson's classic formulation of a Melvillean "quarrel with God." Specifically, terms like "protest theism" (Stan Goldman) or "spiritual agnosticism" (Robert Milder), while varying somewhat in their implications,[11] move beyond rejection of or railing against an absent deity, aiming instead to indicate Melville's more expansive and productive engagement with questions of belief. In the criticism on *Clarel*, we find William Shurr praising the poem's inconclusive and irreducible nature; and more recently, Brian Yothers challenges Hilton Obenzinger's designation of the poem as an "infidel countertext" because the label flattens out *Clarel*'s multiple perspectives, which are not all skeptical or despairing.[12]

In an analogous vein, I argue that casting Melville's relationship to Darwinism and science more broadly as merely a quarrel or critique fails to understand how Melville's persistent questioning of evolutionary theories can also be a tool of both literary experimentation and epistemological inquiry. Goldman and Milder, along with several others, have read Melville's engagement with biblical sources and a nineteenth-century tradition of Holy Land travel writing as simultaneously a challenge to and a reanimation of those narratives.[13] Similarly, I read modern geology as a tool to think with, a way of hypothesizing about Melville's own literary process and craft of truth-telling. Rather than viewing contemporary scientific theories as merely an affront to his worldview, Melville uses the language of science to seek after a truth beyond the scope of scientific inquiry: a truth about human nature and our relationship to an elusive deity. In other words, Melville the author is engaged in a process of mythmaking, attempting to articulate "a truth about the world and humans that lies beyond what we can test and prove."[14] He actively repurposes evolutionary discourse to enrich this pursuit.

Another way of naming this questing spirit in Melville's work is through the metaphor of travel. The importance of travel—as a mechanism for reviving biblical and literary narratives, and as a figure for our fleeting knowledge of both human and divine nature—is elegantly elaborated in Jenny Franchot's essay "Melville's Traveling God" (1999). In contrast to Melville scholars who seek to pinpoint or "fix" his late-career religious position, Franchot argues that Melville's works, which often borrow structurally from the genre of travel narrative, trace that very act of spiritual restlessness—the "wandering to and fro" over deserts of skepticism and belief—that Hawthorne famously describes in his November 1856 journal entry.[15] While Christianity and spiritual quest are key concepts in Melville's fiction and poetry, their formulations are no longer inviolable but "remobilized" as "a form of authorial 'travel.' "[16] Also, unlike earlier scholars, Franchot sees religious quest as inextricable from cultural encounter and formal experimentation; in other words, questions of belief and divine immanence cannot be disentangled from those of human character and literary craft.

In "Wandering To-and-Fro: Melville and Religion" (2005), Emory Elliott similarly highlights the essential but inconclusive spiritual quest enacted through Melville's fiction and poetry. Borrowing Hawthorne's phrase, Elliott argues that Melville's "fictional texts strongly indicate that he knew that his wandering to-and-fro among religious doctrines and philosophical theories would never yield satisfying answers for him, but he appears never to have abandoned the search."[17] Like Franchot, he sees the religious thread in Melville's work as bound up with numerous others, whether psychological, anthropological, or aesthetic.[18] For Elliott, however, an inadvertent distortion of Franchot's work is its overemphasis on the aesthetic implications of Melville's engagement with religion at the expense of its real-world import, ignoring his critique of corrupt nineteenth-century religious institutions.[19]

Just as Franchot and Elliott understand the process of moving through and remixing biblical texts as "a generative authorial model" for Melville,[20] I also see Melville as a traveler through the texts of natural history, engaging questions about the age of the earth, animal extinction, and human origins several years before Darwin's *Origin of Species* was published. In other words, Melville is not merely a passive witness to his age and the aftermath of Darwinian evolution but a constant quester, productively borrowing from the language of modern geology and rewriting naturalist texts to generate his literary experiments. His process reflects what Edward Said describes as *traveling theory*, in which a theory, traveling some distance from its point of origin and encountering a new set of conditions, is transformed, taking on a new position and use. Rather than assuming that "all borrowings, readings, and interpretations are misreadings and misinterpretations," Said casts them instead as simply readings and interpretations forming "part of a historical transfer of ideas and theories from one setting to another."[21] Scientific theory "travels" when the European evolutionary doctrines of Lamarck and Chambers are resisted, accepted, or transmuted in an American (literary) context. For instance, as Ronald Numbers argues, Darwinism came to the United States not as a wholesale import, but rather as a protean signifier that has adapted to various historical, regional, and ideological contexts. For Numbers, the persistence of the term "evolution" (and of the link between Darwin and evolutionary theory) lies in its fluidity of meaning.[22] For our purposes here, traveling theory points to the possibility that Melville's engagement with evolutionary discourse is more than a "creative misreading" but instead an act of theorizing. As will be discussed below, in borrowing from but also transforming the geological discourse of works like Darwin's *Journal of Researches*, Melville opens up narrative possibilities while also developing unique hypotheses about human nature, the deity, and artistic craft.

Voyaging: Melville and Darwin in the Galápagos

Both Darwin and Melville voyaged to the Galápagos Islands as young men. Darwin spent five weeks there in the fall of 1835, part of a four-year stint as unpaid naturalist aboard the *H.M.S. Beagle*. Six years later, the *Acushnet*, a New Bedford whaler carrying the young sailor and soon-to-be-deserter, Herman Melville, made a brief stopover at San Christobal in the Galápagos for fuel and provisions, mostly tortoises, on its way to the Marquesas; he would sail through these equatorial volcanic islands at least twice more as a seaman on other ships before returning to Massachusetts in October 1844.[23] The islands had an imaginative hold on both figures, and they would make discursive returns to the Galápagos later in their careers: Darwin in his 1839 *Journal of Researches* (revised in 1845) and in the 1859 *Origin of Species*; Melville, most notably, in the series of ten sketches called "The Encantadas, or Enchanted Isles," which was serialized in *Putnam's* in 1853 and included three years later in his collection *The Piazza Tales*.

In this essay, I'm interested in how Melville's sketches voyage through the textual and epistemological terrain of Darwin's *Journal*, "wrestling" with it in the same multifaceted sense that Goldman attributes to Melville's struggle with and embrace of biblical sources.[24] Textual clues suggest that Melville is deliberately writing "The Encantadas" with Darwin's 1845 *Journal* in mind.[25] As H. Bruce Franklin concludes, "That Darwin provided materials for *The Encantadas* . . . seems undeniable. It would also seem that Melville meant his reader, as distinguished from what he called 'the superficial skimmer of pages,' to recognize these materials."[26] However, Melville works to obscure this linkage by denying Darwin a place in the shaping of his narrative: "Despite the near certainty that he had read the *Voyage*, the models that

Melville acknowledged for his version of the Galápagos were much older and, by most standards, less authoritative and accurate than Darwin's: first-hand accounts by a buccaneer, a whaling captain, and a captain of the U.S. Navy."[27] Melville's dismissal of all other reports, most notably Darwin's, as "barren, bootless allusions from some few passing voyagers or compilers"[28] suggests how Darwin's account of the islands will be subverted throughout the story, even as it fuels Melville's fictional experiment.

One might ask why Melville would go to the trouble of including Darwin's narrative as a partially obscured intertext, especially as the *Journal* predates the publication of *Origin of Species* by two decades. Given that Darwin only obliquely references evolution in the work, it of course doesn't make sense to attribute prescience or anticipation of Darwin's breakthrough theory of natural selection to Melville's choice of source text. Instead, the comparison reveals how each writer draws on a shared aesthetic, religious, and geological context to make sense of and define his respective craft. Moreover, while the second edition of Darwin's *Journal* did not have the cultural impact of *Origin of Species*, it was nonetheless a commercial success. After Darwin's initial contribution to the *Beagle* expedition notes attracted a wide readership and nearly sold out of its 1,500-copy print run, the work was published as a separate volume in 1839 and again in 1845, with revisions explicitly geared toward a general audience.

Melville's intertextual relationship with the second edition of Darwin's *Journal* is hardly surprising, given the extent to which Melville's writing was deeply embedded in his extensive reading practice and liberal borrowings from a broad range of sources, as scholars like John Samson and David Reynolds have argued.[29] Similarly, in the criticism on Melville and religion, Goldman has shown that Melville's irreverence—including his play, humor, borrowings, and denials—is inextricable from his respect for the raw materials of his narrative and verse experiments, in the sense that he deeply engages them as part of his compositional process.

In taking the position that Melville finds productive source material in Darwin's account of the islands, I differ from historian of science Edward Larson, who casts the portrait of the Galápagos in Melville's "Encantadas" as a foil to Darwin's *Journal of Researches*. According to Larson, Melville adopts a more commonly held view of the islands, one shared by earlier naturalists, as having a pre-Darwinian changelessness, their barrenness also indicating divine disfavor. In contrast, Larson is interested in tracing how Darwin's evolutionary lens "eventually transformed that remote, desolate archipelago into *a sacred site* for science" (italics mine). At stake in this opposition is a sense that Melville and Darwin inhabit distinct spheres, as when Larson writes, "Evolutionary naturalism, devoid of souls and curses, took shape within the scientific culture even as Melville wrote within the literary one."[30] However, I see Melville and Darwin as sharing a larger cultural and epistemological context than Larson gives them credit for here; further, Melville's text enacts his keen awareness of a changing worldview, through his description of a landscape that is on unstable ground, both spiritually and materially. While Larson acknowledges that Melville could have read Darwin's account, he sees in Melville's choice to deny the *Journal of Researches* as a named source a suggestion that the author found it too "spiritually sterile" to list.[31] On the contrary, as I will elaborate below, Melville's textual engagement with Darwin's *Journal* is generative not only of his literary experiments in "The Encantadas" but of his spiritual quest as well. Rather than rejecting Darwin's ideas, in other words, Melville adapts them to create new hypotheses about art and morality.

Revising Darwin's *Journal* thus becomes an act of traveling theory. Melville transforms Darwin's naturalistic observations and proto-evolutionary insights into meditations on artistic craft, particularly the relation between aesthetics and truthful vision in literary narrative. The multiple ways that scientific investigation interweaves with social commentary, psychological insights, and a biblical vernacular are already present in Darwin's narrative; Melville takes inspiration from these parallel threads, this latent tension between taxonomic order and nonlinear voyaging. He discerns and makes visible the "other and darker world" (*Piazza Tales*, 127) submerged within the *Journal*. For instance, in his encounters with the tortoise, that Galápagos native, Darwin is curiously unreflective about the competing modes of vision (and narration) that he employs to observe the island's reptiles. The tortoises, which initially strike Darwin's "fancy" as "antediluvian" in the context of the island's desolate landscape (*Voyage of the Beagle*, 324), are a few paragraphs later the subject of matter-of-fact gastronomic remarks: "the young tortoises make excellent soup; but otherwise the meat to my taste is indifferent" (*Voyage of the Beagle*, 325). Thus, as Melville's paired narrative underscores, *Journal of Researches* "shows Darwin habitually working not . . . from a perceived order in Nature but from a moral order to perceived analogies in Nature. Darwin's Nature is an anthropomorphic world."[32] In contrast, Melville's sketch of the tortoises calls attention to the multiple "optical delusions" through which the creatures serve as both terrifying mystical guide ("with them I lost myself in volcanic mazes") and comestible (*Piazza Tales*, 131–133). He suggests the ultimate failure of either schema alone to provide self-knowledge or a true vision of the world. Instead, the task of literary composition is to create a composite picture through a process that explores the multiple facets of our limited vision.

Repeatedly, Melville points to ambiguities and tensions within Darwin's narrative in order to demonstrate the power of literature to hold multiple truths together simultaneously. One way that he does so is by foregrounding the islands' simultaneous location in both biblical and geological time. On the one hand, we can already sense Darwin's excitement about the islands' significance for his developing theory of natural selection in lines of the *Journal* that marvel at "the amount of creative force, if such an expression may be used, displayed on these small, barren, and rocky islands" (*Voyage of the Beagle*, 344). On the other hand, he still retains a biblical vernacular and time scale in his allusion to the Flood. The two large tortoises encountered on the naturalist's walk "seemed to my fancy like some antediluvian animals"—a language echoed in Melville's descriptions (*Voyage of the Beagle*, 323).[33] Melville adopts Darwin's epithet for the Galápagos tortoises, which are similarly described as "antediluvian-looking" relics of a time before the Flood (*Piazza Tales*, 131). However, this location (or dislocation) of the islands in biblical time is complicated for Melville, becoming a source of fruitful tension that unites the seemingly disparate sketches. Suggesting a world after the Fall, if not a post-apocalyptic one, he describes the islands as a "fit type of all-forsaken overthrow" and notes that "in no world but a fallen one could such a land exist" (*Piazza Tales*, 127). At the same time, the remote northern island of Abington represents a time before the Fall and before human creation: "So far as yon Abington Isle is concerned, Adam and his billions of posterity remain uncreated" (*Piazza Tales*, 141). The ambiguous position of the islands in biblical time—a post-apocalyptic future, a pre-Edenic past—reflects again on the unknown status of the human present.

Another way that Melville shows the Galápagos' uncertain status in time and space is by deliberately getting the geological history of the islands wrong. In the first paragraph of "The Encantadas," he describes the Galápagos as "a group rather of extinct volcanoes than of isles" (*Piazza Tales*, 126); they are, in fact, rather new as island formations go, and their volcanoes are still active. But his inaccurate scientific description contributes to a more psychological mapping of the islands: the observer's sense of the islands' barrenness and desolation, which in turn connects to a sense of abandonment by a divine power. Rock Rodondo, for instance, is not only the site of the narrator's naturalistic observations; it is also identified as Mt. Pisgah. Yet the "Pisgah View from the Rock," based on Moses's vision of the Promised Land,[34] is hardly cheering (or reliable), given the desolation of the surrounding seascape and the "optical delusions" of the island formations. Far from being the vantage point that the author purports is "the very best mode of gaining a comprehensive view of the region round about" (133), the rock becomes a textual space from which to examine the various discourses written on the land and its inhabitants. To borrow a term that Lawrence Buell applies to his reading of *Clarel*, Melville's emphasis here is on the "physiographic sensitivity" of an observer trying to make sense of the disjunction between a landscape's physical realities and the images generated from his own cultural background.[35] Melville's enigmatic, unstable islands are thus analogous to the "vacillations" (146) of the human psyche and identity.

The elusiveness of the landscape—tied to its mutability—extends to a meditation on our tenuous relationship with a remote deity and to our questionable humanity. Take, for example, Melville's parody of the taxonomic chart in the fourth sketch, in which unknown numbers of man-haters and devils are listed along with lizards and spiders as the island's inhabitants. There are trappings of the scientific humor tradition here, calling attention to the naturalist's failure to account for what cannot be observed, or, conversely, his failure to observe what can't be accounted for scientifically. However, Melville challenges not only zoological but also biblical taxonomies. For instance, the narrator describes the marine iguana as "that strangest anomaly of outlandish nature" (*Piazza Tales*, 127) because, according to biblical epistemology, a land animal should not inhabit the ocean; thus, the creature is located outside the bounds of a post-Edenic worldview. Moreover, the adjective "outlandish" later reappears as a descriptor of the penguins and finally the sailors, suggesting that in Melville's alternative state of nature, the human creature is also foreign, non-native, an alien species, perhaps not only for its failure to fit neatly into taxonomic categories but also for its ambiguous relation to a wrathful or indifferent creator.

Amplifying ideas latent in Darwin's *Journal*, therefore, Melville centers "The Encantadas" around the problem of longing in the face of human unknowability and divine remoteness. We can observe this process of traveling theory when we bring Melville's depiction of Rock Rodondo in the third sketch into conversation with an early passage on St. Paul's Rocks, a similar rock formation, in Darwin's *Journal*. In Darwin's account, the latter formation "rises abruptly out of the depths of the ocean" (*Voyage of the Beagle*, 7). For Melville, Rodondo is "some two hundred and fifty feet high, rising straight from the sea ten miles from land" (*Piazza Tales*, 133). In both accounts, the rock formations are strewn with guano upon closer inspection, leading to observations about their avian inhabitants. Darwin finds "on St. Paul's only two kinds of birds—the booby and the noddy" (*Voyage of the Beagle*, 8). Melville's rock, in contrast, offers an abundance of seabirds; in fact, the narrator boasts, "I know not where one can better study the Natural History of strange sea-fowl than at Rodondo. It is the aviary of Ocean" (*Piazza Tales*, 135). There is also a parallel movement in Darwin's St. Paul's Rocks passage from cataloging the "terrestrial fauna," including the birds, to mentioning the fish at the base of the rock (*Voyage of the Beagle*, 9).

But while Darwin's account focuses on understanding the processes by which the rock formation came to have its characteristic incrustations, Melville lingers on its animal life, including its human intruders. In an offhand remark, Darwin mentions that both species of birds on St. Paul's Rocks "are of a tame and stupid disposition, and are so unaccustomed to visitors, that I could have killed any number of them with my geological hammer" (*Voyage of the Beagle*, 8).[36] Melville, in contrast, develops this theme of human predation and violence in an apostrophe to the fish that is both humorous and melancholic: "Poor fish of Rodondo! in your victimized confidence, you are of the number of those who inconsiderately trust, while they do not understand, human nature" (*Piazza Tales*, 136). The word "confidence" here has a particular resonance, given Melville's preoccupation with the confidence trick, or swindle, which is most thoroughly explored in *The Confidence-Man* (1857). While Darwin's naturalist is aloof and unerring, Melville's serves as an entry point for examining the unspoken moral cruelties of the human animal, including its capacity for deception.

Melville's hypothesis in "The Encantadas" is one that Darwin hints at when he discusses the tameness of the island birds: the notion of man as a "dangerous animal" (*Voyage of the Beagle*, 345). If modern geology and comparative anatomy expose our animal kinship and affinities, what is the psychological and literary landscape that results? To explore this interior terrain, Melville picks up on a detail that Darwin glosses over in the *Journal*: the islands are inhabited first by buccaneers, then by whalers, and more recently by a small penal colony. By placing the human in a strange and uneasy relation to the island's creatures, Melville reminds us of our own natural proximity to the animal. Most notably, the figure of the wild man Oberlus, whose "sole superiority . . . over the tortoises was his possession of a larger capacity of degradation; and along with that, something like an intelligent will to it" (*Piazza Tales*, 165), links his physical resemblance to the creatures on Hood's Isle to metaphysical questions about the moral status of human beings.

These questions culminate in the eighth sketch about the Chola widow, in which, after witnessing her husband's and brother's deaths at sea, she is forsaken by the ship's captain who brought them to the island. What is left unspoken and unwritten—the probable rape of Hunilla by passing sailors during her exile on the island—points to human bestiality. This elision picks up on a similar one in Darwin's *Journal*, in which he relegates an unpleasant detail to a footnote. The detail is the probable prostitution of Fuegia Basket, one of two islanders who, as children, were taken to Europe by Captain Fitz Roy "to educate them and instruct them in religion," then returned unceremoniously to their home. Even within the footnote, her prostitution is obliquely referenced and further removed to a parenthetical aside: "Captain Sulivan . . . heard from a sealer in 1842 (?), that when in the western part of the Strait of Magellan, he was astonished by a native woman coming on board, who could talk some English. Without a doubt this was Fuegia Basket. *She lived (I fear the term probably bears a double interpretation) some days on board*" (*Voyage of the Beagle*, 197; italics mine).

In "The Encantadas," the otherness of the islands—a world located in some other time, both geological and biblical—also becomes a vehicle for asking questions about divine (or natural) agency and human responsibility. Thus, the Hunilla sketch includes a meditation on God's nonintervention in human affairs. Evoking the language of covenants, the narrator laments, "Ah, heaven, when man thus keeps his faith, wilt though be faithless who created the faithful one? But they cannot break faith who never plighted it" (*Piazza Tales*, 154–55). But Hunilla has also been read as a figure of Melville's admiration for human endurance.[37] Although the narration above flirts with despair, it doesn't necessarily follow that one should reject faith or deity based on these silences; the answer, if any, is to persist in the voyage.

Ultimately, then, Melville responds to developments in modern geology—and to Darwin's narrative—in order to place psychological truth and questions of human responsibility at the center of his literary project. In the Chola widow sketch, human agency is foregrounded, especially in Melville's cat-and-mouse game with the readers; the narrative twice halts on the verge of revealing Hunilla's full story. This technique forces the reader to fill in the blanks, so that "the reader, by having to write his own story of Hunilla, must define himself in terms of rocks and reptiles."[38] Moreover, Melville's acts of omission in "The Encantadas" mirror a larger trend that Franchot notices in Melville's body of work: his attempts to "vocalize silence,"[39] to model his authorial practice on the Divine Author's withholding of information and air of mystery. In this way, the reader embarks on a quest for meaning in the face of authorial ambiguity, akin to the process of spiritual wrestling with an unknown and unknowable deity.

In "The Encantadas," Melville follows his own advice in "Hawthorne and His Mosses" by obscuring his radical vision of our place in the natural order; in effect, telling the truth "covertly and by snatches."[40] In the interstices of Darwin's narrative, Melville finds sites of illumination, amplification, and covert truth-telling. Through the slipperiness of time and fact in "The Encantadas," Melville not only reshapes Darwin's narrative; he also explicitly creates a state of ambiguity and alterity, a speculative fictional space that allows us to confront deeper moral, psychological, and spiritual truths. Natural science, then, is neither a provocation—a catalyst to the tale's repeated questioning of a benevolent deity and of the human capacity for good—nor is it a satisfactory methodology for answering the questions that deeply interest Melville. Transposed into the fictional world of Melville's "Encantadas," geological hypotheses about the vast age of the earth and our animal ancestry become a means of theorizing about the tensions in our relationship with God and within our human nature, of dramatizing questions of faith that long predate not only evolutionary discourse but also the birth of scientific method.

"Changes and Vanishings": Evolution, Faith, and Craft after 1859

At first glance, "The Encantadas"—a work of magazine fiction that has not garnered the critical attention of "Benito Cereno" or "Bartleby, the Scrivener"—may seem an unlikely companion text to *Clarel*, Melville's longest and most complex poetic effort. And yet, in *Clarel*, published over twenty years after "The Encantadas" and thirty-five years after his stopover at San Christobal, Melville is still voyaging in the Galápagos.[41] In the canto titled "The Island" in part 4, the helmsman Agath offers telltale descriptors of the South American islands to his fellow pilgrims, echoing the language of the much earlier "Encantadas": he notes that "the beach is cinders" (*Clarel*, 4.3.13), just as the earlier story begins by asking the reader to imagine "heaps of cinders" in a vacant city lot to picture the Galápagos Islands' air of desolation (*Piazza Tales*, 126). Agath also describes "the monstrous tortoise drear," which travels the island's well-worn paths wearing a "penal . . . aspect" (*Clarel*, 4.3.61, 69). The account recalls "Two Sides to a Tortoise," the second sketch of "The Encantadas," which evokes the "penal hopelessness" (*Piazza Tales*, 129) of the islands' most iconic inhabitants. This appearance (or apparition) of the Galápagos in *Clarel* reinforces the islands' creative significance for Melville even late into his career. As William Shurr observes, Melville's formative experience of the Galápagos shapes his later symbolic and psychological mapping of the Holy Land.[42]

This continuity also suggests a larger point of connection between the two texts: Melville's preoccupation with barren, enigmatic, and shifting landscapes that are resistant to a totalizing vision, and in which the quest for a hidden deity and an equally elusive humanity is enacted. In *Clarel*, desert and sea are interchangeable ("Sands immense / Impart the oceanic sense" [2.1137–38]),[43] an echo that further links the poem to "The Encantadas." Buell argues that by repeatedly visualizing the desert as a sea, Melville "signals that this and all other poetic and mythic renditions of the land are finally so much overlay—like the intellectual systems that the poem relentlessly sifts at the levels of dialogue and narratorial reflection."[44] His comment equally applies to the formal experiments of "The Encantadas," with its fragmentary, shifting layers that also seem imposed on the island landscape and that enable a literary parsing of natural philosophies and creeds.

I would add, too, that in both works geology functions as a specter in human and divine affairs. In *Clarel* the prominent rock imagery recalls the age of the earth and punningly evokes the biblical and hymnal "Rock of Ages" (2.20.86), now crumbled to mere stones, replaced by an age of rocks epitomized by Margoth and the ascendancy of geological time.[45] Moreover, despite *Clarel*'s desert setting, Melville figuratively evokes the proximity of the sea, the early terrors of which prompted an evolutionary flight to the land. Ishmael calls attention to the sea's psychological and epistemological role in the first chapter of *Moby-Dick*, where it is called "the image of the ungraspable phantom of life; and this is the key to it all."[46] That "ungraspable phantom" is not only our own oceanic origin but also the developmental process itself: life fleeing through endless forms while individuals and species perish.

Although the islands first sketched in "The Encantadas" remain a compelling imaginative terrain in *Clarel*, in the latter work the nature of Melville's relationship to—and uses for—Darwin has changed. In "The Encantadas," Melville explicitly denies Darwin a place in the shaping of his narrative, and, I would add, denies him three times in the persons of the named sources

Cowley, Colnett, and Porter.[47] In contrast, *Clarel* contains a trinity of direct references to Charles Darwin, and he has an altogether different function in the poem. He is no longer a textual source but rather a cultural shorthand or signifier for evolution, reflecting his changed status by the 1870s. While Darwin the author and naturalist is an unnamed but central presence in "The Encantadas," I read the specter of Darwinism in *Clarel*, as well as the poem's too-relentless conceit of science-versus-faith, as something of a ruse disguising the poem's structuring interest in psychological truth and the unfolding of character, both human and divine. Where Darwin's *Journal* serves as an earlier narrative form out of which Melville's literary narrative emerges, I read Darwin's presence in *Clarel* as a signifier of the polarization of science and faith that Melville attempts to represent but also transcend in his verse. Whereas the more fluid language of development and geology initially served as a tool for generating Melville's experimental fictions, in *Clarel* we see Darwin framed as one half of a binary that Melville the poet strains to move beyond.

Denis Donoghue's interpretation of Melville's turn to verse might help to illuminate this point. Consistent with the older idea of Melville's "quarrel" with God, Donoghue positions this turn as a defeatist move, an attempt to find relief and a way out of uncertainty, "to still his beating brain by dividing his world into yes and no."[48] This remark pairs nicely with Delbanco's assertion that Melville embraced "both the yes and no" of his culture,[49] reflected also in his ambivalent stance toward evolution.[50] However, Donoghue goes on to see moments in "his best poems" such as *Clarel* in which "we find him struggling toward a position above both yes and no."[51] Moreover, Donoghue ties this struggle to Melville's poetics, his emphasis on asserting order through conventional poetic forms, which demonstrates the knowledge and will of a human creator in the absence of definitive proof of an intelligent Creator.[52] A clue to the bravery (or bravado) of this poetic stance comes in the definition of art that Melville offers when describing Petra: "Mid such a scene / Of Nature's terror, how serene / That ordered form. Nor less 'tis cut / Out of that terror—does abut / Thereon: there's Art" (*Clarel*, 2.30.40–44).

At the same time, Melville's verse dramatizes the strain itself, repeatedly making visible those formal constraints through an often awkward and disjointed prosody, which Gay Wilson Allen has described as "deliberately hobbl[ing] his muse."[53] Lawrence Buell attributes Melville's embrace of a "poetry of intellectualized, cerebral bound form" as being at the root of contemporary critics' dismissal of Melville's verse, since it reads as less experimental than Melville's literary narratives.[54] However, Donoghue's interpretation allows us to see continuity between Melville's literary narrative and his later verse: the latter is not a rejection of experiment but an alternative form of experimentation, a newly developed hypothesis about how literature might serve as a tool of investigating both this world and the "other, darker worlds" of the human psyche and divine character.

While Darwin is used in *Clarel* as a representative figure for the ambivalence of the age, the goal of the poem is not to dramatize a struggle between faith and science, brought to a boiling point by the publication of *Origin*; rather, it falls to the poet to make visible the psychic effects of the age's incongruities. The couplet that begins the poem's epilogue sums this up neatly: "If Luther's day expand to Darwin's year, / Shall that exclude the hope—foreclose the fear?" (*Clarel*, 4.35.1–2). In this moment, Darwin functions as a hypothesis that does not seem to alter the ultimate goal for the character's quest. In other words, the psychological and spiritual phenomena persist in spite of anything science would do to ostensibly change the frame, and it is this mental and emotional terrain that Melville ultimately stakes as the poet's territory. Once Darwin's impact is contextualized a few lines later as the old debate over "ape and angel" (4.35.12), Melville reveals his continued interest, across a range of forms, in exploring the relationship between literary craft and truthful vision.

Thus, the target of Melville's critique in the poem is not science or Darwin per se, but the "reconciling mood" between evolution and faith that is pervasive in the 1860s and 1870s periodical literature.[55] This mid-century Anglo-American sentiment, which tends to conflate and flatten the differences between these two discourses, is well encapsulated in verse by the Unitarian poet W. H. Carruth's lines, "Some call it Evolution / And others call it God."[56] In Julia Ward Howe's "Kosmos," one of the first poems on evolution written by an American after the publication of *Origin*, the "beasts" are figured as a "prophecy of man," language that both acknowledges the emergence of new forms through natural law and hints at divine intention. In a nod to the nebular hypothesis,[57] an astronomical theory that explained the origin and development of the cosmos based on material forces, she also observes that the sun "conceived the starry spheres / That from her burning bosom sprang." After figuring these natural processes in highly affective, maternal language, the poem closes with a vision of a present, paternal deity: "All power and inspiration move, / Thrilling with light the firmament, / Lifting the heart of man with love."[58] The last word is telling, suggesting the liberal theological emphasis on a benevolent, loving God and diffusing the terrors of a changing cosmogony.

In the context of this assumed reconciliation, a particularly objectionable figure in Melville's poem is the pilgrim Derwent, a jovial Anglican priest who tries "to mediate / 'Tween Faith and science" (*Clarel*, 3.16.167–68). Derwent's false optimism and easy familiarity cause him to be vilified by some of his fellow pilgrims, namely Mortmain, a former 1848 European revolutionary who has become obsessed with human evil, and Ungar, the self-exiled part-Native American Catholic mercenary and former Confederate soldier. Even the naive Clarel, longing for a spiritual guide and fraternal connection, rejects Derwent's overtures at a climactic moment in part 3. This canto is suggestively titled "In Confidence," evoking Melville's interest, mentioned above, in the act of deception that succeeds due to a human drive for intimacy and trust that is nonetheless based on insufficient or improper grounds of knowledge. Derwent is overbold not only in his relations with others such as the moment when, forcing a fraternal feeling to ward off disagreement, "Derwent his arm, / Demure, and brotherly, and grave, / Slips into Rolfe's" (4.23.1–3), but also in the inadequate and changeable foundations of his progressive theological stance. For this reason, Clarel acknowledges to himself, even before their private meeting takes place, a "Truth bitter: Derwent bred distrust" (3.21.69).

Another way of understanding Melville's criticism of Derwent is to see this character as shielding himself from the dark side of the moral universe that is necessary for accessing truth. For instance, the unsuccessful encounter with Clarel prompts Derwent to concede, "Alas, too deep you dive" (3.21.307). The term, which recurs in *Clarel*, recalls a March 1849 letter to Evert Duyckinck in which Melville expresses admiration for Emerson ("I love all men who *dive*") as well as for "the whole corps of thought-divers" (*Correspondence,* 121).[59] What's objectionable, then, about Derwent's response to modern science is that he refuses to look squarely or closely at the lack of fit between these two ways of explaining the world, including their gaps and incongruities, a task that falls instead to the poet of *Clarel*. A more fitting figure of the times is the hunchback Celio, whose physical deformity is suggestive of the mental and moral contortions required to reconcile science and theology.

If Derwent represents a failure of truthful vision through his unwillingness to confront dark, uneasy truths, the geologist Margoth's casual acceptance of a godless universe is also a form of blindness. Margoth is given to reductive statements like "All, all's geology" (*Clarel*, 2.26.13), the repetition of "all" emphasizing his narrow vision, itself a kind of naiveté. Later, in response to Nehemiah's death, Margoth comments that "All's chymestry" (2.39.67)—a statement that ignores the human experiential scale and shows him to be dismissive of affective knowledge, including the human longing for a benevolent deity in times of mourning.

In short, Margoth seems initially to be a straightforward caricature, dismissed by the pilgrims as a "kangaroo of science" (*Clarel*, 2.21.10). The phrase echoes Melville's satirical play on Lord Monboddo's eighteenth-century ideas of development in *Mardi*. Monboddo, appearing as simply "Boddo" in *Mardi*, insisted on man's relationship to the lower primates, but Melville's philosopher Babbalanja reasons, "my ancestors were kangaroos, not monkeys, as old Boddo erroneously opined" (*Mardi*, 507). Continuing his animal associations, Margoth is figuratively made an ass in a comic scene where his geological explanations are interrupted by the donkey's braying,[60] causing Margoth a "decline" in confidence "Arising from late asinine / Applause" (*Clarel*, 2.33.84–85). Although laughable in some respects, Margoth's presence does raise a palpable threat, as the geological hammer he carries functions metonymically. Geology, as wielded by Margoth, is a hammer destroying earlier alternative systems of belief: "the hammer: yes, geology" (2.19.55).

Yet Margoth seems too easy a target, especially given what we have established in our previous discussion of "The Encantadas" about Melville's generative use of scientific language to theorize about literature and morality. Once we note the powerful sway of geological imagery throughout the poem, we can better trace *Clarel*'s interest in a psychological mapping of geology's human implications, akin to what we find in "The Encantadas." For instance, while wandering discontentedly through Jerusalem with his guide Nehemiah, Clarel contemplates the problem of trying to find a stable, material grounding for faith in a shifting world of geological and evolutionary processes, where the very religious monuments on his tour might one day sink back into the primal ocean:

> What object sensible to touch
> Or quoted fact may faith rely on,
> If faith confideth overmuch
> That here's a monument in Zion:
> Its substance ebbs—see, day and night
> The sands subsiding from the height;
> In time, absorbed, these grains may help
> To form a new sea-bed, slug and kelp. (*Clarel*, 1.24.69–76)

The early pages of the poem similarly refer to "time's vast sea" (1.1.81) and "time's swamping sea" (1.2.49); there is a recurring emphasis on the invertebrates and primal forms of the ocean ("sea-bed, slug and kelp" [1.24.76]), as well as their unseen terrors, harkening back to the vastness and ambiguity of time scales, and their implications for organic development, in "The Encantadas." In other words, Melville once again turns space into a proxy for contemplating time.[61]

In *Clarel*, Melville continues to stake a distinct epistemological ground for literature in relation to "prosing Science" (1.36.115). Able, unlike science, to hold alternative truths together simultaneously, the poem dramatizes the dialectic "or false or true" (1.3.13), which suggests that the veracity of the historic site is determined in part by the humanity and tradition that asserts its reality. Brian Yothers demonstrates this characteristic of Melville's art in his reading of an early scene in which Clarel contemplates the Mount of Olives from his window. Finding both the natural and the sacred facets of the landscape equally inscrutable, Clarel links them together as a "double mystery" in need of interpretation but irreducible to a single account.[62]

Furthermore, the poem's relentless opposition of science and faith masks a subtler structural pattern: a series of situations that allow us to grasp and grapple with human personalities and an analysis of character, both human and divine.[63] This is reinforced by the episodic and epistemic nature of a pilgrimage, both through the traveling companions' encounters with strangers as well as opportunities to scrutinize each other, themselves, and the layers of myth and narrative embedded in the landscape. As in "The Encantadas," often these insights in *Clarel* have to do with the distances and silences that prevent us from knowing each other and God, despite the travelers' recurrent longing for closeness and mutual understanding. If, as Goldman notes, "human self-concealment in the poem reflects divided self-concealment,"[64] it is not surprising that Clarel observes, "But if in vain / One tries to comprehend a man, / How think to sound God's deeper heart!" (2.33.109–11).

Agath's description of the Galápagos Islands in *Clarel* mirrors this sense of desolation and doubt in the face of simultaneously enduring and changeable landscapes. He begins by noting that the islands are situated "in waters where no charts avail" (4.3.1), pointing back to the traveling perspective that cannot get settled or find a fixed position.[65] Once again, space and time are equally problematic: despite the recurrent imagery of solitude that suggests an abandoned humanity ("salt creek and ashy inlet bring / More loneness from the outer ring / Of ocean" [4.3.14–16]), Agath persists in a Mosaic account of creation, describing the nearby waters as where "God set that isle which haunteth me" (4.3.4). The volcano, too, conveys the impression of a divine nature that is distant, obscured, or withheld; it "burns unrevealed," as by day the surrounding clouds leave it "dull and sealed" (4.3.10–12).

As in "The Encantadas," the tortoise looms large in Agath's account of the islands as a creature defying easy classification ("of man or beast it scarce may be" [4.3.28]) and subject to the same persistent journey through barren landscapes of the mind. The tortoises, described in "The Encantadas" as "the victims of a penal, a malignant, or perhaps a downright diabolical enchanter (*Piazza Tales*, 132), are similarly noted for their "penal . . . aspect" in *Clarel* (4.3.69), signaling abandonment or punishment by an absent Creator. In both texts, the tortoises are fit figures for humanity's endless seeking after truth in the face of divine mystery; in fact, the description in *Clarel* of the tortoise's "pilgrimage here to and fro" (4.3.87) is reminiscent not only of the storyteller Agath's trait of endurance (4.3.103–7) but also of Hawthorne's journal observation on Melville's "wandering to and fro" over spiritual deserts.

In addition, Clarel's take-away message from the tale recalls Melville's earlier description of the islands as "this other and darker world" (*Piazza Tales*, 127). Here, the image of the Galápagos enables Clarel to reason by analogy from this world to others: "Since *this* world, then, can baffle so— / Our natural harbor—it were strange / If *that* alleged, which is afar, / Should not confound us when we range / In revery where its problems are.—" (4.3.114–18). The Galápagos then, with their uncertain position in space and time, layered over by competing narratives and time scales, are a figure for thinking through (or voyaging among) the related mysteries of the human and divine natures.

Melville's one instance of textual engagement with Darwin in *Clarel* also uses the instability and ambiguity of landscape to explore the theme of human hiddenness and divine silence. Melville has selected a passage not from one of Darwin's more recent publications but from the 1845 *Journal*, suggesting that he is still fitting Darwin into a pre-*Origin* mindset.[66] In Patagonia, Darwin observed: "All was stillness and desolation. . . . One asked how many ages the plain had thus lasted, and how many more it was doomed thus to continue" (*Voyage of the Beagle*, 144–45). He then cites Shelley's "Lines on Mont Blanc" to reinforce his prose observation: "None can reply—all seems eternal now / The wilderness has a mysterious tongue / Which teaches awful doubt." In *Clarel*, Melville picks up on this detail, noting that "Darwin quotes / from Shelley" (2.11.13–14) on the "mysterious doubt—an awful one" (2.11.15) that haunts remote and desert landscapes: "He quotes, adopt it. Is it true? / Let instinct vouch; let poetry / Science and instinct here agree, / For truth requires strong retinue" (2.11.16–19). Here, scientific inquiry is not the agent in provoking "mysterious doubt"; rather, doubt arises from the encounter with desolate and distant nature itself with its silences and blankness, and its vast time scales that do not conform easily to our human one. Moreover, Melville suggests that this uncomfortable truth requires a composite picture, drawing from multiple sources of evidence and discourse.

When Melville writes in part 1 of *Clarel* that "serial wrecks on wrecks confound / Era and monument and man; / Or rather, in stratifying way / Bed and impact and overlay" (1.10.3–6), the "serial wrecks" might point to the layers of former civilizations but also extinct species that came before man, undercutting any sense of the permanence of either human culture or the human form itself. However, this "stratifying" or layering process is also one way of thinking about the poet's choices of meter and diction in which critics have found evidence of his uncertain versifying ability. As Bezanson notes, the deliberate choice of iambic tetrameter creates a constricting or "cramping" effect, as well as doing violence to language in the service of meter; for instance, articles are cut to make the beat work while "to fatten lines," Melville includes "spread-out words" like bewrinkled and ungladsome.[67] Buell makes a similar point that these awkward constraints are a key to the verse's power to communicate psychic violence: "Melville's strict but broken prosodic gridworks, 'Chafing against the metric bound,' as he wrote of Virgil . . . enrich through the very constraints they impose."[68] *Clarel*'s meter contrasts especially with the formal expansiveness of *Moby-Dick*; here, the expansive and unmooring tendencies of modern geology lead to a sense of entrapment, diminishment, and distancing.

Similarly, Melville jarringly contrasts or "overlays" the modern and antiquarian, as in the first canto, which contains "a series of dusty old words, the secondhand stock of a long run of English poets," while also drawing from the language of "shop and factory, from the laboratory, from trading, seafaring, and war."[69] A representative example of the latter, and of the poet's occasional indulgence in the modern and mechanical, flat, and unlovely, comes in the account of Mortmain's youth: "Wear and tear and jar / He met with coffee and cigar" (2.4.46–47). These lines immediately follow the more storied word "prophet," with its Old Testament resonances. At the level of language, then, these juxtapositions underscore the simultaneity of their corresponding worldviews, even if they at times cancel each other out and otherwise challenge sense.

If we step back to consider the role of geology in this later work, *Clarel* indicates a shift toward tradition and abstraction in Melville's late-career trajectory. For instance, the poem's "serial wrecks" that "in stratifying way / Bed and impact and overlay" (1.10.5–6) are a far cry from the "sandwich system" of geology in 1849's *Mardi*, with its richly precise terminology and abundant excesses of natural forms: for example, "sturgeon-forms, cephalaspis, glyptolepis, pterichthys" (112). Darwin, too, as described above, takes on the more distant role of evolutionary icon, losing the status of a hidden but constant interlocutor.

However, *Clarel* is not a radical departure from his earlier work, but an extension of Melville's concerns about the triangulation of truth, science, and art, where faith is one aspect of the poem's epistemology. In other words, we can trace vestiges of earlier forms in Melville's late career, suggesting continuities of development rather than catastrophist ruptures. As in "The Encantadas," *Clarel* examines what it means for human beings to inhabit different time scales and origin narratives simultaneously, to "contain both the yes and no of their culture."[70] The challenge of modern geology becomes not only a vehicle for scientific critique, but also a basis for self-definition: a way to foreground modern literature's access to psychological truth, including the search for human companionship and divine presence.

In the opening pages of his critical biography of Melville, Andrew Delbanco chooses Darwinian evolution as a measure of the cultural ground-shift across Melville's life: "Perhaps the most important intellectual event of Melville's early years was the publication in 1836 of Emerson's *Nature*, which declared . . . a natural world that is the 'incarnation of God.' " By 1890, a year before Melville's death, however, Melville borrowed a William Dean Howells novel from the New York Society Library, "a book written in the shadow of Darwin, who had long since destroyed Emerson's romantic view of creation and replaced it with a vision of the natural world created by chance and filled with brutality."[71]

In the context of his argument, there's nothing to criticize about Delbanco's account: it concisely glosses the nineteenth-century intellectual context before moving on to other subjects. However, the present essay seeks to challenge the passivity of this construction. It explores instead how evolutionary theory "travels" from a European scientific context to an American literary one. Melville actively engages evolutionary discourse to define his craft in works as formally distinct and as remotely situated in time as "The Encantadas" (1853) and *Clarel* (1876). This possibility is difficult to see when we formulate Victorian evolution as a static or monolithic construct. Even Melville scholars like Franchot and Goldman, whose work explores Melville's open-ended and substantive engagement with biblical texts, are tempted to shorthand "Christianity's post-Darwinian ruination" or "that nineteenth-century shibboleth—evolution."[72] By uncoupling the terms "Darwin" and "evolution," however, we can throw into relief a more dynamic and varied nineteenth-century conversation about organic change and geological instability, one that interested Melville long before the publication of *Origin of Species*.

The twin texts of theology and geology are abiding interests of Melville's, key discourses with which he wrestles throughout his career. For Melville, concepts of organic change and geological instability help to enrich and enlarge his literary craft. Rather than quarreling with science, Melville draws on and adapts its language to seek after metaphysical truths about human nature and the individual's relationship with God. In making these claims, I hope to invite further Melville scholarship that looks beyond the easy opposition of science and religion that *Clarel* so disingenuously invokes, to explore instead their convergences and productive tensions in Melville's literary experiments.

Notes

The chapter epigraph is from Charles Darwin, *The Voyage of the Beagle* (New York: Mentor, 1988), 145. Further citations in the text refer to this edition.

1. Andrew Delbanco, *Melville: His World and Work* (New York: Knopf, 2005), 280.

2. Walter E. Bezanson, "Historical and Critical Note," in *Clarel: A Poem and Pilgrimage in the Holy Land*, ed. Harrison Hayford, Alma A. MacDougall, Hershel Parker, and G. Thomas Tanselle (Evanston and Chicago: Northwestern University Press and the Newberry Library, 1991), 506.

3. James R. Corey, "Herman Melville and the Theory of Evolution" (Ph.D. diss., Washington State University, 1968), 85.

4. Herman Melville, *Clarel: A Poem and Pilgrimage in the Holy Land*, ed. Harrison Hayford, Alma A. MacDougall, Hershel Parker, and G. Thomas Tanselle (Evanston and Chicago: Northwestern University Press and the Newberry Library, 2008). Further citations by part, canto, and line number in the text refer to this edition of the poem.

5. For scholarship on this intertextual relationship, see H. Bruce Franklin, "The Island Worlds of Darwin and Melville," *Centennial Review* 11 (Summer 1967): 353–70; Denise Tanyol, "The Alternative Taxonomies of Melville's 'The Encantadas,'" *New England Quarterly* 80 (June 2007): 242–79; William Howarth, "Earth Islands: Darwin and Melville in the Galápagos," *Iowa Review* 30 (Winter 2000–2001): 95–113; Mark Dunphy, "Melville's Turning of the Darwinian Table in 'The Encantadas,'" *Melville Society Extracts* 79 (November 1989): 14.

6. James A. Secord, *Victorian Sensation: The Extraordinary Publication, Reception, and Secret Authorship of "Vestiges of the Natural History of Creation"* (Chicago: University of Chicago Press, 2000), 516.

7. For more on American readers' encounters with pre-Darwinian evolution, see David L. Hull, "Lamarck among the Anglos," in *Zoological Philosophy: An Exposition with Regard to the Natural History of Animals*, by J. B. Lamarck (Chicago: University of Chicago Press, 1984), xliii; John A. DeJong, "American Attitudes Toward Evolution before Darwin" (diss., University of Iowa, 1962), 144; John F. McElligott, "Before Darwin: Religion and Science as Presented in American Magazines, 1830–1860" (diss., New York University, 1973), 261.

8. Peter J. Bowler, *Evolution: The History of an Idea*, rev. ed. (Berkeley: University of California Press, 1989), 149. Bowler and other historians of science have suggested that the "theory" that we read today—the branching open-endedness, the centrality of natural selection—is not necessarily what Darwin's contemporaries would have emphasized even in the late nineteenth century.

9. George H. Daniels, *Science in American Society: A Documentary History* (New York: Knopf, 1971), 225.

10. In an 1851 letter to Hawthorne, Melville defines "visable [*sic*] truth" as "the apprehension of the absolute condition of present things as they strike the eye of the man who fears them not, though they do their worst to him" (Melville, *Correspondence*, ed. Lynn Horth [Evanston and Chicago: Northwestern University Press and the Newberry Library, 1993], 186).

11. For Goldman, *protest theism* refers to a simultaneous struggle against and embrace of deity due to the strength of human need for God. See Stan Goldman, *Melville's Protest Theism: The Hidden and Silent God in* Clarel (DeKalb: Northern Illinois University Press, 1993), 4. Robert Milder defines *spiritual agnosticism* as living "neither with worldly indifference nor with a passionless deferral of belief but with the continuing interrogation of god and the universe" (Milder, *Exiled Royalties: Melville and the Life We Imagine* [New York: Oxford University Press, 2006], 195). Goldman seems to go further in his assessment of the centrality of biblical and theological sources for understanding *Clarel*, while Milder situates the poem more secularly, as contributing to an understanding of the psychological foundations of belief. However, both critics are searching for language to indicate a process of questioning and a skeptical stance that does not end in spiritual despair or exhaustion, as argued by Vincent Kenny, or angry defiance, as claimed by Lawrance Thompson.

12. William H. Shurr, *The Mystery of Iniquity: Melville as Poet, 1857–1891* (Lexington: University Press of Kentucky, 1972), 48; Brian Yothers, *The Romance of the Holy Land in American Travel Writing, 1790–1876* (Aldershot, Eng.: Ashgate, 2007), 111.

13. See Nathalia Wright, *Melville's Uses of the Bible* (Durham, N.C.: Duke University Press, 1949); Ilana Pardes, *Melville's Bibles* (Berkeley: University of California Press, 2008). On the subjects of Holy Land travel writing and nineteenth-century American imaginings of the Near East, see Malini Johar Schueller, *U.S. Orientalisms: Race, Nation, and Gender in Literature, 1790–1890* (Ann Arbor: University of Michigan Press, 1998); Hilton Obenzinger, *American Palestine: Melville, Twain, and the Holy Land Mania* (Princeton, N.J.: Princeton University Press, 1999); Timothy Marr, *The Cultural Roots of American*

Islamicism (New York: Cambridge University Press, 2006); Yothers, *Romance of the Holy Land* (2007).

14. Luke Timothy Johnson, *The Creed: What Christians Believe and Why It Matters* (New York: Doubleday, 2004), 54.

15. Herman Melville, *Journals*, ed. Howard C. Horsforth and Lynn Horth (Evanston and Chicago: Northwestern University Press and the Newberry Library, 1989), 628–29.

16. Jenny Franchot, "Melville's Traveling God," in *The Cambridge Companion to Herman Melville*, ed. Robert S. Levine (Cambridge: Cambridge University Press, 1998), 157.

17. Emory Elliott, "'Wandering To-and Fro': Melville and Religion," in *A Historical Guide to Herman Melville*, ed. Giles Gunn (New York: Oxford University Press, 2005), 170–71.

18. Ibid., 175.

19. Ibid., 202. William Potter extends this criticism to American institutions and practices more broadly; he asserts that there is a "crucial religious element" to Melville's political stance in *Clarel*. See Potter, *Melville's "Clarel" and the Intersympathy of Creeds* (Kent, Ohio: Kent State University Press, 2004), xvi.

20. Franchot, "Melville's Traveling God," 158.

21. Edward Said, *The World, the Text, and the Critic* (Cambridge, Mass.: Harvard University Press, 1983), 168–69.

22. Ronald L. Numbers, *Darwinism Comes to America* (Cambridge, Mass.: Harvard University Press, 1998).

23. Edward J. Larson, *Evolution's Workshop: God and Science on the Galápagos Islands* (New York: Basic Books, 2001), 4.

24. Goldman notes the importance of wrestling as metaphor for Melville. In particular, he discusses the biblical resonances of Jacob's wrestling with an angel of God in Genesis 32, such as crossing a threshold from the human to the divine, but also yoking together hope and pain. Citing the medieval scholar Rashi, he also notes that in Aramaic "to join" is related to both "embrace" and "wrestle." Goldman, *Melville's Protest Theism*, 74.

25. There are also clues outside of the text: a copy was available in the ship's library of the *Acushnet*, and Melville is known to have purchased the 1846 revised American edition in 1847. Melville also quotes Darwin's *Journal* (using the title *Darwin's Voyage of a Naturalist*) in the "Extracts" section of *Moby-Dick*.

26. Franklin, "Island Worlds," 363.

27. Tanyol, "Alternative Taxonomies," 244.

28. Herman Melville, "The Encantadas, or Enchanted Isles," in *The Piazza Tales and Other Prose Pieces, 1839–1860*, ed. Harrison Hayford, Alma A. MacDougall, and G. Thomas Tanselle (Evanston and Chicago: Northwestern University Press and the Newberry Library, 1987), 143. Further citations in the text will refer to this edition.

29. See John Samson, *White Lies: Melville's Narratives of Facts* (Ithaca, N.Y.: Cornell University Press, 1989); David Reynolds, *Beneath the American Renaissance: The Subversive Imagination in the Age of Emerson and Melville* (Cambridge, Mass.: Harvard University Press, 1989).

30. Larson, *Evolution's Workshop*, 10.

31. Ibid., 8.

32. Franklin, "Island Worlds," 366.

33. In the journal Darwin kept during the *Beagle* voyage, which he would draw on for his published work, this sense of competing epistemological frameworks is intensified. Describing the "most clumsy, disgusting Lizards" that inhabit the islands, Darwin notes that "Somebody calls them 'imps of darkness.'—They assuredly well become the land they inhabit." *Charles Darwin's Beagle Diary*, ed. R. D. Keynes (New York: Cambridge University Press, 1988), 353. In *Clarel*, Melville also refers to San Christobal as "that imp-isle" (4.3.48). Darwin's initial impression of the landscape is either a kind of hell on earth or a vision of hell itself: "The country was compared to what we might imagine the cultivated parts of the Infernal regions to be" (*Beagle Diary*, 352). Similarly, Melville's narrator in "The Encantadas" encounters a seemingly post-apocalyptic landscape "looking much as the world at large might, after a penal conflagration" (*Piazza Tales*, 126).

34. This phrase suggests yet another correspondence between "The Encantadas" and *Clarel*. Although the pilgrims are closer to Jerusalem than Mt. Pisgah, it is a desolate view of Jerusalem that prompts Agath's story of "The Island" in *Clarel*: "some chance comparison I've made / In mind between this stricken land / And one far isle forever banned / I camped on in life's early days" (4.3.204–7).

35. Lawrence Buell, "Melville the Poet," in *The Cambridge Companion to Herman Melville*, ed. Robert S. Levine (New York: Cambridge University Press, 1998), 146.

36. The geological hammer will become a figure for Margoth in *Clarel*.

37. Vincent Kenny, *Herman Melville's "Clarel": A Spiritual Autobiography* (Hamden, Conn.: Archon Books, 1973), 27–29.

38. Franklin, "Island Worlds," 367.

39. Franchot, "Melville's Traveling God," 177.

40. Franklin, "Island Worlds," 354.

41. Melville also mentions "The Gallipagos, otherwise called the Enchanted Isles," directly on the opening page of *Mardi*, and obliquely references them in the second volume, which describes an island of "black, beetling crags, rent by volcanic clefts," with a beach "strewn with scoria and cinders" (*Mardi and a Voyage Thither*, ed. Harrison Hayford, Hershel Parker, and G. Thomas Tanselle [Evanston and Chicago: Northwestern University Press and the Newberry Library, 1970], 3, 611).

42. Shurr, *Mystery of Iniquity*, 65.

43. As Obenzinger puts it: "In Melville's pilgrimage to Failure, the desert and the sea, the geographic Alpha and Omega of the romantic landscape according to W.H. Auden, collapse into each other" (*American Palestine*, 78).

44. Buell, "Melville the Poet," 147.

45. Joseph G. Knapp, *Tortured Synthesis: The Meaning of Melville's "Clarel"* (New York: Philosophical Library, 1971), 25.

46. Herman Melville, *Moby-Dick, or, The Whale*, ed. Harrison Hayford, Hershel Parker, and G. Thomas Tanselle (Evanston and Chicago: Northwestern University Press and the Newberry Library, 1988), 5.

47. This isn't an isolated incident; for instance, take Melville's "The New Ancient of Days," one of the astute poetic comments on Darwinism to come out of America in the decades following *Origin*'s publication. Even here, there's a kind of misdirection (or carelessness) when Melville does cite Darwin. The poem

begins with the epigraph "See Lyell's *The Antiquity of Man* and Darwin's *The Descent of Species*." In addition to the conflation of two separate titles by Darwin (i.e., *The Origin of Species* and *The Descent of Man*), neither source contains a reference to Engis Man. For a more general treatment of Melville's use (and intentional misuse) of sources and source titles, see Samson, *White Lies*.

48. Denis Donoghue, *Connoisseurs of Chaos: Ideas of Order in Modern American Poetry*, 2nd ed. (New York: Columbia University Press, 1984), 79.

49. Delbanco, *Melville*, 16.

50. Although *The Confidence-Man* lies outside the scope of this study, the Cosmopolitan's question to the Missouri bachelor Pitch is another example of the yes-no pull: "In the natural advance of all creatures . . . do they not bury themselves over and over again in the endless resurrection of better and better?" (Herman Melville, *The Confidence-Man*, ed. Harrison Hayford, Hershel Parker, and G. Thomas Tanselle [Evanston and Chicago: Northwestern University Press and the Newberry Library 1984], 124). What's intriguing here is that Melville's definition of evolution is premised on the biblical language of burial and resurrection. In addition, Melville's account subtly undercuts the notion of progressive development through the oxymoronic phrase "endless resurrection of better and better."

51. Donoghue, *Connoisseurs of Chaos*, 87.

52. Franchot, "Melville's Traveling God," 177. This is a seeming shift in what Franchot observes in Melville's fiction, in which she sees him mimicking the silences and lacunae of Divine Authorship. But Melville's withholding of information also continues in *Clarel*. Take, for instance, this interruption in Melville's description of one of the pilgrims: "one whose air / Revealed—but, for the nonce, forbear" (2.1.187). This moment recalls the Hunilla sketch described above, where the authorial presence deliberately calls attention to a "revelation" deferred or denied to the reader.

53. Gay Wilson Allen, "Foreword," in Vincent Kenny, *Herman Melville's "Clarel": A Spiritual Autobiography* (Hamden, Conn.: Archon Books, 1973), xii–xiii.

54. Buell, "Melville the Poet," 152.

55. David R. Callaway, "Melville in the Age of Darwin and Paley: Science in *Typee*, *Mardi*, *Moby-Dick*, and *Clarel*" (diss, State University of New York, 2000), 201. Going further, Potter argues that Melville saw this reconciliation between Protestantism and science as a clue to the deeper complicity of these two discourses, a kind of unholy alliance whose assumptions Melville sought to undermine in the poem. See Potter, *Intersympathy of Creeds*, 41–45.

56. William H. Carruth, *Each in His Own Tongue* (New York: Wise-Parslow, 1925).

57. The nebular hypothesis attempted to explain the origins of the universe and planetary bodies by physical means rather than resorting to the need for an intelligent creator. In its broadest sense, it included general models of the universal progressive development shown not only in the cosmos but also on earth and in human society. In this way, the nebular hypothesis could be associated with species development, as two aspects of a more general progressive principle. See Ronald L. Numbers, *Creation by Natural Law: Laplace's Nebular Hypothesis in American Thought* (Seattle: University of Washington Press, 1979), 9–11;

Simon Schaffer, "The Nebular Hypothesis and the Science of Progress," in *History, Humanity and Evolution: Essays for John C. Greene*, ed. James R. Moore (New York: Cambridge University Press, 1989), 134.

58. Julia Ward Howe, "Kosmos," in *Later Lyrics* (Boston: J. E. Tilton, 1886), 131–32.

59. For instance, Rolfe, finding himself too earnestly impassioned, cautions himself, "Let doubt alone; best skim, / Not dive" (*Clarel*, 2.22.102–3).

60. "As came that close / A hideous hee-haw horrible arose / Rebounded in unearthly sort / From shore to shore, as if retort / From all the damned in Sodom's Sea / Out brayed at him. 'Just God, what's that?' / 'The ass,' breathed Vine, with tropic eye" (*Clarel*, 2.33.67–72).

61. Charles Olson, *Call Me Ishmael* (New York: Reynal and Hitchcock, 1947), 14. Olson comments on the association of space and time in Melville's body of work: "Beginner—and interested in beginnings. Melville had a way of reaching back through time until he got himself pushing back so far he turned time into space."

62. Yothers, *Romance of the Holy Land*, 120.

63. Admittedly, this is an idea with roots in the early scholarship on *Clarel*, most notably, Walter Bezanson's still-influential introduction and critical notes to the 1960 Hendricks House edition of the poem. Goldman suggests an interesting emendation, though: that Bezanson and others set up a false choice between the poet's interest in faith and spirituality on the one hand and character and questions of truth on the other.

64. Goldman, *Melville's Protest Theism*, 8.

65. A line that recalls another from *Mardi*: "Oh, reader, list! I've chartless voyaged" (556).

66. We find here further evidence that Melville closely read the *Journal of Researches*.

67. Bezanson, "Historical and Critical Note," 566–67.

68. Buell, "Melville the Poet," 137.

69. Bezanson, "Historical and Critical Note," 567.

70. Delbanco, *Melville*, 16.

71. Ibid., 3–4.

72. Franchot, "Melville's Traveling God," 182; Goldman, *Melville's Protest Theism*, 102.

Faith among the Weeds

Melville's Religious Wildings beyond These Deserts

Martin Kevorkian

When Melville seeks to confer upon Hawthorne his highest praise, he declares the writing of the "Mossy Man" to be as "deep as Dante." "That flowery Hawthorne" plumbs the "deep mystery of sin," like Dante plunging into the pit of hell.[1] And yet the direction of depth in Dante initially deceives. Though to all appearances the pilgrim climbs downwards into the Inferno, in retrospect this descent proves to be but the first stage in an ascent, as he continues in the same absolute direction through the center of the earth and on upwards to the top of the mountain of Purgatory, and thence to Paradise.[2] And the pilgrim receives his vision and undertakes his journey as Love wills, the love of Beatrice acting in concert with love divine. I suggest that a journey begun with Melville's initial valuation of depth in Hawthorne and Dante, affording a true vision of human depravity, leads him ultimately to a great height, one that can be measured in the loving expressions of his late "Rose Poems," as in the climactic celebration of the "Moss-Rose!"—the final word of "Amoroso"—and the subsequent poem's closing image of "The Rose Vine round the Cross."[3]

Recent appreciations of Melville's art after *Moby-Dick* have opened up a critical space for considering the passionate and the spiritual simultaneously, tracing a quest which, as characterized by Clark Davis, "joins religious desire with aesthetic and sensuous appreciation and so strengthens the former through a connection with human emotion."[4] As John Bryant suggests in a 2001 edition, the "Rose Poems," from *Weeds and Wildings Chiefly: With a Rose or Two*, offer a rich field for pursuing such a line of inquiry: "Melville's brilliant but neglected Rose Poems are a set of devotionals in praise of physical and spiritual love . . . A love letter to his wife, Melville's Rose Poems articulate the writer's life-long quandary over faith and doubt in the wholly new terms of transcendence through physical love."[5] Melville's articulation of a "desire / for the garden of God" bears comparison to Dante's culminating vision of the "Celestial Rose," enfolded by the love that animates the universe.[6] Melville finds a witness to faith in the Rose, "Flower, voucher of Paradise, visible pledge, / Rose, attesting it spite of the worm."[7]

This is so despite a critical legacy that has often taken Melville's 1856 discourse in Liverpool, reported by Hawthorne, as his final words on matters of religion, reading them as an articulation of irrevocable despair. The Northwestern-Newberry editors of Melville's journals, for example, refer to "his having made up his mind, as he told Hawthorne 'to be annihilated.'"[8] But in no sense does Hawthorne's account portray Melville, embarking upon a pilgrimage to the Holy Land, as having landed decisively within a perspective of nihilistic materialism: "Melville, as he always does, began to reason of Providence and futurity, and of everything that lies beyond human ken, and informed me that he had 'pretty much made up his mind to be annihilated.'"[9] The "pretty much" may bespeak a disheartened mood, but not a settled mind. The language of approximation opens up the space of possibility shared by faith and doubt alike.[10] In the translation of *Paradiso* that Melville owned and annotated, Dante accounts for a restless, doubting mind as driven by a natural, earthly thirst for heavenly knowledge: "thence does doubt / Spring, like a shoot, around the stock of truth; And it is nature which, from height to height, / On to the summit prompts us" (*Paradiso,* 4).[11] Everything in Hawthorne's account points to such a restlessness in Melville: the individual who has foreclosed possibility does not revert "always" to pursuing questions whose answers lie "beyond human ken." What remains foreclosed by this epistemology and excluded by Melville's persistence is precisely certainty, the certainty of death as annihilation so casually taken for granted in the editorial framing of the Holy Land journals.[12]

In the discussion that follows, I look frequently to Melville's interest in Dante to keep open the spiritual possibilities of Melville's conversations with Hawthorne, since the full range of Dante's poetry that continued to engage Melville's attention better accounts for the range of Melville's late verse than does the traditional emphasis on his affinities for pessimism taken alone. And even a study like William B. Dillingham's account of Melville's "Disenchantment" in his last years, an account that gives such weight to Melville's encounter with pessimist sources, leaves a door (albeit an unlabeled one) open for other influences and moods: "Unquestionably Melville was especially impressed with James Thomson and Arthur Schopenhauer, as his markings in copies of their books and echoes of their ideas in his own writings indicate. On the other hand, Herman Melville was Herman Melville: he never became the disciple of anyone, even a member of his own circle."[13] And of the circle that Dillingham so convincingly establishes, James Thomson himself provides a vector out, even while showing Thomson's own strong affinities for the depths of Dante.

In his illuminating "Introduction to Melville's Marginalia in James Thomson's *The City of Dreadful Night and Other Poems,*" Matthew Giordano discusses the understandable temptation to read Melville's fascination with this poem as diagnostic of a purely pessimistic frame of mind:

> Melville's only substantive markings of the poem come in the form of marginal scorings at the end of the first section . . . In an obvious allusion to Dante's *Inferno*, these ending lines explain that everyone who enters the City of Dreadful Night abandons hope and finds comfort in only one thing:
>
> One anodyne for torture and despair;
> The certitude of Death, which no reprieve
> Can put off long; and which, divinely tender,
> But waits the outstretched hand to promptly render
> That draught whose slumber nothing can bereave. ([Thomson,] "City of Dreadful Night," 7:10–14)
>
> [It is] tempting to read Melville's marking of these lines biographically, as expressing his disappointment with life and his desire for death.

While there may be truth to this reading, other facts of Melville's biography contest it, for Melville did not spend his last decade simply biding time until his death. As Hershel Parker observes, he continued to read voluminously and write productively, caring enough about his poetry to pay out of pocket for the publication of two books of poems, *John Marr and Other Sailors* (1888) and *Timoleon* (1891). If Melville identified somberly with the lines of resignation he marked in "The City of Dreadful Night," this identification seems to represent only part of his perspective in his old age.[14]

If Thomson's City and Dante's *Inferno* represent only a part of Melville's religious stance, Dante's *Paradiso* represents another. In a recent study that makes extensive use of Melville's markings of Dante, Dennis Berthold has observed that Melville "would continue to study the great Tuscan poet all his life."[15] Berthold proposes that "Melville returned to Cary's Dante throughout his career . . . as inspiration for his turn to poetry in the 1850s and beyond."[16] While focusing on "*Mardi*'s Dantean Intertext," Berthold notes that, in this early novel, "Melville could not accompany Dante into Paradise."[17] But as I have argued elsewhere, the Melville of *Clarel*'s pilgrimage seriously considers steps in that direction. Berthold's study provides a clue of a Hawthorne-Dante nexus for enabling that late-career turn toward the *Commedia*'s third realm, as he highlights the 1860 voyage that found Melville reading both *The Marble Faun* and Cary's Dante, and he suggests that Melville's "copious markings, particularly in the heavily sidelined third book 'Paradise,' parallel his late interest in theology."[18] For that interest, Melville found his most notable interlocutor in the "morally companionable" Hawthorne, as Michael Colacurcio so wonderfully characterizes him; though that interest was far, in Hawthorne's eyes, from a "definite belief," as Colacurcio sees the case anew,

Melville's was "a position that left ample room for faith, should it ever be given."[19] In the stanzas of the Rose Poems, we may find that room left open, and filled with love.[20] That openness and that love form an important and largely unwritten legacy of his relationship with Hawthorne.

Granted, Hawthorne's record of the famous conversation on the dunes does strike some dreary notes: "It is strange how he persists—and has persisted ever since I knew him, and probably long before—in wandering to-and fro over these deserts, as dismal and monotonous as the sand hills amid which we were sitting"—and, reading proleptically (as tends to be done with this passage), presumably as dismal and monotonous as the sand hills, metaphysical and geographical, Melville subsequently encountered on his journey and described in *Clarel*. Yet even here, the sand hill setting may register in contrary experiences: "we took a pretty long walk together, and sat down in a hollow among the sand hills (sheltering ourselves from the high, cool wind) and smoked a cigar."[21] While the haunting hollowness of the dunes has resonated the most with subsequent commentary, the sheltering sandscape also provides an occasion for a cozy and leisurely if earnest exchange. And that latter warm mood tends to prevail in the remainder of Hawthorne's account. The two friends spent several days together, and on the subsequent Saturday made an outing to Chester, which Hawthorne narrates with a companionable "we" framing throughout. Visiting the cathedral, they admired the restoration of a tomb "found to have been ornamented with gold and color," which "added vastly to the gorgeous magnificence to which the painted windows, and polished pillars, and ornamented ceilings, contributed so much."[22] If the hollow sand hills point to the difficulties of Clarel's pilgrimage, the beauty of Chester Cathedral points to the Rose Poems, in which Melville would celebrate a vision of radiantly transfigured sepulchers overseen by the "Rose Window," "suffused with rich and soft in dye."[23]

The cathedral tour would not be complete without acknowledgment that the institution was built to feed body and soul together: "Afterwards," Hawthorne writes, "we were shown into the ancient Refectory, which is now used as the city Grammar school," perhaps a spot where one might raise a glass to the "Late Consumptive Usher" who compiled *Moby-Dick*'s Etymology.[24] Ducking into a space adjoining the Refectory, "we went through a small room, in which Melville opened a cupboard and discovered a dozen or two wine-bottles; but our guide told us that they were now empty, and never meant for jollity, having held only sacramental wine." None deterred, the chums move for a change of venue where they may take their own communion, one marked by both jollity and the sacred. They opt for the Yacht Inn, "at which Swift once put up, on his way to Holyhead, and where he invited the clergy of the Cathedral to come and sup with him": "We sat down in a small snuggery, behind the bar, and smoked a cigar and drank some stout."[25] This evening in the snuggery renews the sacrament of their friendship, recalling, for instance, the August night of 1851 when "Melville and I had a talk about time and eternity, things of this world and the next, and books, and publishers, and all possible and impossible matters, that lasted pretty deep into the night; and if truth must be told, we smoked cigars even within the sacred precincts of the sitting room."[26] In such moments, Melville could enjoy the convivial communion with Hawthorne that he had thirsted for since the first letter that he had written to his new boon companion, in January 1851: "Hark—There is some excellent Montado Sherry awaiting you & some most potent Port. We will have mulled wine with wisdom, & buttered toast with story-telling & crack jokes & bottles from morning till night."[27] Or again, in June 1851, in a more clearly eschatological and still more passionate vein:

> Would the gin were here! If ever, my dear Hawthorne, in the eternal times that are to come, you and I shall sit down in Paradise, in some little shady corner by ourselves; and if we shall by any means be able to smuggle a basket of champagne there (I won't believe in a Temperance Heaven), and if we shall then cross our celestial legs in the celestial grass forever tropical, and strike our glasses and our heads together, till both musically ring in concert—then, O my dear fellow-mortal, how shall we pleasantly discourse of all the things which now so distress us.[28]

They will achieve what Melville terms a "comic" vision, a jocular in-law of that eternal perspective that causes Dante to entitle his poem the "Commedia": "Oh, when I lived in that queer little hole called the world" is a lyric that Melville foresees them singing.[29] "Yes," says the man who loves the man who says No in Thunder, "let us look forward to such things. Let us swear that, though now we sweat, yet it is because of the dry heat which is indispensable to the nourishment of the vine which is to bear the grapes that is to give us the champagne hereafter." (Here, perhaps, we encounter an intimation of Melville's associating Hawthorne with the "Vine evangelic" which will bestow its name upon the Hawthorne-pilgrim in *Clarel*.)[30] And reaching an ecstatic pitch of intimacy, Melville delivers in the celebrated letter of November 1851 an address simultaneously his most passionate and his most sacramental: "Whence come you, Hawthorne? By what right do you drink from my flagon of life? And when I put it to my lips—lo, they are yours and not mine. I feel that the Godhead is broken up like the bread at the Supper, and that we are the pieces. Hence this infinite fraternity of feeling."[31] This craving for heavenly communion finds voice even in his wry toast to the Sub-Sub-Librarian, dutiful compiler of the Extracts for *Moby-Dick*. Though he belongs to the "tribe which no wine of this world will ever warm; and for whom even Pale Sherry would be too rosy strong," the narrator enjoins such brethren to "gulp down your tears and hie aloft to the royal-mast with your hearts; for your friends who have gone before are clearing out the seven-storied heavens, and making refugees of long-pampered Gabriel, Michael, and Raphael, against your coming. Here ye strike but splintered hearts together—there, ye shall strike unsplinterable glasses!"[32]

So it is the sacramental evening in the snuggery that ought to blend or contend with the restless conversation in the dunes in striking the final chord for Hawthorne and Melville in 1856. Hawthorne sees Melville one last time the following Monday, and he hits notes of both gloom and cheer regarding his friend's state: "He said that he already felt much better than in America; but observed that he did not anticipate much pleasure in his rambles, for that spirit of adventure is gone out of him. He certainly is much overshadowed since I saw him last; but I hope that he will brighten as he goes onward."[33] Melville hoped so too: not adventure per se, but experiential matter for contemplation, might occasion him to "brighten." Four months later in Florence, after having visited the "tombs of Dante" at Santa Croce, Melville found himself "at dinner table accosted by singular young man . . . He presented me with a flower, and talked like one to whom the world was delightful. May it prove so."[34] Written after a life of much heartache, the Rose Poems show us a Melville who has discovered that capacity for such delight. In "The Rose Farmer," which accompanies the Rose Poems and establishes the condition of their existence, Melville writes on behalf of "we who after ragged scrambles / Through fate's blessed thorns and brambles / Come unto our roses late":[35]

> *Coming through the rye:*
> Hereof the rural poet whistles;
> But who the flute will try
> At *scrambling through the thistles*!
> Nor less upon some roseate way
> Emerge the prickly passage may.[36]

As with the hope voiced at *Clarel*'s conclusion, the faith among the weeds here named, the roseate subject of the rarer poetry here attempted, is one which *may* emerge.

We may here venture a speculative consideration of a puzzling passage in *Clarel*. The character Rolfe (often thought to be modeled on the Melville of the Holy Land journey) has been engaging young Clarel as well as Vine (consistently identified by critics as the poem's Hawthorne figure) on all the usual subjects—the role of religion, the hypothetical demonstrability "that God is not":

> Intense he spake, his eyes of blue
> Adhering, and to eerie hue,
> Like Tyrrhene seas when overcast;
> The which Vine noted, nor in joy,
> Inferring thence an ocean-waste
> Of earnestness without a buoy:[37]

This much sounds familiar—Hawthorne perceiving the restless Melville as lacking the anchor of faith and having pretty much made up his mind to be annihilated. But the narrator continues, tracking the subsequent unfolding of Vine's treatment of this encounter and the interpretation of Rolfe's spiritual life that its words initially produced:

> An inference which afterward
> Acquaintance led him to discard
> Or modify, or not employ.[38]

In this passage, it is almost as if Melville is imagining both Hawthorne's impression of him in that conversation from the start of his pilgrimage, in the hollow of the dunes, and Hawthorne's subsequent understanding of their "good talk" of 1856 (Melville's words) and where it might lead Melville, perhaps to seas less overcast.[39] I have spoken of reading this passage speculatively; one may note the rather curious fact that the narrator too must speak speculatively of it. Though providing access throughout the poem to the inner lives of its characters, the narrator gives us here only a Hawthornean multiple choice: did Vine change his mind completely, and "discard" what has become the dominant final understanding of Melville and religion? Did he merely "modify" the judgment—putting more emphasis on the leeway provided by "pretty much" and less on the prospect of being "annihilated"? Or did he, most curiously of all, simply "not employ"—not put into use, or circulate, the initial inference which he had first formed and still held as most likely? The situation might be put thus: Vine, a poet's faithful simulacrum of a real human, can of course do no more than infer what lives in Rolfe's heart. And the narrator, too, at this crux, finds himself in the same epistemological situation: speaking not as a fictional creator regarding his creation, but as one human being not quite knowing what to make, in retrospect and in absentia, of the silent surfaces that constitute all that another human has presented. One way of understanding the narrator's quandary would be to read it as Melville's own uncertainty produced by the version of Hawthorne's account of the Liverpool-Chester visit that "Melville read in his copy of *Passages from the English Note-Books* (Boston: Fields, Osgood, 1870), II, 155–56 (Sealts 251)."[40] As abridged by Sophia Hawthorne, with her ellipses as they appeared in that edition, the passage still delivers the familiar Melville and his penchant for ontological heroics, and we get Hawthorne's genuine words of praise for his dear friend's character: "Melville, as he always does, began to reason of Providence and futurity, and of everything else that lies beyond human ken. . . . He has a very high and noble nature, and is better worth immortality than most of us. . . . On Saturday we went to Chester together."[41] But we do not get either any words directly attributed to Melville or the seeming note of concern in Hawthorne's reactions to them. No "overcast" Rolfean talk of being "annihilated" on Melville's part appears, and no explicitly unjoyful Vinean "inference" about what struck Hawthorne as at once "strange" and "dismal and monotonous."[42] Reading this passage, Melville might well have wondered at the ellipses. And he might have recalled, from this highly charged meeting, his own strong language about annihilation, and even, perhaps, the uneasiness in his friend's eyes at this all-but-despairing unburthening of his soul—a declaration and response nowhere to be found in the printed text, yet potentially lurking, in those sets of dots, as something someone had deliberately omitted, for whatever reason. Thus might Melville have come to pose the puzzle that faces his narrator in *Clarel*: Did Vine discard, modify, or simply not employ his judgment upon the state of Rolfe's soul as that of a wind-swept "ocean-waste"? If the answer is "modify"—if Melville hoped that that was what Hawthorne hoped—then in the Rose Poems, at least, Melville would make good upon that guess.

In assessing the texture of this late poetic performance, we can affirm Bryant's word choice in specifying that "the Rose Poems take Melville's persistent sexualizing to crystalline heights"—yea, unto the music of the spheres, the vision of the crystalline *primum mobile*, and beyond, to the empyrean.[43] "What we find here is sonnetizing but not Shakespeare's sonnet form, nor do we find the pastoralism of Wordsworth or the narrative of Browning, or even the faith in love of Arnold but a vein of imagistic urgency more clearly connected to Keats, Tennyson, Rossetti, and Swinburne. These poems are about the hot-cold, burning luminosity of love, death, and transcendence all wrapped up in the rose."[44] The faith that emerges is precisely not the secular humanist "faith in love of Arnold," but the faith through love of Rossetti's namesake, Dante.[45] When Bryant reports, in his 2001 gathering, that "Melville's Rose Poems articulate the writer's life-long quandary over faith and doubt in the wholly new terms of transcendence through physical love," one must take that newness as applying to Melville's art, for Bryant elsewhere signals that such fusion does find precedent in the poetic tradition.[46] In "As They Fell," Bryant suggests that Melville makes "'The Devotion of the Flowers to Their Lady' the bedrock of his collection, for it is about Paradise Regained not through ascetism, deprivation, and shame, but as Dante beholding Beatrice would have it, through beauty and the rose."[47] Bryant's astute passing reference merits further consideration, as the comparison to Dante that he evokes does much to illuminate the trajectory from *Clarel* to the Rose Poems.

Clarel strikes its most encouraging note in its final gesture, as the narrator—in a voice of age advising youth—counsels the restless pilgrim to "keep thy heart, though yet but ill-resigned":

That like a crocus budding through the snow—
That like a swimmer rising from the deep—
That like a burning secret which doth go

Even from the bosom that would hoard and keep;
Emerge though mayst from the last whelming sea
And prove that death but routs life into victory.[48]

Scholars have greatly enriched our sense of these final lines by connecting the rising swimmer with resonances that include Polynesian and Buddhist thought. Arguing for "the probable rehabilitative place of eroticism in *Clarel*" that culminates in this conclusion, James Duban observes that "among some of the South Sea Islanders the compound word for hope is beautifully expressive. It is *manaolana*, or the *swimming thought*—faith floating and keeping its head aloft above water, when all the waves and billows are going over."[49] Duban then goes on to argue that Melville's allusions in *Clarel* emphasize "the differences between Western and Polynesian images and religious systems," particularly regarding the "redemptive fusion of sexuality and religion" that Duban finds present only in the latter.[50] But I would, while accepting the relevance of Duban's connections, more favor the approach of William Potter, who notes, in *Melville's "Clarel" and the Intersympathy of Creeds*, that this hopeful conclusion may well be linked to "both Christianity and Buddhism, as well as" to the "sensuality Melville found in his travels to the South Pacific as a young man."[51] An erotic dimension of faith may or may have sat well with the Rev. Cheever whom Duban cites as his contrastive straw man, yet such a fusion is fully compatible with what John Freccero characterizes as "Dante's Christian humanism."[52]

In "Marginalia as Revelation" Lea Newman calls attention to Melville's having copied a quotation from *Purgatorio* 31. Inscribed in Melville's Dante we find a pencil notation, middle leaf, on the printer's imprint, with the page reference to these words' appearance in Cary's translation (which are also marked on that page) : "Tu asperges me. 344"; as the editors of *Melville's Marginalia Online* subsequently note, this inscription is one of only a handful that we can confidently identify as being written by Melville himself, and Newman further observes that Melville's having copied it verbatim gives it unusual weight.[53] Though the inscription has tended to be read as a sign of Melville's guilty self-condemnation, as the words do indeed point to an acceptance of the need for purgative purification, the passage in which the words appear speaks more fully to the beauty of hope in "the swimming thought," and even to the sensuality of the Polynesian "nereids," from *Typee* to *Clarel*, that Duban emphasizes:[54]

The blessed shore approaching then was heard
So sweetly, "*Tu asperges me,*" that I
May not remember, much less tell the sound.
The beauteous dame, her arms expanding, clasp'd
My temples, and immerg'd me, where 'twas fit
The wave should drench me: and thence raising up

> Within the fourfold dance of lovely nymphs
> Presented me so lav'd, and with their arm
> They each did cover me.[55]

As Charles Singleton observes, noting the similarity of the beginning of *Paradiso* to the opening of *Purgatorio* (and indeed the similarity of both to the first canto of the *Inferno*, wherein Dante compares himself to "a man, with difficult short breath, / Forespent with toiling, 'scap'd from sea to shore"), "each of the three *cantiche* can be viewed as a sea—*Inferno* a cruel one, *Purgatorio* a better one, *Paradiso* an ocean."[56] The entire trajectory of the *Divine Comedy* might thus be viewed as "swimming thought" ascendant, until the poet emerges from that "last whelming sea" into the chartless Empyrean of pure light.[57]

Melville had previously invoked this desired ascent explicitly, in *Pierre*, only to have his protagonist reject it. The author-hero Vivia, as imagined by the would-be author Pierre, scoffs, "Is this the end of philosophy? This, the larger, and spiritual life? This your boasted Empyrean."[58] Pierre, believing himself to be the victim of an untenable situation, can find no solace in such unconfirmed promises, as the narrator concludes that "in tremendous extremities human souls are like drowning men . . . the sea is the sea, and these drowning men do drown."[59] Here, unlike Dante, Pierre's author-hero—as imagined, Melville's narrator insists, by one who has immaturely attempted a mature work—fails to ascend.

But the narrator nevertheless offers intimations of what a soul might achieve. Pierre and his inseparable boyhood companion, Glen, at "the age of ten, had furnished an example of the truth, that the friendship of fine-hearted, generous boys . . . sometimes transcends the bounds of mere boyishness, and revels for a while in the empyrean of love."[60] But "for a while" only, as fatal compromises with the social world trample this love the boys share. Similarly, the "adoration" of Pierre for his mother, Mary, "seemed almost to realize here below the sweet dreams of those religious enthusiasts, who paint to us a Paradise to come, when etherealized from all drosses and strains, the holiest passion of man shall unite all kindreds and climes in one circle of pure and unimpairable delight"—but only "seemed," and only "almost."[61] Yet in the sentence that most closely echoes Dante's end point while anticipating the Rose Poems, Melville's narrator writes that "love is both Creator's and Saviour's gospel to mankind; a volume bound in rose-leaves."[62] As Dante ascends to the Celestial Rose, he achieves the final vision in which he "saw in one volume clasp'd of love, whatever / The universe unfolds" (*Paradiso*, 33).[63]

If *Pierre* emphasizes the unattainability (or unsustainability) of empyreal love within the world of human relations, *Moby-Dick*, as Jonathan A. Cook has recently demonstrated, does find such love within the realm of nature: in chapter 87, "the rings of whales . . . duplicate Dante's wheeling rings of fire, the innermost of which is the swiftest 'because of burning love that urges it' (*Paradiso* XXVIII, 45) . . . The innermost circle of sperm whales in this scene, as in Dante's beatific vision, is thus united by love."[64] The Rose Poems give us that "burning love" as realized between humans in a realm both earthly and divine.[65]

The first poem in the cluster, "Ambuscade" opens with images of cold purity, figuring a snowy garden as a "cloister." "And yet" the holy and the passionate appear to be at odds only initially, as the faithful vestment of the "veil-like" robe of snow turns out to have maintained the health and growth of desire:

> And yet, white nun, that seemly dress
> Of purity pale passionless,
> A May-snow is; for fleeting term,
> Custodian of love's slumbering germ–
> Nay nurtures it, till time disclose
> How frost fed Amor's burning rose.[66]

This not-so-chilly "snow," one congruent with "Amor's burning rose," finds an analogue in the "snow-white rose" adorned by "flame" that graces Dante's *Paradiso*.

Here is Cary's rendering of the rose at the opening of canto 31, enfolded from first to last with the image of snow:

> In fashion, as a snow-white rose, lay then
> Before my view the saintly multitude,
> Which in his own blood Christ espous'd. Meanwhile
> That other host, that soar aloft to gaze
> And celebrate his glory, whom they love,
> Hover'd around; and, like a troop of bees,
> Amid the vernal sweets alighting now,
> Now, clustering, where their fragrant labour glows,
> Flew downward to the mighty flow'r, or rose
> From the redundant petals, streaming back
> Unto the steadfast dwelling of their joy.
> Faces had they of flame, and wings of gold;
> The rest was whiter than the driven snow.[67]

Structurally and dramatically, Melville's poem gives a sense of surprising discontinuity not present in Dante's harmonious whole, but ultimately achieves a similar resolution. The "And yet"—the volta—ambushes us in line five, as if the sonnet form implied by such a turn had been abbreviated mid-octave, thence moving to conclusion with a full sestet. That short duration of the apparently discontinuous opening matches the poem's assessment of the white veil's cloistral deferral: not a long, bitter winter, but a mere "May-snow"; under the aspect of the fullness of time, we might say, the time until the wedding day, whether earthly or eschatological, passes quickly as but a "fleeting term" ("Ambuscade," l.7).

The "rose," the poem's final word, provides the firm telos which gives meaning to all that precedes it. Ryan's transcription of the genetic text reveals that only the final line, "How frost fed Amor's burning rose," remains invariant in Melville's many revisions to this poem. All else in "The Ambuscade" constitutes a shuffling of layers of timely deferral. The first verb does not arrive until the poem's third line, and the trail of words before the first full stop registers preponderantly as a series of interchangeable descriptive phrases—"Meek crossing of the bosom's lawn" "Averted revery veil-like drawn," "The cloister of thy virginhood"—made barely legible as a sentence via the interjection that these attributes of snowy setting "well beseem thee" ("Ambuscade," l.3). The ground is frozen, and so is the syntax, covering and re-covering that same ground in an apparently timeless moment. Even past the volta, the syntax continues to tarry with that same actionless image, emerging as clear and complete declaration only after the first explicit marker of time enters the poem, in a statement that defers the verb until its final word: "And yet, white nun, that seemly dress / Of purity pale passionless, / A May-snow is" (ll. 5–7). Only in the strong last line—with hearty beats and resonant r's that link its key terms—do we hear a simple declaration not syntactically inverted by deferral: "frost fed Amor's burning rose."

This theme of a nourishing chill, so emphatically presented to the reader in the shape of a radiant bloom, carries over to the next poem, "Under the Ground," albeit in a somewhat different mood, as we learn that a gardener does indeed, to the speaker's surprise, keep roses in a sepulchre to keep them fresh "against the bridal hour": "A charm in the dank o' the vault there is / Yea, we the rose entomb" ("Under the Ground," ll. 11–12).[68] As preparedness for a wedding occasions this temporary entombment, thus making the practices legible as allegory for the preservation of souls in anticipation of Christ's return (Melville's "against the bridal hour" particularly suggest such liturgical formulations as "against that day" in *The Book of Common Prayer*), one may likewise consider how the white snow covering of "Ambuscade" also echoes the "stoles of snowy white" worn by the saints in heaven (*Paradiso*, 30), in anticipation of their preparation for the resurrection of the flesh.[69] Melville's word choice for the roses in "Under the Ground" also specifically signals a devotional purpose for these garden verses: "there I met the gardener's boy / bearing some dewy chaplets over" (ll. 3–4). In the context of the wedding ceremony for which the roses have been set aside, the "chaplets" would be garlands or wreaths to be worn on the head. But a "chaplet" is also a portion of the rosary comprising five "decades" (of ten Hail Mary's each). The word "chaplet" shares with "chapel" a derivation from the Late Latin *cappa*, specifically the first "chapel" so-called which took its name from the "cape" (*cappa*) of Saint Martin, which it held. That cape is itself associated with the overlap of summer and winter (used to dramatic effect in "Ambuscade" and layered together in *Paradiso,* 31): the "Summer of St. Martin" remembers the warmth in winter that Saint Martin provided by cutting his cape to share with a shivering passerby. Looking ahead in the Rose Poems, the "chaplets" of "Under the Ground" point towards the "Rosary Beads," which close by enjoining ongoing acts of faith against incursions by the deserts of doubt: "Hedge well the Roses, heed the stealth / Of ever-creeping Sand."[70]

The third poem in the cluster, like the first two, treats the paradoxical coexistence of iciness with vitality, but returns to the lighter tone of "The Ambuscade" after the more somber setting of "Under the Ground."[71] If, as in its reference to bearing "chaplets," "Under the Ground" looked forward to an act of faith, "Amoroso" most plainly advocates an act of love. And yet, it does not thereby disqualify its lines from theological significance. Melville's "Amoroso" has, with good reason, been compared first and foremost to Milton's "Il Penseroso" and "L'Allegro."[72] But as Thomas Cole's paired allegorical landscapes that bear these titles may remind us, with their Romanesque framings of Italian sunsets, "Il Penseroso" and "L'Allegro" are Milton at his most Italianate.[73] And "Amoroso" gives us Melville at his most densely Dantesque. In "Melville's *Pierre* and Dante's *Inferno*," G. Giovanni proposes a scenario that seems equally apt for the Rose Poems: "Relying on some knowledge of the *Inferno* on the reader's part, Melville adopts the technique of literary allusion and quotation functioning in place of formal exposition, the literary reference itself becoming contextually an expository symbol."[74] That technique is, one might add, Dante's own, par excellence: as a collection by leading Dantistes declares, Dante's craft is *The Poetry of Allusion.*[75] What Giovanni's study shows us, and which further examination of "Amoroso" should demonstrate: Melville not only alludes to Dante but alludes *as* Dante does. Noting, along with Lea Newman, that we can find among the numerous articles on Melville and Dante not only a nearly exclusive focus on the *Inferno* but also no fewer than three whose titles nominate one or another work as "Melville's Inferno"—*Pierre*, "The Tartarus of Maids," "The Encantadas"—I would affirm that it is time to look beyond Dante's first cantica; we might just recognize intimations of "Melville's Paradiso."[76] And we might begin with a consideration of Melville's Ovid:

> Rosamond, my Rosamond
>   Of roses is the rose;
> Her bloom belongs to summer,
>   Nor less in winter glows,
> When, mossed in furs all cosey,
>   We speed it o'er the snows
>
>   . . . .
>
> While red Arcturus, he
> A huntsman ever ruddy,
>   Sees a ruddier star by me.

O Rosamond, Rose Rosamond,
  Is yonder Dian's reign?
Look, the icicles despond
  Chill drooping from the fane!
But Rosamond, Rose Rosamond,
  In us, a plighted pair,
Frost makes with flame a bond,
  One purity they share.[77]

Is yonder Dian's reign? Are winter snows, or the snowy heavens, governed by the law of chastity? No, as per "Amoroso," and No, as per *Paradiso*. Burning love abides in both, contrary to any exclusionary actions of Diana: "frost makes with flame a bond" to share a purity that is not chastity. Melville's invocation of "red Arcturus" reminds us that Diana's jurisdiction does not extend to the heavens. Arcturus, named for the son that Helice bore by Jupiter, features prominently in the Ovidian narrative that Dante cites and rewrites over the course of the *Commedia*, culminating in a final triumphant appearance in *Paradiso* 31. Helice (aka Callisto) was a chaste follower of Diana, expelled for being, as Rachel Jacoff puts it, "ambushed into eros."[78] Here, we may already begin to think of Helice as the addressee of "The Ambuscade." And if we think along those lines, we may begin to see her tale's appeal for Melville and to puzzle out why this story should resurface in paradise, at the crucial moment of Dante's amazement at the rose, upon which he gazes like one just arrived "from Arctic shores."[79]

In the prior context of the *Purgatorio*'s purifying didacticism, as Rachel Jacoff explains, "Dante concentrates on Diana's chastity as an analogy for Mary's," whereas "Helice's motherhood" registers as a "violation of Diana's standard" (*Purgatorio*, 25).[80] But in the realm of the purified, "in the *Paradiso*, Dante seems to rewrite his own critique of Helice-Callisto by speaking of her in her final metamorphosis as a type of Mary rather than as her opposite. In Ovid, Helice is turned into a bear by Juno's jealousy; just as she is about to be slain inadvertently by her grown son, Jupiter sweeps both mother and son into the sky, where they become the constellations of the Great and Little Bear."[81] Viewed from the context of paradise, this exalted position suggests more than vindication, as "Dante describes the relationship between Helice and her son in language that one might expect to find in a description of Mary's relationship to Jesus" (Jacoff and Schnapp, *Poetry of Allusion*, 245). In Cary's translation, "Helice for ever, as she wheels / Sparkles a mother's fondness on her son" (*Paradiso*, 31).[82] In the printed note at the base of the page, Cary explains that "Helice.] Callisto, and her son Arcas, changed into the constellations of the Greater Bear and Arctophylax, or Boötes. See Ovid, Met. l. ii. fab. v. vi."[83] Arcturus, "the guardian of the Bear," is named for Arcas and the role he is given, and thus reciprocally commemorates that mother-son bond. And his exalted presence thus helps answer Melville's question: is yonder Dian's reign? Jacoff situates the literary and theological point: "The Song of Songs and the tradition of commentary on it provided medieval writers with the major example of the possible fusion of erotic and theological codes. Dante transforms Ovid's *Metamorphoses* into another repository of such possibilities. From the first dream in purgatory it is clear that the repertoire of Ovidian materials will enrich Dante's text imaginatively by offering examples of erotic passion . . . that can be repositioned within a Christianizing context that does not empty them out."[84] Precisely contrary to the expectation that, after the askeses of *Inferno* and *Purgatorio*, the pilgrim might leave behind both classical antiquity and its narratives of passion, Dante's Christian metamorphoses of Ovid only increase with *Paradiso*, as "eros is redeemed rather than rejected, specifically granted validity in Dante's discourse on love in *Paradiso* 26 as the very condition of his ascensional spirituality."[85] As "Amoroso" concludes: "This is Arctic Paradise, / and wooing in the snows!"[86] And that love is guaranteed by the "ruddier star" upon which Arcturus looks in favor, the rose that enfolds the poem and shapes its poetics. In "Amoroso," Melville not only adopts a Dantesque allusive technique that points to *Paradiso* 31, he adapts the rhyme form which Dante invented for the *Commedia*, his terza rima, built on interlocking sets of triple rhymes. Melville bookends the poem with two line-alternated triple rhymes: "rose"(2) "glows" (4) "snows" (6); and "inclose" (20) "snows" (23) "-rose" (25), thus framing "Amoroso" with the same rhyme word, "rose," which opens *Paradiso* 31.

Taking things indoors, Melville's "Rose Window," which merges preacher's text with heavenly dream, locates Dante's Rose in a cathedral setting. Commenting, just after the note on Helice, upon Dante's reference in *Paradiso* 31 to the "wonder" of the "works of Rome," Cary ventures that "it is remarkable that Dante has no allusion to the magnificence of Gothic architecture, which was then in so much perfection."[87] In fact, subsequent readers have found the design of Gothic cathedrals to be implicit in Dante's architectonics and in the imagery of *Paradiso* 31 in particular; as Robert and Jean Hollander note, the idea of "the resemblance of Dante's *candida rosa* [*Paradiso* 31.1] to the rose-wheeled windows of medieval cathedrals" was first articulated within Dante studies as early as 1870, and subsequently developed in numerous commentaries, including Leyerle's hypothesis that Dante had in mind the façade of the basilica of S. Zeno in Verona, with its human figures "rising or falling" like the angels that flit about Dante's Rose, and with its "lovely tracing of light" like the blazing souls who form that flower.[88] While one scholar has objected that the term for "rose window" did not appear in vernaculars until the seventeenth century, the Hollanders respond that this matter of nomenclature "is hardly conclusive evidence that Dante did not think of one of these round, large, beautiful, and many-hued glass structures, piercing stone and splashing the interior with colored light, as the model for his Rose."[89] Nor does the fact that Cary highlights the absence of explicit reference to Gothic windows preclude the possibility that Melville perceives in *Paradiso* 31 such a poetic potential—Cary's calling attention to the strangeness of that apparent omission may have further suggested such a transfigurative identification. Melville's poem provides such an identification: under the influence of the right sermon (a "honied" homily on the Song of Songs, no less), one might be transported from contemplation of a Rose Window to an angelic vision of the Celestial Rose.[90] In fact, the trajectory of Melville's poem moves from homage to gloss on Dante's imagery, tracing the vision of the Rose back to the context of a cathedral window.

The vision within "Rose Window" looks back to both the "seemly dress" of the "white nun" in "The Ambuscade" and the garden tomb of roses awaiting the "bridal hour" in "Under the Ground," portraying the heavenly consummation of those faithful preparations:

> I saw an Angel with a Rose
> Come out of Morning's garden-gate
> And lamp-like hold the Rose aloft.
> He entered a sepulchral Strait.
> I followed. And I saw the Rose
> Shed dappled dawn upon the dead;
> The shrouds and mort-cloths all were lit
> To plaids and chequered tartans red.[91]

Melville concludes the poem with a wonderful return—such as one finds in Dante—to the earthly detail that gives this future scene an immediate incarnational presence in the consecration of the everyday:

> I woke. The great Rose-Window high,
> A mullioned wheel in gable set,
> . . . .
> Aslant in sheaf of rays it threw
> From all its foliate round of panes
> Transfiguring light on dingy stains,
> While danced the motes in dusty pew. ("Rose Window," ll. 20–17)

The foliate sheaf suggests the leaves of both garden and library, the petals of the Celestial Rose and the volume bound in love. The motes dancing in light move between the ecstatic Dance of the Stars suspended in the "beam" of "grace" (Cary, *Paradiso*, 10) and the earthy texture through which Dante infuses his vision of paradise with terrestrial memory, as when he concludes the canto with a simile of Lucretian flux, as "danced the motes" of dust, shifting and glittering in afternoon rays.[92]

Melville's Rose Poems, like the final canto of Dante's *Paradiso*, culminates with a holy song that yet retains such graces of earthly poetry. In

"The Devotion of the Flowers to Their Lady," addressed "O Queen," Melville recalls the vocatives that frame the celebrated "Hymn to the Virgin" of *Paradiso* 33: "O Virgin mother"; "O queen!"[93] While Dante attributes his "Hymn" to Saint Bernard, Melville gives us a "Devotion" "attributed to Clement Drouon, monk, a Provençal of noble birth in the 11th century. In earlier life a troubadour, a devotee of Love and the Rose."[94] Significantly, Melville does not attribute the verses to Clement Drouon, troubadour, in later life a monk. The poem does not, that is, show us the archive of a florid love later renounced. Rather, in this poetic performance, Melville's fictionalized Clement brings to bear the craft of the Provençal troubadour in singing the highest holy praise of that Lady, the Rose, "voucher of Paradise."[95] With "festal" "looks that beguile," the Rose causes "mortals" to "marvel and marvel how came you so bright / Whence the splendor, the joyance— / Florid revel of joyance"; despite exile from Eden, enflaming followers with "desire / for the Garden of God."

In Melville's verse before the Rose Poems, the qualities of such desire have seemed problematic. Wyn Kelley, treating *Clarel*'s "uncertainties about sexuality and love," paraphrases his unsettling inquiries: "Does the love of God require sexual purity? . . . Or can one derive some intimation of heavenly love from love below? . . . Clarel's questions challenge the foundation of religious feeling."[96] To address Clarel's unresolved perplexities, Melville may have found kindred spirits in the heaven of Venus (*Paradiso,* 9), particularly as that realm is animated by the Provençal troubadour tradition which he honors at the close of the Rose Poems.

In this realm we find "the blaze of love perfected," as Clive James renders it.[97] We meet Cunizza, a woman of great passions—as Cary's note explains—wooed by the troubadour Sordello with whom she eloped, and utterly unapologetic for the life of loves that led her to the sphere of Venus: "Yet I naught repine, / Nor grudge myself the cause of this my lot, / Which haply vulgar hearts can scarce conceive" (Cary, *Paradiso,* 9).

As Cunizza speaks, the soul who will go on to explicate what imperfect hearts cannot yet easily understand grows brighter. Cary's translation introduces him as a "joyance," the distinctive term that Melville repeats in "Devotion" and that Bryant privileges as the keyword of the Rose Poems:

> That other joyance meanwhile wax'd
> A thing to marvel at, in splendour glowing,
> Like choicest ruby stricken by the sun,
> For, in that upper clime, effulgence comes
> Of gladness, as here laughter.

This "joyance" represents the soul of "Folco of Genoa, a celebrated Provençal poet, commonly termed Folques of Marseilles, of which place he was perhaps bishop" (Cary notes to *Paradiso* 9; Cary further notes that Dante cited Folques's verses directly in his treatise *De Vulgari Eloquentia*, a key theoretical formulation of Dante's democratic poetics, pursuing the common or "vulgar" tongue as a medium for conveying the highest and most beautiful). Expounding upon pure love, this troubadour rather precisely answers Clarel's question—as to whether heavenly love can eventuate from love below:

> there hides
> No sorrowful repentance here, but mirth,
> Not for the fault (that doth not come to mind),
> But for the virtue, whose o'erruling sway
> And providence have wrought thus quaintly. Here
> The skill is look'd into, that fashioneth
> With such effectual working, and the good
> Discern'd, accruing to this upper world
> From that below.[98]

Melville, by positioning himself in "Devotion" as inheritor of a troubadour, also places himself in the position of Dante (that is, Dante similarly inherits and quotes from that tradition in conveying his philosophy of love). Cary identifies Dante's debts to the troubadors throughout the notes—citing, for example, the Provençal poet who makes the same allusion to Ovid—and quotes Dante's praise of Provençal as having cultivated, "in a more perfect and sweet language, the vernacular poetry."[99] More generally highlighting the *Commedia*'s project of continuing to elevate living language (rather than Latin) to communicate love both earthly and divine, Cary's introduction to the "Life of Dante," annotated in Melville's hand, emphasizes Dante's "large and philosophical principles" for writing in the vernacular, which hitherto had been "scarce supposed to possess dignity enough for instruction."[100]

As Allison Cornish argues, writing on "The Allure of the Stars," "One of the most important and original things about Dante's literary project is his recuperation of sensual, earthly love—a love incited by pleasure, particularly of the eyes—as salvific and educational."[101] Cornish extends this recuperation to the linguistic and literary medium that Dante chooses to convey his vision: "In general, we might say that just as Dante uses Beatrice, a real woman of supreme physical attractiveness (*sommo piacere*), as the vehicle for his salvation, so he employs vernacular poetry (whose traditional subject is erotic) as the vehicle of his message."[102] Melville analogously draws upon the troubadour tradition to sum the "florid revel of joyance" in the Rose.

As we have attempted to show, the gathering thus concluded presents an alternative to the hollow sandhills of metaphysical despair often associated with late Melville; the collection offers "Rosary Beads" to be prayed faithfully, for such malaise is ever at hand:

Grain by grain the Desert drifts
Against the Garden-Land;
Hedge well thy Roses, heed the stealth
Of ever-creeping sand.[103]

In this endeavor to nourish and cherish the roses, *Weeds and Wildings* as a whole concludes with salutes to two custodial figures, the farmer and the friend. If "The Rose Farmer" shows us the prospect of "some roseate way" that may emerge "through the thistles," the final words of "L'Envoi" hail that dear companion who would share the poet's belated, newfound appreciation for faith among the weeds:

Time, Amigo, does but masque us–
Boys in gray wigs, young at core.
. . . .
Wiser in relish, if sedate
Come gray-beards to their roses late.[104]

At one point Melville had conceived of "L'Envoi" as the opening piece for *Weeds and Wildings Chiefly: With A Rose or Two*; as its farewell gesture, it brings the collection back to the volume's epigraph, borrowed from Hawthorne's *Dolliver Romance*: "Youth is the proper, permanent, and genuine condition of man."[105] While the Rose Poems, as occasional verse, certainly do form a Valentine for Lizzie—as Bryant's imaginatively reconstructed narrative vividly recounts—they may also be thought of as undertaking a spiritual quest under the sign of Hawthorne.

Dante concludes his pilgrimage guided by the friendly gray visage of Bernard, alight with what Clive James calls a "reassuring fire": "Joy benign Glow'd in his eye, and o'er his cheek diffus'd."[106] We may note that finally not Beatrice but Bernard, in his love for the rose and its queen, enkindles Dante's faith as never before: "Bernard gaz'd / With so exceeding fondness, as infus'd / Ardour into my breast, unfelt before."[107] For Melville, Hawthorne served as a privileged interlocutor and confessor on matters of faith, and perhaps as its inspiring model as well.[108]

In a fall afternoon of 1851, Hawthorne had retired to "Love Grove, to read the papers. While thus engaged, a cavalier on horseback came along the road, and saluted me in Spanish; to which I replied by touching my hat, and went on with the newspaper. But the cavalier renewing his salutation, I regarded him more attentively, and saw that it was Herman Melville!"[109] After supper, Hawthorne put Julian to bed, and he and Melville had one of their talks "about time and eternity, things of this world and the next."[110] "L'Envoi"'s hail to the Amigo evokes this friendly salutation and ongoing conversation: a conversation that we may suspect ultimately did much to make possible Melville's embrace, in the Rose Poems, of sacred love.

Notes

1. Herman Melville, "Hawthorne and His Mosses," *The Literary World* 7, no. 185 (August 17, 1850): 125 and 7, no. 186 (August 24, 1850): 147.

2. Even from the start of the descent, the language that Dante uses to describe the slope of the path has presented translators with challenges. *Inferno* Canto II twice describes the way ahead as "alto," which most modern English translators render as "deep" (e.g., Charles Singleton, Robert Pinsky). But the Reverend Henry Francis Cary, whose translation Melville owned and annotated, chose the arguably more literal "high" for the first appearance of this term (line 13 of the translation; line 12 of the original); Clive James has recently joined Cary in this dissenting choice; Dante, *The Divine Comedy*, trans. Clive James (New York: Liveright, 2013), 9. Though Cary appears to have been Melville's primary source for Dante, Melville's annotations to Cary show an awareness of and sensitivity to differences of translation, as when Melville copies into the margin of *Inferno* Canto III "John Carlyle's version of the line"; Dante, *The Vision; or Hell, Purgatory, and Paradise: Translated by the Rev. Henry Francis Cary, M.A.: A New Edition, Corrected: With the Life of Dante, Chronological View of His Age, Additional Notes, and Index* (London: Bohn, 1847; Sealts Number: 174), autographed, marked, and annotated by Herman Melville; collection of Mr. William Reese; introduction to Melville's marginalia in this copy by Steven Olsen-Smith, melvillesmarginalia.org. John Aitken Carlyle's prose translation of Dante, accompanied by the original Italian, sidesteps the high/deep dilemma in Canto II by rendering the word "alto" as "arduous": up or down, a way down that ultimately will prove to be a way up, the climb will be difficult; Dante, *Dante's Divine Comedy: The Inferno: A Literal Prose Translation with the Text of the Original Collated from the Best Editions, and Explanatory Notes*, trans. John Aitken Carlyle (Chapman and Hall, 1867), 14, 24.

3. Herman Melville, "*Weeds and Wildings Chiefly: With a Rose or Two," by Herman Melville: Genetic Text and Reading Text, Edited from the Manuscripts, with Introduction and Notes*, by Robert Charles Ryan (Ph.D. diss., Northwestern University, 1967), 38. Further quotations are cited parenthetically in the text. In both "Moss-Rose" and "Rose Vine," the Rose, object of the poet's passionate veneration, pairs with one of Melville's literary identities for Hawthorne, the "sweet Man of Mosses" that Melville heralds in "Hawthorne and His Mosses" and the character Vine in *Clarel*, there associated with the "Vine evangelic"; Herman Melville, *Clarel: A Poem and Pilgrimage in the Holy Land*, The Northwestern-Newberry Edition, vol. 12, ed. Harrison Hayford, Alma A. MacDougall, Hershel Parker, G. Thomas Tanselle, Historical and Critical Note by Walter E. Bezanson (Evanston and Chicago: Northwestern University Press and the Newberry Library, 1991), 223. Melville was generally given to playfully invoking the kinds of floral references that names in the Hawthorne family invited, as in his July 17, 1852, effusion that "the Hawthorne is a sweet flower;may it flourish in every hedge," in a letter that also concluded with "compliments" to Hawthorne's daughter, the "Rose-bud"; Herman Melville, *Correspondence*, The Northwestern-Newberry Edition, vol. 14, edited and annotated by Lynn Horth, revised and augmented from *The Letters of Herman Melville* (1960) edited by Merrell R. Davis and William H. Gilman (Evanston and Chicago: Northwestern University Press and the Newberry Library, 1993), 230–31.

4. Clark Davis, *After the Whale: Melville in the Wake of "Moby-Dick"* (Tuscaloosa: University of Alabama Press, 1995), 144. For a further discussion of Robert Milder's excellent suggestion—in *Exiled Royalties: Melville and the Life We Imagine* (Oxford: Oxford University Press, 2006), 133—to consider "spiritual drives" alongside other desires, without reducing the former to mere symptoms, see my *Writing beyond Prophecy: Emerson, Hawthorne, and Melville after the American Renaissance* (Baton Rouge: Louisiana State University Press, 2013), 221. This line of thinking also owes a debt to Samuel Otter, *Melville's Anatomies* (Berkeley: University of California Press, 1999), 255; and Jonathan Cook, "Melville and Religious Experience: A Response," *Leviathan* 12, no. 3 (October 2010): 135–36.

5. Herman Melville, *Tales, Poems, and Other Writings*, ed., with an introduction and notes, John Bryant (New York: Modern Library, 2001), 554.

6. In highlighting the Dantesque echoes of the rose, my study seeks to complement, with a slightly altered inflection on religious experience, William B. Dillingham's "Associating with the Rose," in *Melville and His Circle: The Last Years* (University of Georgia Press, 1996). Helpfully correcting the notion of a final descent into unmitigated skepticism and despair, Dillingham observes that "Melville's circle in these late years was diverse enough to accommodate both a 'sublime old infidel,' as he affectionately referred to the twelfth-century Persian poet Omar Khayyám, and a contemporary Anglican clergyman, Samuel Reynolds Hole [author of *A Book About Roses*] . . . He could embrace both . . . because he discerned that they were not opposites but complements . . . They manifested collectively a coherent vision that Melville perceived as a variation on his own religiouslike set of convictions about art and the imagination, the emblem of which became the rose" ("Associating with the Rose," 140). "Religiouslike" indeed—and if so very like, why not reciprocally consider what one might call his artistic and imaginative set of convictions about religion? In amplifying the associations of the rose, Dillingham does not cite Dante, but foregrounds Sadi's *The Gulistan, or Rose-Garden*, acquired 1868, in which Melville marked "a passage dealing with the power of the rose to raise those who keep company with it above the baseness of life" ("Associating with the Rose," 140). That upward vector is indeed compatible with Dante's vision, an elevation that Dillingham characterizes as the "intoxification of religious experience" ("Association with the Rose," 141). The word "intoxification" bears a measure of pejorative skepticism (if not precisely a reference to the influence of a poppy derivative, something potentially along such lines), but Dillingham does categorize the experience as "religious," without apparently feeling the need to qualify this state of transport as being merely "like" such a one.

7. Melville, *Tales, Poems, and Other Writings*, ed. Bryant, 572. The Rose thus also echoes the faithful Palm in *Clarel*, as read by Wyn Kelley in *Herman Melville: An Introduction* (Oxford: Blackwell, 2008), 159; discussed in *Writing beyond Prophecy*, 217.

8. Herman Melville, *Journals*, the Northwestern-Newberry Edition, vol. 15, Texts Revised with Historical Note and Annotations by Howard C. Horsford with Lynn Horth (Evanston and Chicago: Northwestern University Press and the Newberry Library, 1989), 401. The editors here discuss Melville's "parodic tone" in referring to the doctrine of resurrection (in connection with viewing a garden)

as "symptomatic of his having made up his mind . . . 'to be annihilated.' " As F. O. Matthiessen noted long ago, too-brief quotations of Hawthorne's report of Melville's remark on annihilation have been a prime source for "many distortions" to late biography (including both the idea that Melville was suicidal and that there had been a final "break" with Hawthorne): "For Melville to give up idealism for materialism, to accept the doctrine of the annihilation of the soul at death, would be a hard decision; and as Hawthorne suggests, he never really made it"; F. O. Matthiessen, "Reassertion of the Heart," in *American Renaissance* (Oxford: Oxford University Press, 1941), 489, 490–91. Matthiessen's corrective attempts in this influential study notwithstanding, assertions of bleak finality recur with regularity in connection with this passage and late Melville. Yet I am here arguing for something quite different than, for example, the perennial strand in Melville criticism that views *Billy Budd* as a "testament of acceptance." I would emphasize Merlin Bowen's observation that the content of that "testament" and its doctrine of acceptance excludes religious considerations, even if it traffics in reading religious symbols: "What somehow goes unnoticed is that the action of hanging Billy Budd is undertaken in clear opposition to Vere's own conscience and in obedience to 'the exacting behest' not of God but of social expediency"; Merlin Bowen, "Captain Vere and the Weakness of Expediency," in *Critical Essays on Melville's "Billy Budd, Sailor,"* ed. Robert Milder (Boston: G.K. Hall, 1989), 62. I am likewise indebted to conversation with Brad King on this topic. I would also make a distinction of genre: when Matthiessen writes that in "Billy Budd" Melville could "accept" the evil of the world "with a calm impossible to him in *Moby-Dick*," the contours of that acceptance still conform to the plot of a "tragic end" (*American Renaissance*, 512). Reading later Melville alongside Dante, and reading Dante all the way through, as Melville later did, one may discern the possibilities of hope for a divine comedy rather than acceptance of human tragedy. The recuperative strain of commentary for which I am arguing more closely resembles that advanced by Stan Goldman in *Melville's Protest Theism: The Hidden and Silent God in "Clarel"* (DeKalb: Northern Illinois University Press, 1993), a book which greatly influenced my discussion of *Clarel* in *Writing beyond Prophecy*. For the present study, I have found further encouragement in Walter Donald Kring's well-documented study of *Herman Melville's Religious Journey* (Raleigh, N.C.: Pentland, 1997). Kring's account offers a Melville who worked "his way through doubt and despair to a reasonable and satisfactory religious belief," and includes such fascinating detail as that All Souls, where Elizabeth and Herman attended Unitarian services, continued to celebrate communion (v, 134–35). I will suggest that the "Rose Poems" reflect a Melville who pursued a Dantesque trajectory through despair and continued to seek Hawthornean communion.

9. Melville, *Journals*, 628.

10. For the usefulness of considering the proximity of faith and doubt while reading Melville, I am indebted generally to Robert Milder's *Exiled Royalties*, mentioned above, and his discussion of Paul Tillich's insight that "the situation of doubt, even of doubt about God, need not separate us from God. There is faith in every serious doubt, namely, the faith in the truth as such"; Milder accordingly proposes that the " 'faith' that *Clarel* testifies to is not in God or immortality (though the poem retains a hope of both) but in the sanctifying power of living in a state of intellectual and spiritual aspiration" (*Exiled Royalties*, 194). More

specifically for the present text, Milder proposes a related balance in "Old Man Melville: The Rose and the Cross," in *New Essays on "Billy Budd,"* ed. Donald Yannella (Cambridge: Cambridge University Press, 2002). But, by emphasizing Melville's affinities with Dante, I consider the "and" (of the rose and the cross) to be more fully synthesizing, less a weighing of alternatives on one hand "and" the other. Reading "The Rose Window," Milder asks, has the speaker "arrived at a visionary faith? We can't be sure . . . All that is certain is the pageant of color the speaker sees upon awakening—dust motes transfigured by the roseate light streaming through 'the great Rose-Window high.' One may read the poem, with John Bryant, as illustrating 'the power of faith, beauty, art, and the rose to transfigure matter into spirit,' or one may read it the opposite way as implying that immortality is conjectural at most but the glories of sense experience palpably real" (*Exiled Royalties*, 90). While acknowledging, with Milder, that we can't be sure, I would shade toward Bryant's reading, as, for instance, those very dust motes of the waking moment return us to the substance of Dante's vision of Christ as described in Paradise, with the earthliest of metaphors conveying the divine: "He sees Christ's outline come alive and live / . . . Lights moved that sparkled as they met and passed / Brightly, as, here, we see the particles / Of matter in the sunbeam, slow and fast, / Straight and askew. / Inside the shaft that sometimes streaks the dark" (*Paradiso* 14; James, trans., *Divine Comedy*, 423). Milder, like Dillingham placing emphasis on Omar Khayyám but not mentioning Dante, sees a clear opposition between a "secular hedonism" and "Christian miracle" (*Exiled Royalties*, 91–92). Yet for Dante, and the Melville who follows his poetry attentively to Paradise, the terms of aesthetic pleasure and faith form a sacred confluence drawn together by love.

11. Cary, ed., *The Vision*, 376.

12. Hawthorne's further commentary on Melville's restlessness follows the remark: "he informed me that he had 'pretty much made up his mind to be annihilated'; but still he does not seem to rest in that anticipation; and, I think, will never rest until he gets hold of a definite belief" (Melville, *Journals*, 628). For a consideration of this trope in another text close to Melville's heart, *Hamlet*, see Robert Watson, *The Rest Is Silence: Death as Annihilation in the English Renaissance* (Berkeley: University of California Press, 1994). For an important and thoroughgoing recent discussion of how a resistance to certainty, an interweaving of skepticism and faith considered within a context of religious pluralism, pervades Melville's oeuvre (including the later poetry), see Brian Yothers, *Sacred Uncertainty: Religious Difference and the Shape of Melville's Career* (Evanston, Ill.: Northwestern University Press, 2015).

13. William B. Dillingham, "Disenchantment," in *Melville and His Circle: The Last Years*, 86.

14. "James Thomson's *The City of Dreadful Night and Other Poems*," ed. Matthew Giordano, *Melville's Marginalia Online*, ed. Steven Olsen-Smith, http://melvillesmarginalia.org/UserViewFramesetIntro.php?id=43.

15. Dennis Berthold, *American Risorgimento: Herman Melville and the Cultural Politics of Italy* (Columbus: Ohio State University Press, 2009), 92.

16. Ibid., 70.

17. Ibid., 92.

18. Ibid., 70.

19. Michael Colacurcio, "Charity and Its Discontents: Pity and Politics in Melville's Fiction," in *There Before Us: Religion, Literature, and Culture from Emerson to Wendell Berry*, ed. Roger Lundin (Grand Rapids, Mich.: Eerdmans, 2007), 79.

20. As an anonymous (and, in the true sense, charitable) reader's report discerns, the present essay hopes to offer an "explanation of how the experience of human love might explain Melville's continued connection to Christian ideals" (Editorial correspondence, Nov. 6, 2014).

21. Melville, *Journals*, 628.

22. Melville, *Journals*, 632.

23. Ryan, *Weeds*, 40, ll. 15–27. In the context of such transfiguration, the editors of the present volume helpfully remark that the trajectory from *Clarel* to the Rose Poems includes continuity as well as reversal, a continuity discernable in *Clarel*'s own reversals: "there are numerous moments of beauty in *Clarel*, including ones where Melville revises his own initially negative view of a particular place in favor of a more sympathetic one (see for example the Church of the Holy Sepulchre)" (editorial correspondence, October 7, 2013). I would add that Clarel's capacity to discern spiritual beauty in such settings often corresponds with the presence and perspective of Vine, as when, viewing the Sepulcher of Kings, "a waste where beauty clings / Vining a grot," Clarel is struck by a man of "meditative mein": "A low wind waves his Lydian hair: /A funeral man, yet richly fair— / . . . Beauty yet harmonized in grace"; "And they exchanged quick sympathies / Though but in glance, moved by that act / Of one whose faith transfigured fact" (*Clarel*, 87–88, 90).

24. Melville, *Journals*, 632.

25. Ibid., 632–33.

26. Nathaniel Hawthorne, *The American Notebooks*, The Centenary Edition of the Works of Nathaniel Hawthorne, vol. 8, ed. Claude M. Simpson, et al. (Columbus: Ohio State University Press, 1973), 448.

27. Melville, *Correspondence*, 176.

28. Ibid., 191–92.

29. Ibid., 192.

30. Ibid., 192; *Clarel*, 223.

31. Melville, *Correspondence*, 212.

32. Herman Melville, *Moby-Dick: Or, The Whale*, The Northwestern-Newberry Edition of The Writings of Herman Melville, vol. 6, ed. Harrison Hayford, G. Thomas Tanselle, and Hershel Parker (Evanston and Chicago: Northwestern University Press and the Newberry Library, 1988), ix–xx.

33. Melville, *Journals*, 633.

34. Ibid., 114, 115.

35. Ryan, *Weeds*, 44.

36. Ibid., 44, ll.1–6 (complete first stanza of "The Rose Farmer").

37. Melville, *Clarel*, 101.

38. Ibid., 101.

39. Melville, *Journals*, 51.

40. Ibid., 624.

41. Ibid., 627.

42. Melville, *Clarel*, 101; Melville, *Journals*, 628.

43. John Bryant, "Ordering the Rose: Melville's Poetic Revisions," *Melville Society Extracts* 117 (July 1999): 15–18, http://people.hofstra.edu/John_L_Bryant/Melville_Extracts/Volume%20117/extracts117_jul99_pg18.html.

44. Bryant, "Ordering the Rose," 118.

45. The "hot-cold" poem finds its apotheosis in Dante's successor, Petrarch, though, as Lea Newman notes, "To date no evidence has been found to suggest that Melville read Petrarch; his works are not listed in Sealts' *Melville's Reading*. Cary's essay and chronology provide the link between Petrarch and Dante; the introductory material also emphasizes Dante as one of the Priors of Florence"—hence the allusion to "Petrarch and his Priors" in *Mardi*; Newman, "Melville's Copy of Dante: Evidence of New Connections between the *Commedia* and *Mardi*," *Studies in the American Renaissance 1993*, ed. Joel Myerson (Charlottesville University Press of Virginia, 1993), 311. Thus, Melville's hot-cold poetry, as Bryant characterizes it, would seem more likely to have developed from Dante—in parallel to Petrarch, as it were—and particularly from the imagery in *Paradiso* of snow and flame as discussed in the present essay. For the broader legacy, see Leonard Forster, *The Icy Fire: Five Studies in European Petrarchism* (Cambridge University Press, 1969).

46. Bryant's notes to Melville, *Tales, Poems, and Other Writings*, 554.

47. John Bryant, "Melville's Rose Poems: As They Fell," *Arizona Quarterly* 52, no. 4 (Winter 1996): 65.

48. Melville, *Clarel*, 499.

49. James Duban, "From Bethlehem to Tahiti: Transcultural 'Hope' in *Clarel*," *Philological Quarterly*, 70, no. 4 (Fall 1991): 479, 476 (quoting an 1860 New York newspaper).

50. Ibid., 477, 479.

51. William Potter, *Melville's "Clarel" and the Intersympathy of Creeds* (Kent, Ohio: Kent State University Press, 2004), 175–76, citing also Laurie Robertson-Lorant.

52. Rachel Jacoff and Jeffrey T. Schnapp, eds., *The Poetry of Allusion: Virgil and Ovid in Dante's "Commedia"* (Stanford, Calif.: Stanford University Press, 1991), 76; see also the final page of "An Introduction to the *Paradiso*" in *Dante: the Poetics of Conversion*, ed. Rachel Jacoff (Cambridge, Mass.: Harvard University Press, 1986), 220: "The restless drive of Dante's verse reaches its climax and its repose with the word 'Love' in the last verse, just as the desire that is in human terms insatiable finds its satisfaction in the love of God. What follows after the word represents a fall to earth . . . Dante's personal fulfillment of his own most intimate desires is perfectly harmonized with the love that is the motive force of the entire universe, of the sun and the other stars. Spatially, to speak of the sun and stars is to return to our perspective, looking up at the heavenly bodies which had long been surpassed by the pilgrim's journey to the Empyrean. The word 'Love' is therefore the link that binds the heaven to earth and the poet to his audience, containing within it the substance of the poem."

53. Lea Bertani Vozar Newman, "Marginalia as Revelation: Melville's 'Lost' Copy of Dante and a Private Purgatorial Note," *Melville Society Extracts* 92 (1993): 4.

54. Duban, "From Bethlehem to Tahiti," 479.

55. Cary, ed., *The Vision*, 344. Cary's notes for *Paradiso* 33 also point to the attendant "Nereïdes admirantes" of Catullus's poem on Neptune (526).

56. *Paradiso 2: Commentary*, vol. 6 in Dante Alighieri, *The Divine Comedy*, trans., with a commentary, Charles S. Singleton (Princeton, N.J.: Princeton University Press, 1975) 39.

57. Melville, *Clarel*, 499.

58. Herman Melville, *Pierre, or, The Ambiguities*, The Northwestern-Newberry Edition, vol. 7, ed. Harrison Hayford, Hershel Parker, and G. Thomas Tanselle, Historical Note by Leon Howard and Hershel Parker (Evanston and Chicago: Northwestern University Press and the Newberry Library, 1971), 303.

59. Ibid., 303.

60. Ibid., 216.

61. Ibid., 16.

62. Ibid., 34.

63. Cary, ed., *The Vision*, 526. See also the anticipation of this ascent in *Paradiso* 23.73, 80, which moves from "sea" to "fair Garden" and, ultimately, "Sacred Rose" (James, trans., *Divine Comedy*, 470; also *Paradiso* 28 concludes by with the figure of arriving upon shore from a sea of doubt, James, 498).

64. Jonathan A. Cook, *Inscrutable Malice: Theodicy, Eschatology, and the Biblical Sources of "Moby-Dick"* (DeKalb: Northern Illinois University Press, 2012), 144–45. Here Cook contrasts the affectionate cetacean idyll with Ahab's hate (Cook, 145; citing the work of Marius Bewley, 144); one might note that Pierre's version of Ahabian absolutism also sinks his soul.

65. As Ryan and Bryant report, the Rose Poems were initially conceived as part of a larger collection, perhaps to have been entitled "Meadows and Seas" (Bryant notes to *Tales*, 605). We might thus think of the Roses as emerging not just from the Weeds, but also, as Dante would have it, from the whelming seas.

66. Ryan, *Weeds*, 37, ll. 5–10.

67. For other passages in Dante that anticipate this final image, see the movement from "winter" to "rose" (James, trans., *Divine Comedy*, 418), the recurrence, without apology to Elvis, of the phrase "burning love" (James, 417, 482), and the juxtaposition of blazing flames, fires and flowers (James 463, 468, 471).

68. Ryan, *Weeds*, 37.

69. Cary, ed., *The Vision*, 513; see also the notes to Canto 30 line 129 of Robert and Jean Hollander's *Paradiso* (New York: Anchor Books, 2007), 839.

70. Ryan, *Weeds*, 41.

71. Bryant also notes the alternating pattern of the sequence; and while both the subject matter and tone do oscillate as he observes, I do not find the absolute difference of purpose which he attributes to "Under the Ground." Bryant insists that Melville, in the second Rose Poem, condemns what he depicts, whereas I find that Melville's meditations on rose preservation offer a quiet exposition on the pragmatism of both the florist and the faithful.

72. For example, in Ryan's commentary and Bryant's "As They Fell."

73. Though these titles declare Milton's Italianism most explicitly, much of his other poetry also notably hails Dante in particular. Cary highlights throughout his translation of the *Commedia* the many connections between Milton and Dante; his notes to *Paradiso* 30 and 31 alone contain five cross-references to *Paradise Lost*. Melville would thus have encountered, through Cary (as well as by his own lights), a very Miltonic Dante in this region of his heaviest borrowing for the Rose Poems.

74. G. Giovanni, "Melville's *Pierre* and Dante's *Inferno*," *PMLA* 64, no. 1 (March 1949): 71. Providing good warrant for Melville's optimistic expectation regarding his contemporary readers' familiarity with Dante, Giovanni cites Emerson's observation that, specifically since the appearance of the complete Cary translation, "all studious youths and maidens have been reading" Dante. Kathleen Verduin further historicizes Emerson's statement in her brilliant study of "Dante in America: The First Hundred Years," in *Reading Books: Essays on the Material Text and Literature in America*, ed. Michele Moylan (Amherst: University of Massachusetts Press, 1996), 16–51; the Emerson quotation appears on 21.

75. Jacoff and Schnapp, *The Poetry of Allusion*.

76. Newman notes that one salutary "exception to the critical focus on 'The Inferno' is Charlene Avallone's analysis of the imagery from 'Purgatorio' and 'Paradiso' to be found in 'The Piazza'" (Avallone, "Melville's 'Piazza,'" *ESQ: A Journal of the American Renaissance* 22 [Fall 1976]: 221–33, esp. 222–23) (Newman, "Melville's Copy of Dante," 333n2). Christopher Sten, in arguing that *Moby-Dick* embraces the epic of "spiritual quest, of the search for a transcendent order or significance in human life, as in the Divine Comedy," also seems prepared to consider the fuller sweep of the poet's pilgrimage; Sten, *Sounding the Whale: "Moby-Dick" as Epic Novel* (Kent, Ohio: Kent State University Press, 1996), 2.

77. Ryan, *Weeds*, 38, ll.1–10.

78. Jacoff and Schnapp, *Poetry of Allusion*, 244.

79. Cary, ed., *The Vision*, 515.

80. Jacoff and Schnapp, *Poetry of Allusion*, 244.

81. Jacoff and Schnapp, *Poetry of Allusion*, 245. The words "Great Bear" appear as a pencil annotation to *Paradiso* 31 in Melville's copy of Dante, though this inscription has been identified by the editors of *Melville's Marginalia Online* as not in Melville's hand (and, the editors suggest, may have been made by a later reader). In any case, the annotation bears no additional information than that conveyed by Cary's own footnote to the passage. Lea Newman, in connection with this marked passage of the *Paradiso*, and quoting Cary's note, speaks of "The attention Melville paid to . . . astrological and astronomical details" (Newman, "Melville's Copy of Dante," 335. The "Documentary Note" of caution regarding *Melville's Marginalia* may be found at http://melvillesmarginalia.org/UserViewFramesetNote.php?id=11).

82. Cary, ed., *The Vision*, 515.

83. Melville owned a translation of Ovid—by Dryden, Pope, Congreve, Addison, and Others, in the Harper's Classical Library, Sealts #147.

84. Jacoff and Schnapp, *Poetry of Allusion*, 245–6.

85. Ibid., 246.

86. Bryant comments on Lizzie's amended (and perhaps censorious) "wooing in the snow" as less poetic and less explicit than Melville's original "sparking" ("As They Fell," 84). The *Oxford English Dictionary* does list an 1859 U.S. usage of "sparking" as "courting, paying attentions"; though not particularly vulgar in the context of McClintock's *Beadle's Courtship* as cited by the *OED*, "sparking" does register as more informal than "wooing" and hence more "intimate" as Bryant suggests ("As They Fell," 84). Additionally we may miss in "Amoroso" the way "sparking" had played against "Arctic" (and worked in concert with "Arcturus")—and also the way that this image of scintillation had given a

Dantesque quality to this snow scene. For the recurrent sparking against snow-white backgrounds that accompanies *Paradiso*'s loving floral displays, see, for example, James, trans., *Divine Comedy*, 477–78: love, desire, spark; 507: flower beds, scintillating; 508: spark.

87. Cary, ed., *The Vision*, 515n4.

88. Hollander, *Paradiso*, 858.

89. Hollander, *Paradiso*, 858.

90. Ryan, *Weeds*, 40, l.6.

91. Ibid., 40, ll. 12–19.

92. James, trans., *Divine Comedy*, 423.

93. Ryan, *Weeds*, 41, l.1; Cary, *Paradiso*, 33.

94. Ryan, *Weeds*, 41.

95. Ibid., 41–42.

96. Kelley, *Introduction*, 157.

97. James, trans., *Divine Comedy*, 392.

98. The troubadour goes on to speak in praise, for instance, of the faithful harlot, whose effectual good achieved is remembered, while any fault is forgotten: "Know then, the soul of Rahab is in that gladsome harbour, to our tribe United, and the foremost rank assign'd" (Cary, *Paradiso*, 9).

99. See Cary's notes to *Inferno* 31.1 and *Purgatorio* 26.132; Cary also points to the troubadors in, for example, notes to *Purgatorio* 7.110, *Purgatorio* 26.113, and *Paradiso* 6.136 (Cary, ed., *The Vision*, 387). On Dante's inclusion of the troubadors as transcultural, a celebration of Persian love poetry, see W. S. Merwin's *Purgatorio* (New York: Alfred A. Knopf, 2000), xv.

100. Cary, ed., *The Vision*, xxviii, xxxi.

101. Allison Cornish, *Reading Dante's Stars* (New Haven, Conn.: Yale University Press, 2000), 12.

102. Ibid., 12.

103. Ryan, *Weeds*, 41.

104. Ibid., 49.

105. Ryan, *Weeds*, 1. Milder helpfully reads into the record Eleanor Metcalf's comment on the note that Melville kept by his desk, "Keep true to the dreams of thy youth": "'These dreams,' granddaughter Eleanor Metcalf commented, 'grew out of the deepest needs of the whole man' and 'reflected a desire to nourish the roots of life. . . . In other words, they were religious in nature'"; Milder, "Old Man Melville," 95. Metcalf's sense of this private note may supply a gloss on the epigraph for *Weeds and Wildings* that Melville borrowed from Hawthorne, a shared dream of youth of which these poems partake.

106. James, trans., *Divine Comedy*, 513; Cary, *Paradiso*, 31.

107. Cary, *Paradiso*, 31.

108. For instance, the famous passage on annihilation itself points strongly to an ongoing feature of the Melville-Hawthorne relationship, when Hawthorne reports "Melville, *as he always does*, began to reason of Providence and futurity, and of everything that lies beyond human ken"; that is, Melville consistently confided in Hawthorne regarding his struggles of faith (Melville, *Journals*, 628; emphasis added). More speculatively, one may note, from early on, associations in Melville's writing between Hawthorne and religious curiosity. In chapter 43 of *Redburn* (1849), the young protagonist "came to a hawthorn lane, leading

down very prettily to a nice little church; a mossy little church; a beautiful little church . . . The porch was viny as an arbor." (Edwin Haviland Miller notes that Melville alluded to Hawthorne's "A Rill from the Town Pump" in *White-Jacket*, and thus encountered Hawthorne's writing earlier than may be supposed from "Hawthorne and His Mosses"; Miller, *Melville* [New York: George Braziller, 1975], 174; David B. Kesterson has provided a helpful survey of this nexus, www.hawthorneinsalem.org/ScholarsForum/HawthorneandMelville.html.) Whether or not this passage has Hawthorne in mind, its imagery aligns with Melville's association of his friend—whether thorny, mossy, or viny—with his uncertainties at the threshold of worship. To point to another association: in the 1852 letter in which Melville celebrates his friend's floral identity—"the Hawthorne is a sweet flower"—he also finds noteworthy that he encountered Hawthorne's latest volume "in the hands of a clergyman" (Melville, *Letters*, 230).

109. Hawthorne, *American Notebooks*, 447–48. Bezanson also cites this passage from Hawthorne's *American Notebooks*, in which Melville "saluted me in Spanish," to annotate the use of an "Amigo" greeting in *Clarel* (*Clarel*, 588).

110. Hawthorne, *American Notebooks*, 448.

Religious Communities

Melville and the Unitarian Conscience

Dawn Coleman

In chapter 29 of *Moby-Dick*, Stubb ruminates on Ahab's strange behavior after the captain has ordered him below with the contemptuous exclamation "Down, dog, and kennel!" Ahab sleeps only three hours a night and his sheets are always "rumpled and tumbled," "the coverlid almost tied in knots," and the pillow hot. Stubb concludes, "I guess he's got what some folks ashore call a conscience; it's a kind of Tic-Dolly-row they say—worse nor a toothache."[1] Superficially the joke is on Stubb, so carefree and amoral he does not know what a "conscience" is and can comprehend it only as a "Tic-Dolly-row," or tic douloureux, a facial neuralgia that jolts sufferers with unpredictable, crippling pain. Yet just as Pip after his abandonment speaks in illuminated ramblings that reveal the artificiality of social hierarchies and the absurdity of human endeavor, so the offhand remarks of Stubb, a hale, down-to-earth everyman innocent of book knowledge, defamiliarize conventional thinking. More than a joke, Stubb's conjecture renders conscience strange, dissociating it from moral and religious discourses and positing it as a wholly physiological ailment.

From *Moby-Dick* forward, Melville approached conscience as a puzzle, a religious concept that, like so many others, turned kaleidoscopic under his skeptical eye. In what follows I explore his interest in conscience first by considering his lifelong relationship with Unitarianism, which celebrated conscience as the moral core of human nature and a primary means of knowing God. Unitarianism played a larger role in his thought than we have tended to recognize, both as a lived experience interwoven with family and marital identity and—as the recent discovery of his hand in the six-volume *Works* (1848) of Unitarian minister William Ellery Channing (1780–1842) suggests—as a vital intellectual tradition that gave him much to ponder.[2] From there, I present the larger context of nineteenth-century Unitarian views on conscience, then demonstrate how Melville's fiction of the 1850s, in particular *Pierre*, reflects Unitarian moral thinking on conscience, primarily in a shared critique of intuitionism. My last stop is *Billy Budd*, in which Melville returns to the question of conscience with renewed, secularizing vigor. This story rejects the notion that conscience is an innate, God-given monitor, or even an essential element of human nature, while holding fast to it as a painful physical reality (Stubb's Tic-Dolly-row redux) and as an indispensable political principle.

Melville's Lived Unitarianism

Melville's connections with Unitarianism are worth reviewing because their aggregate force makes evident how thoroughly his life narrative was intertwined with this tradition. Melville first learned of Unitarianism through his father, Allan Melvill, who came from a religiously liberal Boston family that attended Brattle Street Church during the ministries of the renowned Joseph Buckminster and Edward Everett.[3] Raised in the Dutch Reformed Church of Maria Gansevoort, Melville at age twenty-eight reconnected with liberal religion through his marriage to Elizabeth Knapp Shaw, a ceremony performed by the Unitarian Alexander Young, minister of New South Church, where the Shaw family attended.[4] After the Melvilles settled in New York City, they attended the First Congregational Church of New York City, known from 1845 to 1855 as the Church of the Divine Unity and afterward as All Souls.[5] During this time the renowned minister Henry Whitney Bellows (1814–1882; fig. 1) led the church. Church records indicate that in February 1850, Melville paid $14.15 in rent on pew 117, one of the church's more affordable pews; the sum covered the Melvilles' rent for the latter half of 1849.[6] Former All Souls minister Walter Kring points out that although church attendance would have been expected of a "proper New York family," neither that fact alone nor Elizabeth's family affiliation with Unitarianism entirely explains their congregational choice, as Melville's mother and sisters attended Dutch Reformed churches and his brother Allan and his wife Sophia attended an Episcopalian one. Kring reasonably posits that Melville "actually *preferred* Reverend Bellows' sermons to any available alternatives."[7] The arrival of the Melvilles' first child may have prompted their pew rental; Malcolm was born in February 1849 and received baptism from Bellows that September.

During these early years of marriage, and arguably in later decades as well, Melville engaged with Unitarianism not only experientially, but also intellectually. Sometime in 1849 or 1850, Melville picked up the third volume of Elizabeth's copy of William Ellery Channing's *Works* and penciled a marginal response, a four-line inscription (erased at some later point) that challenged Channing's claims for Jesus's uniqueness in "The Evidences of Revealed Religion" by raising the competing example of "Mahomet."[8] Extrapolating from his reliance on Pierre Bayle for an anomalous, outdated reading of Muhammad, we can date his reading of this essay to a period between April 1849 and June or July 1850. We thus know that Melville encountered Channing's thought during the crucial, formative years leading up to *Moby-Dick*, and though this inscription in the third volume is the only marking definitively in his hand, the set abounds in marginalia that may belong to him. In addition to a half-dozen inscriptions by Elizabeth, the set contains nearly 450 separate markings, mainly scoring, bars, and parentheses, which may be in either Elizabeth's hand or Herman's. Forty-seven of the set's fifty-nine essays are marked in some way. Although decisive attribution is impossible, the set is a

Fig. 1. Henry Whitney Bellows, September 1861.
Courtesy Andover-Harvard Theological Library.

rich, provocative potential source for Melville, especially since many of the flagged passages resonate with his characteristic preoccupations: the nature of genius, the peculiar gifts of Milton, the role of a national literature, slavery, and more. It is difficult to believe that he had these essays on his shelf and did not read them.

That Melville read Channing promises to enrich dramatically our understanding of his relationship to Unitarianism. Channing (1780–1842; fig. 2) holds title as "the single most important figure in the history of American Unitarianism," the minister who most outspokenly defended the liberal movement in New England Congregationalism in the 1810s and 1820s and who served as the liberal standard-bearer until his death in 1842.[9] Yet his active mind and eye for moral subtlety extended his scope and cultural significance beyond Unitarian circles. Andrew Delbanco traces the tensions that gave his work its originality: between temperamental conservatism and religious radicalism, between belief in the common person's divinity and Federalist aversion to the people en masse, between dissatisfaction with institutions and fear of antinomianism. Independent-minded and politically bold, Channing belies the notion that Unitarianism was a byword for head-in-the-sand romantic optimism. Perhaps more than any other American theologian of his day, he

Fig. 2. William Ellery Channing, from the 1815 portrait by Gilbert Stuart. Courtesy Andover-Harvard Theological Library

perceived the murkiness of moral questions: indeed, his "very essence" was "his sensitivity to half-truths and dualities."[10] His individualistic resistance to party spirit made him a model of solitary and, at times, iconoclastic moral and intellectual endeavor—and a natural kindred spirit for Melville.

The essays, sermons, lectures, and letters collected in Channing's *Works* reflect these contemplative, humanistic tendencies. The set contains, of course, Channing's career-defining repudiations of orthodox theology: "Unitarian Christianity" (1819), the pivotal ordination sermon for Jared Sparks in Baltimore that infuriated the orthodox with its credo that one must use reason in interpreting the Bible; the fire-throwing "Moral Argument against Calvinism" (1820), which impugned orthodox Congregationalism for trafficking in terror and promoting a distorted, unjust view of God; and "Likeness to God" (1828), his fullest statement on human dignity.[11] The set also includes learned essays on literature and history, such as those on Milton (1826), Napoleon Bonaparte (1827), and the theologian and homiletician François Fenelon (1829); "Remarks on National Literature" (1830), which Emerson built on for "The American Scholar" (1837); and the much-circulated "Self-Culture" (1838), a call for perpetual spiritual growth originally delivered as a lecture to workingmen.[12] Of especial interest are the seven essays on slavery that, taken together, reveal the progressive radicalism of Channing's antislavery advocacy; these include an open letter to Henry Clay opposing the annexation of Texas (1837) and "The Duty of the Free States, or Remarks on the Creole" (1842), a full-throated argument for human rights that Delbanco, after detailing Channing's evolving antislavery thought in the early 1840s, calls the "culminating document of these years, perhaps of Channing's life" (*William Ellery Channing*, 142). Taken as a whole, at nearly 2,500 pages and covering an impressive range of vital social and political topics, the *Works* showcases Channing as one of antebellum America's major thinkers. With this set in hand, we will want to consider how Melville's democratic humanism, ethical sensibilities, and literary interests were fed by, and grew outward from, an informed dialogue with Unitarian writing and belief.

Although the role that Channing's *Works* may have played in Melville's writing after 1848 has yet to be fully explored, we know that Melville's personal connections with Unitarianism persisted from the late 1840s through the end of his life. In Pittsfield, where the Melvilles moved in 1850, the Unitarian minister Orville Dewey baptized the three children born after Malcolm (Stanwix, Elizabeth, and Frances), an event Melville recorded in his Bible's "Family Record" in September 1863.[13] Besides being a family friend of Lemuel Shaw who happened to live in Sheffield, just thirty miles away, Dewey was the retired pastor of the Church of the Messiah, or the Second Congregational Church of New York City, the city's other Unitarian congregation.

When the Melvilles returned to the city in late 1863, Elizabeth and occasionally Herman began attending All Souls again. Elizabeth rented a pew from 1865 to 1873, when she wrote the church treasurer citing financial constraints and asking to be released from paying pew rent.[14] She also received baptism from Bellows in March 1872.[15] The regularity of Melville's own attendance remains difficult to determine: William Braswell reported that Melville's granddaughter, Eleanor Metcalf, wrote to him that her grandfather "would on rare occasions go to All Souls' Church in Fourth Avenue, but for many years during the latter part of his life he did not do even this."[16] Since no record of church members during Bellows's long pastorate (1839 to 1882) survives, we cannot know whether he or Elizabeth were members of All Souls either before or after their time in Pittsfield. Record-keeping improved when Bellows's successor, Theodore Chickering Williams (1855–1915; fig. 3), gained the pulpit in 1883. And so it could be discovered, though not until 1975, that Melville was listed as a member of All Souls in 1884.[17] He also rented pew 138, valued at $800, under his own name in 1887, and in March 1890, Elizabeth rented a pew valued at $250, which she held until her death in 1906.[18] In September 1891, Williams performed Melville's funeral service at the Melvilles' home.[19]

Critics have often downplayed Melville's relationship to Unitarianism as a vestige of his paternal inheritance and social formality of his adult life, while seldom considering how it might have influenced his fiction and poetry.

Fig. 3. Theodore Chickering Williams, ca. 1885.
Courtesy Andover-Harvard Theological Library.

Although recent scholarship has begun to explore the resonance between Melville's thought and Unitarianism, the field has a long history of reading Melville's attitude toward the denomination as antagonistic.[20] Most strikingly, biographer Hershel Parker writes that Melville "always found Unitarianism repugnant" and has described him as "persistently aggrieved at the Boston and New York Unitarians," sweeping statements that read Melville as oddly close-minded and that conflate a wide range of theological and social positions.[21] Parker's Melville is on a hair-trigger around Unitarians: uniformly contemptuous of Dewey because of Dewey's seeming indifference to the poor and failure to avow abolitionism, disgusted by British Utilitarianism and American Unitarianism for their supposedly similar "countinghouse mentality toward all things moral," and angry at Emerson for "employing standard Unitarian thought," which leaves him "rag[ing] in his marginalia [of Emerson's essays] as he could not safely rage against anything Lizzie reported from Henry W. Bellows's latest sermon."[22] For Parker, the bottom line is clear: Melville loathed Unitarians as pretentious, selfish hypocrites, and any involvement with them was no more than a concession to Elizabeth.

That such a careful scholar as Parker can perceive only Melville's differences from Unitarianism is perplexing, though perhaps no more so than the long history of silence surrounding the influence of this religious tradition on his work. The neglect may be partly due to the fact that the world first learned of Melville's pew rental and membership at All Souls in an essay by Walter Kring and Jonathan Carey that also revealed the scandalous information, gleaned from a letter from Elizabeth's half-brother Samuel Shaw to Bellows, that Elizabeth considered Melville insane and was contemplating a separation from him.[23] Kring and Carey's essay, which included Shaw's letter to Bellows along with Elizabeth's letter to Bellows thanking him for his "active interest" in her situation and expressing gratitude for counsel that would allow her to endure "whatever further trial may be before" her, forced the question of whether Melville physically abused his wife.[24] This disquieting possibility eclipsed more theoretical considerations of Unitarianism's influence on Melville. For instance, none of the scholarly commentaries in *The Endless, Winding Way in Melville*, Donald Yannella and Hershel Parker's volume reprinting Kring and Carey's essay, weighs interpretive questions related to Melville's Unitarian affiliation. But to be fair, the significance of even Melville's outrageous domestic behavior would not receive the consideration it deserved until more than a decade later in Elizabeth Renker's groundbreaking 1994 *American Literature* essay.[25]

The habitual lack of interest in Melville's Unitarian connections may also be due to dusty prejudices about Unitarians and a tendency to conflate all nineteenth-century Unitarians with those who denounced transcendentalism in the 1830s. More than forty years ago, historian Conrad Wright leveled a critique that still holds, charging that literary scholars often misconstrue nineteenth-century Unitarians by accepting at face value the testimony of the transcendentalists who parted ways from them: "Emerson's references to 'the pale negations of Boston Unitarianism' and 'the corpse-cold Unitarianism of Brattle Street' have seemed to lovers of picturesque phraseology to be an adequate characterization of the faith of Channing's generation, and to make firsthand investigation of the record of that generation unnecessary."[26] Nineteenth-century Unitarianism continues to be treated as a dull business, as a temporary refuge of respectability for bloodless Boston Whigs who attended churches built on the ethical scraps of a deracinated Christianity, conformist WASPs who shunned both the more vibrant, emotionally rich communities of traditional piety and the devil-may-care iconoclasm of transcendentalism. Often Unitarianism is remembered alongside the orthodox charge that it was a "halfway house to infidelity" or Erasmus Darwin's quip that it was "a featherbed to catch a falling Christian," further examples of vivid metaphors serving as intellectual shorthand.[27]

Yet Melville would have had good reason to regard Unitarianism as worthy of thoughtful engagement. Besides the fact that this faith represented a connection to his father, as well as to Elizabeth, their children, and the Shaws, it was also far less dogmatic and more accepting of doubt than his mother's Calvinism, and was less the disputative anti-Trinitarianism of caricature than an Enlightenment-born movement to resist orthodoxy's pessimistic view of human nature by affirming human dignity and a loving God.[28] Nor were all mid-nineteenth-century Unitarians "corpse-cold." Although they upheld the rational religion inherited from New England Congregationalist ministers such as Charles Chauncy and Jonathan Mayhew, who condemned the "enthusiasm" and conversionism of the Great Awakening, many were notably pietistic, or intent on orienting the heart toward charity and reverence.[29] Further, as Lawrence Buell explains, Unitarians, with their education and social prestige, fueled a great deal of early to mid-nineteenth-century American literary culture, laying the groundwork for receptivity to European romanticism and an interest in poetry and imaginative literature. Buell notes that one-half of all "major" New England writers were Unitarians and that Unitarians sponsored and dominated the publisher Ticknor and Fields, as well as landmark publications such as the *North American Review* and the *Atlantic Monthly*.[30]

Given that Melville related less to the denomination in the abstract than to specific individuals and to one church in particular, we must also look more closely at Bellows and All Souls to see the merits Melville might have found there. Socially progressive and civic-minded, Bellows was the nation's leading Unitarian minister in the latter half of the century. A Harvard Divinity School graduate whose brief first pastorate was in Mobile, Alabama, he denounced slavery from the pulpit during the debates leading up to the Compromise of 1850 and, when the war came, served as president of the United States Sanitary Commission from 1861 to 1878.[31] He also perceived the rationalistic and secularizing tendencies of his age and, rather than denying or denouncing them, sought to reconcile them with Christianity. His "Suspense of Faith" sermon preached to Harvard Divinity School alumni in 1859, a watershed in Unitarian history comparable to Emerson's Divinity School Address in 1838, declared that the radical individualism espoused by Emerson had had its day and that the crisis of faith besetting modern Americans could be remedied only by a stronger, renewed liberal church.[32] In 1865 he spearheaded the creation of the National Conference of Unitarian Churches, which consolidated Unitarianism as a denomination (the American Unitarian Association formed in 1825 convened individuals, not churches). He envisioned the National Conference as a tent big enough to cover both biblicist Unitarians who saw themselves as liberal Christians and the radicals who, whether skeptical or transcendentalist, interpreted religion in more naturalistic terms and refused to assign a privileged position to Jesus or to historical Christianity.[33] Remembered in denominational histories primarily as an organizer, Bellows was also known in his day as an eloquent preacher zealous for intellectual and spiritual freedom. In raising money for Antioch College in Ohio, for instance, he exhorted his fellow Unitarians to support a school that would reach students from parts of the country not "sicklied o'er with the New England subtleties of debate" and that would nurture those who have "free thoughts and new religious ideas."[34] Without sharing Bellows's theocentrism or commitment to the church as an institution, Melville likely appreciated the minister's political and religious liberalism, ecumenicity, and privileging of intellectual freedom.

Melville may also have warmed to the spirit of inclusion and intellectual tolerance at All Souls. According to Kring, the church's reformed bylaws of 1846 stated that those who wished to take communion or to join the church did not need to declare any creed or profession of faith at all. Indeed, the Methodist minister John Fletcher Hurst, trying to sum up mid-century Unitarian beliefs in his *History of Rationalism* (1865) and with Bellows in his sights, expressed frustration that the Unitarians lacked clear criteria for membership and a coherent theological program. He complained, "The Unitarians neither exact nor desire conformity to authority; in fact they have no authority. Reason is left to place its own construction upon the truths of revelation."[35] During this period at All Souls, anyone who wished to become a member simply informed the pastor of his or her intent, a rule that lasted until the church's adoption of a minimalist, one-line covenant in 1922.[36] Thus Melville's name in Williams's membership book did not signal adherence to specific beliefs but merely a desire to be identified as a church member. Since Bellows's membership record has gone missing, one cannot assume that Melville's 1884 membership suggests any change of heart regarding All Souls or Unitarianism or even any particular appreciation of Williams, though Melville may have been newly drawn to the church by this educated young man who would eventually publish a volume of original poetry (1910) and a translation of Virgil's *Georgics* and *Eclogues* (1915). In short, although we do not know either Melville's membership status at All Souls through 1882 or his exact attitude toward the church, it is difficult to imagine that he recoiled from this creedless, progressive congregation—or from Unitarianism as a denomination—as "repugnant."

Recognizing affinities between Melville and the Unitarians clears the way for the possibility that he met this tradition with mingled appropriation and resistance, as he did so many other religious perspectives. Yet I do not wish to identify Melville *as* a Unitarian, since to classify a person as either in or out of a religious tradition, a true believer or an apostate, is to impose the terms of confessional Protestantism and so distort the ambiguities of religious identity. In seeking to understand Melville's relationship to Unitarianism, we might turn instead to recent work on American religious liberalism that stresses the permeability of its boundaries. In the edited volume *American Religious Liberalism* (2012), cultural historians Leigh Eric Schmidt and Sally Promey have argued for a capacious definition of religious liberalism that moves beyond familiar ecclesiastical narratives to include metaphysical religion, quasi-religious movements, print culture, the arts, and literature as equally legitimate participants in what counts as religious history. This decentering of churches makes visible the fluidity of religious liberalism—the difficulty of determining who is within its bounds, its love-hate relationship with centrifugal forces such as secularism and cosmopolitanism, and the tremendous variety of extra-ecclesiastical practices, including imaginative literature, that address religious questions, sometimes with pronounced skepticism. Keeping in mind both Melville's sporadic yet persistent relationship to Unitarianism and the porosity of religious liberalism, we can attend with renewed sensitivity to his shifting, multifaceted relationship to Unitarian thought.

The Unitarian Conscience

Of the many Unitarian ideas that shaped Melville's thinking, the idea of conscience is one of the most salient, in that it serves, alongside reason, as a first principle in Unitarian theology. While circulating freely in secular discourses, "conscience" has had strong associations with Christianity ever since the late fourth century, when Jerome used the Latin term *conscientia* to translate the Greek *syneidesis* in the Vulgate. The political scientist Edward Andrew observes that conscience "is a Western and almost exclusively Christian word," without equivalent in Sanskrit, Chinese, or Japanese.[37] Typically interpreted through the Middle Ages as the knowledge one shared with (*con + scientia*) the church and as thus undifferentiated from dogma, the concept came to prominence during the Reformation as the justification for individual religious dissent. Martin Luther's reply to Johann von Eck at the Diet of Worms exemplifies this shift. When Eck begged Luther, "Lay aside your conscience, Martin; you must lay it aside because it is in error," the accused replied, "My conscience is captive to the Word of God: I cannot and will not retract anything, since it is neither safe nor right to go against conscience. I cannot do otherwise, here I stand, may God help me, Amen."[38] As Luther's declaration suggests, notwithstanding the Reformation's rallying cry of *sola scriptura*, the conscience that guided scriptural interpretation was the key to resisting ecclesiastical authority. Despite the efforts of various Reformers to limit conscience so as to mitigate the threat that radical subjectivity posed to the social order, by the time of the English Civil War (1642–51), the "revolutionary, antinomian, and subjectivist" interpretation of conscience was in full flower.[39] In America the fruit was evident in phenomena such as Roger Williams's founding of Providence in 1636 on the stated principle of "liberty of conscience" and in the Antinomian controversy of 1636–38, during which Anne Hutchinson, testifying before the General Court of Massachusetts, claimed "immediate revelation" as the grounds for her spiritual discernment and her faith in this revelation as a matter of "conscience."[40] Among philosophers, a backlash against the socially destabilizing individualism of conscience ensued, with Thomas Hobbes, John Locke, David Hume, and Adam Smith all pairing conscience with reason and subordinating it, in varying degrees, to civil law and social consensus.

Inheriting this robust philosophical and religious conversation, nineteenth-century Unitarians invoked conscience both to justify the break from orthodoxy, on the classic Reformation grounds that freedom of conscience legitimated religious difference, and, following eighteenth-century thinkers such as the Scottish philosopher Thomas Reid and British Unitarian Richard Price, to affirm it as evidence of humanity's inherent goodness.[41] They held that if God had endowed people with conscience, or the ability to discern divine justice, they could not, as the Calvinists claimed, be totally depraved. "The Moral Argument against Calvinism" (1820) centered on this point. There Channing turned the tables on the orthodox who charged that Unitarian abandonment of doctrine led to immorality by attacking Calvinist belief in original sin and a punitive God as itself destructive. In "Likeness to God," Channing took the argument a step further: not only did conscience link humans to the divine by interpreting "God's love and virtue and hatred of sin," but humans could know God only by reference to their own moral nature. Conscience was "the lawgiver in our own breasts, which gives us the idea of divine authority, and binds us to obey it."[42] David Robinson notes that, despite appearances, Channing did not wish to claim that humanity makes God in its image, but to repair the breach between the divine and human that Calvinism insisted upon.[43] Maintaining that conscience served as a link to God also allowed Unitarians to continue believing in moral absolutes even as they abandoned Trinitarian theology and other dogmas of Protestantism.[44]

Yet conscience was unstable ethical ground, especially for those, like the Unitarians, committed to rationality. Andrew demonstrates that from Luther on, conscience has been a rogue, operating on its own particularistic, antinomian terms regardless of attempts to circumscribe it with rationality or the law.[45] Following Locke, Unitarians habitually coupled "reason and conscience" with scant discussion of the conflict between the two: Bellows, for instance, could declare that "reason and conscience" were "always good seed; always sacred and divine in their rights . . . the elder Scriptures in men's hearts."[46] At the same time, as Daniel Walker Howe explains, Unitarians tried to safeguard conscience from unreason by stressing its presumptive debt to the counsel of parents and ministers, one's reading of the Bible, habits of right conduct, and acquired skill in moral judgment. They also held that while the moral sense intuitively revealed general truths, such as the golden rule, any application of these truths—that is, one's specific duties in a given situation—required careful examination and should be "calculated by prudential reason, on the basis of factual knowledge and experience."[47] They were thus unfazed by the differences among consciences, which reflected different levels of moral development. As Bellows remarked in a sermon, in a passage whose conceit intriguingly echoes that in Plotinus Plinlimmon's "Chronometricals and Horologicals" pamphlet in *Pierre*:

> How easily might God have regulated all the consciences in the universe by his own, as all the astronomic clocks in England are electrically controlled by the clock at Greenwich observatory? We could

> then have told the moral time at head-quarters, i.e. in God's own mind, to an absolute certainty, by simply looking at the dial in our own souls! One common chime would have sounded out the hours from all the moral belfries in the Universe, and Heaven and earth and all places and posts in God's dominions would have struck noon and midnight with simultaneous stroke![48]

Unlike Plinlimmon, Bellows did not accept human deviation from the divine standard as inevitable in a fallen world.[49] Rather, he explained that God did not choose to set consciences by the supernatural equivalent of Greenwich Mean Time because the greater divine achievement lay in allowing people to develop their moral intelligences gradually, which gave them a more complete, authentic reverence for God. Cultivating one's conscience depended on intelligence, strong will, and "the development of all the great human faculties and the harvesting of all the richest previous experiences."[50] The mature conscience also weighed the opinions of others, an often difficult enterprise. Channing described this challenge in "Remarks on Associations" (1833), in a passage scored in the Melvilles' Channing:

> Our greatest and most difficult duty, as social beings, is, to derive constant aid from society without taking its yoke; to open our minds to the thoughts, reasonings, and persuasions of others, and yet to hold fast the sacred right of private judgment; to receive impulses from our fellow-beings, and yet to act from our own souls; to sympathize with others, and yet to follow our own consciences.[51]

Unitarian theories of conscience thus sought to reconcile two antagonistic values, one a legacy of the Reformation, the other of the Enlightenment: the sacredness of individual moral conviction and the virtue derivable from society and dialogue.

The Unitarian perspective on conscience can be contrasted with that which predominated among transcendentalists, for whom the opinions of others, not to mention the guidance of the Bible and elders, were held to be all but irrelevant. For transcendentalists, conscience was an immediate intuition of the truths of Spirit, a revolutionary force liable to prompt one to break from society, especially in defiance of slavery. Such conviction marks, for instance, "Civil Disobedience," in which Henry David Thoreau asks, "Must the citizen . . . resign his conscience to the legislator? Why has every man a conscience, then?" and Theodore Parker's famous antislavery sermon, "The Function and Place of Conscience, in Relation to the Laws of Men."[52] These transcendentalist exemplars reveal the limitations of the Unitarian willingness to entertain multiple points of view, as Unitarians were generally less inclined to grant the perspective of slaves the same weight as that of masters or to believe that conscience demanded the immediate abolition of slavery.

Notwithstanding these failures of moral judgment, one can appreciate the humility underlying the Unitarian belief that moral discernment required dialogical thinking.

Conscience in *Pierre*

Melville's fiction of the early 1850s recurs frequently to questions of conscience, a concern that seems a natural outgrowth of his reading in Channing and exposure to Unitarian thought at All Souls in 1849. Of course, numerous books read between 1848 and 1851 may also have fueled his interest in conscience: for instance, *Hamlet*, where "conscience does make cowards of us all"; *Richard III*, whose titular king is, like Ahab, assailed by conscience in the dead of night; *Paradise Lost*, in which God declares, "And I will place within them as a guide / My umpire conscience"; and Pierre Bayle, who in his *Dictionary* followed Milton in regarding conscience as the ultimate guide to conduct.[53] Melville may also have begun to revolve issues of conscience after the formation of the antislavery "Conscience Whig" party in Massachusetts in 1848 and, after 1850, the abolitionists' protest that the Fugitive Slave Law violated the rights of conscience. Amidst this swirl of conscience rhetoric, Unitarian moral discourse would have served Melville as a personally significant, intellectually resonant point of departure for his ethical reflections. Whatever its precise degree of influence on him, reading his work in its light suggests how his own largely secular ethical perspective could emerge from his contemporaries' theistic yet strongly humanistic one.

While Melville did not share the Unitarian belief that conscience actively links humans to God or that it reveals God, his fiction of the early 1850s treats it as a force integral to personal identity and moral decision-making and implies that its proper development requires a careful consideration of others' perspectives, not merely a strong sense of inner conviction. His fiction of that period conveys these ideas primarily through a particular type of negative example: a man in a position of authority who justifies himself by invoking conscience, with these self-justifications serving as a delusional cover story for a destructive will to power. Such characters rely on a transcendentalist sense of conscience, hearkening to an unreliable inner voice of conviction while little heeding what Channing called "the thoughts, reasonings, and persuasions of others." Trapped in their own heads, they make terrible decisions.

Ahab is a prime example of this pattern. Making monomaniacal vengeance the rule of the *Pequod*, he represses not only what may be an inner corrective voice troubling his sleep (what Stubb speculates is his conscience), but also, more deliberately, his waking knowledge of his financial obligation to the ship's owners. Repeatedly rejecting Starbuck's ethical admonitions in favor of his own inner drives, he redefines conscience as will and dominance:

"My conscience is in this ship's keel!" a declaration that collapses the ship, the men, and his will into his "conscience" (*Moby-Dick*, 474). It is this failure to recognize conscience as a sense of morality shaped in response to the claims of others that eventually destroys the ship.

The counterpoint to Ahab's stifled, stunted conscience is Ishmael's healthy, flexible one. After Ishmael uses the golden rule to decide that he should worship Yojo with Queequeg, he follows Queequeg's lead in kindling wood, offering burnt biscuit, salaaming, and kissing the statue's nose, after which they undress and go to bed "at peace with [their] own consciences and all the world" (*Moby-Dick*, 52). Idolater though Ishmael may be—and certainly neither Channing nor any other confessed Christian would approve of Yojo-worship—his philosophy is sound, congruent with Unitarian teachings in that they are based on rationality and a process of give-and-take. Melville writes his approbation on Ishmael's body, in sound sleep and physical comfort.

In *Pierre*, questions of conscience receive more sustained attention. This novel recasts Ahab's misguided, monomaniacal conviction as young Pierre's holy fervor to sacrifice himself for Isabel in the name of "Truth, Love, Pity, Conscience," a self-immolation that, like Ahab's failed quest, is a tragic self-delusion that eventually destroys not the errant purist alone, but those around him, too (*Pierre*, 49). The novel is less sympathetic to Pierre—and more forgiving of its supposed Unitarian cleric, Reverend Falsgrave—than critics typically recognize. As James Duban has demonstrated, Melville uses Pierre, who misperceives his repressed sexual desires as the intuitions of a heavenly mandate, to critique transcendentalist subjectivism.[54] For instance, we learn from a passage whose free indirect discourse might lure us into temporary approbation, that Pierre is "one of those spirits, which not in a determinate and sordid scrutiny of small pros and cons—but in an impulsive subservience to the god-like dictation of events themselves, find at length the surest solution of perplexities, and the brightest prerogatives of command" (88).[55] Such lines satirize claims to moral certainty based on the equivalent of a lightning bolt to the soul and, given that Pierre is a callow nineteen-year-old, implicitly deprecate the transcendentalist approach to conscience as adolescent folly. Yet it is worth noting that even the transcendentalists were suspicious of divine edicts vouchsafed to young people: Theodore Parker cautioned that conscience, all-wise as it was, could be "immature, in the young, who have not had time for the growth and ripening of the faculty."[56]

True to his transcendentalist conscience, Pierre grapples alone with the mystery of Isabel, refusing to consult, as Unitarian moral philosophy recommended, tradition, elders, propriety, or a reasonable consideration of consequences. Convinced of his own superior morality and overly anxious to protect his idealized image of his dead father, he rejects the guidance of his mother and his minister, both of whom might have offered sensible counsel to check his rash behavior had he taken them into his confidence. As it is, Pierre presents his dilemma only obliquely, as when he asks his mother at breakfast whether the legitimate child should shun the illegitimate. Mrs. Glendinning, whom we need not see as the monster Pierre perceives her to be while he is in the throes of his late-adolescent rebellion and inchoate sexual awakening, responds with the advice, congruent with Unitarian philosophy, to weigh public mores and private judgment: "'Ask the world, Pierre'—said Mrs. Glendinning warmly—'and ask your own heart'" (*Pierre*, 101). If her recommendation is rather worldly, it is also, as a general guide to moral decision-making, completely reasonable, especially for an impetuous nineteen-year-old. Since she does not know the dilemma he faces, she can say nothing more pertinent.

Falsgrave, too, might have proven a valuable guide to Pierre in his moral bewilderment, despite critics' reflexive dismissal of him as a toady. Hershel Parker has influentially read him as Melville's righteous critique of "nominal Christianity," in particular Unitarians like Dewey who supposedly showed an "un-Christlike deference to the opinions of the rich and un-Christlike concern for the poor."[57] Yet why must young Pierre, whom Parker reads much more carefully, be the only figure of moral and psychological complexity in this novel? We might instead see Falsgrave in the light of Melvillean ambiguity, nowhere more evident than in this baldly subtitled novel. Falsgrave's gentlemanly deportment, delicate hands, affinity for the society of cultured women, and hint of indolence set the stage for his exposure as a hypocrite—the "snowy bosom" must be the whited sepulcher hiding corruption within (*Pierre*, 99)—but the novel ducks and dodges this too-predictable unveiling, which the "reverend rake" type of mid-century popular fiction would have led readers to expect.[58] In *Pierre*, the genteel clergyman is indeed imperfect, primarily in being too deferential to the beautiful patroness who has built his church, paid his salary, and attracted his personal notice to the point that he has proposed marriage. As this last fact suggests, he, like young Pierre, conducts his moral reasoning not as pure spirit, but as a human being, with a body alive to desire. And just as Pierre's psychosexual turmoil, ridiculous as it may be at points, invites compassion, so with Falsgrave Melville discourages readers from the cheap pleasures of contempt. Though limited and fallible, Falsgrave turns out to be a well-meaning professional trying to live by his understanding of Christian duty. The narrator affirms that Falsgrave is "well worthy" of the Glendinnings' esteem, and the novel leaves open the possibility that, as Pierre speculates at breakfast, Falsgrave might be "capable of giving him worthy counsel in his strait" (99).

Tradition and usage would make Falsgrave a spiritual father of sorts for Pierre, yet Pierre never seeks out this counsel. Indeed, the most important fact about Falsgrave is that he represents a missed opportunity. At breakfast, Pierre surprises the minister with his loaded question about the legitimate child's obligation to the illegitimate, causing him to look at Pierre "searchingly," a hint that he may know more about Glendinning family secrets than the young master suspects, and to offer a vague answer in line with the Unitarian commitment to the primacy of reason in moral deliberation: "though conscience may possibly dictate freely in any known special case; yet, by one universal maxim, to embrace all moral contingencies—this is not only impossible, but the attempt, to me, seems foolish" (*Pierre*, 101–2). Though equivocal, the assertion that correct moral deliberation requires knowledge of specifics is also, like Mrs. Glendinning's counsel, eminently sensible. The minister's prudence finds its visual analogue in his cameo brooch decorated with an intertwined serpent and dove, an allusion to Jesus's command to his disciples: "Behold I send you forth as sheep in the midst of wolves: be ye therefore wise as serpents, and harmless as doves" (Matt. 10:16). The suggestion that Falsgrave among his parishioners is the sheep among wolves reverses the readerly expectation, fueled by popular fiction, that the respectable, well-spoken minister is a fraud, a sinful man deceiving the innocent, a predator roving the flock. Here, the "sheep" is a minister from a humble background—Falsgrave is "the child of a poor northern farmer who had wedded a pretty sempstress" (98)—who, in seeking to fulfill his moral duties, needs all his wits about him to avoid falling victim to the wolfish displeasure of his parishioners, especially the moneyed and powerful. The fact that his brooch was given him by "an appreciative friend" suggests that he does his job well, while the white napkin hiding the brooch hints at the social proprieties that cloak his worldly-wise yet Christian philosophy (102). Rather than conclude, as one critic has it, that Falsgrave exemplifies an "expedient virtue," which is to assign an undue weight to his secular and self-serving motives, we might instead regard him as providing a glimpse of what it might mean to be a mature, principled, yet pragmatic navigator of moral difficulties.[59] Through Falsgrave, Melville implies that liberal Christian ministers, and perhaps Unitarians in particular, are ordinary men striving to reconcile reason, social forms, and moral duty: neither prophets, denouncing injustices regardless of consequences, nor charlatans. Falsgrave resembles no one so much as the lawyer in "Bartleby," who must also negotiate his moral responsibilities in a knotty situation. As with the lawyer, if we condemn Falsgrave too readily, we miss the subtlety with which Melville limns the contingencies inherent in scenes of complex moral reasoning.

Whatever Falsgrave's redeeming virtues, Pierre, infatuated with Isabel and impatient with anything but an absolutism that feeds his desire, can see in the minister only craven, supercilious hypocrisy. After the cryptic breakfast-table conversation, Pierre next seeks out Falsgrave not in a calm afternoon meeting at the parsonage, the customary setting for pastoral consultations, but at midnight on the minister's doorstep. Having just left Isabel, Pierre is agitated and accusatory and demands to know what will happen to unwed mother Delly Ulver. When Falsgrave says she will depart the community and declines to discuss the matter further given the hour and his young guest's imperious behavior, Pierre sniffs, "I perfectly comprehend the whole, sir" (163). He censures the minister's heartlessness and announces that he has decided not to speak with him on a matter nearer his heart. He once thought Falsgrave might "sincerely and honestly counsel" him but now knows otherwise: "a hint from heaven assures me now, that thou hast no earnest and world-disdaining counsel for me. I must seek it from God himself, who . . . never delegates his holiest admonishings." Pierre concludes his monologue by telling the minister, twenty years his senior, that he judges not him but his profession, "entangled" as it is with "fleshly alliances" (164), which, as Brian Higgins and Hershel Parker point out, is "intensely ironic" given Pierre's own developing entanglement with Isabel.[60] In the next chapter, the narrator underscores Pierre's outrageous behavior, remarking that Pierre's aggressive mood has led him to invade Falsgrave's "profound midnight slumbers" and "most discourteously [make] war upon that really amiable and estimable person" (166).[61] What Falsgrave's advice might have been, had Pierre returned at another time as invited, is left a mystery; Pierre awakens the next morning brimming with the conviction that he must sham-marry Isabel. His intuitionist moral epistemology immediately begets dreadful ethics: he transforms his possible sister into his wife, and that, through coercion. When Pierre informs Lucy and his mother that he has decided to marry Isabel before consulting with Isabel herself, he holds Isabel's reputation hostage, making him, not her, the novel's clearest seducer. He declares to Isabel, too truly: "already have I plunged! now thou canst not stay upon the bank" (191). The subsequent unraveling of fate, or folly, does not vindicate this "plunge," taken in the name of conscience yet driven by the eager desire for physical contact.

A fuller study of Melville's fiction could analyze conscience in *Moby-Dick* and *Pierre* in more detail and trace how the pattern of the powerful, isolated man steaming ahead in its name recurs, transformed, in "Bartleby" and *Benito Cereno*. Briefly, in "Bartleby," the lawyer's endless moral deliberations and obsessive, solitary ruminations—"What shall I do? what ought I to do? what does conscience say I *should* do with this man, or rather ghost?"—create an effect as claustrophobic as the office walls yet lead to no action that stops Bartleby's death, though perhaps to a few that accelerate it.[62] In *Benito Cereno*, the figure of the mentally isolated, morally misguided man reappears as Captain Delano, whose satisfied reflection on his own moral purity—"'Who would murder Amasa Delano? His conscience is clean'"—suggests how the faith of Northern whites in their own unsullied consciences had reinforced their contempt for slaveholders, exacerbating national tensions whose only resolution would be found in civil war.[63] From the late 1850s through the 1870s, conscience seems a less urgent concept for Melville: it is an empty signifier in *The Confidence-Man* and surprisingly absent in *Battle-Pieces* and *Clarel*, though of course both texts engage profound questions of moral decision-making.

Conscience in *Billy Budd*

Conscience returns in force in *Billy Budd*. This renewal of interest may be due to Melville's seemingly stronger connections to Unitarianism in the late 1880s and early 1890s, as suggested by the All Souls pew rental and membership book, as well as by an entry in the New York Society Library ledger indicating that Octavius Brooks Frothingham's *Boston Unitarianism, 1820–1850* (1890) was charged to the account of Herman and Elizabeth Melville from January 30 to February 5, 1891.[64] The volume is a contextual biography of the author's father, Nathaniel Frothingham (1793–1870), the well-known pastor of Boston's First Church from 1815 to 1850, and O. B. Frothingham (1822–1895) may himself have been of interest to Melville. A former Unitarian minister with transcendentalist beliefs, he pastored the Third Unitarian Society in New York (1855–59) and helped organize the Free Religious Association, as well as serving as its first president (1867–78). With an open-mindedness one suspects Melville would have appreciated, Frothingham believed churches should be "arenas for mental challenge and encounter with faith of all kinds."[65] To be clear, in noting Melville's heightened attention to Unitarianism in the 1880s, then turning to *Billy Budd*, I do not wish to suggest that he was seeking reconciliation with Christian faith, or Unitarianism, or even God. Melville in his final two decades was who he ever was: skeptical, searching, democratic, intellectually acquisitive, morally inquisitive, and labyrinthine in his literary artistry. The precise influence on *Billy Budd* of his association with All Souls, perusal of Frothingham, and, possibly, continued or resumed contemplation of Channing, is impossible to gauge with certainty. But we can safely assume that all of these sources contributed to his thinking about the ethical issues at the story's heart, in particular the question of conscience, or whether human beings possesses some inner mechanism that can be relied upon to guide the way to justice. Implicitly in dialogue with the Unitarianism that had been a significant presence in his family and social world for decades and that seems to have held heightened interest for him in the late 1880s, Melville worked out in *Billy Budd* a sophisticated secularization of conscience, one that rejects the Unitarian belief that it is an intrinsic element of human nature that connects humanity to God, yet retains the concept as a political principle essential to liberal societies and as, for most people, a pre-linguistic, embodied force that monitors the justice of one's actions.

The novel's seeming moral opposites, Claggart and Billy, are limit cases through which Melville examines the imperfect applicability of the Unitarian belief in the universality of conscience. One is naturally good, the other, evil, but both are outliers, odd cases, fascinating in their individuality and no guide to human nature in general. Claggart is the clearer challenge to Unitarian moral philosophy. When his hate rises against Billy after the soup-spilling incident, the narrator, commenting on the apparent disproportion between the foretopman's mistake and the master-at-arms's hunger for revenge, asks, "But how with Claggart's conscience? For though consciences are unlike as foreheads, every intelligence not excluding the scriptural devils who 'believe and tremble' has one. But Claggart's conscience being but the lawyer to his will, made ogres of trifles."[66] The Unitarians countenanced a diversity of consciences, but men such as Claggart are strong counterarguments to the claim that conscience is a universally accessible divine authority and revelation. Whereas Ahab might be said to have a conscience that tries to surface in his fitful sleep, Claggart has no conscience Unitarians would recognize as such. He is a psychopath, a madman, a "peculiar human creature the direct reverse of a saint!," one who by every indication is fatally flawed, evincing the rare and terrifying "natural depravity" described by Plato (74–76). Claggart has not, as Unitarian theology would maintain regarding such a man, corrupted an originally pure conscience or failed to develop an immature one; his conscience is the "peculiar" one "assigned to be [his] private mentor" (80). Whoever made this assignment—God, Fate, Nature, or the marplot of Eden—Claggart had the deck stacked against him from the start.

Claggart represents the worst of humanity without a conscience as traditionally understood; Billy, the best. Like Claggart, Billy lacks the capacity for self-questioning moral reflection not because he is depraved but because as a good-hearted child of nature, he needs no mystical element to reconnect him with a supposed divinity. No inner division demands remedy: "Of self-consciousness he seemed to have little or none" (52). Even at the moment of his greatest inner conflict, he does not search his soul. On trial when he hesitates in response to being asked whether he knew anything about "incipient trouble," his negative reply reflects only an "erring sense of uninstructed honor" and "the blind feeling now his that nothing really was being hatched" (106–7). The narrator notes Billy's departures from martial duty, but Billy himself does not. Thus *Billy Budd* suggests that just as for a cursed few—the naturally depraved—there was never original purity, so for a blessed few—the young, beautiful, good-natured, happy-go-lucky, and beloved—there was no fall. Claggart and Billy might look like throwbacks, Melville's reversion to mythic or romantic types, but, given the story's analytical narrator and realistic detail, they are better read as a naturalistic rethinking of types. By nature, the story implies, a few men really are diabolical and a few, angelic. In both cases, the traditional idea of conscience as an inner, divine voice has little explanatory power.

Captain Vere is the story's primary vehicle for dissecting the workings of conscience in more typical mortals, those not morally anomalous by nature. Though not credited with conscience in name, Vere is a man of principle and study, with a store of "positive convictions" arrived at through a "line of reading" that has given him "confirmation of his own more reserved thoughts—confirmation which he had vainly sought in social converse" (62). However admirably studious, Vere is also unwittingly self-interested, reading not to encounter new ideas, reflect on his own beliefs, or widen his perspective—it is telling that he avoids fiction and poetry altogether—but to confirm biases formed by his aristocratic background. Vere thus cultivates his conscience so that it speaks only on behalf of the era's conservatism. He holds these views in good faith: out of solicitude for the world at large, he "disinterestedly opposed them [revolutionary ideas] not alone because they seemed to him insusceptible of embodiment in lasting institutions, but at war with the peace of the world and the true welfare of mankind" (63). His conscience gives voice to the echo-chamber of reactionary ideas in which he has ensconced himself. With Vere, Melville ponders how tempting it can be to listen to the opinions only of the like-minded, then repose in the strength of one's beliefs. Good intentions and moral probity notwithstanding, the conscience that supervises these convictions is too partial to be a reliable guide to justice.[67]

When the moment of crisis comes, and Claggart lies dead on the deck, Vere plays out Melville's well-established narrative pattern of the powerful, isolated man whose moral intuition eventuates in tragedy. Aghast at Billy's fatal blow, he stands "motionless . . . absorbed in thought," then, "starting, he vehemently exclaimed: 'Struck dead by an angel of God! Yet the angel must hang!' " (101). It is an appalling declaration, a hasty conclusion worthy of Pierre. But Vere is even more disturbing than Melville's earlier flawed protagonists. His conscience is not immature, like Pierre's, or idiosyncratically disordered, like Ahab's or Claggart's, but, in line with his conservative beliefs, systematically subordinated to imperial power. In one of the most chilling yet incisive passages in Melville's fiction, Vere articulates the core of his moral reasoning, such as it is. He addresses the drumhead court in his impromptu star chamber: "But something in your aspect seems to urge that it is not solely the heart that moves in you, but also the conscience, the private conscience. But tell me whether or not, occupying the position we do, private conscience should not yield to that imperial one formulated in the code under which alone we officially proceed?" (111). Vere's deference to law and insistence on rationality do more than represent a troubling acquiescence to wartime exigencies: they expose the split in modernity between reason and conscience from which the Unitarians averted their eyes. Although Unitarians wrote as if reason and conscience were mirror images of one another, a linkage underwriting the idea of "rational religion," Vere indicates otherwise. Reasonably, deliberately, conscientiously, he seeks to erase conscience. One of his chief tactics is to shift his rhetoric from conscience to "private conscience," a sleight-of-hand that, especially when set against the notion of an imperial conscience, should sound an alarm bell for readers. This substitution stacks the deck by reducing conscience to a radical subjectivity that operates outside rational, public discussion; in effect it conflates all claims to conscience with the solipsistic moral intuitionism Melville had critiqued in Ahab and Pierre. In shrinking and stigmatizing conscience, Vere echoes Hobbes, with whose writings Melville was familiar.[68] Hobbes denounced the idea that "'private Consciences, which are but private opinions'" could legitimately oppose the law, which is "the publique Conscience, by which [a man in civil society] hath already undertaken to be guided."[69] For Hobbes, claims of conscience invited civil disorder, since the man who followed his conscience would not "dare to obey the Soveraign Power, farther than it shall seem good in his own eyes." Vere follows this reasoning to the letter.

Denial of conscience in all its forms is integral to the conservative politics for which Vere is fighting. Much like Hobbes, Edmund Burke held that individuals entering civil society would, as Andrew explains, "renounce the right of private judgment and execution of the laws of nature."[70] Ineluctably individualistic, conscience threatens to lead to anarchy. Thus it makes perfect sense that Vere, fighting revolutionary France and contemptuous of common sailors, cannot brook "private conscience." Siding with traditional authority over freedom of conscience, vested power over principled dissent, Vere would have, with full faith in the rightness of his decision, excommunicated Luther, burned Servetus, and exiled Anne Hutchinson. To give conscience leeway would be to sanction individualism and republicanism, to endorse Thomas Paine's *Rights of Man*, which had praised the French National Assembly for, "like America," establishing "UNIVERSAL RIGHT OF CONSCIENCE, AND UNIVERSAL RIGHT OF CITIZENSHIP."[71] The name of Billy's merchant ship reminds readers of the freedom lost when the claims of conscience are excluded. Thus the story drives home the point that although consciences vary greatly, each one bearing the stamp of its owner, and although some people, like Billy and Claggart, have no conscience to speak of, the concept is nonetheless a fundamental political principle for free societies, an indispensable metaphor for individual liberty.

But is conscience no more than a metaphor, a fiction underwriting the individualism upon which democratic societies are built? Is there no impulse to justice in the human heart? *Billy Budd* suggests that most people do possess a sense of justice, which they experience not supernaturally, as a connection to God, or even intellectually, as the result of careful ratiocination, but physiologically, as embodied ease or agitation. The story is full of bodies protesting their active or incipient complicity with injustice.[72] In one of the most telling moments, the men of the drumhead court cannot sit still when Vere exhorts them to ignore the private conscience: they "moved in their seats, less convinced than agitated by the course of an argument troubling but the more the spontaneous conflict within" (111). What is this involuntary restlessness, arising from inner tension and exacerbated by repellent speeches, if not a "kind of Tic-Dolly-row," or uncontrollable, physical twitching prompted by an aversion to doing wrong, which one might also call conscience? This bodily knowledge of impending participation in moral error is evident throughout the trial: in the three officers' "simultaneously stir[ring] in their seats" and exchanging anxious looks after Billy leaves; in Vere's pacing the cabin; in the "something" in the officers' faces that prompts Vere to remind them to follow the imperial conscience; in the sailing master's "faltering" speech when asking if the court might not convict yet mitigate the penalty; perhaps, too, in the agony on Vere's face after the captain leaves his private interview with Billy, so pronounced it strikes the senior lieutenant as a "startling revelation," a suggestive visual analogue of the Unitarians' sense of conscience as a spark of divinity or God-given monitor (109, 111–12, 115). At Billy's hanging, Vere suppresses with unnatural stiffness his recognition of the leading role he has played in this unjust death (123–24). Only later, sedated and at the brink of death, can Vere's body assert the knowledge of guilt. "'Billy Budd, Billy Budd,'" is not spoken, it "would seem," in the "accents of remorse," but the lack of conscious contrition does not exonerate (129). The body testifies against Vere though mind and heart remain impenitent. Vere's troubled death contrasts with Billy's clarion blessing and unwonted stillness at the moment of hanging, both of which symbolize what the narrator earlier calls his "essential innocence," or, more precisely, his lack of an internal moral sense that would register a repressed knowledge of transgression through twitchings and stirrings (117, 121). Without awareness of guilt, Billy suffers no half-repressed inner conflict or accompanying bodily agitation.

Residually religious and ambivalently secular, "conscience" remains a live wire in public discourse as many terms and tenets of Protestantism do not. We continue to debate the claims of conscience with respect to issues of religious freedom, military service, voting, whistle-blowing, jury deliberation, and other personal yet public judgments. The judgment of the U.S. Supreme Court in *Burwell v. Hobby Lobby* (2014) that closely held corporations have consciences, too, makes consideration of this foundational concept in Western history newly important for public life. To contemplate Melville on conscience is to perceive the moral and intellectual continuity between his moment and our own, as well as between his work and a long history of post-Reformation writing on the limits of subjectivity in moral epistemology, one that includes, most pertinently for Melville, the sermons and essays of nineteenth-century American Unitarians such as Bellows and Channing. As I have suggested, Melville used his fiction of the early 1850s to think through a Unitarian perspective on conscience, writing stories that implied, often indirectly, that conscience should be a moral conviction arrived at not through a flash of inspiration but through reckoning with multiple viewpoints. If in *Billy Budd* he wished to illustrate the inadequacy of the conscience hypothesis to explain the moral inner workings of all people, he was nonetheless doubly committed to it as a human right and as a widely shared subconscious, corporeal guide to justice.

Conscience is only one of the most obvious points of entry in considering how Channing and Unitarianism shaped Melville's social ethics, biblical hermeneutics, critiques of orthodox theology, and literary ambitions. Future investigations of these connections will not, one trusts, reduce Melville's spectacularly creative fiction to a Unitarian tract, but rather strengthen our understanding of how Melville engaged with thoughtful fellow dissenters from religious orthodoxy. Seen as emerging from this conversation, his work illuminates the outer limits of liberal Protestantism and the creative, humanistic possibilities of post-Protestant secularity.

Notes

1. Herman Melville, *Moby-Dick; or The Whale*, vol. 6 of The Writings of Herman Melville, ed. Harrison Hayford, Hershel Parker, and G. Thomas Tanselle (Evanston and Chicago: Northwestern University Press and the Newberry Library, 1988), 127–28. Further citations come from this edition.

2. On the discovery of Melville's hand in this set and an analysis of its significance, see my "Mahomet's Gospel and Other Revelations" (*Leviathan* 17, no. 2 [2015]: 74–88) and my critical introduction to the set on *Melville's Marginalia Online*. The discussion of the Channing set below draws on these essays.

3. William H. Gilman, *Melville's Early Life and "Redburn"* (1951; New York: Russell and Russell, 1972), 22. Gilman also notes that Melville's grandfather, Major Thomas Melvill, "read regularly *The Christian Register*, organ for the religious liberalism of Jared Sparks, William Ellery Channing, and Henry Ware" (ibid.), and that Thomas Melvill Jr., Herman's uncle, referred in an 1833 letter to Lemuel Shaw to a "volume of Buckminster's Sermons much used by my parents" (Gilman, *Melville's Early Life*, 298n97).

4. Hershel Parker, *Herman Melville: A Biography*, vol. 1, *1819–1851* (Baltimore: Johns Hopkins University Press, 1996), 153. Parker misidentifies James Freeman Clarke, rather than Young, as minister at New South Church in 1847 (1:543). Clarke pastored Boston's Church of the Disciples from 1841 to 1850; see Henry Warner Bowden, *Dictionary of American Religious Biography*, 2nd ed. (Westport, Conn.: Greenwood, 1993), 115. Regarding Lemuel Shaw's Unitarianism, an early biographer reports that though Shaw sided with Unitarianism over transcendentalism and regularly attended Young's church, he declined to become a communicant. Like Melville, Shaw may have had reservations about the tenets of even liberal Protestantism; see Frederic Hathaway Chase, *Lemuel Shaw: Chief Justice of the Supreme Judicial Court of Massachusetts, 1830–1860* (Boston: Houghton Mifflin, 1918), 314–15.

5. The church changed its name to "The Unitarian Church of All Souls" in 1975; see Walter Kring, "Introduction" to *The Endless, Winding Way in Melville: New Charts by Kring and Carey*, ed. Donald Yannella and Hershel Parker (Glassboro, N.J.: Melville Society, 1981), 7.

6. Walter Kring and Jonathan S. Carey, "Two Discoveries concerning Herman Melville," *Proceedings of the Massachusetts Historical Society*, 3rd ser., 87 (1975): 138; see also Walter Kring, "Introduction," 9.

7. Walter Kring, *Herman Melville's Religious Journey* (Raleigh, N.C.: Pentland, 1997), 46–47. Kring, minister of All Souls from 1955 to 1978, held that

Unitarianism played an important role in Melville's life, but this claim has had little impact on Melville studies, perhaps because it was not accompanied by new literary interpretations of Melville's work. See Brian Yothers on this point in *Melville's Mirrors: Literary Criticism and America's Most Elusive Author* (Rochester, N.Y.: Camden House, 2011), 85.

8. See my "Mahomet's Gospel" for details.

9. David Robinson, *The Unitarians and the Universalists* (Westport, Conn.: Greenwood, 1985), 229.

10. Andrew Delbanco, *William Ellery Channing: An Essay on the Liberal Spirit in America* (Cambridge, Mass.: Harvard University Press, 1980), 53–54.

11. William Ellery Channing, *The Works of William E. Channing, D.D*, 8th ed., 6 vols. (Boston: Munroe, 1848), 3:59–103, 2:217–41, 3.227–55. A digital scan of the Channing set can be viewed on *Melville's Marginalia Online*.

12. Ibid., 1:3–68, 1:69–166, 1:167–215, 1:243–80, 2:347–411.

13. Jay Leyda, *The Melville Log: A Documentary Life of Herman Melville, 1819–1891*, 2 vols. (1951: New York: Gordian, 1969), 2:662.

14. Kring and Carey, "Two Discoveries," 139.

15. Ibid.

16. William Braswell, *Melville's Religious Thought: An Essay in Interpretation* (New York: Pageant, 1959), 7.

17. See Kring and Carey, "Two Discoveries," for the original report of Williams's membership book; Kring offers the 1884 date in his introduction to the essay's republication (5).

18. Kring and Carey, "Two Discoveries," 139.

19. Hershel Parker, *Herman Melville: A Biography*, vol. 2, *1851–1891* (Baltimore: Johns Hopkins University Press, 2002), 920–21.

20. Notable commentary on Melville and Unitarianism includes that of T. Walter Herbert Jr., who, building on William Gilman's interpretation of Allan Melvill's Unitarianism as defined by its cosmic optimism (Gilman, *Melville's Early Life*, 22–23), interprets the discrepancy between Allan Melvill's faith in God's providence and his catastrophic business failure as one source of Melville's ironic disillusionment with religion (*"Moby-Dick" and Calvinism: A World Dismantled* [New Brunswick, N.J.: Rutgers University Press, 1977], 45–56); John Seelye, who, similarly equating Unitarianism with optimism, emphasizes Melville's resistance in *Moby-Dick*, *Pierre*, and *The Confidence-Man* to Unitarian idealism and faith in social action ("*Pierre*, *Kavanagh*, and the Unitarian Perplex," in *Melville's Evermoving Dawn: Centennial Essays*, ed. John Bryant and Robert Milder [Kent, Ohio: Kent State University Press, 1997], 375–92); and Masafumi Yoneyama, who notes the affinities between Unitarian biblical criticism and the hermeneutic techniques mocked in "Jonah Historically Regarded," as well as Ishmael's parody of the principles underwriting William Paley's *Natural Theology*, which served as a Harvard textbook central to Unitarian education ("Melville's Critique of Unitarianism in *Moby-Dick* and *Pierre*," *Studies in American Literature* 36 [2000]: 15–35). Yoneyama also claims that Plotinus Plinlimmon in *Pierre* represents Unitarian utilitarianism and, more persuasively, that *Pierre* critiques Unitarian belief in the perfection of Christ and Unitarian optimism about human improvement. More recent scholarship has traced significant connections between Melville's work and Unitarian thought. See James Duban on Melville's debt to Unitarian

theology in *Clarel* and his annotations to the New Testament ("The Oracle of God Within," *Literature and Theology* 28, no. 4 [2014]: 425–37); Brian Yothers in *Sacred Uncertainty: Religious Difference and the Shape of Melville's Career* (Evanston, Ill.: Northwestern University Press, 2015) on the influence of Henry Bellows's religious progressivism and tolerance in *Clarel* (188); and my discussion in *Preaching and the Rise of the American Novel* (Columbus: Ohio State University Press, 2013) of the parallels between Channing's "Likeness to God" sermon and Ishmael's celebration of the divine unity of humanity (150–52).

21. H. Parker, *Herman Melville*, 2:896, 2:68; see also Brian Higgins and Hershel Parker, *Reading Melville's "Pierre; or, The Ambiguities"* (Baton Rouge: Louisiana State University Press, 2006), 15.

22. H. Parker, *Herman Melville*, 2:65–68, 2:69, 2:501.

23. See Kring and Carey, "Two Discoveries."

24. Ibid., 141.

25. Elizabeth Renker, "Herman Melville, Wife Beating, and the Written Page," *American Literature* 66, no. 1 (1994): 123–50; see also Elizabeth Renker, *Strike Through the Mask: Herman Melville and the Scene of Writing* (Baltimore: Johns Hopkins University Press, 1996), 49–68. Renker details how twentieth-century scholars dismissed and trivialized reliable oral histories of Melville's abuse of Elizabeth, then spells out the connection between Melville's frustrations with writing and with the women who surrounded him as he wrote.

26. Conrad Wright, *The Liberal Christians: Essays on American Unitarian History* (Boston: Beacon, 1970), 39.

27. Gary Dorrien, *The Making of American Liberal Theology: Imagining Progressive Religion, 1805–1900* (Louisville, Ky.: Westminster John Knox, 2001), 88; qtd. in Adrian Desmond and James Moore, *Darwin: The Life of a Tormented Evolutionist* (New York: Norton, 1991), 5.

28. See Barbara Packer on the motives behind the liberal Christians' split from the orthodox in the early nineteenth century ("The Transcendentalists," in *The Cambridge History of American Literature*, vol. 2, *Prose Writing 1820–1865*, ed. Sacvan Bercovitch [New York: Cambridge University Press, 1995], 331–49); Philip Gura in *The Wisdom of Words: Language, Theology, and Literature in the New England Renaissance* for an analysis of Unitarian scriptural exegesis as exemplified in the influential anti-Trinitarian polemic of Andrews Norton (Middletown, Conn.: Wesleyan University Press, 1981), 15–31; and David Robinson in *The Unitarians and the Universalists* (Westport, Conn.: Greenwood, 1985) and Dorrien in *The Making of American Liberal Theology* for comprehensive surveys of nineteenth-century Unitarian thought, a valuable complement to literary analyses of the movement focused on Unitarianism as a precursor to transcendentalism.

29. On Unitarian piety, see Dorrien, *Making of American Liberal Theology*, 41–43; and Robinson, *The Unitarians and the Universalists*, 41–42.

30. Lawrence Buell, "The Literary Significance of the Unitarian Movement," *ESQ* 33, no. 4 (1987): 212–13; see also discussions of Unitarianism throughout his *New England Literary Culture: From Revolution to Renaissance* (New York: Cambridge University Press, 1986).

31. See Walter Kring's *Henry Whitney Bellows* on the minister's opposition to slavery (vol. 2 of *A History of the Unitarian Church of All Souls* [Boston: Skinner House, 1979], 103–9).

32. Robinson, *The Unitarians and the Universalists*, 88–90.
33. Wright, *The Liberal Christians*, 83–91.
34. Henry Whitney Bellows, *The Reformed Church of Christendom, or the Duties of the Liberal Christians to the National Faith at this Crisis of Options . . .* (Boston: American Unitarian Association, 1865), 19.
35. John Fletcher Hurst, *History of Rationalism; Embracing a Survey of the Present State of Protestant Theology* (New York: Carlton and Porter, 1865), 546.
36. Kring, *Henry Whitney Bellows*, 480. The "Bond of Union" adopted in 1922 read, "In the freedom of the truth and in the spirit of Jesus we unite for the worship of God and the service of man" (ibid.).
37. Edward G. Andrew, *Conscience and Its Critics: Protestant Conscience, Enlightenment Reason, and Modern Subjectivity* (Toronto: University of Toronto Press, 2012), 12.
38. Qtd. ibid., 15–16.
39. Ibid., 23–33, 32.
40. Andrew R. Murphy, *Conscience and Community: Revisiting Toleration and Religious Dissent in Early Modern England and America* (University Park: Pennsylvania State University Press, 2001), 67. David D. Hall, ed., *The Antinomian Controversy, 1636–1638: A Documentary History*, 2nd ed. (Durham, N.C.: Duke University Press, 1990), 337.
41. See Daniel Walker Howe's *The Unitarian Conscience: Harvard Moral Philosophy, 1805–1861* for a discussion of the Enlightenment-era thinkers who shaped the ethical reasoning of the Harvard-trained men behind the Unitarian movement (1970; Middletown: Wesleyan University Press, 1988), 27–68.
42. Channing, *Works*, 3:234.
43. David Robinson, "The Legacy of Channing: Culture as a Religious Category in New England Thought," *Harvard Theological Review* 74 (1981): 228.
44. Howe, *Unitarian Conscience*, 55–56.
45. Andrew, *Conscience and Its Critics*, 6–8.
46. Henry W. Bellows, *Re-Statements of Christian Doctrine in Twenty-five Sermons* (Boston: American Unitarian Association, 1870), 94.
47. Howe, *Unitarian Conscience*, 55.
48. H. W. Bellows, *Costliness of God's Moral Government, Preached in All Souls' Church, New York. September 24th, 1871* (Baltimore: John P. Des Forges, 1871), 11. Compare Herman Melville, *Pierre; or The Ambiguities*, vol. 7 of The Writings of Herman Melville, ed. Harrison Hayford, Hershel Parker, and G. Thomas Tanselle (Evanston and Chicago: Northwestern University Press and the Newberry Library, 1971), 210–15. Further citations come from this edition.
49. That this passage in Bellows's sermon employs the same metaphor as Plinlimmon's pamphlet suggests several possible explanations beyond sheer coincidence: that Bellows had used this metaphor before and that Melville, hearing it in the late 1840s, adapted and elaborated it in *Pierre*; that Bellows read *Pierre*—plausible given the Melvilles' association with the church—and found the metaphor too good to pass up; or that both writers drew on a common source, possibly Emerson's "The Transcendentalist," which posits as advantageous "that we should now and then encounter rare and gifted men, to compare the points of our spiritual compass, and verify our bearings from spiritual chronometers" (Ralph Waldo Emerson, *Essays and Lectures*, ed. Joel Porte [New York: Library

of America, 1983], 208). Merton Sealts Jr. notes the possible influence of this line in Emerson on the guiding motif of Plinlimmon's pamphlet in *Pierre*: see *Melville's Reading*, rev. ed. (Columbia: University of South Carolina Press, 1988), 67–68.

50. Bellows, *Costliness of God's Moral Government*, 11.

51. Channing, *Works*, 1:281–332, 1:292. Other marked passages in the Melvilles' copy of Channing's *Works* that focus on conscience include "On Catholicism" (2:284:3–8), "On Spiritual Freedom" (4:70:29–32), "Self-Denial" (4:110:28–31), and "Charge for the Ordination of the Rev. John Sullivan Dwight" (5:310:1–5). Several marked passages in this last sermon share the heroic spirit of Father Mapple's peroration: e.g., "I now say, preach with moral courage. . . . Speak what you account great truths frankly, strongly, boldly" (5:309:27–31).

52. Henry David Thoreau, "Civil Disobedience," in *Walden, Civil Disobedience, and Other Writings: Authoritative Texts, Journal, Reviews and Posthumous Assessments, Criticism*, 3rd ed., ed. William Rossi (New York: Norton, 2008), 228. Theodore Parker, *The Function and Place of Conscience, in Relation to the Laws of Men; A Sermon for the Times, Preached at the Melodeon, on Sunday, September 22, 1850* (Boston: Crosby and Nichols, 1850).

53. William Shakespeare, *Hamlet: Text of the Play, the Actors' Gallery, Contexts, Criticism, Afterlives, Resources*, ed. Robert S. Miola (New York: Norton, 2011), 3.1.82. John Milton, *Paradise Lost: Authoritative Text, Sources and Backgrounds, Criticism*, ed. Gordon Teskey (New York: Norton, 2005), 3.195. Andrew, *Conscience and Its Critics*, 90–91.

54. Duban, *Melville's Major Fiction: Politics, Theology, and Imagination* (DeKalb: Northern Illinois University Press, 1983), 149–91.

55. One of the most interesting challenges in reading this novel is differentiating the narrator's voice and free indirect discourse, a novelistic strategy Melville here uses for the first time in a sustained way. The narrator warns against the error of conflating the two: "the thoughts we here indite as Pierre's are to be very carefully distinguished from those we indite concerning him" (167). Yet the line between Pierre's thoughts and those of the narratorial "we" can be exceedingly difficult to discern, often shifting within paragraphs or even sentences. Melville in this novel is slipperier than even Henry James will be, whether because psychologically subtler or simply less concerned to sort out differing subjectivities. He thus intensifies the formal ambiguity inherent in *style indirect libre*, which in blurring the line between character and narrator invites readerly identification with flawed characters: most famously, Madame Bovary; here, two years before Flaubert's scandalous novel, Pierre. Melville would revisit and refine his use of free indirect discourse in *Benito Cereno*.

56. T. Parker, *The Function and Place of Conscience*, 12.

57. H. Parker, *Herman Melville*, 2:67; see also Higgins and Parker, *Reading "Pierre,"* 16. Elsewhere I discuss why Melville may not have regarded Dewey as an outright villain: despite Dewey's failure to come out as antislavery, he was, like Melville, sensitive to art, literature, and moral complexity (Coleman, *Preaching*, 129–31).

58. See Karin E. Gedge, *Without Benefit of Clergy: Women and the Pastoral Relationship in Nineteenth-Century American Culture* for an overview of reverend rakes (New York: Oxford University Press, 2003), 80–85. The many

hypocritical ministers in mid-century fiction include the Rev. F. A. T. Pyne in George Lippard's *The Quaker City* (1845), St. John Rivers in *Jane Eyre* (1849), Arthur Dimmesdale in *The Scarlet Letter* (1850), and Nathan Warburton in Alice Cary's *Hagar* (1852).

59. Nancy Sweet, "Abolition, Compromise, and 'The Everlasting Elusiveness of Truth' in Melville's *Pierre*," *Studies in American Fiction* 26, no 1 (1998): 21. Sweet convincingly reads Pierre's moral crisis, and the pervading tension within the novel between "expediency and idealism," as a commentary on white America's moral dilemma regarding slavery (ibid., 22). Seen in this light, as a de facto apologist for the slavery-tolerating status quo, Falsgrave might indeed seem a scoundrel. Yet as Sweet details, the novel does not champion idealism, and "Melville offers no simple resolutions for a world torn between the altruistic need to adhere to a 'higher law' and the selfish need to preserve and perpetuate itself" (ibid., 23).

60. Higgins and Parker, *Reading "Pierre,"* 92.

61. Especially in light of such narratorial affirmations of Falsgrave's worthiness, we should not read the name "Falsgrave" as a shorthand for moral delinquency, as Parker does in saying it is one "Bunyan or Hawthorne might have invented" (H. Parker, *Herman Melville*, 2:67), a reading that, besides conflating Hawthorne's often ironic and shifting allegories with Bunyan's religious codes, casts Melville as unrecognizably moralistic. We might instead read the name as an allusion to the studied demeanor the prudent minister must wear in society, the polite mask that hides his social and ethical calculations, deliberations that do not in and of themselves discredit him.

62. Herman Melville, *The Piazza Tales and Other Prose Pieces, 1839–1860*, vol. 14 of The Writings of Herman Melville, ed. Harrison Hayford, Alma A. MacDougall, and G. Thomas Tanselle (Evanston and Chicago: Northwestern University Press and the Newberry Library, 1987), 38.

63. Ibid., 77.

64. Sealts, *Melville's Reading*, 177.

65. Bowden, *Dictionary*, 191.

66. Herman Melville, *Billy Budd, Sailor (An Inside Narrative)*, ed. Harrison Hayford and Merton M. Sealts Jr. (Chicago: University of Chicago Press, 1962), 80. Further citations come from this edition.

67. Here I resist the common critical inclination to regard Vere sympathetically, as a good man racked by his unfortunate duties. Andrew Delbanco, for instance, has written that Vere is "a man of 'exceptional moral quality,' who strives to uphold the law and justice" (*Melville: His World and Work* [New York: Knopf, 2005], 307). However Vere may endeavor to uphold law and justice to the best of his lights, these lights are dim given that he has, through deliberate, sustained study, made himself incapable of acting on any notion of justice that would elevate individual rights over the declared good of the state. Symptomatic of the misreading of those who admire Vere, Delbanco misquotes the novella. The narrator does not say that Vere is a man of "exceptional moral quality," but rather remarks, as Vere appraises Claggart, "Though something exceptional in the moral quality of Captain Vere made him, in earnest encounter with a fellow man, a veritable touchstone of that man's essential nature" (Melville, *Billy Budd*, 96). The point is that something "exceptional," or distinctive, in Vere's moral

nature gives him keen insight into character when dealing with a person face to face. This line draws attention to a positive aspect of Vere's character—call it intuition or judiciousness—but it is not the blanket praise Delbanco's altered quote suggests. For a less forgiving, more compelling recent interpretation of Vere's character, see Stanton Garner, *The Two Intertwined Narratives in Herman Melville's "Billy Budd": A Study of an Author's Literary Method* (Lewiston, N.Y.: Edwin Mellen, 2010).

68. See Sealts, *Melville's Reading*, on Melville's allusions to Hobbes in *Omoo* (26, 31).

69. Thomas Hobbes, *Leviathan, or the Matter, Forme, & Power of a Commonwealth Ecclesiasticall and Civil*, ed. Ian Shapiro (New Haven, Conn.: Yale University Press, 2010), 194.

70. Andrew, *Conscience and Its Critics*, 138.

71. Thomas Paine, *Rights of Man: Being an Answer to Mr. Burke's Attack on the French Revolution*, 2nd ed. (London: J. S. Jordan, 1791), 82; accessed through *Eighteenth Century Collections Online*, Gale.

72. My reading of Melville's use of involuntary bodily responses as an index to moral justice takes inspiration from Matthew Rebhorn's essay, "Minding the Body: *Benito Cereno* and Melville's Embodied Reading Practice," which discusses how Melville presents the body as shaping consciousness and rational cognition in *Benito Cereno* (*Studies in the Novel* 41, no. 2 [2009]: 157–77). In *Billy Budd* Melville pushes his theory of what Rebhorn calls "the embodied mind" further, exploring the idea that embodiment shapes not only thought, but also the putatively spiritual realm of moral reasoning.

Melville and the Mormons

Zachary McLeod Hutchins

Literary critics aware of Herman Melville's recurring interest in the doctrine and history of the Church of Jesus Christ of Latter-day Saints (LDS) have come to widely varying conclusions about the relationship between this uniquely American writer and uniquely American faith. Robert Rees suggests that Melville crafted *Mardi* (1849) as a mythic counterpoint to the Book of Mormon (1830) by drawing on Joseph Smith's account of an ancient American prophet named Alma, and Richard Rust has documented parallels between Smith and Melville, emphasizing their common quest for religious truth.[1] However, Hilton Obenzinger argues that Melville voices revulsion for Mormon doctrine and particularly "the plural wives of Nauvoo" through Nathan, the Illinois farmer of Melville's epic poem *Clarel* (1876).[2] Melville's opinion of the Mormon faith, like his opinion of religion more generally, seems to have oscillated over the course of his life.

Tracking Melville's reflections on Mormon doctrine across the trajectory of his career suggests that an initial sympathy for the LDS church transitioned to disapproval and revulsion during the 1850s, when Brigham Young and James Strang led two different branches of the sect founded by Smith in well-publicized acts of resistance to federal authority. Efforts to assess Melville's relationship with the LDS church thus depend, at least in part, on the question of which Melville one is considering—the young novelist or the seasoned lecturer and poet. Charting the course of that relationship indicates that Melville's exposure to LDS theology may have played a role in the conception of both *Mardi* and *Pierre* (1852) and suggests that Melville is more indebted to the Mormon imaginary than readers have previously supposed.

From New York to Nauvoo

As an adolescent coming to maturity in Albany, just east of the intense revivalism consuming New York's Burned-over District, Melville probably learned at a relatively young age about Smith and the Mormon church he founded in Fayette, New York, on April 6, 1830. Just three weeks later Smith's first volume of scripture, an abridged translation of writings by ancient American prophets, came under attack by *The Rochester Republican* in a column reprinted by other New York papers: "BLASPHEMY.—'*Book of Mormon*' alias *The Golden Bible* . . . . The 'author and proprietor' is one Joseph Smith Jr. . . . The volume consists of about 600 pages, and is divided into the books of Nephi, of Jacob, of Mosiah of Alma, of Mormon, of Ether, and of Helaman."[3] Confronted with a wave of negative publicity, Smith and many of his followers moved to Ohio in 1831, but New York newspapers continued to track this native son and the religious movement he had sparked. During a proselytizing trip to New York City in October 1832, Smith stopped to preach in Albany where a teenaged Melville spent the fall working as a bank clerk while a cholera epidemic raged in the city—divine punishment, Smith suggested in a contemporary revelation, for the wickedness of Albany's inhabitants.[4]

Resistance to Smith's calls for repentance, together with the financial panic of 1837, eventually forced him to leave Ohio for Missouri, where a war between church and state soon erupted.[5] New York newspapers reprinted accounts from Missouri that painted Mormon suffering at the hands of the state in pathetic terms, deprecating the executive order issued by Missouri governor Lilburn Boggs calling for "the *expulsion or extermination* of the Mormons," and reports that "the Mormons were set upon and murdered" led at least one correspondent to the conclusion that "the poor deluded Mormons are 'more sinned against than sinning,' in the matter of this war."[6] Subsequent reports described the unjust and inhumane treatment of Smith and his followers in detail:

> The Mormons upon the approach of the mob sent out a white flag, which being fired on by the mob, Jo Smith and [Sidney] Rigdon, and a few other Mormons of less influence, gave themselves up to the mob. . . . The prisoners being secured, the mob entered the town and perpetrated every conceivable act of brutality and outrage—forcing fifteen or twenty Mormon girls to yield to their brutal passions!![7]

Forced to abandon their property in the dead of winter, Missouri Mormons fled across the icy Mississippi River to Commerce, Illinois, where Smith eventually rejoined them, after spending several months in prison. Melville, who would later identify empathetically with Smith's suffering and exiled followers, may have read these and other newspaper accounts or, during a trip to Illinois in the summer of 1840, heard the story firsthand.

Leon Howard and John W. Nichol have persuasively argued that Melville's journey from upstate New York via the Erie Canal and Great Lakes to Galena, Illinois, where his uncle, Thomas Melvill Jr., lived, included a journey down the Mississippi River to Cairo, Illinois, during his return east; such a trip would have taken Melville past—and perhaps into—the bustling port city of Commerce, which Smith had renamed Nauvoo.[8] In July 1840, when Melville likely arrived in Illinois, Missouri mobs had crossed the river to renew their attacks on the Mormon refugees, kidnapping and beating four

Illinois church members before hanging one until he nearly died. Newspapers across the country carried accounts of the violence and it seems all but certain Melville would have heard local discussions of the attack.[9] Exacerbating the suffering caused by mob violence and a local recession was the fact that Nauvoo had been built on a mosquito-infested marsh, and Smith's congregants suffered a debilitating outbreak of malaria in the summer of 1840. If Melville did make his way into the growing port city, he would have found a people beset by enemies without and devastated by illness within, huddling in half-completed buildings.

After his return to Lansingburgh, New York and his eventual departure for the Pacific aboard the *Acushnet* in early 1841, Melville likely lost track of domestic news of the Mormons, but upon his return, he learned of their continued clashes with frontier settlers from Francis Parkman's *The California and Oregon Trail* (1849). By 1846, mobs had murdered Smith and once again driven the Mormon community from their homes in Nauvoo. Under the direction of Young most members of the fledgling church packed up their meager belongings and trekked across the prairies to the solitude of present-day Utah, and Melville found a brief account of their desert wanderings in Parkman's narrative. Melville's 1849 review of Parkman peopled the west with "the veritable grandsons of Daniel Boon; with the Mormons; with war-parties; with Santa Fe traders; with General Kearney; with runaway United States troops; and all manner of outlandish and interesting characters."[10] Parkman's travelogue describes most pioneers "as good Christians and as zealous Mormon-haters" who fear violence from "the much-dreaded Mormons," but his accounts of actual encounters with Latter-day Saint refugees hardly live up to this advanced billing. When Parkman finally meets with a band of Mormon settlers outside Fort Pueblo, they seem far more interested in complaining about their trials and laboring to establish yet another homeland than in threatening others:

> After half an hour's riding, we saw the white wagons of the Mormons drawn up among the trees. Axes were sounding, trees were falling, and log-huts going up along the edge of the woods and upon the adjoining meadow. As we came up the Mormons left their work and seated themselves on the timber around us, when they began earnestly to discuss points of theology, complain of the ill-usage they had received from the "Gentiles," and sound a lamentation over the loss of their great temple of Nauvoo. After remaining with them an hour we rode back to our camp, happy that the settlements had been delivered from the presence of such blind and desperate fanatics.[11]

Parkman's conclusion about the Latter-day Saints—violent, desperate fanatics—is the product of prior reporting and prejudice rather than his own experience; he has already sided with the "Mormon-haters." But Melville, who seems to have read Parkman with his 1840 excursion through Mormon country in mind, retained a more sympathetic perspective.

Curiously, Melville's review of Parkman—who really has very little to say about the Mormons—inserts the Latter-day Saints into a section of the narrative from which Parkman had excluded them. Melville writes that Parkman's company boards "a steamer, crammed with all sorts of adventurers, Spaniards and Indians, Santa-Fe traders and trappers, gamblers and Mormons" (*Piazza Tales*, 232). However, the passage Melville must have had open in front of him when he paraphrased Parkman is devoid of Mormons; Parkman's steamboat holds "Santa Fé traders, gamblers, speculators, and adventurers of various descriptions, and her steerage was crowded with Oregon emigrants, 'mountain men,' negroes, and a party of Kanzas Indians."[12] One possible explanation for this odd insertion is that Melville incorporated his own memories of a Mississippi steamboat trip past the Latter-day Saint settlement at Nauvoo into Parkman's account, synthesizing textual and personal experience. Whatever the motive that moved Melville to incorporate additional mentions of the Mormons in his review, he clearly had the Latter-day Saints on his mind in 1849.

Alma, Abraham, and an Apostolic Church

Melville's awareness of and apparent sympathy for Mormon suffering may have been induced or augmented by one of the many newspaper articles written by Thomas Kane in 1848 and 1849. Matthew Grow notes that Kane, a non-Mormon apologist for the church, wrote of the Saints' suffering in such pathetic terms that among New England intellectuals, it briefly became "fashionable to sympathize with the downtrodden Mormons." Figures such as Wendell Phillips, Ralph Waldo Emerson, Walter Channing, and John Greenleaf Whittier encouraged Kane in his apologetics.[13] Melville's insertion of Mormon exiles into his review of Parkman, and his subsequent sympathetic identification with Mormon suffering in an 1850 letter to Evert Duyckinck thus reflects his participation within a larger current of popular opinion.

In contemplating the critical and popular failure of his third novel, which some reviewers subjected to harsh criticism, Melville compared the banishment of *Mardi* to the serial expulsions of Smith, Young, and their followers from New York, Ohio, Missouri, and Illinois. As he wrote his friend Duyckinck in early February 1850 to present him with a copy of the novel:

> Again: (as the divines say) political republics should be the asylum for the persecuted of all nations; so, if Mardi be admitted to your shelves, your bibliographical Republic of Letters may find some contentment in the thought, that it has afforded refuge to a work, which almost everywhere else has been driven forth like a wild, mystic Mormon into shelterless exile.[14]

This empathetic association with the LDS refugees deprecated by Parkman suggests that Melville viewed the Mormon church collectively as a type of Ishmael banished to the desert by Abraham, a figure with whom he would identify in *Moby-Dick*.[15] In 1850, whatever Melville thought about the doctrines taught by Smith and Young, he could not help but recognize his own desires for intellectual freedom in their flight to the west.

Robert Rees offers substantial evidence suggesting that Melville had read portions of the Book of Mormon by 1850 and that he was both familiar with and sympathetic to its teachings. Smith's first volume of scripture contains a history of several ancient prophets who led multiple groups of religious seekers from the Levant to the Americas and from thence to the islands of "the west sea"—to Polynesia.[16] This Mormon explanation for the sacred origins of Native peoples populating the Americas and Pacific islands would have intrigued a young Melville returning from the Marquesas and the Sandwich Islands in 1844, and textual parallels between *Mardi* and the Book of Mormon suggest that he may have used this volume of American scripture as one source of inspiration for the mythologies that fill his third novel.[17] As Rees argues, a Mormon influence seems particularly apparent in Melville's account of Alma, the prophet and Christ figure worshipped in Maramma and Serenia—two of the many islands visited by Melville's protagonist Taji and his companions (Media, a king; Babbalanja, a philosopher; Mohi, a historian; and Yoomy, a poet) in their archipelagic wanderings.

In the Book of Mormon, which describes a visit made by the resurrected Jesus Christ to the Americas, the ministry and teachings of two prophets named Alma (Alma the Elder and Alma the Younger, a father-son pair) comprise the volume's longest narrative and its center. Numerous similarities between this pair and Melville's Alma, first noted by Rees, suggest that *Mardi* is at least partially indebted to the Book of Mormon:

> The most important parallel between Melville's Alma and the Mormon Almas is that both are clearly associated with Christ. In addition, both are prophets and teachers; both rebuke kingship to administer to the poor; both are concerned with regenerating the heathen; both condemn prayer without righteous living; both emphasize that it isn't necessary to worship in temples or synagogues; and both are concerned over those of high station.[18]

Beyond these parallels noted by Rees, both Melville's Alma and the Mormon Almas are introduced at the burning of religious heretics.

In the Book of Mormon, Alma the Elder is introduced as a wicked priest who has perverted Christian teachings to his own benefit. When a true Christian arrives to condemn Alma and his fellow false priests, Alma's peers sentence the Christian to death by fire.[19] Alma objects to the sentence handed down by his peers and for protesting is likewise condemned to die. However,

Alma escapes the flames, and guilt-stricken at the death of this martyr, he repents and dedicates his life to Christ. Alma the Younger, like his father, strays as a youth, persecuting Christians until he is converted to the faith by a vision of Jesus. After this experience Alma the Younger becomes a missionary and, in his journeys, witnesses the fiery martyrdom of Christians condemned by corrupt officials: "And they brought their wives and children together, and whosever believed or had been taught to believe in the word of God they caused that they should be cast into the fire." Alma's missionary companion, Amulek, urges him to draw on the power of God and halt the immolations, but God forbids Alma, explaining that he allows these innocents to be killed because they go to a heavenly reward and so "that the judgments which he shall exercise upon [their tormentors] in his wrath, may be just."[20] In the Book of Mormon, both Almas condemn the burning of believers by corrupt officials who have perverted the doctrines of Christ but cannot intervene; their only recourse is a demonstration of true Christian living.

In *Mardi*, Melville's Alma—a Christlike figure who teaches the people of Mardi to worship Oro, a type of God the Father—is likewise associated with the burning of heretics at the first appearance of his adherents on the island of Maramma. When Taji and his companions explore the island, they find a priest chastising a young man for talking out of turn: "let him speak no more; but bow down, and grind the dust where he stands; and declare himself the vilest creature that crawls. So Oro and Alma command."[21] The youth rejects this directive together with the associated doctrines of original sin and innate depravity, insisting that "because [Oro] is thus omnipotent, and I a mortal, it follows not that I am vile. Nor so doth he regard me. We do ourselves degrade ourselves, not Oro us" (*Mardi*, 347). For this apparently heretical speech, Alma's followers on Maramma commit the boy to flames. Yoomy, like Amulek pleading with Alma the Younger, begs Media to use his authority as king and command the killers to stop, but Media, like Alma, demurs. Disturbed by this murder and the memory of similar crimes, Babbalanja rejects the worship of Alma, at least in part because his "own sire was burnt for his temerity, and in this very isle? Just Oro! It was done in the name of Alma" (*Mardi,* 349–50). Babbalanja's father, unlike Alma the Elder, has not escaped death by fire. But like Alma the Younger, this skeptical and rebellious Babbalanja eventually embraces the teachings of Alma—Christ—through a vision. When Melville's travelers reach the island of Serenia, Babbalanja initially hesitates to dock at "that land of enthusiasts," a place where "Mardians pretend to the unnatural conjunction of reason with things revealed; where Alma, they say, is restored to his divine original" (*Mardi,* 622–23). But on Serenia Babbalanja learns that the priests of Maramma have perverted the Christian teachings of Alma and experiences a vision that converts him to the true faith. When Taji, Media, Mohi, and Yoomy sail on, they leave Babbalanja behind on Serenia, a convert to the doctrines of Alma.

The Mormon parallels in Melville's novel multiply if *Mardi* is read in the context of other revelations received and taught by Smith. Babbalanja's vision includes an account of pre-mortal existence at odds with prevailing nineteenth-century conceptions of life before birth but consistent with doctrine revealed by Smith in his translation of Egyptian papyrus scrolls purportedly narrating the life of Abraham. Smith's followers bought the papyri, with four mummies, from a traveling showman named Michael Chandler in July 1835; on one of the scrolls Smith found and translated an account of Abraham's life in Egypt as an astronomer in the court of Pharaoh.[22] For the rest of his life, Smith proudly displayed the mummies and papyri to visitors, and several 1840 travelers to Nauvoo reported hearing the prophet explain the story associated with these objects. A writer from Quincy, Illinois recalled his own introduction to the papyri, when Smith

> walked to a secretary, on the opposite side of the room, and drew out several frames, covered with glass, under which were numerous fragments of Egyptian papyras, [*sic*] on which, as usual, a great variety of hierogryphical [*sic*] characters had been imprinted. These ancient records, said he, throw greater light on the subject of Christianity. . . . There, said he, pointing to a particular character, that is the signature of the patriarch Abraham.[23]

Smith's translation of these hieroglyphics includes a discourse on "Kokaubeam, which signifies stars, or all the great lights, which were in the firmament of heaven." Melville's possible exposure to Smith's ideas about Abraham and Egyptian astronomy during his 1840 travels through the Mormon homeland of Illinois may be hinted at in his 1850 letter to Duyckinck.[24] Immediately after comparing *Mardi* to "a wild, mystic Mormon," Melville suggests that his friend tie "a bit of old parchment (from some old Arabic M.S.S. on Astrology) . . . round each volume" of the novel (*Correspondence*, 154). In the 1840s, Joseph Smith may have owned the only manuscript in the United States close to this description, so Melville's transition from Mormons to ancient Near Eastern reflections on astrology either represents a remarkable coincidence or a recollection of Melville's own visit to Nauvoo, where curious newcomers regularly viewed Smith's collection of Egyptian artifacts.[25]

The heterodox content of Babbalanja's vision in *Mardi*, which reinscribes one of Mormonism's most unusual doctrines, is also worth consideration. As Melville's philosopher soars through the heavens, he see "spirits in their essences; sad, even in undevelopment. With these, all space is peopled;—all the air is vital with intelligence, which seeks embodiment" (*Mardi*, 636). Belief in an existence before birth had, as Terryl Givens notes, experienced a resurgence in the nineteenth century behind the rise of romantic and transcendentalist philosophers. But even the doctrine's most prominent and radical advocates represented the shift from a spiritual life into mortality as a tragedy. For example, when William Blake's Thel experiences mortality with the option of returning to her pre-mortal state, she "recoils with a shriek and flees back to the safety of Har."[26] Melville's characterization of the shift from a spiritual preexistence to embodiment as a positive form of progress that alleviates sorrow matches Mormon belief but diverges from virtually every other conception of a pre-mortal life. Even the Neoplatonic influence of Dante's *Paradiso*, a major source for *Mardi*'s mystic symbolism, cannot account for Melville's conception of life before birth.[27]

In the Book of Abraham, Smith characterizes the transition into mortality as a reward for the faithful and an opportunity to progress towards theosis. Speaking in the voice of this eponymous patriarch, Smith declares that

> the lord had shewn unto me, Abraham, the intelligences that were organized before the world was; and among all these there were many of the noble and great ones, and God saw these souls that they were good, and he stood in the midst of them, and he said, these, I will make my rulers. . . . and he said unto those, who were with him, we will go down, for there is space there, and we will take of these materials, and we will make an Earth whereon these may dwell.[28]

This material incarnation is a reward that alleviates the sorrow of disembodied spirits because, as Smith taught, "spirit and element inseperably [*sic*] connected receiveth a fullness of Joy, and when separated man cannot receive a fullness of Joy."[29] Smith's monism rejects the Christian and Platonic identification of materiality as an inherently corrupt condition and dismisses representations of the Fall as a tragedy: "Adam fell, that men might be; and men are, that they might have joy."[30] Givens describes this Mormon belief in embodiment as the benevolent development of disembodied spirits, together with a rejection of original sin, as a "unique" combination in theological and philosophical history, but Melville's description of Alma worship in *Mardi* likewise lumps the rejection of original sin with the joyous incarnation of preexistent spirits under a single theological rubric.[31] Either Melville independently invented an original theological system strikingly similar to that outlined by Smith less than a decade earlier or *Mardi* is more indebted to Mormon thought than readers have previously acknowledged.

As his first sustained foray into the realm of the romantic imagination, *Mardi* represents a significant moment in Melville's intellectual development, and the Mormon presence in that novel is suggestive.[32] Even if he thought of the Book of Mormon and Smith's account of Abraham as nothing more than fables, Melville may have recognized in those additions to and revisions of scripture a model for the mythologies of *Mardi*. By comparing the novel to "a wild, mystic Mormon" and suggesting it be bound in an old Arabic astrologer's parchment, Melville may have hinted at the book's origin as much as its reception, belatedly recognizing that a public which had rejected Smith's new American mythologies as blasphemy would be unlikely to accept an allegory informed by the emerging Mormon canon. This apparent incorporation of ideas from Smith's new scriptures suggests that Melville had already consciously modeled his first soarings into the realm of imagination and prophecy after the creative flights of another American seer.[33]

After the composition of *Mardi* and the Parkman review, Melville's interest in Mormonism apparently disappeared during the writing of *Redburn* (1849), *White-Jacket* (1850), and *Moby-Dick* (1851), only to surface again with *Pierre* (1852).[34] In *Pierre*, Melville depicts an enigmatic philosopher named Plotinus Plinlimmon, like the philosopher Babbalanja in *Mardi*, confronted with LDS doctrine and scripture. But instead of following Babbalanja's example by converting, when Plinlimmon receives a package containing "a very fine set of volumes—Cardan, Epictetus, the Book of Mormon, Abraham Tucker, Condorcet and the Zend-Avesta," the philosopher returns his gift unopened.[35] Unlike Babbalanja, who renounces his itinerant life for the peace of Serenia, Plinlimmon decides that he has no need for Mormon or any other religious doctrine, having already found a home in the Church of the Apostles—a rundown structure now converted into apartment and office space. Being a resident of the Apostles, as Melville suggests the complex was commonly known, Plinlimmon and every other resident is already "familiarly styled an *Apostle*" and by association they collectively become

> organized in a peculiar society, which, though exceedingly inconspicuous, and hardly perceptible in its public demonstrations, was still secretly suspected to have some mysterious ulterior object, vaguely connected with the absolute overturning of Church and State, and the hasty and premature advance of some unknown great political and religious Millennium. (*Pierre*, 268–69)

Pierre Glendinning also takes up residence in the Apostles, where he lives with a small group of women including Isabel, an allegedly long-lost half-sister pretending to be his wife and for whom he feels an incestuous attraction; Delly Ulver, a serving-woman whose sexual indiscretions have left her friendless and in need of Pierre's protection; and eventually Lucy Tartan, Pierre's rejected former fiancée. Melville's mention of Mormon scripture, together with his focus on nineteenth-century incarnations of the primitive apostolic church and his portrayal of an apparently polygamous household, suggests that he was re-creating the scandalous moral history of the Latter-day Saints in *Pierre*.

Plinlimmon's refusal to open a package containing the Book of Mormon might seem an implicit condemnation of LDS doctrine and principles. However, in a novel whose eponymous protagonist staunchly defends moral absolutism and chronometrical ideals, rejection by a horological relativist such as Plinlimmon may actually be a tacit endorsement of Smith's scripture and the other volumes contained in that package.[36] In his representation of Plinlimmon, a hypocrite who forbids his followers to drink wine but drinks freely himself, Melville anticipates the satirical attacks of *The Confidence-Man* (1857) against the temperance movement, transcendentalist philosophy, and evangelical religion. But as Bruce Rosenstock argues with respect to *Pierre*, Melville's denunciation of corrupt social reformers does not preclude a concomitant belief in the pursuit of an idealized "America as the symbol of a rebirth of faith."[37] Pierre dedicates his life to the ethics of Christ's Sermon on the Mount in pursuit of that dream and dies in its defense, a victim of social mores forbidding the presumptive immorality of his cohabitation with Isabel, Delly, and Lucy.

Discussions of the deviant sexual behaviors hinted at in *Pierre* are both long-standing and wide-ranging. Contemporary readers condemned the novel for promoting incest on two fronts. As Duyckinck complained in his review of *Pierre*, "Mrs. Glendinning and Pierre, mother and son, call each other brother and sister, and are described with all the coquetry of a lover and mistress. And again, in what we have termed the supersensuousness of description, the horrors of an incestuous relation between Pierre and Isabel seem to be vaguely hinted at."[38] Modern readers have elaborated on the possible motivations for Melville's scandalous depiction of incest and argue that the novel dramatizes homoerotic desire; but few have addressed the presumptive sexual crimes for which Pierre was ostracized by other characters in the novel itself.[39]

When Lucy's mother comes to dissuade her daughter from living with Pierre, Isabel, and Delly, she suggests that this living arrangement makes a mockery of holy matrimony. Addressing Isabel, she spits, "And for thee, madam, I have no words for the woman who will connivingly permit her own husband's paramour to dwell beneath her roof. For thee frail one [Delly], thou needest no amplification.—A nest of vileness! And now, surely, whom God himself hath abandoned forever [Lucy], a mother may quit, never more to revisit" (*Pierre*, 329). The assumption of Lucy's mother, her brother Frederic, and her scorned lover Glen Stanly is that all three women are willing sexual partners for Pierre. Melville's readers may have been outraged by the author's intimations of incest, but most of the characters in his novel have no notion of Isabel's problematic relationship with Pierre; within the novel's pages, the sexual crime for which society condemns Pierre, Isabel, Lucy, and Delly is that of an unsanctified but recognizably biblical polygamy.[40] In other words, the infamy of Pierre's incestuous obsession with Isabel has obscured the more immediate crime: his participation in an apparently polygamous relationship.[41] In Lucy's mother, Melville thus provides an early representation of the horror that elective polygamy inspired in non-Mormon American citizens. As Nancy Bentley relates, after Utah Mormons publicly embraced polygamy in 1852, the "specter of white women apparently choosing to enter polygamous marriages confounded fundamental beliefs of the novel-reading public." Lucy's choice to move in with Delly, Isabel, and Pierre captures the moral dilemma faced by a society learning that women sometimes willingly chose to enter polygamous relationships.[42]

In the weeks after Lucy's addition to the household, Pierre, Isabel, and Lucy remain in their small apartment so that Pierre can work feverishly on the book that he is writing, but when they finally leave its confines, they do so as a threesome, with Pierre in the middle and a woman on either side. Lucy meekly offers to leave the ostensibly married couple alone, walking before the pair, but he insists: "'Nay, one on each arm'—said Pierre—'come!'" Melville provides a witness to this polygamous picture when "a cheek-burnt, gamesome sailor passing, exclaimed—'Steer small, my lad; 'tis a narrow strait thou art in!'" (*Pierre*, 349). Lucy misunderstands the sailor's remark and assumes that this stranger simply meant to comment on the narrowness of the street, but Melville's language here points to the problem of Pierre's romantic attachment to both Isabel and Lucy. From the sailor's perspective, by attempting to squeeze two women into the position that society dictates can only be occupied by one partner at a time, Pierre has made the "strait" of marriage look narrow indeed.

But with this anonymous sailor's words, Melville also seems to sanctify Pierre's apparent polygamy, endorsing his attempt to live a chronometric Christian lifestyle. Melville's characterization of Pierre's polygamous dilemma as a "narrow strait" carries with it an obvious nautical connotation but also recalls the exhortation of Jesus Christ: "strait is the gate, and narrow is the way, which leadeth unto life, and few there be that find it" (Matt. 7:14). Thus Pierre's presumptive sexual excesses and apparent polygamy are ironically sanctioned by his Christian absolutism. A central problem of *Pierre*, as Ellen Weinauer argues, is that of marriage—of "owning women."[43]

In the early months of 1852, when Melville finished *Pierre*, polygamy was a practice that had come to be identified by non-Mormons as a defining characteristic of the LDS church. Rumors that Mormons had abandoned monogamy circulated during the time of their exodus to Utah, but sympathy for their suffering and the apologetics of Thomas Kane had forestalled condemnation. In an 1850 essay, Whittier acknowledged popular speculation surrounding Mormon sexual practices, then dismissed that speculation in the face of Kane's assurances and Brigham Young's able leadership: "They have shrewd, intelligent men at the head of affairs, and are evidently losing a great deal of the fanaticism of their early time. . . . The author of the 'Discourse' before us, denies emphatically the charges which have been preferred against their habitual purity of life." In the spring of 1851, another editorialist in the Pittsfield *Sun* praised the "Mormon founders of Deseret [for] doing what the Puritans did in Massachusetts two centuries ago," celebrating the industry of LDS pioneers.[44] But by 1852, the tide of public opinion had turned against Young and the Mormons, as Congress objected to the admission of Utah as a state "on the ground that the Mormon religion—particularly that feature recognizing polygamy—is anti-Republican."[45] Orson Pratt, a Mormon apostle, would not officially embrace and publicly defend the doctrine on behalf of the church until August 1852, but the existence of Mormon apostles with multiple wives was an open secret in the months and years prior to that announcement.[46] Along with his friend Nathaniel Hawthorne, whose *Blithedale Romance* was written and published at approximately the same time as *Pierre*, Melville was immersed in the contemporary discourse on marriage and familiar with multiple sects advocating free love, but his intimations of polygamy in *Pierre* are paired with other theological positions widely associated with the LDS church.[47]

If, in the 1850s, polygamy was a distinguishing feature of the LDS church, the faith's other infamous and distinctive feature was its insistence that modern-day prophets and apostles worked miracles and guided the church just as they had in biblical times. In the character of Pierre, an honorary Apostle and polygamist by virtue of his living arrangements, Melville combined the defining characteristics of contemporary Mormon belief. A possible return to the Mormon background of *Mardi* makes sense because, in Pierre's labors as an ambitious but unsuccessful romantic writer, Hershel Parker has found a figure of Melville in the throes of writing *Mardi*: Pierre's struggle to write a great work of literature is "something like a melodramatic version of [Melville's] own immature attempt to write a mature book, *Mardi*."[48] Pierre seems like an honorary Mormon at least in part because the Melville who wrote *Mardi* had self-identified with Mormon suffering and the grandiosity of Smith's religious imagination. But whereas *Mardi*, the Parkman review, and the Duyckinck letter seem to represent an interest in Mormon doctrine and history, *Pierre* seems more like an autopsy of that interest. The Melville who narrates Babbalanja's unexpected conversion experience seems genuinely intrigued in the prospect of inexplicable spiritual occurrences that culminate in serenity—Serenia—despite the accompanying social ostracism. The Melville who describes Pierre's conversion to "chronometrical" ideals is less interested in the prospect of experiencing religious conviction than in analyzing the mental processes by which such conviction arrives.

Almost unanimously, Melville's reviewers complained that the processes by which Pierre arrived at his decisions—to accept Isabel as his sister, renounce Lucy, declare Isabel his wife, and later accept Lucy into their household—were irrational and immoral. Charles Hazewell in the Boston *Daily Times*, for example, denounced the novel as "a miserable affair. There is nothing rational or probable, hardly anything possible, about it. The motives for the conduct of any of the parties are such as would consign the best of them to the madhouse."[49] But Pierre's apparent irrationality was not, as Hazewell implied, a failure of Melville's creative faculties; rather, Melville intentionally designed his novel as an examination of the human desire to make intuitive ethical judgments, rather than reason, the basis for action.[50] Neither the Mormon belief in revelation, apostles, and polygamy, nor, for that matter, any act grounded in religious faith, can be reduced to strictly rational grounds, and Melville's construction of an irrational Pierre demonstrates that fact. *Pierre* implicitly condemns the Mormon faith specifically and Christianity generally as irrational, even as it acknowledges a compelling human desire for supra-rational, chronometrical ethical ideals to which we can aspire. If Pierre's irrational, headlong plunge into the trappings of Mormonism represents Melville's desire for ethical and metaphysical certainty, Pierre's ostracism and suicide indicates the author's awareness that pursuing such certainty would inevitably lead to undesirable consequences. That disrepute and death are the result of Pierre's irrational religious quest signals Melville's own reluctant prioritization of reason over religion.

Melville seems to have respected the zeal that pushed Pierre into heading an apparently polygamous household within the Apostles (*Pierre*, 283). But whatever lingering empathy or admiration Melville might have felt for suffering Mormon polygamists, driven with their apostolic leaders into exile for their religious convictions, faded in the years following the publication of *Pierre*. The sympathy of Melville and others, aroused by newspaper coverage of the Mormon expulsion from Nauvoo during the late 1840s, quickly eroded with reports of Mormon criminality and resistance to federal authority.[51]

The Politics of Polygamy

Because multiple claimants to Smith's authority had arisen in the wake of his death, the actions of many different LDS communities were commonly attributed to Mormons. Sensational news about the two largest groups, led by Brigham Young in the Utah territory and James Strang in Michigan, regularly appeared in Pittsfield, Massachusetts newspapers. Thus Melville, perusing the *Sun*, might have read that Strang's "Mormons have been committing numerous depredations on the fishermen, burning their dwellings, robbing them of their fish in barrels, destroying their salt, and stealing their nets, boats, clothes, money, and provisions" without realizing that this group differed from Utah "Mormons who [having] a conscientious conviction of the right and necessity of more wives than one, may excuse his violation of law, upon the same plea which is offered to the man who disobeys the Fugitive Slave Law."[52] The attribution of Strangite criminality to the generic label "Mormon" made it difficult for an average citizen to distinguish the generally passive resistance of Utah Mormons from acts of violence attributed to other LDS splinter groups.[53] Notwithstanding this confusion, Melville seems to have made an attempt to differentiate between the followers of Young and Strang in their movements. *The Confidence-Man* (1857) thus acknowledges the existence of both groups. Travelers on the riverboat *Fidèle* remark on the presence of a "Green prophet from Utah" as well as a city called the New Jerusalem "in northern Minnesota . . . originally founded by certain fugitive

Mormons."[54] Neither group is given much attention by Melville, but his brief description of these Mormon outposts is certainly less condemnatory than his treatment of other social groups and institutions in the novel, and much kinder than contemporary Republican political discourse, which characterized polygamy and slavery as twin relics of barbarism.[55] Melville's willingness to differentiate between the two groups without condemning either suggests that he remained an informed and relatively neutral observer of the splintered Mormon community.

This differentiation between Strang and Young in 1856, when Melville wrote *The Confidence-Man*, is a demonstration of personal interest in the niceties of two distant religious groups, but familiarity with Mormon movements would become a matter of public interest and civic duty between 1857 and 1858, when it briefly appeared that Utah—and not South Carolina—would be the first member of the Union to secede. After William Drummond resigned from Utah's territorial Supreme Court in March 1857, he accused Young, in his capacity as Utah's governor, of undermining the rule of law, federal authority, and the republic itself. In response, the newly elected James Buchanan authorized a military expedition to quell Young's putative Mormon rebellion.[56] The Utah War, as this excursion and its associated skirmishes came to be known, captured the attention of a nation. Reporters warned in the fall of 1857 that Young's Utah Mormons "will receive material aid from the Indians, and their ultimate design is to throw off all allegiance to the Union and establish themselves as an independent Government."[57] Fear-mongering journalists reported wildly inaccurate accounts of Mormon military capabilities, describing the importation of secret devastating weapons from Russia to Utah by LDS scientists and forecasting a general uprising by allied Native American nations in Oregon and Washington.[58] As a result, public sentiment against Young's Saints built to a crescendo, and this threat of Mormon-induced political instability, even more than the public distaste for polygamy, seems to have been the trigger that turned Melville against Mormonism.[59]

When Melville returned to the lecture circuit in December 1858 with an address on "The South Seas," he offered a brief but emphatic condemnation of the Latter-day Saints in his presentation. In the wake of Young's resignation in April 1858 as Utah governor and the triumph of federal power, Melville speculated that the Saints might seek refuge in the South Seas:

> The Mormons of Salt Lake City have likewise thought of these secluded islands upon which to increase and multiply—or this has been recommended to them, showing the drifting of the imagination in that direction. . . . As for the plan suggested not long since, of making a home for the Mormons on some large island in Polynesia, where they could rear their pest houses and be at peace with their "institutions," the natives will resist their encroachments as did the Staten Islanders that of Quarantine. If sensible men wish to appropriate to

> themselves an uninhabited isle, that is all right, but I do not know of a populated island in the hundred millions of square miles embraced in the South Seas where these "fillibusterers" would not be imperatively and indignantly expelled by the natives. (*Piazza Tales*, 417)[60]

On the one hand, Melville's criticism demonstrates an awareness of Mormon theology when he correctly suggests that the biblical command to "multiply, and replenish the earth" (Gen. 1:28) motivates Mormon polygamy instead of ascribing the practice to an unnatural Orientalist lust, as did so many of his contemporaries.[61] On the other hand, Melville no longer seems to care—as he did in *Pierre*—about the motivations for apparently irrational religious behavior. By 1858 the negative effects of Mormon conduct had become more important to Melville than the causes.

Melville's characterization of polygamy and associated Mormon doctrines as an infectious plague signals the final and complete dissolution of an earlier sympathetic identification with Smith's followers. But the terms of this disavowal suggest that Melville breaks with the Mormons over politics more than religion. In casting Young's Mormon followers as filibusterers, Melville allies the LDS community with the revolutionary efforts of William Walker, a United States citizen who organized military expeditions aiming to seize control of Nicaragua and Honduras in the 1850s.[62] Melville undoubtedly knew very well that popular rumor identified Sonora, Mexico, as the likely destination of Young's Mormon refugees—not some South Pacific island.[63] In the last months of 1858, when Melville began speaking on "The South Seas," Sonora was also rumored to be Walker's next target, establishing a tie between Mormons and this face of filibustering.[64] Melville's address solidifies that link and confirms an essentially Republican association between slavery and polygamy.

By 1858, because the Utah Saints were almost universally unpopular, both the Republican and Democratic parties sought to identify the other's adherents as Mormon-sympathizers. Notwithstanding the Republican platform of 1856, which termed polygamy barbaric, Democratic propaganda sought to characterize Mormon conceptions of marriage as essentially Republican: "The only part of the Union that stands out against the democracy and the administration of Buchanan is Utah. . . . This will form a nucleus for the republicans in 1860. In the meantime, if they are not successful in promulgating their opinions, they have only to wait for their Mormon brethren to propagate them."[65] Republicans, for their part, alleged that Democrats tacitly endorsed Mormon resistance by withholding government support for a military solution to Young's rebellion:

> Next, upon the filibuster question and the Utah army bill, we find the Southern fire eaters among the most intractable and inconsistent of filibusters. In the one case they are ready to involve the country in all

> the perils of a general war; in the other they are so very squeamish that they cannot vote a few regiments of troops to restore law and order among the Mormons and Indians for fear of creating an army dangerous to the liberties of the country. Such are the stultifications of our hair-splitting fire eaters of the South.[66]

By identifying the Saints and filibustering as linked evils, Melville sides with the Republican Party in this political struggle. Democrats generally supported filibuster activity as a potential means of introducing slave-holding territories and states into the Union, so Melville's condemnation of filibustering as a Mormon tool of degenerative cultural imperialism works as an implicit critique of Democratic positions.[67] His discussion of Mormon relocation plans thus offers an early hint of Melville's dissent from the traditional family affiliation with the Democratic Party, in addition to illustrating his shift from sympathy to antipathy for the Latter-day Saints.[68]

Although the Utah War thrust Mormon theology to the center of public consciousness in 1857 and 1858, the conflict's anticlimactic resolution—Young's peaceful, if somewhat delayed, abdication of the governorship—together with the escalation of hostilities between North and South, soon left the Saints in relative obscurity. Melville might eventually have heard his brother-in-law, John Hoadley, recount the story of a private interview with Young in 1872, granted when Hoadley passed through Salt Lake City, or he might have listened to his sisters, Fanny and Catherine, describe their experiences among polygamists on the same trip. After the interview, Hoadley concluded that

> the inevitable individuality of man, will bunch them up into a half a dozzen [*sic*] societies of varying manners, some of which will take their place among the various dissenting denominations, and become as harmless and inoffensive as Ana-Baptists, Pseudo Baptist, Campbellites, Moravians, Dunkers, Quakers, Shakers, Sanderainians [?], Swedenborgians, who knows what?[69]

By the end of the Civil War, the Mormon threat to conventional American mores and political sovereignty had largely passed; neither Melville nor the general public would again find the Mormons so compelling as they had in the 1840s and 1850s. There is, accordingly, little reason to think that Melville's private opinion of the Mormons changed substantially between 1858 and his death in 1891.

A lack of ongoing interaction did not prevent Melville from including observations on Mormon life and culture in the poems of his later years. In *Clarel*, as Hilton Obenzinger has noted, the Jewish convert, Holy Land settler, and former Illinois farmer named Nathan rejects the Mormon faith, apparently repulsed by rumors of polygamy. The LDS community in Nauvoo apparently disturbs Nathan:

a sect about him stood
In thin and scattered neighborhood;
Uncanny, and in rupture new;
Nor were all lives of members true
And good. For them who hate and heave
Contempt on rite and creed sublime,
Yet to their own rank fable cleave—
Abject, the latest shame of time;
These quite repelled, for still his mind
Erring, was of no vulgar kind.[70]

If we accept Nathan's opinion as Melville's, the author's youthful interest in Mormon cosmology had, by 1876, given way to derision. The excesses of Mormon sectarianism, theology, and polygamy, features that Nathan characterizes as heaving contempt on the sublime rites and creeds of Christianity, now induced revulsion in Melville.

In the 1870s, anti-polygamy sentiment in the United States intensified, shaped by two decades of anti-Mormon lecturers and the eyewitness testimony of young girls like Elizabeth Cotton. After converting to the Mormon faith in England and emigrating to Utah, Cotton wrote a letter describing the horrors of polygamy that circulated widely:

> Many of the men have eight or ten wives, and he sleeps with one two nights and another two nights, and so on, and this is Mormonism. . . . What they preach about is———, thieving, and cutting anybody's throat, and if you ask anything about it you are told it is none of your d—d business. I know one young woman of 15, who has had four husbands in five months, and that gives you an idea of Mormonism.[71]

Cotton's letter and similarly inflammatory depictions of polygamist excess displaced any public sympathy for Mormon suffering with righteous indignation.

In his poetry of the 1880s, when Melville metaphorically represents the sexual excesses of Oriental harems, he accordingly links those sexual transgressions to Mormon polygamy. His understanding of the causes of polygamy had shifted since 1858, when he attributed the practice to obedience to the biblical mandate of Genesis. Describing a Persian rose farmer who casually deflowers stems just as they are budding, Melville represents widespread unrest: "What agitation! Every rose / Bridling aloft the passionate head!" Pressed for the reason these roses rebel against the farmer's treatment, Melville's narrator responds, "Pray ask of her who'll hint it clear— / A Mormon's first-wife making moan."[72] The rumored sexual predation of adolescent girls only confirmed Melville in rejecting Mormon polygamy, albeit whimsically in this case. By the end of his life, Melville believed that the practice had more to do with lust than with a "strait" religious dictate.

Melville's apparent dismissal of biblical rationales for polygamy likely also reflects a prolonged shift toward religious skepticism. In "The New Ancient of Days," Melville satirically forecasts the ultimate displacement of religion by science, portraying the rise of a fossilized skeleton who attempts to overthrow religious leaders. As the animated man of bone narrates humanity's descent from crabs and apes, Melville depicts his plot to unseat the pope, Joseph Smith, the Buddha ("Jos"), and Mohammed ("Mahone"), among other religious leaders:

> Obstreperous grown, he'd fain dethrone
> Joe Smith, and e'en Jones Three;
> Against even Jos and great Mahone
> He flings his fossiliffer's stone
> And rattles his shanks for glee.
> I'll settle these parvenu fellows, he-he!

Even as he proclaims the ascendance of this living fossil, Melville seems disturbed at the prospect of scientism unseating religion, asking if, by a "Hyena of bone," the "Great Pope" and "the Grand Pan-Jam be overthrown / With Joe and Jos and great Mahone, / . . . then, my masters, where should we be?"[73] Darwin's doctrine of natural selection forces Melville to imagine a world lorded over by hyenas, hardly a match for the imaginative vistas of Serenia and Babbalanja's vision of a Mormon-like pre-mortal life four decades earlier. This posthumously published poem, Melville's final word on Mormon theology and culture, acknowledges an innate desire for ecclesiastical "masters" or a divine God who can place human life in an eternal perspective; that he would identify the Mormon Church as a religious tradition comparable to the Roman Catholic Church, Buddhism, or Islam is a testament to Melville's perception of the movement's significance. But "The New Ancient of Days" also frankly depicts the difficulty of reconciling religious yearnings with a rational reading of the extant fossil record. Melville thus ends his life and his relationship with Mormon theology in an ideological no-man's land, caught in the crossfire between scientific evidence and spiritual desire.

A Posthumous Coda

Melville's death in 1891 changed the terms of his engagement with the Mormon faith. Unable to voice his opinions about Smith's followers from the grave, he effectively ceded control of the relationship, and on May 3, 1924, Herman Melville was posthumously baptized, by proxy, a member of the Church of Jesus Christ of Latter-day Saints; Mormons claimed Melville as their own.[74] The novelist who penned *Mardi* might have welcomed a posthumous induction into the Church of Jesus Christ of Latter-day Saints, grateful that his wandering soul, like his third novel, had found refuge in a welcoming asylum. But the lecturer and poet seems likely to have taken a dimmer view of his presence in the "pest houses" reared by polygamous unions—notwithstanding the church's official renunciation of polygamy in 1890, just before Melville's death.

Still, there is reason to believe that the mature Melville would have tolerated and perhaps welcomed posthumous baptism, if only because the sacrament signifies his continuing presence in the celebrant's memory. When a young man unaffiliated with any religious sect dies in *Clarel*, Catholic friars "had held to unprotesting lips / In mistimed zeal the crucifix." This posthumous conversion is "criticised" by "some," but also seems to fulfill the dead man's deepest desire: "Remember me! for all life's din / Let not my memory be drowned" (I.40.12–13, 20, 25–26). Melville had so long survived his brief fame as the man who lived among the cannibals that one obituary mistakenly dubbed him Henry Melville; he might have welcomed the knowledge that *someone* would remember him thirty years after his death, even if it was the Mormons.

More importantly, the Mormons who saw to his posthumous baptism were family—or at least seemed to think so. Reflecting again on the attribution of religion to the dead, Melville almost endorses the practice in the words of Rolfe, the character most often identified with Melville himself, as a harmless comfort to the living:

> if at this spent man's death-bed
> Some kind soul kneeled and chapter read—
> Ah own! to moderns death is drear,
> So drear: we die, we make no sign,
> We acquiesce in any cheer—
> No rite we seek, no rite decline.
> Is't nonchalance of languid sense,
> Or the last, last indifference?
> With some, no doubt, 'tis peace within;
> In others, may be, care for kin:
> Exemplary thro' life, as well
> Dying they'd be so, nor repel. (*Clarel* I.40.51–62)

Those responsible for Melville's entry into the ranks of the wild, mystic Mormons believed themselves to be kin gathering the lost souls of their relatives; his soul was not seized by spiritual "filibusterers" colonizing the afterlife. Church policy in the 1920s required that all posthumous baptisms be approved by a relative of the deceased, and one Alexander Melville is listed on the form authorizing Herman's entry into a Mormon afterlife.[75] A common ancestor for the two men has not surfaced, and Alexander likely claimed Herman as a cousin without documentary evidence of the relationship, but both have roots in the Scottish county of Fife; so a family bond may yet be uncovered.[76]

When Alexander Melville and his relatives brought the author of *Moby-Dick* into the LDS church, they seem to have done so with the intent of welcoming a long-lost family member home. When queried, Alexander Melville's surviving posterity could not recall that their ancestor had any particular appreciation for his putative cousin's works. The Melville Revival didn't include a precocious Utah chapter; the Mormons seem to have been less interested in what Melville thought of them than in providing an asylum for his wandering soul—as Duyckinck had, years earlier, given refuge to *Mardi*.

Notes

The author would like to thank Tim Marr, Ed Whitley, Kylan Rice, Richard Rust, Sam Otter, Eliza Richards, the many librarians at Brigham Young University, and the editors of this volume for their assistance, questions, and feedback; it is an essay bettered by their generous aid.

1. See Robert A. Rees, "Melville's Alma and the Book of Mormon," *Emerson Society Quarterly* 43, no. 2 (1966): 41–46; Richard Dilworth Rust, "'I Love All Men Who Dive': Herman Melville and Joseph Smith," *BYU Studies* 38, no. 1 (1999): 151–69.

2. Hilton Obenzinger, *American Palestine: Melville, Twain, and the Holy Land Mania* (Princeton, N.J.: Princeton University Press, 1999), 100.

3. "Blasphemy," *Ithaca Journal,* April 28, 1830, 3. On the American tradition of pseudobiblical writings within which the Book of Mormon falls, see Eran Shalev, *American Zion: The Old Testament as a Political Text from the Revolution to the Civil War* (New Haven, Conn.: Yale University Press, 2013), 84–117.

4. Richard Lyman Bushman, *Joseph Smith: Rough Stone Rolling* (New York: Alfred A. Knopf, 2006), 188. The Smith revelation announces that "I the Almg [Almighty] have laid my hand up on the nations to scourge them for there wickedness and plagues shall go forth and it shall not be taken from the earth." Subsequent passages specifically identify Albany, Boston, and New York as havens of wickedness. See *Revelation Book 2* in *The Joseph Smith Papers* (Church Historian's, 2013), 38–40, josephsmithpapers.org.

5. Just months after Smith left Ohio in January 1838, local mobs attempted to burn down the Mormon temple in Kirtland but mistakenly fired a nearby Methodist church instead. See "Church Burnt by Mistake," *The Emancipator,* June 21, 1838, 31.

6. "The Mormons," *Hudson River Chronicle,* November 27, 1838, 2. Other commentaries reciprocally accused the Mormons of inhumane depredations; see "News!! from the St. Louis Gaz," *Hudson River Chronicle,* November 20, 1838, 2.

7. "Horrible Revelations!" *The Mercury and Weekly Journal of Commerce,* January 3, 1839, 4.

8. Leon Howard, *Herman Melville: A Biography* (Berkeley: University of California Press, 1951), 37; John W. Nichol, "Melville and the Midwest," *PMLA* 66,

no. 5 (1951): 613–25. For a more comprehensively documented account of this journey, see Hershel Parker, *Herman Melville: A Biography,* vol. 1, *1819–1851* (Baltimore: Johns Hopkins University Press, 1996), 166–79.

9. See "Horrible Outrage," *New-Bedford Mercury,* August 7, 1840, 1.

10. Herman Melville, *The Piazza Tales and Other Prose Pieces, 1839–1860*, ed. Harrison Hayford, Alma A. MacDougall, and G. Thomas Tanselle. (Evanston and Chicago: Northwestern University Press and the Newberry Library, 1993), 233. Citations from this edition will appear hereinafter in the text.

11. Francis Parkman, *The Oregon Trail*, ed. William R. Taylor (New York: Library of America, 1991), 39, 87, 275; see also 333.

12. Parkman, *The Oregon Trail*, 10. Spaniards are not mentioned in this particular quote but, unlike Mormons, appear two paragraphs later in Parkman's prose.

13. Matthew J. Grow, *Liberty to the Downtrodden: Thomas L. Kane, Romantic Reformer* (New Haven, Conn.: Yale University Press, 2009), 84; Whittier penned a positive review of Kane's 1850 pamphlet, *The Mormons*, for the *National Era* that was republished in the Pittsfield *Sun* just days before Melville moved to Arrowhead in October 1850. See John G. Whittier, "Miscellaneous," *The Pittsfield Sun,* October 3, 1850, 1.

14. Herman Melville, *Correspondence*, ed. Lynn Horth (Evanston and Chicago: Northwestern University Press and the Newberry Library, 1993), 154. Smith himself may have been one of the divines that Melville had in mind. Smith regularly lamented that the republic did not protect him or his people from persecution, arguing that the Constitution's singular flaw is that, "although it provides that all men shall enjoy religious freedom, yet it does not provide the manner by which that freedom can be preserved . . . those who have the misfortune to be weak or unpopular are left to the merciless rage of popular fury." Of course, Melville's words also seem to echo Thomas Paine, whose deist leanings were anything but divine: "This new world hath been the asylum for the persecuted lovers of civil and religious liberty from *every part* of Europe." See Joseph Smith, *Joseph Smith's Teachings: A Classified Arrangement of the Doctrinal Sermons and Writings of the Great Latter-day Prophet*, ed. Edwin F. Parry (Salt Lake City, Utah: Deseret News, 1912), 24; Thomas Paine, *Thomas Paine Reader*, ed. Michael Foot and Isaac Kramnick (New York: Penguin Books, 1987).

15. See Ilana Pardes, *Melville's Bibles* (Berkeley: University of California Press, 2008), 73–97. More broadly, this implicit link between Mormons and Ishmael (Muhammad's ancestral connection to Abraham) reflects contemporary characterizations of Mormons as Muslims; see Timothy Marr, *The Cultural Roots of American Islamicism* (New York: Cambridge University Press, 2006), 6, 185–218.

16. The Book of Mormon, trans. Joseph Smith Jr., ed. Laurie F. Maffly-Kipp (New York: Penguin, 2008), 412.

17. The earliest documented claim that Polynesian islanders, like Native Americans, were descended from Book of Mormon peoples came in 1851, but the establishment in 1844 of proselytizing missions to the Society Islands suggests that this doctrine may have earlier roots. See Norman Douglas, "The Sons of Lehi and the Seed of Cain: Racial Myths in Mormon Scripture and Their Relevance to the Pacific Islands," *Journal of Religious History* 8, no. 1 (1974): 99–104; R. Lanier Britsch, *Moramona: The Mormons in Hawaii* (Laie, Hawaii: Institute for

Polynesian Studies, 1989); John-Charles Duffy, "The Use of 'Lamanite' in Official LDS Discourse," *Journal of Mormon History* 34, no. 1 (2008): 118–67; Hokulani K. Aikau, *A Chosen People, a Promised Land: Mormonism and Race in Hawai'i* (Minneapolis: University of Minnesota Press, 2012).

18. Rees, "Melville's Alma and the Book of Mormon," 44–45.

19. The Book of Mormon, 192–94.

20. Ibid., 266–67.

21. Herman Melville, *Mardi; and a Voyage Thither*, ed. Harrison Hayford, Hershel Parker, and G. Thomas Tanselle (Evanston and Chicago: Northwestern University Press and the Newberry Library, 1970), 346–47. Citations from this edition will appear hereinafter in the text.

22. A synthetic account of this translation of Abraham is available in H. Donl Peterson, *The Story of the Book of Abraham: Mummies, Manuscripts, and Mormonism* (Salt Lake City, Utah: Deseret Book, 1995). Since the rediscovery of fragments of Smith's papyri in the twentieth century, Egyptologists have identified one of the texts from which Smith produced his account of Abraham as the "Breathing Permit of Hor." See Robert K. Ritner, "'The Breathing Permit of Hor' Thirty-four Years Later," *Dialogue* 33, no. 4 (2000): 97–119.

23. Quoted in Peterson, *The Story of the Book of Abraham*, 185.

24. "The Book of Abraham," *Times and Seasons,* March 15, 1842, 720. On Smith's astronomy in the Book of Abraham, see Bushman, *Joseph Smith: Rough Stone Rolling*, 452–58.

25. Maxine Moore argues that Melville derived his understanding of astrology primarily from contemporary almanacs and contends that the Duyckinck letter discloses an "astrological riddle" in the book. See Maxine Moore, *That Lonely Game: Melville, "Mardi," and the Almanac* (Columbia: University of Missouri Press, 1975).

26. Terryl L. Givens, *When Souls Had Wings: Pre-Mortal Existence in Western Thought* (New York: Oxford University Press, 2010), 244–45.

27. On Melville's use of Dante in Babbalanja's vision, see "Melville's Copy of Dante: Evidence of New Connections between the *Commedia* and *Mardi*," in *Studies in the American Renaissance 1993*, ed. Joel Myerson (Charlottesville: University Press of Virginia, 1993), 305–38, especially 325–30.

28. "The Book of Abraham," 720.

29. See *Revelation Book 2* in *The Joseph Smith Papers*, 67, josephsmithpapers.org.

30. The Book of Mormon, 64.

31. Givens, *When Souls Had Wings: Pre-Mortal Existence in Western Thought*, 217.

32. Merrell Davis dates the shift in *Mardi* from travelogue to fiction back to the spring of 1848, and it is at least possible that this is the date at which Melville read the Book of Mormon, alongside Shakespeare, Montaigne, and Coleridge, at the relative beginning of his self-administered education in literature. See Merrell R. Davis, *Melville's "Mardi:" A Chartless Voyage* (New Haven, Conn.: Yale University Press, 1952), 62–63.

33. For some reason, Rowland Sherrill leaves *Mardi* out of his consideration of Melville as a self-conscious prophet, a puzzling omission given that this novel is the first to leave the realm of practical prediction and soar into the ethereal and

unknowable; any account of Melville as prophet should begin with *Mardi* and his exposure to figures such as Smith and William Miller. See Rowland A. Sherrill, *The Prophetic Melville: Experience, Transcendence, and Tragedy* (Athens: University of Georgia Press, 1979).

34. Of course, Melville's insistence that *Moby-Dick* is a new, American gospel opens the possibility that Melville's magnum opus began as a second, more successful attempt to follow Smith's example in offering an original volume of American scripture. On the biblicality of *Moby-Dick* see Jonathan A. Cook, *Inscrutable Malice: Theodicy, Eschatology, and the Biblical Sources of "Moby-Dick"* (DeKalb: Northern Illinois University Press, 2012).

35. Herman Melville, *Pierre, or The Ambiguities*, ed. Harrison Hayford, Hershel Parker, and G. Thomas Tanselle (Evanston and Chicago: Northwestern University Press and the Newberry Library, 1971), 291. Citations from this edition will appear hereinafter in the text.

36. Rees, "Melville's Alma and the Book of Mormon," 41–42; on Melville's portrayal of Plinlimmon as satire, see Brian Higgins, "Plinlimmon and the Pamphlet Again," *Studies in the Novel* 4 (1972): 27–38.

37. Bruce Rosenstock, "Melville's Transcendentals: Kant and Radical Evil in *Pierre; or the Ambiguities*," *Leviathan* 12, no. 3 (2010): 33.

38. Evert A. Duyckinck, in *Herman Melville: The Contemporary Reviews*, ed. Brian Higgins and Hershel Parker (New York: Cambridge University Press, 1995), 431.

39. For the most recent discussions of incest in *Pierre*, see Paul Hurh, "The Sound of Incest: Sympathetic Resonance in Melville's *Pierre*," *Novel* 44, no. 2 (2011): 249–67; and Wendy Stallard Flory, "Melville and Isabel: The Author and the Woman Within in the 'Inside Narrative' of *Pierre*," in *Melville and Women*, ed. Elizabeth Schultz and Haskell Springer (Kent, Ohio: Kent State University Press, 2006), 121–40. On the novel's homoerotic elements, see James Creech, *Closet Writing/Gay Reading: The Case of Melville's "Pierre"* (Chicago: University of Chicago Press, 1993).

40. Pierre is explicitly linked to Old Testament patriarchy and polygamy by his own allusions to the plight of Esau: "Pierre cursed himself . . . because he had himself, as it were, resigned his noble birthright to a cunning kinsman for a mess of pottage, which now proved all but ashes in his mouth" (*Pierre* 289). The birthright that Pierre has resigned is his potential marriage to Lucy; he has become an Esau figure and, like Esau, ends up bringing three women into his household—first two outcasts (Judith and Bashemath in the Bible, Delly and Isabel in the novel) and then a choice more appropriate to his lineage (Mahalath in the Bible, Lucy in the novel). See Genesis 26:34, 28:9. My analysis here is partially indebted to a conference paper presented by Joseph Meyer at the 2013 convention of the American Literature Association.

41. One contemporary reviewer may have alluded to Pierre's polygamy in describing the novel's controversial passages as "pleasant excursions into Mahomet's paradise." See "New York *Herald*, 18 September 1852," in *Herman Melville: The Contemporary Reviews*, 438.

42. Nancy Bentley, "Marriage as Treason: Polygamy, Nation, and the Novel," in *The Futures of American Studies*, ed. Donald E. Pease and Robyn Wiegman (Durham, N.C.: Duke University Press, 2002), 342. That nineteenth-century

Mormon women willingly chose to enter polygamous relationships was demonstrated by Belinda Marden Pratt, *Defence of Polygamy, by a Lady of Utah, in a Letter to Her Sister in New Hampshire* (Salt Lake City, 1854). For a discussion of Eliza R. Snow's poetic defense of LDS views on gender, see Edward Whitley, *American Bards: Walt Whitman and Other Unlikely Candidates for National Poet* (Chapel Hill: University of North Carolina Press, 2010), 67–112.

43. Ellen Weinauer, "Women, Ownership, and Gothic Manhood in *Pierre*," in *Melville and Women*, ed. Elizabeth Schultz and Haskell Springer (Kent, Ohio: Kent State University Press, 2006), 142.

44. Whittier, "Miscellaneous," 1; "What They Think of Uncle Sam Abroad," *The Pittsfield Sun,* March 6, 1851, 3.

45. "Thirty-Second Congress," *The Pittsfield Sun,* April 8, 1852, 2.

46. See David J. Whitaker, "The Bone in the Throat: Orson Pratt and the Public Announcement of Plural Marriage," *Western Historical Quarterly* 18 (1987): 293–314.

47. Beyond the marital experiments conducted at Brook Farm and in Salt Lake City, a community of perfectionists in Oneida, New York, and proponents of free love in Indiana also attracted national attention for their unusual sexual practices.

48. Hershel Parker, *Herman Melville: A Biography,* vol. 2, *1851–1891* (Baltimore: Johns Hopkins University Press, 2002), 84.

49. "[Charles Creighton Hazewell]. Boston *Daily Times*, 5 August 1852," in *Herman Melville: The Contemporary Reviews*, 422.

50. On the intentional obscurity and ambiguity of Melville's language in *Pierre*, see Elizabeth Duquette, "*Pierre*'s Nominal Conversions," in *Melville and Aesthetics*, ed. Samuel Otter and Geoffrey Sanborn (New York: Palgrave Macmillan, 2011), 117–36.

51. On the proliferation of anti-Mormon sentiment in the 1850s, see Gary L. Bunker, *The Mormon Graphic Image, 1834–1914: Cartoons, Caricatures, and Illustrations* (Salt Lake City: University of Utah Press, 1983); and Terryl L. Givens, *The Viper on the Hearth: Mormons, Myths, and the Construction of Heresy* (New York: Oxford University Press, 1997).

52. "Mormon Depredations," *The Pittsfield Sun,* June 9, 1853, 2; "Legal Resistance to Unrighteous Law," *The Pittsfield Sun,* June 22, 1854, 2.

53. There were, of course, violent acts committed by Utah Mormons—most notably the Mountain Meadows Massacre. My point is simply that potential sympathy for Young's followers in their largely nonlethal resistance to federal authority was eroded by the misdeeds of Strang's disciples because both groups were referred to as Mormons; differentiation was difficult. On the Mountain Meadows Massacre, see Will Bagley, *Blood of the Prophets: Brigham Young and the Massacre at Mountain Meadows* (Norman: University of Oklahoma Press, 2002); and Ronald W. Walker, Richard E. Turley Jr., and Glen M. Leonard, *Massacre at Mountain Meadows* (New York: Oxford University Press, 2008).

54. Herman Melville, *The Confidence-Man; His Masquerade*, ed. Harrison Hayford, Hershel Parker, and G. Thomas Tanselle (Evanston and Chicago: Northwestern University Press and the Newberry Library, 1984), 7, 50.

55. See Sarah Barringer Gordon, *The Mormon Question: Polygamy and Constitutional Conflict in Nineteenth-Century America* (Chapel Hill: University of North Carolina Press, 2002).

56. For a brief synopsis of Drummond's role in provoking the Utah War, see Michael S. Durham, *Desert between the Mountains: Mormons, Miners, Padres, Mountain Men, and the Opening of the Great Basin* (Norman: University of Oklahoma Press, 1997), 203–6.

57. "The Mormons Preparing to Fight," *The Pittsfield Sun,* November 5, 1857, 2.

58. "The Mormon Infernal Machine," *The Pittsfield Sun,* November 19, 1857, 1; "From California &c.," *The Pittsfield Sun,* February 18, 1858, 2.

59. As Peter Coviello recently recalled so forcefully, nineteenth-century anti-polygamy rhetoric characterized the institution as a means of enslaving white women; cast in these terms, it seems almost inevitable that the author of *Benito Cereno* and "The 'Gees" would eventually come to reject polygamy. See Peter Coviello, *Tomorrow's Parties: Sex and the Untimely in Nineteenth-Century America* (New York: New York University Press, 2013), 104–28.

60. Melville's speech links Mormons to the advocates of free love, a tie that might plausibly derive in part from a newspaper article that appeared in the weeks immediately preceding his first lecture on the South Seas. See "Indiana Divorce," *The Pittsfield Sun,* November 25, 1858, 2.

61. On Oriental representations of Mormon polygamy, see Marr, *The Cultural Roots of American Islamicism*, 202–18.

62. On the filibustering movement more broadly, see Rodrigo Lazo, *Writing to Cuba: Filibustering and Cuban Exiles in the United States* (Chapel Hill: University of North Carolina Press, 2005).

63. For reports that Young and Utah Mormons would emigrate to Sonora, see "Late and Important from Utah," *The Pittsfield Sun,* June 17, 1858, 3; "In a Letter to Secretary Cass," *The Pittsfield Sun,* June 17, 1858, 2; "From the Utah Army," *The Pittsfield Sun,* July 15, 1858, 3.

64. One warning that Walker would invade Sonora can be found in "The Scare-crow Walker," *San Francisco Bulletin,* September 16, 1858, 2.

65. "The Only Part of the Union," *The Pittsfield Sun,* December 24, 1857, 2.

66. "The Difficulties of the Administration," *The New York Herald,* April 9, 1958, 4.

67. On Mormons, filibustering, and Sonora, see also "The Western Territories," *The Pittsfield Sun,* December 17, 1857, 1; and "The Mormon Question," *The Deseret News,* February 17, 1858, 398.

68. Melville's mother characterized the clan as "a Democratic family" in trying to secure Herman a political appointment during the 1850s. See Parker, *Herman Melville: A Biography,* vol. 2, *1851–1891*, 346.

69. Quoted in Parker, *Herman Melville: A Biography,* vol. 2, *1851–1891*, 742. Parker's transcription of "Sanderainians" is almost certainly an error for "Sandemanians," a sect founded in eighteenth-century Scotland and practicing primitive Christianity.

70. Herman Melville, *Clarel; A Poem and a Pilgrimage*, ed. Harrison Hayford, Alma A. MacDougall, Hershel Parker, and G. Thomas Tanselle (Evanston and Chicago: Northwestern University Press and the Newberry Library, 1991), I.17.183–92. Citations from this edition will appear hereinafter in the text.

71. Elizabeth Cotton, "What an English Girl Thinks of Mormonism," *The Pittsfield Sun,* May 20, 1858, 1.

72. Herman Melville, *Collected Poems of Herman Melville*, ed. Howard P. Vincent (Chicago: Hendricks House, 1947), 308.

73. Melville, *Collected Poems*, 376. The authoritative, forthcoming Northwestern-Newberry edition of Melville's unpublished poems replaces "Jos" with "Fos," a plural and vernacular reference to the Buddha; Robert Madison, an editor of that volume, provided this helpful clarification of the text.

74. "Index Card to Salt Lake Temple Records," No. 15862, Book 27, Page 556, in the *Temple Index Bureau* collection, Microfilm 1263221, Harold B. Lee Library, Brigham Young University. The LDS church teaches that all posthumously performed ordinances must be accepted by the spirit of deceased recipients, which means that from a Mormon perspective the church did not claim Melville so much as extend him a personal invitation to heaven.

75. "Index Card to Salt Lake Temple Records," No. 15862, Book 27, Page 556, in the *Temple Index Bureau* collection, Microfilm 1263221, Harold B. Lee Library, Brigham Young University. Problematically, these records also indicate that Alexander (1821–1911) was dead by the time Herman was posthumously inducted into the church; it is unclear whether Alexander gave his consent for Herman's baptism while still alive or whether one of Alexander's sons and grandsons authorized the baptism in his father or grandfather's name. One of Alexander's great-grandsons, James Keith Melville, was a proxy in the 1934 baptism of Herman's brother Allan. See "Index Card to Salt Lake Temple Records," No. 19997, Book [illegible], Page 952, in the *Temple Index Bureau* collection, Microfilm 1263221, Harold B. Lee Library, Brigham Young University. Herman Melville's baptism also does not conform to several of the regulations regarding the posthumous induction of members that were subsequently issued in 1934. These regulations specified that baptism could only be authorized by direct descendants; to ensure compliance, those performing the rite were encouraged to specify their relations to the dead. Alexander Melville is listed as a "relative" of Herman Melville, a term that was acceptable but discouraged because of its vagueness. See *The Development of LDS Temple Worship, 1846–2000: A Documentary History*, ed. Devery S. Anderson (Salt Lake City, Utah: Signature Books, 2011), 235–37.

76. Herman Melville was a descendant of Thomas Melville (1700–1769) of Fife, and Alexander Melville was born in Fife, though many of his Melville ancestors hailed from Midlothian.

Melville's Asia, Melville's Missionaries

Brian Yothers

That Herman Melville was an outspoken critic of missionaries, and especially the American Protestant missionaries celebrated by many of his more conventionally devout contemporaries in the United States, is so well established as to be a commonplace in Melville scholarship. Perhaps because the point seems moot, particularly in relation to the early years of Melville's career as a writer, some of the more obscure as well as more positive aspects of Melville's engagement with the nineteenth-century missionary encounter have yet to be fully explored. In what follows, I consider how Melville wrestled with the vital cultural and religious issues raised by the encounter between European and North American missionaries and the peoples of Asia, Africa, and the South Pacific, not just in his first two novels, but throughout his long and varied career. I begin and end, not with the South Sea narratives *Typee* and *Omoo*, but with Melville's representations of missionaries from his career as a poet, most centrally in his long poem *Clarel*. Starting from this unusual vantage point, it is possible to see how the missionary encounter informs Melville's career as a whole and to come to a more comprehensive and accurate view of some of his complex religious engagements and negotiations with his era.

Starting with a text like *Clarel*, which is less frequently discussed than Melville's prose fiction and is less discursive in its commentary on missionaries than *Typee* and *Omoo*, may seem an odd choice, but it also provides a corrective to our frequent tendency to neglect the latter portion of Melville's career, or to assume a straightforward trajectory from Melville the youthful radical to Melville the older and increasingly conservative poet. What I mean to show here is the way in which certain strands in Melville's religious thought remain consistent even as they develop, and beginning with the author of *Clarel* in his fifties rather than the author of *Typee* and *Omoo* in his twenties affords us a better vantage from which to view his career in its entirety. For Melville, the relationship between religious skepticism and ethical passion is always both ambivalent and intense. Melville's representations of missionaries, both as antagonists and as exemplars of a human character type that can be viewed with sympathy and admiration as well as satire and irony, serve as an excellent microcosm of his broader religious thought. Meanwhile, one of Melville's central themes, the dialogues among cultures, is highlighted early and late in his representations of missionaries.

Most centrally, what starting with *Clarel* shows us is that Melville's fundamental concern when representing missionaries is not a conventional critique of hypocrisy or fanaticism. Rather, Melville's objection to Christian missions reflects his antipathy toward the idea of conversion as the solution to cultural and religious difference and his embrace of a wide-ranging pluralism, and by the time Melville published *Clarel* in 1876, his pluralism had become sufficiently capacious that he could honor his erstwhile adversaries even while satirizing their conversionist intent. Meanwhile, as the story of Titus Coan and his son Titus Munson Coan that I discuss at the end of this essay shows, at least some of the missionaries could find room for Melville in a similarly ambivalent embrace, thus illustrating the way in which nineteenth-century culture wars could become folded into less confrontational negotiations. The story of Melville and the missionaries thus becomes, not a morality tale of faith versus infidelity or obscurantism versus progress, but rather of a series of accommodations with difference that helps to explain Melville's complex cultural dialogue with the faiths of Asia, a dialogue that receives its most extensive treatment in *Clarel* but persists throughout his career.

Reading Nehemiah, Holy Land Missionary

Melville's 1876 poem *Clarel* examines, with irony and anguish, the confrontation of Protestant Christianity with other traditional Christian faiths and the religious traditions of Asia. As such, it captures a central strand of Melville's career, from its beginning with *Typee* to its posthumous conclusion in *Billy Budd* and Melville's other unpublished works. For Melville, the dissensions within Christianity and the confrontation between Christianity and alternative religious traditions from around the world inform his writing and his religious thought at every stage of his career, and in *Clarel* this obsession becomes manifest as never before or after. If the confrontation between Christianity and its religious competitors and among the faith traditions within Christianity is central in *Clarel*, the mechanism that makes it so, both thematically and dramatically, is the missionary encounter. Melville narrates such encounters throughout his career, from the bitter anti-missionary satire that often recurs in *Typee* and *Omoo* to the quizzical ironies of *Moby-Dick*, the short fiction, and *The Confidence-Man*. Melville's representation in *Clarel* of both the Protestant missionary Nehemiah and the religious traditions of the Holy Land provides an important frame for understanding the role of the missionary encounter in Melville's work.

Like some of the other long poems of the American and British nineteenth century—we may consider Robert Browning's *The Ring and the Book* as a transatlantic corollary—*Clarel* often challenges critics because of its ambition and complexity. It provides, however, a kind of key to central questions about religion, nationalism, human self-development, and the nature of art that recur across Melville's career. The fact that the elderly American missionary Nehemiah is integral to the plot through much of the first half of Melville's 18,000-line verse novel suggests just how crucial the missionary encounter is to all these questions; and Melville's persistent representation of Asian religious traditions, especially in dialogue with Nehemiah's ill-fated missionary endeavors, illustrates how much the missionary encounter is bound up with questions of interreligious and cross-cultural dialogue for Melville.

Melville's title character, a young American theology student tormented by doubt, meets Nehemiah after he has already had considerable opportunity to question his inherited faith. In a very short time, he has been exposed to the bewildering range of options for religious belief in Asia: Jewish, Muslim, Roman Catholic, and Eastern Orthodox residents and pilgrims all embody differing faiths, and all suggest possibilities for doubt that are shaped by the traditions from which they spring. Moreover, when Clarel reflects on the various pilgrims he sees in Palestine (Jewish immigrants from America and India, Roman Catholic and Eastern Orthodox Christians visiting the Church of the Holy Sepulcher, Muslim pilgrims leaving Jerusalem for Mecca), he also considers those pilgrimages that he can see only in his mind's eye: the Hindu pilgrimage to the Ganges and Buddhist pilgrimages in China. He finds this urge to pilgrimage and religiously motivated travel more generally expressive of a general human tendency—an "intersympathy of creeds"—that cuts across religious traditions, an observation that, as William Potter suggests, places comparative religion at the thematic core of Melville's narrative poem.[1] At the same time, Clarel recognizes in some of the pilgrims a manifestation of disappointment, doubt, and disillusionment—a corresponding ecumenical tendency toward skepticism—that appears to transcend the bounds of virtually any single religious tradition.

When Nehemiah appears, then, Clarel is seeking an experience of transcendence that can reframe all his doubts and uncertainties (and by extension the uncertainties of some of the multireligious, multicultural, and multiethnic seekers he has encountered) within the context of faith. He seeks this experience through pilgrimage itself, in hopes that the land of Palestine can communicate spiritual truths by means of his physical presence. Immediately before he meets Nehemiah, Clarel contemplates the story in the Gospel of Luke of Christ's post-resurrection meeting with his disciples at Emmaus:

> "Christ lived a Jew, and in Judea
> May linger any breath of him?
> If nay, yet surely it is here
> One best may learn if all be dim."
> Sudden it came in random play
> "Here to Emmaus is the way;"
> And Luke's narration straight recurred
> How the two falterers hearts were stirred

Meeting the Arisen (then unknown)
And listening to his lucid word
As here in place they traveled on.
That scene, in Clarel's temper, bred
A novel sympathy, which said—
I too, I too; could *I* but meet
Some stranger of a lore replete,
Who, marking how my looks betray
The dumb thoughts clogging here my feet,
Would question me, expound and prove,
And make my heart to burn with love,
—Emmaus were no dream today! (1.7.52–53)[2]

This passage is worth quoting at length because of the light it sheds on the reasons that Melville uses an American Protestant missionary as Clarel's initial guide in the Holy Land. The passage begins with an invocation of place as a source of knowledge: Jesus's Jewishness and the location of the poem in biblical Judea are used to suggest that place may itself communicate some sort of knowledge of the divine that would otherwise prove elusive. The very fact that Jesus's Jewishness is acknowledged means not only that Clarel's approach differs from that of many Christian pilgrims throughout history but also that it meshes with patterns in the writings about Palestine produced by nineteenth-century Protestant missionaries. Place is not by itself enough, however, for Clarel requires a personal encounter to make his heart "burn" with a luminous moment of divine recognition, like that experienced by Jesus's disciples at Emmaus when they came into personal contact with the resurrected Christ as described in Luke 24:13–35. Nehemiah fills this role, which in the Gospels is filled by Christ himself, but he is, not surprisingly, inadequate to fulfill the weight of expectation that Clarel has placed upon him.

Nehemiah's inadequacy is not evident from the first. In what comes close to being a parody of the conventional speedy answer to the believer's prayer for faith, Nehemiah appears instantly after Clarel's plea for a modern-day meeting on the road to Emmaus, and "seemed, illusion such was given, / Emerging from the level heaven, / And invested with its liquid calm" (1.7.60–62). The optical illusion seems to make Nehemiah a divine messenger, and his otherworldliness is intensified by the fact that in his simplicity, he is upheld by faith, which makes him seem preternaturally youthful: "Scarce aged like time's wrinkled ones" (1.7.64). The fact that he does not carry a staff echoes Christ's words to his disciples upon sending them out into Judea ("Provide neither gold, nor silver, nor brass in your purses, / Nor scrip for your journey, neither two coats, neither shoes, nor yet staves: for the workman is worthy of his meat" [Matt. 10:10]), and the fact that he is carrying a "solitary Book" rather than a crucifix or icon indicates his Protestantism. His opening address to Clarel seems to connect him to Clarel's prayer: "'Young friend in Christ, what thoughts molest / That here ye droop so? Wanderest / Without a guide where guide should be? / Receive one, friend: the book—take ye" (1.7.76–79). Nehemiah appears to provide Clarel an authoritative guide, and to do so in the best Protestant form; for what he offers Clarel is the apparent solidity of the written Word, in combination with the personal address to Clarel from a "friend" of his immortal soul. The form in which the written word is presented, however, undermines this very solidity. The book, the narrator observes, is "gray / And weather-stained in woeful plight— / Much like that scroll laid bare to blight, / Which poet pale, when hope was low, / Bade one who into Libya went / Fling to the wasteful element" (1.7.81–86). One aspect of this description is clear: we are given the comical image of a weathered man presenting a weathered volume to a young man who is wrestling with the doubts of youth, thus providing another layer of irony to the response that Clarel receives to his prayer.

There may be more to this passage than is initially apparent, though, and when we attend closely to the extended simile, we begin to grasp it. The "poet pale" to whom the narrator alludes in the passage above is, as Walter Bezanson first noted, John Keats, and the "scroll laid bare to blight" is Keats's poem *Endymion*.[3] What have Keats and *Endymion* to do with an aging religious fanatic who passes out tracts to Muslims and Jews in nineteenth-century Palestine? The answer lies in part in the passage from which Melville drew his allusion, and in part in Keats's *Endymion* itself. Like *Clarel*, and indeed like much of Melville's work, *Endymion* may seem so ambitious as to be quixotic. As Walter Jackson Bate has observed, when Keats wrote the poem, he wished "to use the poem as a large, demanding 'test' or 'trial.'"[4] Such a test or trial would be not unlike the large, demanding task that Melville was taking upon himself in writing *Clarel*, a much more ambitious poem than he published before or afterward. Keats published *Endymion* to negative reviews, and Melville's own history of receiving negative reviews for work like *Moby-Dick*, *Pierre*, and *The Confidence-Man* may be reflected in his choice of Keats's *Endymion* as an analogy for Nehemiah's failures as a missionary.[5] In a frequently quoted letter, Melville wrote to Nathaniel Hawthorne, "Though I wrote the Gospels in this century, I would die in the gutter," thus establishing a direct connection between Melville's sense of authorial frustration and the aims of propagators of the Christian gospel.[6] If Nehemiah is a holy fool for Christ, Melville and Keats may both be seen as holy fools for an artistic dream that was invested with a religious intensity and earnestness.

Melville's lone annotation in his copy of Keats's *The Eve of St. Agnes* is also instructive. Melville wrote, quoting Ernest Renan, "to appear for a moment, to reflect a soft and profound refulgence, to die very young—this is the life of a god."[7] This reflection on Keats is suggestive of another sort of analogy with missionaries and missionary literary culture: one of the more popular and widely circulated subgenres of missionary writing was the memoir of a missionary who had died young. Indeed, the missionary narrative that was most widely used in the recruitment of American missionaries in the nineteenth century was Leonard Wood's "A Sermon, Preached at Haverhill (Mass.) in Remembrance of Mrs. Harriet Newell, Wife of the Rev. Samuel Newell, Missionary to India: Who Died at the Isle of France, November 30, 1812." Initially published in 1814, the sermon went through numerous reprintings under a variety of titles and helped to inspire other women who also became the subject of posthumous memoirs to join the missionary endeavor. Harriet Newell was only nineteen when she died, sharing with Keats a remarkably brief life as well as broad posthumous renown.[8] If Melville was more sympathetic and less skeptical about his fellow poets and novelists than about missionaries, there are nonetheless certain structural congruities between the idealistic careers of nineteenth-century Anglo-American missionaries and those of contemporaneous romantic writers. The prospect of death at a young age, the opportunity for travel to exotic realms, the sense of sacrifice for a cause that is incomprehensible to many of one's peers (but also carries with it the prospect of future glory)—all these connect the enterprise of the missionary with that of the romantic poet.

What Melville does in *Clarel*, then, is to make the missionary a figure of thwarted romance and frustrated aspiration. Melville is concerned with what English literature's most famous example of the prematurely deceased romantic poet has in common with an aging Protestant missionary on a quixotic quest, and it is precisely the vaunting, seemingly absurd, ambition behind each of their books that solves the riddle. If Keats aspired to poetic greatness, Nehemiah's spiritual aspirations have their own poetry. The Melville who composed *Clarel* had spent a decade and a half sacrificing for his new literary vocation as a poet to an audience that seemed indifferent to his efforts, just as he had earlier devoted his efforts as a novelist to an audience that had become more alienated, if not actively hostile. Small wonder then that Melville could feel a curious connection to a man whose own efforts at communication with an audience whose values differed from his own were proving fruitless, even if that man held to a version of Christian orthodoxy with which Melville had little sympathy.

If Melville presents the missionary Nehemiah as the counterpart to the aspiring but frustrated romantic poet, this sort of representation of missionaries was not foreign to nineteenth-century American literary culture. In an 1848 article for *Godey's Magazine and Lady's Book*, Rufus Wilmot Griswold offers a comparable evocation of romance relative to the missionary endeavor, but with a contrasting affective quality. For Griswold, the biographer, literary executor, and maligner of Edgar Allan Poe, the missionary was a figure of chivalric romance, a fit topic for a nineteenth-century heroic narrative that could rival the *Chanson de Roland* or the *Nibelungenlied*. In his essay, "The Knights Errant and the Female Missionaries of North America," which narrates the emergence of the American Protestant missionary movement out of the "Haystack Revival" at Williams College (the "memorial" referred to in the beginning of the quotation), Griswold used romantic medievalism as a foil for the courage that missionaries, and especially women, displayed in fields around the world:

> This memorial was followed by the founding of the American Board of Commissioners for Foreign Missions, and the institution of that new Order, whose deeds of devotion and heroism have as much surpassed the noblest acts of the old Templars, as the knight errantry of the middle ages did the barbarism of the Teutonic tribes before Charlemagne. "The age of chivalry," said Burke, in a famous passage of his Reflections, "is passed." But it was not and is not so. The fields of Buena Vista, Resaca-de-la-Palma, and Churubusco, have witnessed a thousand instances of that pride, enthusiasm, recklessness of life, and thirst for glory, which in the days of the Paladins strewed with bones the mountains and the valleys and the bottom of the seas from Poland to Palestine; while the highest type of chivalric character has been abundantly illustrated in every year since the foundation of the Board, by deeds of daring and endurance for the love of God, from which the heroes of the Niebelungelied, would have shrunk back appalled in their bravery for self.[9]

For Griswold, himself an ordained minister as well as an important arbiter of literary taste, the story of American missionaries was morally and ethically uncomplicated, and was destined for ultimate success despite more immediate obstacles. The medieval romance is a model here insofar as this is the story of brave deeds and lost lives, but with a triumphant end in sight that has been providentially foreordained. For Melville, as developed in the story of Nehemiah, the complications were many and the prospects for success few; for Nehemiah's ultimate goal is, like his biblical namesake, the "rebuilding" of Jerusalem in preparation for Christ's Second Coming. Nehemiah may have a sense of absolute certainty regarding his mission, but events provide a powerful counterforce that helps to justify Clarel's own doubts.

Nehemiah cannot resolve Clarel's doubts, but he nonetheless provides another component of Melville's extended anatomy of faith and doubt that develops throughout the poem. We learn quickly that Nehemiah is a figure more likely to complicate than resolve Clarel's doubt. Nehemiah identifies himself as "the sinner Nehemiah," but as the narrator remarks, he could more easily be seen as a saint, and indeed he is seen in precisely this way by most of those who encounter him, whether they regard him as sane or mad. The narrator observes, with a balance of pathos and humor, that "say what cynic will or can, / Man sinless is revered by man / Thro' all the forms which creeds may lend. / And so secure nor pointed at, / Among brave Turbans freely roamed the Hat" (1.9.73–78). The response that Nehemiah elicits both exalts the purity of his own personality and undermines the missionary imperative itself, since the various "forms which creeds may lend" are shown to shed similar light on his character.

However admirable Nehemiah is as a character, he fails utterly to provide the return to faith for Clarel that his benign appearance seems to suggest when they first meet. His tracts prove substantially less enduring than Keats's poetry, and in one instance are rejected as food even by a camel: when Nehemiah offers an Arabic-language tract to a Bedouin, his camel, in an odd parody of Christian communion, "misjudging, snapped it up, / And would have munched, but let it drop" (2.13.37–38). Nehemiah himself dies on the shore of the Dead Sea, sleepwalking to his death after having a heavenly vision of the New Jerusalem. The description of his death is at once darkly comic and ironic in that the missionary who meant to awaken those who were separated from the light of Christianity (as he understood it) himself walked in his sleep to his own demise; and yet it is strangely touching in that he is granted a sort of apocalyptic beatific vision before his death (2.38.15–45).

In the end, then, Nehemiah's religious madness, however saintly, remains madness, and Melville's view of the missionary effort in Palestine continues to be the one that he suggested in his 1856 *Journal* when describing the Dicksons, a family of American missionaries settled in Palestine:

> Old Dickson seems a man of Puritanic energy, and being inoculated with this preposterous Jew mania, is resolve to carry his Quixotism through to the end. Mrs. D. don't seem to like it, but submits.—The whole thing is half melancholy, half farcical—like the rest of the world.[10]

If Melville's attitude is tolerant, ascribing a level of low comedy to the Dicksons that is, after all, congruent with its equivalent in the rest of the world, he still plainly sees their mission of the conversion of the Jewish and Muslim populations of Palestine as a species of insanity, and one that Nehemiah shares.

Nehemiah's saintly madness, in fact, parallels similar aspirations and agonies on the part of two characters who serve as his doubles in the Jerusalem cantos: Celio and Nathan. Like them, Nehemiah dies early in the poem, indicating perhaps that each of the models for conversion that these three characters individually represent will not offer Clarel a solution for his crisis of faith.

Clarel shares his doubt and attendant anguish with the figure of Celio, a crippled Italian orphan raised by Franciscan monks. Celio and Nehemiah are paired with each other because of their proximity to each other in the early cantos of Melville's poem, and also because each represents a distinct pole of the missionary encounter: Nehemiah as the bringer of the "good news" of the Christian gospel, and Celio as the unwilling recipient of this good news, a victim of missionary zeal. The religious stance of each is associated specifically by the narrator with suffering: Nehemiah is said to have taken up his mission in Palestine because of his "stricken heart," the result of some "forepast bane" (1.8.8,11). If the source of Nehemiah's suffering is unknown, Celio's suffering is manifestly both physical and existential, as a cripple and an orphan. As a result of his parentless state, Celio was taken in by Franciscan monks and brought up as a Catholic. This upbringing had mixed results in that he comprehends certain aspects of Catholic teaching on an intellectual level at the same time as he has rebelled against these same teachings on an affective level. In religious services, Celio "but conformed; he showed no zest / Of faith within, faith personal" (1.12.30–31). If Celio seems detached in the context of religious services, it is not for a lack of personal emotional intensity: when soliloquizing, Celio can be truly impassioned. Considering the combination of Christ's existential appeal with the presence of suffering in the world, Celio muses

> Nor less some cannot break from thee;
> Thy love so locked is with thy lore,
> They may not rend them and go free:
> The head rejects; so much the more
> The heart embraces—what? the love?
> If true what priests avouch of thee,
> The shark thou mad'st, yet claim the dove. (1.13.65–71)

In Celio's understanding, Christ himself looks not unlike Nehemiah: a figure to be loved, but one whose message cannot be squared with the sharkish qualities of the existing world. Celio, then, is the Christian who does not fully convert, and his torment results from his partial acceptance of a message that can only cause pain if it is not fully embraced. If Nehemiah and Celio occupy opposite poles in their attitudes toward the Christian faith, an inner experience of anguish is ultimately what unites and drives them.

If Celio is, like Nehemiah, a kind of poet of the soul, and if he serves as a foil for Nehemiah in his status as a victim of the zeal of Christian missionaries (albeit of a different denomination from Nehemiah), Nathan, the American convert to Judaism, provides a still more complicated instance of the ambiguities of conversion. Nehemiah is the character who shares Nathan's story with Clarel, and the fact that Nehemiah is on some level the narrator of this story perhaps explains the air of incredulity that seems to pervade the narration. Born into a Protestant family of New England Congregational stock, Nathan found his way through nearly every religious transformation and conversion which an American might experience during the mid-nineteenth century, ending with Judaism. Melville's narrator in *Clarel* sums up his fervent wrestling for a belief that could sustain him: "Alone and at Doubt's freezing pole, / He wrestled with the pristine forms / Like the first man" (1.17.193–95). As with Nehemiah and Celio, Nathan's religious position is the response to profound personal distress. Notably, the three of them—Protestant missionary, Catholic agnostic, and Christian convert to Judaism—are positioned at radically divergent points on the doctrinal spectrum, but their suffering and the relationship of their suffering to their actions make them analogous to each other. Nathan's conversion to Judaism presents several major challenges to Nehemiah's belief system, most of all because this conversion belies the narrative at the heart of liberal and conservative varieties of Protestantism alike during the nineteenth century, which was a story about the inevitability that earnest seekers of all faiths would ultimately find their way to Protestantism, whether because of its superior biblicism or its superior rationality.

A poem from Melville's earlier *Battle-Pieces, and Aspects of the War* (1866) illuminates the potential for the missionary encounter to lead to reversals and moral ambiguities in a manner that resembles Nehemiah's discomfiting encounter with Nathan. In the midst of Robert E. Lee's concluding statement in "Lee in the Capitol," the Confederate general relates the story of a "Moorish maid" who faces a forced conversion at the hands of Christian crusaders.[11] She is faced with the choice of either losing her life or abandoning her father, and she chooses to remain faithful to her father, demonstrating that for her, interpersonal bonds mean more than life itself, and more than religious affiliation. The seeds of the tension between the creedal and the interpersonal that recur so frequently in *Clarel* are sown in this poem, and as in *Clarel*, they emerge from the tensions and uncertainties associated with conversion.

Christian missions as a topic are inextricably linked to those who are targeted for conversion, and throughout *Clarel* Melville depicts potential converts in ways that emphasize the richness of their own traditions and impulses toward faith and doubt. Nehemiah may interpret his encounters with Islam, Judaism, Catholicism, and Eastern Orthodoxy through the matrix of the encounter of truth with error, but his interlocutors of various faiths have a corresponding ability to frame the encounter in their own terms. The way in which Nehemiah's behavior is interpreted is significant in that he is seen as a kind of holy fool, both touched and protected by God.

What does it mean to start a consideration of Melville's representations of missionaries with Nehemiah and *Clarel* rather than with his earlier, more critical representations in *Typee* and *Omoo*? One difference is that starting with *Clarel* alerts scholars to the ambivalence with which Melville regarded missionaries and teaches readers to be alert to the uncertainties that appear in embryonic form in these earlier texts. Moreover, when we talk about Melville, whether in relation to missionaries, or Asian religions, or any other feature of his work, we are always best off if we remember that we are not talking about a figure whose views are fixed at the moment that he publishes any one of his novels, but rather about a man who was continually rethinking his views on religious, political, social, and aesthetic topics over the course of his career. Another benefit is that *Clarel* reminds careful readers of Melville's work that the missionary encounter is a two-way negotiation: European and American missionaries are not simply bestowing light on people "sitting in darkness," as their own propaganda at times implied (a device fiercely parodied by Mark Twain), nor were they merely conduits for imperialism, as it may seem to us today; rather, they were engaged in a complex negotiation for power and meaning with the peoples among whom they lived and worked.

As with Melville's representations of missionaries throughout his career, there are clear historical precedents for the figure of Nehemiah. In his Holy Land journals, Melville commented upon several Protestant settler-missionaries who were active in Jerusalem in the 1850s. First of all was the most likely direct model: "The old Connecticut man wandering about with tracts &c—knew not the language—hopelessness of it—his lonely bachelor rooms—he maintained that the expression 'Oh Jerusalem!' was an argument proving that Jerusalem was a byeword &c."[12] In addition, Walter Dickson of Groton, Massachusetts, is extensively quoted in Melville's journal in relation to the ingathering of Jews to prepare for the Second Coming. Dickson, in turn, was inspired in his mission by the former Millerite Clorinda Minor (whom he misidentified as "Mrs. Minot"), author of *Meshullam! Or Glad Tidings from Jerusalem* (1851), a report back to her supporters in Philadelphia arguing that the conversion of the Jews and Second Advent were at hand.[13] It is possible, nonetheless, that other potential models for Nehemiah came from outside Ottoman Palestine and can provide us with a means of connecting Melville's most ambitious poem with his early forays along the dividing line between fiction and nonfiction in *Typee* and *Omoo*.

Sailors, Islanders, Missionaries: *Typee*, *Omoo*, and Sailors' Magazines

By the time we look at *Clarel* in most accounts of Melville's work, it is easy to forget the centrality of sailors to his first encounters with missionaries. The relationship between sailors and missionaries was often antagonistic, but the two communities could also come together in curious ways. I want to suggest a less obvious potential model for a figure like Nehemiah than those who had been resident in mid-nineteenth-century Jerusalem, one whose existence has the potential to connect earlier and later representations of missionaries in Melville's work. Unlike the Holy Land missionary-settlers described above, Frederick O. Nelson cannot be claimed with any certainty as a direct source for Nehemiah, but his story is at least highly suggestive in relation to Melville's Holy Land missionary in *Clarel*. Nelson was a former American sailor who, improbably, became an American missionary to Protestant

Sweden. Letters from and about Nelson appear in the *Sailor's Magazine* in the early 1840s, at the very time when Melville was himself a sailor and thus likely to be exposed to such publications, and his story has some suggestive parallels with Nehemiah's. Like Nehemiah, Nelson was a tract-distributing expatriate, and if Melville was aware of him, his status as an ex-sailor who devoted his life to Protestant missions would have made him a fascinating model for a figure like Nehemiah. In his letters to the *Sailor's Magazine*, Nelson wrote about his aspirations and struggles as an American Protestant missionary in Lutheran Sweden (a curious field for Protestant missionary endeavor, to say the least). He regarded the Swedish church as hopelessly cold and impervious to feeling, and his goal of "converting" Sweden was to lead Scandinavian Lutherans into the enthusiastic, affective Christianity of the Second Great Awakening—what Nelson referred to in his own letters as "experimental religion."[14]

Nelson's case brings us to another vital matter: the way in which missionary literary culture and the literary cultures of sailors could intertwine in the nineteenth century. As Mary K. Bercaw Edwards has documented in *Cannibal Old Me*, the relationship between sailors and missionaries could be highly fraught and even hostile. *The Temperance Advocate and Sailor's Friend*, a periodical in which, as Daniel Aaron first pointed out, *Typee* received early and negative reviews, provides an excellent example of this tendency. The two consistent matters about which sailors are exhorted in missionary publications are temperance and Sabbath-breaking, and in the *Friend*, Titus Coan wrote at some length and on several occasions about the second of these matters.[15] Coan is especially significant in this regard because he served as a missionary both to the indigenous peoples of the Pacific and to the European and American sailors who frequently interacted with these indigenous peoples. Coan worked in locations across the Pacific, including the Sandwich Islands, Tahiti, and the Marquesas—the three main locations about which Melville wrote. As a missionary to the Pacific and a writer who criticizes sailors' morality, especially with regard to temperance, Coan might be expected to be a vigorous opponent of Melville; as we shall see, the story is more complex than that.

The sea, then, provides an important means of comparing Melville's early and late depictions of Christian missions. As I have tried to suggest, in *Clarel* Melville approaches Christian missionary endeavor with considerable ambivalence, expressing a sympathy for individuals that is highly seasoned by skepticism about the futility of imposing alien religious systems on native peoples. Can we identify any further continuities between the older Melville who was the sympathetic (and sardonic) creator of Nehemiah, and the younger author who earned the enmity of foreign missions societies? Answering this question requires a deeper engagement with *Typee* and *Omoo*, and a considerations of the ways in which polemic and analysis may coincide in those early novels.

Satirizing Missions: *Typee* and *Omoo*

Starting with *Clarel* is particularly valuable as we consider where in Melville's discussions of missionaries in *Typee* and *Omoo* he may go beyond simple critique into a reflection on the nature of intercultural dialogue itself. Melville's attacks on missionary hypocrisy and avarice are both well-known and obvious, but the understanding of how cultures interact implied by these passages requires more unpacking. When, for example, Melville describes the mutual incomprehension that missionaries and Marquesans demonstrate in the early chapters of *Typee*, he emphasizes the ways in which each group is behaving in a manner that is consistent with the moral norms of their society. The focus is less exclusively on the missionaries and their hypocrisy (although this is certainly a point of focus) than on the meeting of cultures with incommensurate standards for judging the morality of both actions and beliefs. In this way, Melville's early work includes the consideration of differing religious traditions in contact and conflict that only grows more intense and wide-ranging throughout his career. Moreover, the moral judgments in the early novels are likewise congruent with those expressed in *Clarel* and beyond. In *Clarel*, Melville regards Nehemiah, Celio, and Nathan (and many other characters) alike with compassion mingled with irony, and this perspective is not absent amid the moral indignation of *Typee* and *Omoo*.

The scholarship dealing with the representation of missionaries in *Typee* and *Omoo* is substantial, and it tends to emphasize Melville's critique of the hypocrisy of Christian missions, coupled with a corresponding critique of Melville's veracity launched by those whom he had criticized. One of the earliest essays on the confrontation between Melville and the prolific missionary literary culture of his day was Daniel Aaron's "Melville and the Missionaries" (1935), which stressed the highly negative tone of many reviews of *Typee* in missionary and missionary-affiliated publications.[16] Just over half a century later, John Samson pointed out that, in addition to its more straightforward attacks on missionary arrogance and hypocrisy, *Omoo* can be read as a formal satire on missionary narratives.[17] T. Walter Herbert's treatment of Melville in the Marquesas also emphasized the ways in which Melville criticized Western presumptions of cultural superiority. More recently, Albert Tricomi has used Melville as a point of departure for his full-length study of representations of missionaries in American literature, suggesting that Melville's bracing critiques of the missionary enterprise in these texts is decisive for our understanding of Melville's treatment of religion more broadly. Finally, Sujit Sivarandam has noted the ways in which Melville's critique of their architecture is a part of his wider satirical treatment of missionaries.[18] The scholarly consensus thus reflects a view of Melville's relationship to American missionaries as broadly antagonistic in a manner reminiscent of early hostile reviews of Melville's first two novels in the missionary press.

This consensus is largely accurate, but we might consider whether there are hints of Melville's later ambivalence even in Melville's early works.

Typee begins and ends with highly critical representations of American missionaries in the Pacific—in the Marquesas at the beginning, and at greater length in the Sandwich Islands at the end. In the opening chapter, we read of a missionary woman who is "not sufficiently evangelized" to forgive Marquesan islanders who have assaulted her to verify her gender. In this instance, Melville highlights the contrast between Marquesan and North American codes of modesty, as the Marqesan islanders regard the missionary woman's clothes—the "sacred veil of calico," as Tommo describes them—as being a deception, whereas for the missionary woman nudity is a moral violation.[19] He also, however, calls attention to the gap between the ethical code of the Christian gospels as a nearly impossibly difficult standard to which to adhere—it would indeed require a great deal of forgiveness for the missionary to overcome her humiliation in this instance—and Christianity as a faith tradition identified with European and North American culture, which can then be bestowed by missionaries upon grateful converts.

The arrogance of the missionary's view, as understood by Melville, becomes apparent when Melville's narrator Tommo engages in an extended anti-missionary polemic in chapter 26 of *Typee*. Tommo rebukes the missionaries, and indeed European and American imperialism more generally, for their treatment of indigenous islanders, proclaiming "the small remnant of the natives had been civilized into draught horses, and evangelized into beasts of burden."[20] The use of the term "evangelized" here is significant relative to Melville's earlier comments on the missionary woman who was unable to forgive her attackers. The native Hawaiians have been forced into a grotesque parody of the ethics of the Sermon on the Mount. They are serving the missionaries, not out of mutual Christian love but as victims of the violence of imperialism, and if the woman in the earlier anecdote had proved unable to adhere to the sternest demands of her religious traditions, the recipients of the zeal of missionaries in the Pacific had been compelled to do so. Tommo then turns to a more specific vignette, one which also parallels the earlier story of the missionary woman, this time involving a New England matron in the mission field. This woman had grown up on a farm where she thought "nothing of driving the cows to pasture" but is now unwilling to walk herself, and beats the men drawing her cart in a reversal of the ethics of nonviolence and doing to others what we would have them do to us.

In the appendix that concludes *Typee*, when describing the state of affairs in Hawaii, Melville gives vent to further indignation at the abuses that he attributes to American missionaries, describing Gerrit P. Judd as "a sanctimonious apothecary-adventurer" and the missionaries as a group as "a junto of ignorant and designing Methodist elders in the councils of a half-civilized king."[21] What Melville rejects utterly in *Typee* is religion as an identity rather than an ethical code, particularly when wedded to self-interested political power.

Omoo lacks the more extended polemics of *Typee*, but its humorous discussions of missionaries can be if anything even more biting. For example, in a late chapter, Melville presents us with a British missionary sermon, as related to the narrator by a Tahitian islander. The islander's account is presented in a simplified version of English, meant to represent a Tahitian form of pidgin. While this could be read as a source of comedy at the islander's expense, what seems more likely is that it is a means of defamiliarizing the missionary sermon in order to highlight the way that it relies on brute power and material interests for its logic. The islander reports that the missionary uses his sermon as an opportunity to attack the British Empire's French rivals and to glorify Great Britain: "Good friends, very bad times in Tahiti; it make me weep. Pomaree is gone—the island no more yours, but the Wee-Wees' (French). Wicked priests here, too; and wicked idols in women's clothes, and brass chains." The attack on the French is followed immediately by British self-exaltation: "Good friends, this very small island, but very wicked, and very poor; these two go together. Why Beretanee so great? Because that island good island, and send *mickonaree* [missionaries] to poor *kanaka* [islanders]."[22] What Melville satirizes here, and elsewhere in *Omoo*, is faith in the service of Mammon, cultural chauvinism, and mental stagnation.

What brings these passages from *Typee* and *Omoo* together is their wry presentation of the contact among cultures that mutually misunderstand each other, in some cases innocently, and in some cases deviously and strategically. Missionaries willfully misread numerous aspects of Marquesan, Tahitian, and Hawaiian behavior in order to make the islanders appropriately "heathen" subjects for conversion. Conversely, indigenous converts reimagine Christianity in ways that fit within their own inherited traditions in some cases, and in others pit the new religion against the old in order to undo traditions that appeared burdensome. What Melville objects to in the missionary enterprise in the Pacific in his early novels is the institutionalized arrogance that the examples he adduces represent. What he embraces, whether he sees it in the sailors, the indigenous peoples of the Pacific, or even the missionaries themselves, is goodwill, cooperation, and a sincere and impartial quest for truth.

Missionaries are not just present in *Typee* and *Omoo* through Melville's representations of them, however. They are also woven into the fabric of his narrative as source materials and modes for Melville's own work. As numerous critics beginning with Charles R. Anderson have noted, Melville makes use of the *Polynesian Researches* of William J. Ellis and *A Visit to the South Seas, in the U.S. Ship Vincennes, in 1829 and 1830* by Charles S. Stewart.[23] Stewart and Ellis both provide accounts of the Pacific islands that are detailed and careful in their ethnography and their treatment of local customs and folkways. Melville's simultaneous literary use of these figures and satirical attitude toward their mission of conversion comes close to his treatment of

Nehemiah in *Clarel*: insofar as the missionaries are thoughtful interlocutors with the cultures of the Pacific islands, Melville relies upon them as sources; insofar as they seek conversion as a central goal, he is a consistent critic. Melville is indeed a formidable critic of the missionary enterprise in *Typee* and *Omoo*, but he is also writing out of a wider discussion of the Pacific in nineteenth-century America to which missionaries are important contributors. Melville both rejects the view of Christianity as an exclusive source of meaning and salvation that undergirds the missionary enterprise and leaves room for individual missionaries who display traits that he values such as curiosity, intellectual honesty, and courage.

Missionaries in the Background in *Moby-Dick*

Moby-Dick remains the most important work in the Melville canon for testing any assertion made about Melville as a literary artist. Missionaries may not seem as central to the plotting of Melville's masterpiece as they are in *Typee* and *Omoo*, but the intellectual connection with Asia is readily apparent, and the missionary encounter lurks in the background. How important is Asia in *Moby-Dick*? H. Bruce Franklin has argued in *The Wake of the Gods* for the importance of comparative mythology, including both South and West Asian religious traditions, for understanding *Moby-Dick*, although he downplayed the South Asian element in the novel, focusing instead on Egyptology. And in *Moby-Dick: A Hindu Avatar*, H. B. Kulkarni sets forth a case that the novel as a whole expresses Hindu religious thought, and that the ultimate lesson of *Moby-Dick* is the "reconciliation of good and evil, love and hate into the highest existence of the spirit."[24] The emphasis that Franklin and Kulkarni have placed on the encounter with Asia is easily understandable: in *Moby-Dick*, Vishnu is referred to as a whaleman, Hindu pictures of the whale are compared with Christian pictures, and Fedallah and his phantom crew are from India and Southeast Asia, respectively. The interplay between the United States and Asia that was most directly visible in the nineteenth century in the encounter between colonized peoples and European and North American missionaries is threaded throughout Melville's great whaling novel.

Examining the multireligious composite that Melville creates in the character of Queequeg reveals the broader role of Asia and of the missionary encounter broadly construed in *Moby-Dick*. Queequeg is said to be of royal lineage, and he is a seeker after knowledge who is willing to consider conversion from his own inherited traditions, but who ultimately rejects this prospect, concluding that "it's a wicked world in all meridians." As a sincere seeker who actively looks for opportunities to understand and evaluate Christianity, Queequeg seems like the ideal potential convert; ironically, it is this very set of qualities, which make him resemble "George Washington cannibalistically developed," that cause him to remain non-Christian.[25]

Two stories capture the covert role that the missionary encounter plays in *Moby-Dick*. First, Ishmael chooses to worship Queequeg's deity Yojo, thus making Queequeg the missionary in their friendship, a story that Ishmael relates in his characteristic seriocomic manner:

> I was a good Christian; born and bred in the bosom of the infallible Presbyterian Church. How then could I unite with this wild idolator in worshipping his piece of wood? But what is worship? thought I. Do you suppose now, Ishmael, that the magnanimous God of heaven and earth—pagans and all included—can possibly be jealous of an insignificant bit of black wood? Impossible! But what is worship?—to do the will of God—that is worship. And what is the will of God?—to do to my fellow man what I would have my fellow man to do to me—that is the will of God. Now, Queequeg is my fellow man. And what do I wish that this Queequeg would do to me? Why, unite with me in my particular Presbyterian form of worship. Consequently, I must then unite with him in his; ergo, I must turn idolator. So I kindled the shavings; helped prop up the innocent little idol; offered him burnt biscuit with Queequeg; salamed before him twice or thrice; kissed his nose; and that done, we undressed and went to bed, at peace with our own consciences and all the world. But we did not go to sleep without some little chat.[26]

The passage is a striking reversal of the conventional missionary encounter, and it is justified in terms of the Christian New Testament, specifically the Sermon on the Mount, referred to by Melville in *Pierre* as the "greatest real miracle" of all the world's religions. Ishmael is, paradoxically, required by his Christian faith to violate the Christian proscription of idolatry, and the pagan is in this scenario the missionary who wins a convert.

An ironic counterpart to this scene is Ishmael's discussion of Queequeg's "Ramadan." Here it is Queequeg who plays the role of the missionary, chiding Ishmael for his lack of faith. Ishmael skeptically dismisses Queequeg's prayer and fasting, arguing that it will likely only be a source of indigestion. By making the Christian the skeptic in this scene, Melville reminds his readers that matters such as skepticism and belief are often a matter of one's position: Queequeg's fidelity to Yojo is incommensurate with Christianity, and Ishmael's moderate attachment to Christianity, while it may not stop him from praying to Yojo, disqualifies him from a thoroughgoing attachment to Queequeg's faith. Evident throughout this series of exchanges is Melville's tendency to abstract ethical precepts that he admired in Christianity from the status of Christianity as an identity marker. Here as in *Typee* and *Omoo*, amidst the irony and satire, a serious case is being made for engagement, dialogue, and finding analogies between seemingly opposed religious positions.

Missionaries in the Later Poetry

Returning to *Clarel* and the various published and unpublished writings that Melville produced late in his life brings the question of Melville's treatment of both the missionary encounter and the rich array of Near Eastern and Asian faith traditions full circle. Even after Nehemiah's death, *Clarel* deals with missions and with Asian religions in the broader sense suggested by *Moby-Dick*. The missionary impulse comes to the fore in conversations with the Dominican monk, this time from a sympathetically rendered Catholic point of view. The Dominican monk serves as a perilously attractive voice for the Catholic tradition from the point of view of Melville's Protestant pilgrims. In general, Melville shows an interest in the later portions of *Clarel* in the ways in which the existence of multiple Christian theological traditions make the missionary impulse within Christianity problematic even as he represents multiple points of contact between Christianity and other world religions.

Still later in Melville's literary and religious itinerary than *Clarel*, Melville's final collection of published poetry, *Timoleon*, serves to illustrate the competing imperatives of Melville's attachment to the traditions associated with his personal history and engagement with wide-ranging religious and philosophical alternatives. In the brief poem "Buddha," for example, Melville juxtaposes a biblical quotation from the epistle of James with a brief sketch of Buddhist thought, writing:

> Swooning, swim to less and less,
> Aspirant to nothingness,
> Sobs of the worlds, and dole of kinds
> That dumb endurers be—
> Nirvana! Absorb us in your skies,
> Annul us into thee.[27]

If the poem's reading of Buddhism is necessarily limited, it nevertheless captures a central aspect of Buddhist thought: the necessity of an escape from desire and its associated ills through enlightenment. "Buddha" illustrates Melville's syncretic method in its use of Christian and Buddhist modes of belief and action. The quotation from the epistle of James reads: "For what is your life? It is even a vapor that appeareth for a little time and then vanisheth away." Melville's use of the New Testament verse as the epigraph for a poem paying tribute to Buddhism suggests congruence between Christian and Buddhist thought, presenting them as complementary statements of a truth that is fully confined within neither tradition.

Especially when read in tandem with "Buddha," Melville's late fragment "Rammon" shows that his consideration of missionary encounters can involve thoroughgoing reversals. This fragment is built around the biblical figure of King Solomon and incorporates Buddhism as a missionary religion which, it is worth remembering, it has often been. Solomon is, of course, renowned in the Hebrew and Christian traditions for his wisdom, and one of the more striking stories regarding him that appears in the Hebrew scriptures and is referenced in the Christian New Testament is his encounter with the Queen of Sheba, an event that brings Solomon into contact, at least potentially, with the wider intellectual ferment across the Asian continent.

Rammon's dialogue with Buddhism develops out of Solomon's philosophy of the vanity of human existence as expressed in the book of Ecclesiastes and his encounter with Asia emblematized in the Bible by the Queen of Sheba. Rammon, the "unrobust child of Solomon's old age," has been prepared for his encounter with Buddhism by his own inherited disposition and his acceptance of his father's thought. Melville's narrator expresses Rammon's pre-contact inclinations in a manner reminiscent of the Christian supersessionist idea that the Hebrew Bible (as Old Testament) provides a preparation for the Christian New Testament:

> Vanity of vanities—such is this life. As to a translated life in some world hereafter—far be that thought! A primary law binds the universe. The worlds are like apples upon a tree; in flavor and tint perchance one apple perchance may somewhat differ from another, but all partake of the same sap. One of the worlds we know. And what find we here? Much good, a preponderance of good; that is, good it would be if it could be winnowed from the associate evil that taints it. But evil is no accident. Like good it is an irremovable element. Bale out your individual boat if you can, but the sea abides.[28]

Rammon's reflections on the nature of human existence and suffering have prepared him to find analogies within Buddhism. Solomon, as a "lax Hebrew," allows advanced religious ideas that blend with certain aspects of Judaism to enter his kingdom, most notably in the person of "that travelled and learned Indian dame, not less communicative than inquisitive, the Princess of Sheba" (*Collected Poems* 412). The narrator further stresses that "through her it was that the doctrine of the successive transmigration of souls came to circulate . . . among a people whose theocratic lawgiver was silent as to any life to come (*Collected Poems* 412). Melville thus highlights the idea that Buddhism could have become a part of a young Hebrew prince's intellectual milieu via the Hebrew kingdom's economic and cultural exchanges with Asia, and he points to an aspect of the Hebrew faith in Solomon's time that would become uncomfortable for Christian writers to acknowledge: the lack of a developed doctrine of an afterlife. When Rammon hears of the teachings of the Buddha, he is drawn to them in part by intellectual assent and in part by temperamental susceptibility to ideas that highlight the inescapability of suffering in human experience, but also and preeminently by the character of the Buddha. As the narrator reflects:

> But the wonderful conceptions of Prince———— [Siddhata?] were backed by something equally marvelous, his personality and life. These singularly appealed to Rammon also born a Prince, and conscious too that rank had not hardened his heart as to the mass of mankind, toilers and sufferers, nor in any wise intercepted a just view of the immense spectacle of things.
>
> But, in large, his thought of the Buddha partook of that tender awe with which, long after Rammon's time, the unconventional Christians were impressed by the story and character of Christ. It was not possible therefore for him to regard any doctrine, however repugnant to his understanding and desire, authentically ascribed to so transcendent a nature.[29]

This passage highlights Melville's interest in personality as a determining factor in religious choices. Figures whose character is admirable, whether the Buddha or Jesus Christ, draw people to them more through the force of their example and the admiration to which it gives rise than through a particular set of doctrines regarding the afterlife. The fact that Melville compares Rammon's reverence for the Buddha so directly with the religious enthusiasm of the early Christians who adored Jesus out of a personal sense of love and reverence for him makes this aspect of Melville's religious thought clear. As I have argued elsewhere, Melville's expressions of skepticism with regard to Christian doctrine in his marginal notations in *The New Testament and the Book of Psalms* are balanced by a personal reverence for Jesus both as an admirable human being and as a crafter of parables.[30] There seems to be a similar love and reverence manifest in Melville's invocations of the Buddha here, a reverence that is Melville's as well as Rammon's, and that specifically applies to the Buddha as a source of truth.

The bare fact of Buddhism's chronological priority over Christianity is no doubt also part of the point here: Melville was consistently interested in ways in which elements within the monotheistic religions are anticipated or paralleled by more ancient faiths. Here again, Melville's annotations in his copies of the Bible are instructive. In his copy of *The New Testament and the Book of Psalms*, Melville marked passages where Paul referred to non-Christian philosophers, and evidently used biblical commentaries to track down the philosophers in question.[31] That Buddhism has chronological priority over Christianity is itself a reason for Melville to question the desirability of the conversion of the world to Protestant Christianity in the second half of the nineteenth century, but there is a deeper reason for skepticism here. The possibility posed by the narrator that interest in an afterlife entered Jewish religious thought through an exposure to Buddhism and its doctrine of reincarnation suggests that the genealogy of Christianity is not what its adherents suppose. If Christianity is formed in part out of trace elements of Asian religions within Judaism, then this genealogy calls into question both the likely success and even the wisdom of nineteenth-century American Protestant efforts to convert adherents of Hinduism and Buddhism in South Asia. As a model for interreligious dialogue, Melville seems to find Rammon's syncretism more alluring than a strategy built around conversion.

Viewing the fragment on Rammon, the Queen of Sheba, and Buddhism in connection with both Queequeg's quest for religious truth in *Moby-Dick* and the emergence of Nathan as a major figure in *Clarel* is highly instructive. The logic of the Protestant missionary encounter in the nineteenth century derives from a progressive view of revelation: God is revealed first in the Old Testament, and then, more perfectly, in the New Testament; Judaism replaces polytheism and is succeeded by Christianity; Christianity is expressed in the Catholic Church, but more perfectly in Protestant churches; Protestant missions will ultimately pave the way for the Second Coming of Christ and the end of the travails of history. Rammon's story, however, undermines this narrative. Rather than being prepared by his Jewish faith for a linear movement toward Christianity as in Christian supersessionist narratives, Rammon, like Queequeg, is a freethinking religious dissident who turns to a religion that is distinct from the entire Western monotheistic tradition, and like Nathan, actively reverses the standard progressive pattern, moving from Judaism to a non-Western religious tradition in the same way that Nathan moves from Christianity to Judaism. Unlike Nathan in relation to Judaism, Rammon does not experience Buddhism as an alternative gospel to be propagated, but like Nathan in relation to Judaism, he does experience Buddhism as an alternative means of succor in the face of doubt, anxiety, and depression.

Writing about Rammon late in life, Melville portrays a form of religious encounter that resists the model of proselytism and instead suggests an eclectic response to interreligious conversations that relies upon analogy rather than doctrinal precision. In this way, Melville reflects a larger move toward secularization in nineteenth-century culture, but not via what Charles Taylor has called a "subtraction narrative"—the myth of the creation of a secular society by means of a simple removal of religion. Rather, he considers a context for religion in an encounter among religious possibilities that allows for varying modulations of faiths and doubts shaped by experience, reason, and personality—a kind of missionary encounter in which two distinct religious cultures enter into conversation with each other, without the prospect or necessity of actual conversion.[32]

The Two Faces of the Missionary Encounter

In evaluating the evolving role that missionaries played in Melville's religious thought, it is worth considering an event from Melville's life that did not find its way into his fiction or poetry. In 1859, in the interval between

Melville's career as a novelist and his career as a published poet (although he was already writing poetry at this time), Melville received a visitor who was closely associated with his past literary success as a novelist. Titus Munson Coan, the son of one of the most famous nineteenth-century American missionaries in the Sandwich Islands, was accompanied by a friend, John Thomas Gulick, who also had spent time in the South Pacific and who had a similar interest in hearing Melville's tales; both were undergraduates at nearby Williams College. Coan was surprised that the man who had done more than any other to spread interest in the Marquesas in North America had little to say about the regions that had made him famous in the early stages of his career.

The missionary children (a group that scarcely seems to exist in Melville's depiction of missionaries in his early novels) hoped that Melville would be prepared to share stories from his adventures in the South Pacific that would go beyond what they had already read in his fiction, but they were, as Coan explained in his account of the meeting, disappointed. Instead of regaling them with stories from the Pacific, Melville instead spent the conversation discussing his own reading in classical philosophy and his own reflections on the nature and meaning of human existence. As Coan remarked, "The shade of Aristotle arose like a cold mist between myself and Fayaway." Surprisingly enough, Titus Munson Coan would go on to become one of Herman Melville's earliest biographers.[33]

The fact that the son of Hawaii's most famous nineteenth-century American missionary would choose to visit Melville at all is worthy of some comment. The hostile reaction to Melville's first two novels in the missionary press is well known, but the guardedly sympathetic reaction that some missionaries appear to have had to Melville may be surprising to anyone who assumes that this exhausted Melville's reception among missionaries. In the elder Titus Coan's own memoirs, he writes that Melville was "romantic" and points out some possible missteps in his description of the Marquesas, but he also praises both the quality of Melville's writing and seems to accept that Melville's accounts are largely, if not entirely, accurate. Coan saw Melville as an interlocutor, not a thoroughgoing antagonist, and thus did not engage in the sorts of ad hominem attacks that religious journals often did. Also noteworthy regarding the Coan family is that they were correspondents of Charles Darwin and provided data for his researches from their travels in South America. Melville's critiques of Christian missions can thus be seen to be an extension of discussions within mainstream American religious culture, rather than an absolute departure from them. If Melville could view Darwin with both literary interest and ambivalence, this trait was shared by at least some of his contemporaries among American missionaries.[34] Some of these same missionaries could view Melville's writings with enthusiasm rather than either the defensiveness or the outrage shown in many early reviews of his first two novels. Titus Munson Coan himself was one such example, in that he praised *Typee* as a "masterpiece" and claimed that *Typee* and *Omoo* succeeded in communicating "the most vivid truth expressed in the most telling and poetic manner."[35]

I have begun and ended this essay with two examples of Melville's complex relation to Christian missions: at the end, his conversation with two men associated with his past as a writer of prose fiction that dealt critically with the missionary enterprise, and at the beginning, his sympathetic portrayal of an American missionary's last days in his longest and most ambitious poem. These two points serve to illuminate broad swathes of Melville's career in that they reveal something about both Melville's treatment of the missionary enterprise and of the larger but related matter of the cultural confrontation between largely non-Christian Asia and Christian Americans. On one level, Melville approached the question of American missionary endeavors from the standpoint of a liberal, reforming Christianity outraged by the hypocrisies of much of institutional religion in nineteenth-century America—a position that brings him close both to confirmed critics of the Christian faith like Mark Twain and to devoutly religious figures like Harriet Beecher Stowe. (If we too often forget that the skeptical ironist Mark Twain and the devout Stowe were neighbors in late nineteenth-century Connecticut who had more in common with each other than is often recognized, our misperceptions relative to Melville's curious mix of ironic skepticism and fierce ethical passion can be equally misleading.)[36] On another level, Melville wove the missionary encounter into a larger set of questions about what it would mean to live in a pluralistic world and what possibilities existed for widely divergent cultures and faiths to learn from and instruct each other. If one strand here is represented by the female missionary in *Typee* who commandeers native peoples like oxen to pull her cart, a countervailing strand is Ishmael on his knees before Yojo with Queequeg, or the narrator in "The Encantadas" metaphorically kneeling before the raped and abandoned Hunilla and exclaiming: "Humanity, thou strong thing, I worship thee, not in the laurelled victor, but in this vanquished one"[37] Passionate protest against religiously sanctioned injustice, whatever the theological underpinnings, and a passionate embrace of human courage and solidarity, whatever the deity invoked, both characterize Melville's writing. Insofar as the missionary impulse can be used in support of injustice and exploitation, Melville rejects it; insofar as the attendant cross-cultural contact allows for human solidarity, Melville cautiously embraces it.

What Melville offers us in *Clarel* through the figure of Nehemiah and elsewhere in his later work is an example of how these strands can both coincide and unite, not just through a Christian European or North American who instructs those who have not heard of Christianity (with recognizable connections to imperialism), nor even merely through the Western readers who enhance their knowledge through learning about the alternative religious and philosophical traditions of Asia (perhaps a subtler form of imperialism). In

Clarel, Nehemiah as well as his interlocutors becomes an object of knowledge, suggesting, however tentatively, a world in which religious difference, contact, and dialogue are matters of negotiation rather than conversion or conquest. In his later years, Melville implied that the American missionaries he satirized in his youth could be, if not the "knights-errant" invoked by Rufus Wilmot Griswold, at least one more source of illustration for the always complicated, and often profoundly moving, human quest for the divine amid its many temporal entanglements.

Notes

1. William Potter, *Melville's Clarel and the Intersympathy of Creeds* (Kent, Ohio: Kent State University Press, 2005), examines Melville's use of comparative religion in the poem.

2. Herman Melville, *Clarel, a Poem and Pilgrimage in the Holy Land*, ed. Harrison Hayford, Alma A. MacDougall, Hershel Parker, and G. Thomas Tanselle (Evanston and Chicago: Northwestern University Press, and the Newberry Library, 1991); references to this edition will be cited by part, canto, and line in the text.

3. "Discussions," in *Clarel*, 724.

4. Walter Jackson Bate, *John Keats* (Cambridge, Mass.: Harvard University Press, 1979), 174.

5. On negative reviews of Keats's poetry, see Bate, *John Keats*, 149.

6. Keats had a personal connections to Christian missions. Keats's friend and sometime correspondent Benjamin Bailey was a missionary in colonial Ceylon, finishing his career as an archdeacon who was expelled from his prominent role because of his publication of inflammatory anti-Buddhist propaganda. See Bate, *John Keats*, 196–97; for Bailey's anti-Buddhist polemic, see his inflammatory *Six Letters of Vetus: To the Editor of the Ceylon Times: On the Re-Connexion of the British Government with the Budhist Idolatry of Ceylon* (Colombo, 1852).

7. John Keats, *The Eve of St. Agnes*, front flyleaf annotation, in Wilson Walker Cowen, *Melville's Marginalia* (New York: Garland, 1987), 130. The Documentary Note for the volume by Steven Olsen-Smith at *Melville's Marginalia Online* (http://melvillesmarginalia.org) identifies Ernest Renan's *St. Paul*, as translated by Ingersoll Lockwood (New York: Michel Levy Freres, 1869), as the source of Melville's annotation.

8. Leonard Woods, *A Sermon Preached at Haverhill (Mass.) in Remembrance of Mrs. Harriet Newell, Wife of Rev. Samuel Newell, Missionary in India, Who Died at the Isle of France, November 30, 1812, To which Are Appended Memoirs of Her Life* (Boston: Samuel T. Armstrong, 1814).

9. Rufus Wilmot Griswold, "The Heroism of the Knights-Errant, and of the Female Missionaries of America," *Godey's Magazine and Lady's Book* (August 1848), 37; *American Periodicals Series Online*, 61.

10. Herman Melville, *Journals*, ed. Howard C. Horsforth and Lynn Horth (Evanston and Chicago: Northwestern University Press and the Newberry Library, 1989), 94.

11. Herman Melville, *Published Poems*, ed. Robert C. Ryan, Harrison Hayford, Alma MacDougall Reising, and G. Thomas Tanselle (Evanston and Chicago: Northwestern University Press and the Newberry Library, 2009), 163–69.

12. Melville, *Journals*, 85.

13. Melville, *Journals*, 92. See *Journals*, 442, for Walter Dickson, and 441 for Clorinda Minor. For an extended discussion of the latter, see Brian Yothers, *The Romance of the Holy Land in American Travel Writing, 1790–1876* (Burlington, Vt.: Ashgate, 2007), chap. 3.

14. Frederick O. Nelson, *Sailor's Magazine* (April 1841), 244–46, and (July 1841), 353. See also *Sailor's Magazine* (June 1842), 303–4, for more on Nelson.

15. Titus Coan, *The Temperance Advocate and Seaman's Friend,* vol. 1, no. 9:45.

16. Daniel Aaron, "Melville and the Missionaries," *New England Quarterly* 8 (September 1935): 404–8.

17. John Samson, "Profaning the Sacred: Melville's *Omoo* and Missionary Narratives," *American Literature* 56 (December 1984): 496–509. See also Juniper Ellis, "Melville and the Missionaries," *SPAN: Journal of the South Pacific Association for Commonwealth Literature and Language Studies* 48–49 (1999): 140–49; Erin T. Suzuki, "Frauds and Gods: The Politics of Religion in Melville's *Omoo* and *Mardi*," *ESQ: A Journal of the American Renaissance* 53 (Fourth Quarter 2007): 360–86.

18. See Albert H. Tricomi, *Missionary Positions: Evangelicalism and Empire in American Fiction* (Gainesville: University Press of Florida, 2011). For a consideration of Melville's discussion of missionary architecture and its relevance to his wider critique of Protestant missions, see Sujit Sivasundaram, *Nature and the Godly Empire: Science and Evangelical Mission in the Pacific, 1795–1850* (New York: Cambridge University Press, 2005). For a history of Protestant missions in the nineteenth-century Middle East, see Ussama Makdisi, *The Artillery of Heaven: American Missionaries and the Failed Conversion of the Middle East* (Ithaca, N.Y.: Cornell University Press, 2009).

19. Herman Melville, *Typee, A Peep at Poynesian Life*, ed. Harrison Hayford, Hershel Parker, and G. Thomas Tanselle (Evanston and Chicago: Northwestern University Press and the Newberry Library, 1968), 6–7.

20. Melville, *Typee*, 196.

21. Ibid., 255

22. Herman Melville, *Omoo: A Narrative of Adventures in the South Seas*, ed. Harrison Hayford, Hershel Parker, and G. Thomas Tanselle (Evanston and Chicago: Northwestern University Press and the Newberry Library, 1968), 173–74.

23. Charles Roberts Anderson, *Melville in the South Seas* (New York: Columbia University Press, 1939) was the seminal work in this area. More recent discussions include Geoffrey Sanborn, *The Sign of the Cannibal: Melville and the Making of a Postcolonial Reader* (Durham, N.C.: Duke University Press, 1998); and Jill Barnum, Wyn Kelley, and Christopher Sten, eds., *"Whole Oceans Away": Melville and the Pacific* (Kent, Ohio: Kent State University Press, 2007).

24. H. B. Kulkarni, *Moby-Dick: A Hindu Avatar* (Logan: Utah State University Press, 1970), 66.

25. Herman Melville, *Moby-Dick, or the Whale*, ed. Harrison Hayford, Hershel Parker, and G. Thomas Tanselle (Evanston and Chicago: Northwestern University Press and the Newberry Library, 1988), 55–56.

26. Melville, *Moby-Dick*, 52.
27. Melville, *Published Poems*, 281.
28. Herman Melville, *Collected Poems*, ed. Howard P. Vincent. (Chicago: Hendricks House, 1947), 412. Cited in text by page number.
29. Melville, *Collected Poems*, 412.
30. Brian Yothers, "One's Own Faith: Melville's Reading of *The New Testament and Psalms*." *Leviathan: A Journal of Melville Studies* 10, no. 3 (October 2008): 39–59.
31. For Melville's annotations and markings in *The New Testament and the Book of Psalms*, see http://melvillesmarginalia.org.
32. See Charles Taylor, *A Secular Age* (Cambridge, Mass.: Harvard University Press, 2007), for a full development of the author's argument against "subtraction narratives."
33. See Merton M. Sealts, *The Early Lives of Melville* (Madison: University of Wisconsin Press, 1974), for a discussion of Coan's role as an early Melville biographer.
34. For the Coans' correspondence with Charles Darwin, see the *Darwin Correspondence Project*, http://www.darwinproject.ac.uk.
35. Sealts, *Early Lives of Melville*, 118.
36. The writings of Harriet Beecher Stowe and Mark Twain correspond to two strong impulses implicit in much of Melville's work. Stowe consistently differentiates between a doctrinally defined Christianity that fails to attend to such pressing matters as the enslavement of human beings and the ethical and affective Christianity that she prescribes. While vehemently critical of religious establishments of every sort, Twain still makes exceptions in his anti-religious satire for figures who define themselves through empathy and compassion rather than through supernaturalism and doctrinal distinctions.
37. Herman Melville, *The Piazza Tales and Other Prose Pieces, 1839–1860*, ed. Harrison Hayford, Alma A. MacDougall, and G. Thomas Tanselle (Evanston and Chicago: Northwestern University Press and the Newberry Library, 1987), 157.

Melville among the Heathens

Religion, Race, and Representation in the South Seas

Richard A. Garner

> "Hurra, my lads! It's a settled thing; next week we shape our course to the Marquesas!" The Marquesas! What strange visions of outlandish things does the very name spirit up! Naked houris—cannibal banquets—groves of cocoa-nut—coral reefs—tatooed chiefs—and bamboo temples; sunny valleys planted with bread-fruit-trees—carved canoes dancing on the flashing blue waters—savage woodlands guarded by horrible idols—*heathenish rites and human sacrifices.*
>
> —Herman Melville, *Typee: A Peep at Polynesian Life*

Melville's *Typee*[1] presents a series of representational dilemmas to the contemporary reader, quandaries which continue to reappear throughout his writing on the South Seas. Take for instance Queequeg's opening lines to Ishmael in *Moby-Dick*: "Who-e debel you . . . you no speak-e, dam-me, I kill-e."[2] With little effort the contemporary critic can read this passage as a racist caricature, where Queequeg's manner of speaking embodies an orientalist appropriation of vernacular speech. From *Typee* and *Omoo* to *Moby-Dick*, Melville's texts pepper readers with orientalist figures, suspect inflections of Polynesian speech, and questionable judgments on supposedly savage religious practices such as tattooing, taboo, and ritual cannibalism.[3] Yet, since Carolyn Karcher's *Shadow over the Promised Land*, scholars have regularly and forcefully read Melville as an antiracist, anticolonialist writer. At the same time, while Karcher argues that *Typee* inverted "the cultural assumptions Melville had inherited about the relative merits of civilization and savagery, Christianity and heathenism, white and nonwhite,"[4] others have launched a strong critique of this position, arguing that "in Oceania, for instance, insofar as Melville is discussed at all, it is less as an anti-racist defender of human rights than as an author whose terms of critique of colonialism reinscribe its assumptions."[5] Was his work, then, a radical critique of prevailing conditions or did it ultimately reinforce the very representational structures that made the violence it sought to critique possible?

Let us begin to address this question by looking at a scene that is central to much of the action which concludes *Typee*. Here, Tommo is under pressure to endure the ritual facial tattooing common among his Typee hosts: "I was fairly driven to despair; nothing but the utter ruin of my 'face divine,' as the poets call it, would, I perceived, satisfy the inexorable Mehevi and his chiefs" (220). The language here is instructive, with its invocation of despair alongside the figures of poetry and divinity. While the tone of the passage remains jocular—as Tommo witnesses someone having their eyelids tattooed, he quips upon "the exquisite sensibility of these shutters to the windows of his soul, which he was now having repainted" (218)—it nevertheless expresses a real anxiety for Melville's narrator, one that becomes increasingly insistent as his tale progresses. It is also an anxiety that ultimately revolves around the question of religion, and presents the reader with some of the troubling colonial representations that critics find so problematic:

> At last, seeing my unconquerable repugnance, he ceased to importune me. But not so some other of the savages. . . .
>
> . . . The whole system of tattooing was, I found, connected with their religion; and it was evident, therefore, that they were resolved to make a convert of me.
>
> In the decoration of the chiefs it seems to be necessary to exercise the most elaborate pencilling; while some of the inferior natives looked as if they had been daubed over indiscriminately with a house-painter's brush. I remember one fellow who prided himself hugely upon a great oblong patch, placed high upon his back, and who always reminded me of a man with a blister of Spanish flies stuck between his shoulders. . . .
>
> Although convinced that tattooing was a religious observance, still the nature of the connection between it and the superstitious idolatry of the people was a point upon which I could never obtain any information. Like the still more important system of the "Taboo," it always appeared inexplicable to me. (220–21)

Here, Melville's narrator is adopting the role of a detached observer, humorous in mien, but nevertheless conveying to his readers a set of empirical facts; immediately following this passage, he goes on to a general discussion of the taboo throughout Polynesia that continues for the rest of the chapter.

But at the edges of these specific, factual observations, the hermeneutic Tommo brings to his ironic empiricism exposes how even a sympathetic observer can import Western ways of seeing into the encounter with the other. In analogizing the tattooist's inscriptions on the body as penciling and daubing, Tommo recasts the practice in the lexicon of Western art, though in an unflattering manner: penciling lacks the gravitas that would be appropriate to the social station of the Marquesan chiefs, while the daubing is portrayed as mere craft, house painting. And it is in the smallest details that the stakes of these interpretations come to light. The difference is subtle, but crucial: in the tattooing of eyelids, the reader does not experience a scene of painting, but of *re*-painting. Between painting and repainting is an entire ontology of the body, a Western and Christian body originally painted (made) in the image of God. Not only is this original image painted over, but it is done so indiscriminately, in a fashion that makes the body and its meaning fundamentally ambiguous, just as the social practice of taboo in which that body is caught remains fundamentally ambiguous. The visual economy in which the "face divine" participates is obscured, and the reciprocity of the gaze which defines that economy—the mutual intelligibility of the soul—is occluded, an eclipse of being where the divine art is effaced by a poor, all-too-human imitation of nature. We also see more personal, visceral responses creep into Tommo's account. He evinces a physical disgust at the religious practices of the Marquesans, refers to them as superstitious idolaters, and mocks the tattoos of some "inferior natives."

Although it seems that such a passage would be hard to reconcile with the antiracist readings of Melville's work, a recourse to historical contextualization will present us with a far more complex picture. This essay's historical archaeology of discourse on the South Seas argues that Melville's deployment of the discourse of colonialism is ultimately strategic and effective, though it does so without relieving the text of its baggage or ignoring the serious dangers that Melville's strategy entails.[6] Moreover, it reads Tommo's encounter with the religious community of the Typee as a foundational moment in Melville's aesthetic trajectory. Through a juxtaposition of the two religious communities—Christian missionaries on the one hand and the Marquesans on the other—Melville inaugurates a radical critique of his own cultural background, a critique which will await its fullest expression in *Moby-Dick*. Yet even then, the full import of this critique only becomes clear when Ishmael's vision is seen as a continuation of the work that began among the Typee (as the latter part of this essay will argue through a comparison of Kory-Kory and Queequeg).

In the process of this examination, one of the key interventions of this essay—simultaneously so obvious as to be banal, and so necessary as to be crucial—is its argument that religious and racial discourses of this epoch cannot be treated separately. By focusing on how race and religion intersected in the nineteenth-century conceptualization of the South Seas, we can not only see precisely where Melville either called into question or reproduced the particular representational practices of his time, but also what the operative racial episteme of the moment entailed. While it is becoming increasingly commonplace to read this period as coterminous with the rise of scientific racism, in many ways Melville's society is still beholden to an earlier regime of knowledge. Race is still viewed from within a hermeneutic governed by Enlightenment humanism, which, though still enmeshed with what Foucault called disciplinary power, is not quite yet biopolitical (where biopolitics is defined, after Foucault, as a mode of power that regulates not just the bodies of individuals as the disciplines do, but the life of populations as a whole, thus making the management of the biological life of the species—birth and death rates, hygiene, public health and safety, environment conditions, and so on—the central imperative of politics). After undertaking a reformulation of the terrain of racial discourse in Melville's time, we may evaluate the discontinuity not only between Melville and his culture, but also the discontinuity within the writer's own works. In the process, I argue for a distinct evolution in Melville's conceptualization of religion, race, and culture by way of his original, disconcerting encounter with the religious communities of the Marquesas. Indeed, the two categories—religion and race—are as inextricable for Melville as they were for his culture as whole; being primarily cultural, religious difference is the fundamental marker of distinction among races. And while *Moby-Dick* radicalizes the conclusions of the earlier South Seas works, it does so not by rejecting them, but by building on their strategies and deploying them as ethopoiesis, a moment of ethical transformation made uniquely possible by aesthetics.

While this essay ultimately argues for Melville's work as a radical critique of the episteme within which he wrote, it also proposes a methodological intervention into the framing of the question itself. Implicit in this racio-religious representational dilemma are deeper questions about how our relation to the past structures the ways we are able to answer this question—or rather, how that answer can qualify as truth. By what measure could we span the epistemic gap between Melville's culture and our own? How can scholars engage the history and aesthetics of literature without reducing the politics of the past to the contours of the present? By attempting to establish the discursive structure that gave Melville's statements their meaning, this method attempts to unearth the stratified layers of meaning that objects accrete over time. This presupposes that across historical periods the very nature of such central concepts as *cannibalism* or *race* can change dramatically and rapidly, such that any analysis which attempts to drag them across that chasm of meaning obscures both their construction in the past and their operation in the present. This problem as it relates to *Typee* and *Omoo* can be segmented into four distinct categories—missionaries, culture/race, cannibalism, and sentiment—each of which will be taken up in turn.

Discourse on the South Seas: *Typee*, *Omoo*, and the Nineteenth Century

Heathenish Rites

In Melville's time, missionaries were at the vanguard of the growing wave of colonial expansion into Polynesia. While important logistically for the seafaring system of international trade, as well as for a few important commodities such as sandalwood and bêche-de-mer,[7] the South Sea Islands were primarily popularized as a destination along two vectors: tales of exploration and missionary enterprises. Indeed, the latter takes up the former as a method of recruitment in crucial and important ways. Rod Edmond has noted that tales of exploration such as Captain William Bligh's were used by newly founded groups such as the London Missionary Society to choose the South Pacific as the most amenable destination for its first enterprises.[8] As one South Seas missionary would write to the London Missionary Society about their recruiting practices: "You make them believe . . . they are going to heaven; and when they arrive, instead of heaven, they find black men and fiends and barbarized missionaries."[9] While the bitterness in this passage is obvious, the source of that bitterness is located slightly offstage, in the romantic representations deployed to persuade Europeans to uproot their lives and undertake the arduous tasks of travel and settlement. And since it is such boots-on-the-ground interests that drove the colonial project in the South Pacific—"without their presence the interest of western governments would have been negligible"[10]—the discourse which justifies and frames this missionary work is an important backdrop against which to read the various representational tropes deployed by Melville.

In gauging the initial reactions to its publication, it is hard to read *Typee* as anything but a broadside against the missionary enterprises of his day. Even though Melville was forced to bowdlerize the American edition of his text, "the vehemence with which he was attacked for his criticism of missionaries" was notable, especially when compared to the more hospitable reviews of the secular press.[11] This foundational theme of Melville's early works has led one critic to call them "the most sharply anti-missionary, anti-colonialist perspective we have from any canonical nineteenth-century American novelist."[12] Furthermore, Melville's frontal assault on the proprieties of the day's religious expansionism is not just in itself a strong case for the progressive side in "the question of whether the book should be considered 'colonialist' (residually pro-Western empire building) or 'postcolonialist' (anti-Western dominance)."[13] It also provides a window into a deeper critique of his era's racial episteme and clarifies the stakes involved in representations that may, on first glance, appear colonialist and/or racist.

Take for instance the following passage from *Typee*, lamenting that "the progress of the Hawiians and Tahitians to utter extinction is accelerated in a sort of compound ratio" by Western contact (193). On its face, it would seem to be an ideal example of the "vanishing Indian" trope so prevalent in North American settler colonialism,[14] and even sympathetic critics such as Edmond see this trope as merely a transposition into "the myth of the dying Polynesian."[15] It was nevertheless a deep indictment of the specific logic of the missionary enterprise, whose discursive coordinates differed from those of settler colonialism. Polynesian extinction not only directly contradicted the Christian civilizing mission that undergirded missionary work; it also contained the secondary implication that the godly were the vector by which "vices and diseases [were] introduced among these unhappy people" (193). *Omoo* would continue Melville's critique of the fruits of Western contact with the Polynesians, which "must accelerate the final extinction of their race."[16] Yet despite doing so in a more moderate tone, its cultural impact would be more robust. *Omoo* not only "effectively challenged the nostrums the general public had been hearing from the missionary societies," but it did so in a manner that readers and reviewers took to heart, even spurring calls for reform from within the evangelical community.[17] This critique of the missionary enterprise also highlights a central context for Melville's writing, namely, the concepts of savagery and civilization that shaped his intellectual milieu.

Tattooed Chiefs and Bamboo Temples

The interpretation of both language and culture, insofar as these can be separated, plays a major role in the reflections of Melville's protagonists in *Typee* and *Omoo*. Yet subtending these interpretations is a deeper anti-civilizational rhetoric that emerges from the broader intellectual milieu of the late nineteenth century, taking up questions of empiricism, romanticism, and racism. The importance of this anti-civilizational critique—what Charles Robert Anderson called Melville's "brief against civilization"[18]—only becomes apparent when we first take note of the discontinuities that underscore the concept of race at the time.

As T. Walter Herbert has argued, the concept of civilization operative in the nineteenth century was narrower than today's, denoting not a duality between civilized and savage, but a continuum of gradations along a spectrum between the two.[19] While Herbert's text is largely silent on the question of race, it does offer an important clue to the racial episteme of Melville's society. The savage is not a racial category, but a civilizational one, a figure that reflects an episteme still framed more by the Enlightenment than by modernity—natural history as opposed to biology.[20] In this sense, a savage is still one with the universal man of the Enlightenment, *Homo economicus* stripped of society. Absent the trappings of civilization, he resides at the base of the social hierarchy and does not necessarily represent a force that threatens it.[21] He is a product of classifying, of hierarchy, of natural history, and not yet a product of the norm, the population, and biology. In the dual figures of savagery and civilization, we can see a notion of race that has not yet undergone the "openly biological transcription" that begins in Melville's time but will only achieve its full transformation and ascension "in the racist biologists and eugenicists of the late nineteenth century."[22] In other words, while Melville certainly writes of race and deploys several tropes from within the discourse of race, we are dealing with an earlier, distinct racial episteme. In Foucault's terms, race in Melville's age was not yet biopolitical.[23]

So when Melville writes that "civilization, for every advantage she imparts, holds a hundred evils in reserve," he provides contemporary readers the lens through which the hierarchy of life he describes should be viewed (*Typee*, 124). In fact, the term "race" rarely crops up in Melville's tale, despite his attention to cultural detail and comparison. When it does, it clearly points toward the older, civilizational meaning. When Tommo speculates on an "extinct and forgotten race" responsible for some ruins on the island of Nukuheva, it is clear that he is thinking in terms of an older, preceding civilization (155). Or, when he conjectures that the Typee and Happar might be of different races it is already telling that the term "race" can be divided so finely (66); even when he speaks of differences in skin color, it is in the service of an argument that the people of the bay have been "made the victims of the worst vices and evils of civilized life" (182). Again, when he compares the Marquesans to Native Americans, and juxtaposes them to the "Anglo-Saxon hive," it is likewise to note that "civilization" has "extirpated the greater portion of the Red race" (195).

Nowhere in the text is there a biological transcription in evidence; from within the racial episteme that Melville writes, *Typee* is a strictly antiracist text insofar as it is an anti-civilizational one. In addition, this critique of civilization is at the same time a critique of the religious drive behind the colonial process; race is much more intimately bound up with religious community than it is with biologism. This correlation is illustrated by the comparison to Native Americans, wherein the extirpation of their "paganism" is directly proportional to the extirpation of their very lives, a link made even stronger by the preceding passage:

> Heaven help the "Isles of the Sea!"—The sympathy which Christendom feels for them has, alas! in too many instances proved their bane.
>
> How little do some of these poor islanders comprehend when they look around them, that no inconsiderable part of their disasters originate in certain tea-party excitements, under the influence of which benevolent-looking gentlemen in white cravats solicit alms, and old ladies in spectacles, and young ladies in sober russet low gowns, contribute sixpences towards the creation of a fund, the object of which is to ameliorate the spiritual condition of the Polynesians, but whose end has almost invariably been to accomplish their temporal destruction! (195)

Melville is direct in his critique of the effects of the religious/colonial status quo, even if he will ultimately qualify these pronouncements. But before addressing his equivocations—and the important references to the parlor and sympathy within the passage itself—we need to examine how some crucial tropes are refigured by this rereading of race via the civilizational regime.

First, the question of language with which the essay opened. Queequeg's seemingly caricatured and broken English is a problem other scholars see in

Melville's treatment of the Marquesan language, which "includes many non-Marquesan or nonsense words."[24] Similarly, take the following speech by Jim, the harbor pilot for Papeetee Bay, as Tommo/Typee/Omoo's ship lands at Tahiti: "Ah! you pemi, ah!—you come!—What for you come?—You be fine for come no pilot.—I say, you hear?—I say, you ita maitai (no good)."[25] Going back to Charles Robert Anderson, Melville has developed a reputation with scholars for having a "bad ear" for the languages he encountered. On the other hand, anthropologist Emanuel J. Drechsel has recently argued that Melville's linguistic representations may be better than previously thought, if only because what he was re-presenting was not Marquesan or Tahitian, but a "Maritime Polynesian Pidgin, i.e. an interlingual medium based on makeshift ('broken') . . . versions of Hawaiian, Marquesan, Tahitian, Māori . . . and used primarily in contact between Pacific Islanders on the one hand and European or American explorers and colonists on the other during much of the nineteenth century, if not earlier."[26] Thus, what often seems like a stilted English or a poorly rendered Marquesan is something else altogether, a hybrid form of communication created organically through the interaction of diverse peoples in a contact zone. This does not exculpate Melville for his failings as a translator, but it does cast them in a new light. To return to Queequeg and Ishmael, it highlights not the differences that separate the two, but the way their relationship transcends those forms of difference. Their relationship highlights what they do share: a contact language (in their case, what seems to be a European maritime pidgin), but also the language of mutual work and the intimacy of male friendship. And the same is true of Tommo and Kory-Kory, who seems to speak almost no English, yet—far from what Mary Bercaw Edwards characterizes as little more than "a talking sedan chair"[27]—forms an active and sympathetic character at the heart of the emotional and narrative tension of the text. While Melville seemed to only recognize the distinctness of his pidgin vocabulary from the actual Marquesan language belatedly and somewhat vaguely,[28] he nevertheless presented what he did know in a manner whose accuracy satisfied many critics familiar with this form of speech both then and now.[29]

Perhaps more importantly, it highlights how relationships are created across seemingly insurmountable social, cultural, and linguistic barriers—a theme at the heart of Melville's work, and one which bears directly on the question of representation. As Claire Colebrook has noted, "a strain of nostalgia and utopianism runs through . . . forms of anti-representationalism."[30] All forms of representation, even in situations of ideal communication, will always be imperfect; they will always be tinged with violence. Obviously such cultural encounters were much more fraught in the situation of increasing European contact with Polynesia. The discourse surrounding such encounters was not something of Melville's invention, and would have continued regardless of his picking it up and re-presenting it. Knowing the manner in which Melville stitched together his own experiences with a plethora of well-known texts of the period allows us to see Melville's practices of representation as a form of colonial counter-text. Indeed, throughout Melville's early representations of Polynesia, we can see him "playing off the way it had been constructed by others."[31] Thus, in the scene in which the young women of Nukuheva swim out to meet Tommo's ship, we can see him directly parodying Charles S. Stewart's *A Visit to the South Seas*. Stewart also relates Captain Finch's cruise through the Marquesas on the *U.S.S. Vincennes*, on which Melville's cousin Thomas sailed, where Finch frankly ranks the Marquesans in terms of a racial hierarchy—a judgment Melville explicitly deviates from and counters in his rewriting of the text. And when we read Bercaw Edwards's comparison of the French colonial records to *Typee*—with their overlapping and diverging names, dates, and judgments on the politics and culture of the islands—we can almost see Melville purposefully rewriting these actual, banal records, with their narrower but no less influential audience.

A remarkable aspect of both *Typee* and *Omoo* is the oscillating extremes of the social situations Melville's protagonists find themselves in, from deplorable living conditions at sea, to island captivity by a Marquesan tribe, to sea again but this time with a mutiny, and back to island captivity but now by a colonial government. As Carol Colatrella has noted in *Literature and Moral Reform*, one reason that Melville's work retains so much of its salience in our own era is that we remain deeply enmeshed in the disciplinary regimes that emerged in Melville's era. In one sense, it is his awareness of the penal nature of ship discipline, its profound capture of the sailor's body, that makes Melville's captivity narrative of a different order than those that have come before him in American letters. If anything, his captivity at the hands of savages seems downright genteel when juxtaposed to his captivity at the hands of enlightened society. Indeed, one of his primary protests against the work of the missionaries is the Western regime of punishment they import alongside their civilizing project. In *Omoo*, Melville considers the string of imported laws as tantamount to the "abolition of their national amusements and customs," out of which no good and much ill emerges:

> Doubtless, in thus denationalizing the Tahitians, as it were, the missionaries were prompted by a sincere desire for good; but the effect has been lamentable. Supplied with no amusements, in place of those forbidden, the Tahitians, who require more recreation than other people, have sunk into a listlessness, or indulge in sensualities, a hundred times more pernicious, than all the games ever celebrated in the Temple of Tanee.[32]

And even though what will become biopolitical racism exists only in a nascent form, where Melville does engage the link between race, civilization, and the population—for example, in the statistics of decline surrounding the vanishing Polynesians—he also directly critiques these nascent epistemologies of biopolitical racism and calls them into question by arguing that they are not the solution to, but the cause of "permanent factors which . . . sapped the population's strength . . . wasted energy, and cost money."[33] If biopolitical racism "first develops with colonization," then here, even before this project has crystallized, we can see Melville exposing the violence endemic to this colonial project, with all its little regimes of failed hygiene and arbitrary discipline.[34] In doing so, his critique focuses on the defense of Polynesian religious communities over and against the Christian ones. Given the choice between the best intentions of the missionaries and the Temple of Tanee, Melville consistently sides with and invokes the latter.

Melville's writing, when measured against his own milieu, appears distinctly counter-hegemonic in the realms of religion, sexuality, race, and colonial politics. More than just the representations of the language he heard and spoke while sojourning in the South Seas, Melville also represents to his reader the cultural practices that he encountered. These practices are almost all intimately bound up with the Marquesan religious cosmogony and, just as importantly for our purposes, Melville understood them as such. On one side, certain critics have characterized Tommo's relation to the culture of the Marquesas as an "inability to see it as other than eccentric or bizarre,"[35] while others have argued that his ultimate experience is an exoticizing one of a "world that cannot be made knowable."[36] On the other side, other critics have read Tommo as a prefiguration of the twentieth-century post-structuralist anthropologist.[37] Often, this judgment circles around the interpretation of the following passage: "For my own part, although hardly a day passed while I remained upon the island that I did not witness some religious ceremony or other, it was very much like seeing a parcel of 'Freemasons' making secret signs to each other; I saw everything, but could comprehend nothing" (177). What is often glossed over is that Melville has already given us a hermeneutic for interpreting this quandary in his "Preface," where he tells his readers that he attempts to present "such matters just as they occurred, and leaves every one to form his own opinion concerning them" (xiii). Here Melville argues against hermeneutic mastery, warning the reader against that discourse of the master which would overcode and prejudge his South Seas encounters, and in doing so, cultivate the good, colonial subjectivities driving the imperial mission of his day. Which is not to say that his forms of representation are perfect—far from it—but that they present readers with a model for negotiating the inevitable violence of representations in a contact zone, one which eschews an ethics of purity for one that favors openness and reflexivity in the face of the other.

But even if Melville, in the guise of Tommo, eschews the deployment of his narrative as an apparatus of imaginary capture that would instruct his readers in the proper way to think and feel on the subject he presents, this does not mean that he has himself mastered the epistemological and emotional experiences he is organizing in the narrative. Throughout both *Typee* and

Omoo, Tommo equivocates in his critique of civilization, such as in the following passage taken from amidst the discussion of Native Americans: "Let the savages be civilized, but civilize them with benefits, and not with evils; and let heathenism be destroyed, but not by destroying the heathen" (*Typee*, 195). On one level, the reader should take these statements for what they were: conciliatory gestures. Even the rhetorical form of the double-chiasmus in this passage implies both a form of symmetry, and thus stability, at the same time as it inverts the relation of domination implicit in the terms it juxtaposes: savages/civilized, heathenism/destroyed. And if one stacked up the whole list of pronouncements pro and con on civilization and its benefits from the texts, the sheer weight of the latter would bury the former. Yet this duality remains unquestionably problematic, even weighted as it is toward the anti-civilizational; it points to a tactical political moderation but also to a seeming inability to break, ultimately, from the colonial project. Nowhere is this issue more starkly dramatized than the question of cannibalism, which remains central to debates on the politics of Melville's early novels up to the present day.

Cannibal Banquets

Cannibalism continues to be a representational problem in the interpretation of *Typee*. While *Omoo* largely abandons this theme, it plays a central role in Tommo's resolution to escape from the Typee—his "last horrid revelation" (238). Whether or not it was actually an integral part of Typee ritual observance,[38] cannibalism was located as such within the civilization discourse of the period. For Melville, the practice—or, at the very least, fear of the practice—represents a quilting point for the myriad strands of conflict between the Marquesan and Christian religions; the invocation of a final "revelation," where the unveiling of the bones of the ritual victim parallels the final judgment of the Christian deity, presents this opposition in its starkest, most apocalyptic form.

But before we can locate the figure of cannibalism within Melville's broader anti-civilizational critique, we once again require recourse to the discursive formation against which cannibalism appeared in the nineteenth century. Methodologically, Geoffrey Sanborn's *The Sign of the Cannibal* does for cannibalism at length what this essay attempts to do for racio-religious representations in brief, serving as a model for reestablishing themes in the context from which they emerge in order to measure them—and their effect—from within their own milieu. As an archaeology of cannibal discourse in the nineteenth century, his book attempts "to do more than identify the existence of newness" with regard to the radical nature of Melville's postcolonial sensibility; it attempts "to identify the degree of its emergence with respect to the other elements of the discourse" of cannibalism in the period. In so doing, he maps the discursive territory that was available to Melville for articulating the nature of cannibalism, which divided itself into the following concepts: "lust, denial, famine, vengeance, superstition, and the desire to terrorize."[39] Each category condenses an etiology for the consumption of human flesh: lust, purely gustatory; famine, a desperation response to hunger; vengeance, a desecration of the enemy's corpse; superstition, either ancestor incorporation (positive) or enemy destruction (negative); terror, a weapon to frighten enemies; and denial, which rejected the existence of cannibalism as a social institution.

This background is crucial in situating Melville's representation of cannibalism because it not only contextualizes the choices he did make, but also the one he did not: denial. The debate in Melville's time existed on a savage/humane continuum where the lust explanation—that cannibals not only existed, but ate human flesh merely because they enjoyed its taste—operated on the "transcendentally savage" end of the spectrum, whereas denial represented a "transcendentally humane" perspective. There was no doubt as to the famine explanation; reliably occurring as it did to Europeans—audiences were particularly titillated by stories of shipwreck cannibalism—it served to mark off the other forms only in contrast. Superstition was less often invoked as an explanation, but it did play a particularly important role in the justification of missionary enterprises, a fact which should serve to remind us that cannibalism is an object of concern both as a pagan religious practice and as an important social problem solved by Christian conversion. After first establishing the discursive terrain on which Melville operated, Sanborn very quickly sees that the crucial question is why Melville does not choose what appears to our modern sensibilities as the most radical answer: a denial that the Typee are cannibals at all.[40] And this is indeed the crucial question, insofar as it frames the problem of representation in Melville in a manner that not only shows what was at stake politically from within his own milieu, but also his broader strategy for addressing the problem of knowledge and otherness circulating around representations of the South Seas. What makes Melville's choice even more stark is that, as Bercaw Edwards has argued, the scene of cannibalism he describes is an interpolation of a scene from David Porter's *Journal of a Cruise Made to the Pacific Ocean*.[41] Except that Melville seems to use Porter's account to make the exact opposite claim, namely, that the Typee *are* cannibals. Whereas Porter states that cannibalism is "a practice so unnatural" that it justifies violence, he nevertheless absolves the Typee of the practice even though it would have been a useful excuse for the violence he perpetrated against them.[42] Moreover, the fact that Melville is rewriting a scene from Porter in chapter 32 of *Typee* at the very least calls into serious question whether he witnessed a similar event. In other words, the preponderance of evidence seems to indicate that Melville's inclusion of the scene of cannibalism, the "last horrid revelation," was a deliberate choice, and one that deviated from his own experiences of the Marquesas.[43]

When examined more closely, however, what seems to be a representational choice that plays into the dominant narratives of the period appears quite different. In fact, we can see that Melville is attempting to offer a critique of missionary colonialism not by claiming that it disrupts an ideal, Edenic culture; instead of denying the existence of cannibalism, he will imply that cannibalism exists, yet attempt to portray cannibals as sympathetic, sentimental figures. While Melville's account of the South Seas is regularly described as romantic, the text complicates both romanticism in the literary sense and the more common sense (i.e., idealized, romanced). To get a sense for the manner in which Melville writes against a certain tendency within the romantic literary tradition is best illustrated by a comparison of some representative passages. The first from Melville:

> Our journey was soon at an end; for, scaling a sudden height, we came abruptly upon the place of our destination. I wish that it were possible to sketch in words this spot as vividly as I recollect it. Here were situated the Taboo groves of the valley—the scene of many a prolonged feast, of many a horrid rite. Beneath the dark shadows of the consecrated bread-fruit trees there reigned a solemn twilight—a cathedral-like gloom. The frightful genius of pagan worship seemed to brood in silence over the place, breathing its spell upon every object around. (*Typee*, 91)

Unlike many of his contemporaries and predecessors, Tommo does not find in nature a transcendental return to some kind of spiritual peace. From Goethe's "famous description of the cathedral of nature" in the second letter of *The Sorrows of Young Werther*,[44] to Emerson averring that "in the woods, we return to reason and faith,"[45] the image of the woods as a cathedral had in Melville's time become established as a common trope. Longfellow would write that "the vast cathedral of Nature is full of holy scriptures, and shapes of deep, mysterious meaning" and Thoreau would likewise note that, upon a winter walk, "the withdrawn and tense sky seemed groined like the aisles of a cathedral."[46] Against this backdrop, Melville's description of a "cathedral-like gloom" takes on a surfeit of significance, only heightened by his invocation of "genius." Melville is rewriting both the tropes of nature-as-cathedral as well as the romantic genius that is often invoked by such a setting. Jonathan A. Cook has noted another important correlate to *Typee*'s melancholy reaction to paradise—its resonance with the biblical Eden. Insofar as a foundational part of the book's "appeal is also doubtless its imaginative incorporation of mythic elements," paradise itself becomes an ambivalent space.[47] In the cathedral of nature, it is not just a particular conception of nature that is being rewritten, but a conception of the cathedral as well. Furthermore, this religious rewriting is not confined to Melville's description of the Taboo groves, but this sense of oppression and melancholy permeates his descriptions of the natural splendor of Marquesan nature, as for instance when Tommo relates that the sight of beautiful tropical birds "always oppressed me with melancholy" (216).

In short, Melville is deliberately writing a narrative of savagery and otherness that does not rely on models in the Rousseauian tradition of the noble savage, and in fact goes out of its way to eschew those models for a practical, empirical form of representation. Stated from the outset, this mode of representations has as its goal the task of actively working against such mastery, refusing an overcoding of the text in order to allow the audience to form their own opinions. As Tommo advises his readers, tongue firmly in cheek: "I recommend all adventurous youths who abandon vessels in romantic islands during the rainy season to provide themselves with umbrellas" (48). As Sanborn has noted, by way of William Charvat's reading of *Moby-Dick*, this gesture is tied into the pedagogical method Melville deploys throughout his text, which he calls *processual speculation*. An attempt to present the scope of available alternatives, and a commitment to choose no singular, totalizing approach to the world, this project is perhaps best summarized in Melville in the following passage discussing the "counterpoise" of sperm and right whale heads alongside a ship: "So, when on one side you hoist Locke's head you go over that way; but now, on the other side, hoist in Kant's and you come back again."[48] It is crucial, as Sanborn argues, to see this as the process in play as Tommo shifts through the various explanations of cannibalism throughout *Typee*. His opinion on the subject is not static, but changes as his sojourn progresses.

Nevertheless, the question remains: why not denialism? Why vengeance or, even more radically, terror as the explanation for cannibalism? Bercaw Edwards offers two slightly more prosaic reasons for this choice: first, it is a reflection of the fact that this tale began its life as sailor talk, as an oral form prone to exaggeration and honed upon retelling the tale to multiple audiences;[49] second, that it allowed Melville to spice up the tale by adding elements from yet another genre, namely, the gothic.[50] In other words, there were narratological, even commercial reasons for this choice, ones that highlight the milieu of narration from which the text emerged—to which one might add Melville's association with the Knickerbocker School and its skepticism of the transcendentalist's view of nature. Sanborn, on the other hand, focuses on the pedagogical method, and the politics implied by *processual speculation*. Ultimately, the problem with denialism was twofold: it was linked to a fading form of Enlightenment thought, and in particular one that was closely tied to the idealization of the noble savage. John Barrow denied cannibalism, as did John Atkins in his *Voyage to Guinea, Brasil, and the West Indies* (1735), because it contravened the theoretical tenets of an episteme that was slowly being eclipsed. Barrow, for whom cannibalism was "too monstrous to be believed," began from a theoretical premise on human nature and proceeded to organize the empirical data from that prior set of assumptions.[51] However, this "laudable but misguided attempt to think the best that could be thought about human nature" led to Barrow's position being "defined as a blinkered humanism, . . . stripped of much of its power to disturb the certainties of the discourse on savagery" (Sanborn, *Sign of the Cannibal*, 36).[52]This broader shift in the intellectual currents of the time was tied to the perceived excesses of the French Revolution (and, though unmentioned by Sanborn, the Haitian Revolution), which was in turn tied up with the idea of the noble savage and the state of nature. Melville's defense of the Marquesans and other Polynesians would already enter the public stage linked to "an effeminate and dangerous idealism" that would slant readers' perception toward viewing him as an overly theoretical "Rousseauian throwback" (*Sign of the Cannibal*, 87). Melville not only wanted to avoid the taint of theory, but also to prevent the reflexive resistance a denialist tale would inevitably provoke; indeed, as Sanborn argues, both the demands of the market and his own opposition to totalizing theories would have made the choice an odd one for Melville both as an author with an eye on public reception as well as one with an ethical argument to advance. Thus, "Melville introduces the denial of cannibalism because he wants to make the entire discursive field an object of critical attention, and . . . he backs away from it because it is incompatible with his project of processual speculation and potentially damaging to his book's reception" (*Sign of the Cannibal*, 89).

Hence what makes a methodology such as Sanborn's so necessary: what appears to our modern sensibilities as the radical solution is in fact a much more conservative one. It is more conservative in principle because it eschews empirics for an essentialized view of human nature and an attendant totalizing theory of society, a view that is fast being eclipsed in a major epistemic transition. Yet it is also more conservative in effect because, no matter how radically and purely against the pernicious discourses of cannibalism denialism may have been, such a position would have been received as a dead letter by the public. For Melville's critique of civilization to gain any traction at all, it had to be not a Rousseauian critique, but an empirical one—one that based itself on the "unvarnished truth" (*Typee*, xiv). No matter how much modern readers desire Melville to make their own epistemological and political choices, those options were simply unavailable to him. Forced to work within the discursive terrain available, Melville instead chose to stitch together a critique of civilization that, without abandoning its suspect categories wholesale, sought to transform them in specific and purposeful ways. It is in this fashion that we should read the orientalist—or perhaps, Pacificist—representations of Melville's texts, that is, that their deployment is a means to subvert them, as Sanborn notes: "the only reason Melville identifies himself with the Orientalist desire of his readers is so that he can bring them to see, in the failure of his voyeuristic desire, the failure of theirs" (*Sign of the Cannibal*, 79). For Melville it is far more radical to accept the premise of cannibalism's existence and attempt to transform its signification than to reject it outright, which, in any case, would be a form of intellectual totalization.

Naked Houris

Which is where the question of sentiment enters into the equation. It is also where this essay's interpretation of the work done by *Typee* apropos of cannibalism begins to differ in subtle yet important ways from that of Sanborn's, which ultimately sees the tale as a "romance of spontaneous masculine sensibility" (*Sign of the Cannibal*, 101). Sanborn posits that Melville affirms the vengeance concept of cannibalism as a rejection of domesticity, because otherwise Typee men "would be, for all practical purposes, indistinguishable from the women" (*Sign of the Cannibal*, 89). Yet it seems difficult to reconcile the slippage between the argument that Melville chooses vengeance as a counter to a creeping domesticity and, at the same time, the argument that Melville only creates a scene of cannibalism as a counter-practice to colonial domination. While Sanborn clearly establishes the terrain on which the debate over the status of cannibalism in Melville can be productively carried out, he cannot, however, have it both ways. It cannot be the case that Melville was all along meticulously pitching his argument to his audience as an anti-Rousseauian defense of the South Sea Islanders, but that, in the end, he is really making an argument about representational terror that stakes out political and theoretical ground that is unseen and nearly unseeable to his contemporaries. Instead, it seems far more likely, both in terms of Melville's broader tactics and in terms of the text itself, that Melville does not use cannibalism to reject sentiment, but uses sentiment to reject the subjugation of cannibals.

D. H. Lawrence famously read Tommo's escape as an inability to break the "long chain" of civilization represented by the figures of "Home and Mother."[53] Yet what we see instead is a text that embraces the tropes of sentiment as a way to short-circuit other, more pernicious discourses on the subject. Sentimentalizing cannibalism is a natural outgrowth of Melville's empiricist critique of civilization. If cannibalism is inevitable, the only option is to resignify it, and what Lawrence sees as Melville's failure is actually his strategy all along. And Sanborn is correct; Tommo's narrative undeniably "bears a striking resemblance to the language of domesticity" (*Sign of the Cannibal*, 89). It also seems clear that Melville's representations are designed to combat the view of cannibalism as an act that "obscures the humane capacity for sentiment" (*Sign of the Cannibal*, 59). Henry Bolingbroke would adopt this view of cannibalism as fundamentally at odds with the operation of sentiment when he argued thus: "Man is the object of our strongest affection—the tenderest emotions of the heart."[54] This theoretical postulate emerged alongside numerous purportedly empirical representations of cannibalism. In her *Life in Feejee, or, Five Years among the Cannibals*, Mary Wallis relates the following tale of cannibalism: "The body of Wilson and his woman were taken ashore where they were cooked and eaten; the lives of the children were spared that they might be fattened before they should be killed."[55] Charles Darwin relates a similar tale of cannibalism from Tierra del Fuego: "when pressed in winter by hunger, they kill and devour their old women before their dogs . . . they are pursued by the men and brought back to the slaughter-house at their own firesides!"[56] In other words, this "cannibal talk" which circulated throughout society took on a distinct resonance within the broader discourse of sentimentalism and domesticity: cannibalism as a devourer of Home and Mother.[57]

Against this discourse, Melville re-creates an oft-overlooked scene of domestic tranquility and affection. There may be other sentimental accounts of living with cannibals in the literature of the day, but if there are, then Meville's was certainly foremost among them. While readers expect to meet the fierce tribe of Porter's *Journal*, they instead spend much of their time in an almost quintessentially domestic scene; Typee as "Happy Valley" (124). Especially after the departure of Toby, Tommo is ensconced in a Typee family, one that creates relations of care and reciprocal sympathy that nineteenth-century readers would have associated with sentimental novels. A queer family, to be sure, but a family nevertheless.[58] Fayaway is an obvious embodiment of feminine grace and devotion, and Tommo sees her as a woman who participates in the economy of reciprocal sentimental interiority: "her mind was swayed by gentle impulses hardly to be anticipated from one in her condition; that she appeared to be conscious there were ties rudely severed, which had once bound us to our homes; that there were sisters and brothers anxiously looking forward to our return" (108). This connection casts Fayaway's exotic sexuality, with its mix of innocence and forwardness, in a different light as well, insofar as she remains within the sentimental economy despite her sexuality—a connection that is altogether deadly in the seduction novels popular in America after the Revolution. Sophia Hawthorne famously saw "Fayaway in his face," and the reception of her as a character—and the imagined sexual link between Fayaway and Melville—seems to indicate that she resonated as a figure that both participated in as well as challenged the sentimental economy.[59] Kory-Kory is also figured as a devoted caregiver, who "never for one moment left my side" and regularly bathes and tends to his invalid charge (109). Kory-Kory's depiction is often framed as a prototypical colonialist relationship à la Robinson Crusoe and Friday, a judgment which is sometimes taken to hyperbolic extremes—in one case, Tommo becomes "literally . . . guilty of racial slavery."[60] Setting aside for a moment Tommo's status as, in the larger scheme of things, Kory-Kory's captive, as well as the homoerotic undertones of their whole relationship, Kory-Kory's ministrations bear a striking resemblance less to slavery than a familiar figure from sentimental novels, the domestic nurse who, through her patient and loyal attentions, brings back a family member from the brink of a deadly ailment. Marheyo and Tinor duly serve as surrogate father and mother figures; Marheyo at one point gives Tommo "a paternal hug" and Tinor is referred to from early on as "dear, good, affectionate old Tinor!" (121, 85). Melville makes this contrast explicit in the comedic "baked baby" scene, in which Toby goes into a panic over the contents of a dish served to them at a religious feast (94).

This scene also highlights the way that all these discourses become intimately enmeshed one with the other. If cannibalism in *Typee* is primarily represented as a religious element of Marquesan culture, it nonetheless resonates with all these broader cultural discourses. When Melville enters the Typee Valley—the valley of the cannibals—he is entering a space where the social bonds of sympathy should cease to operate according to the conventions of his time. The sign of the cannibal circulates within the broader culture of Melville's day to block all forms of sympathy, breaking the great chain of moral sentiments. In cannibal talk, a body is reduced to a mere object for another to use, an instrumentalized vehicle for the other's desire; consequently, all violence becomes justifiable against cannibalism as the worst form of savagery, a judgment which again and again is deployed in the service of colonial violence. Melville's narrative counters this disruption of the circuit by sentimentalizing the cannibals, by showing them to be Kory-Kory and Fayaway, Marheyo and Tinor; it rebuilds the bonds of sympathy over and against all those civilizing narratives that would destroy them. It does so not by idealizing them, but by showing that even amidst violence, they remain beings in sympathetic relation to other beings—just like everyone else. It is from this perspective that we should reread the final scene of Tommo's escape. The violence with which the tale concludes only appears contradictory if we assume that Melville is presenting an idealized depiction of Marquesan culture and not a realistic one, where violence and sympathy remain inextricable, as they do in Melville's own culture—a connection Melville takes pains to establish when he links the parlor sympathy of Christendom's "tea-party excitements" to the violence of the missionary enterprise. Before Tommo can reach the boat that takes him to his final violent encounter with Mow-Mow in the bay, he is surrounded by hostile men in a scene charged with potential violence. This is where the famous references to Home and Mother appear, but they turn out to be not what motivates Tommo to risk the danger of escape, but what his Typee friends invoke when aiding his flight:

> Before I had proceeded a hundred yards I was again surrounded by the savages, who were still in all the heat of argument, and appeared every moment as if they would come to blows. In the midst of this tumult old Marheyo came to my side, and I shall never forget the benevolent expression of his countenance. He placed his arm upon my shoulder, and emphatically pronounced the only two English words I had taught him—"Home" and "Mother." I at once understood what he meant, and eagerly expressed my thanks to him. Fayaway and Kory-Kory were by his side, both weeping violently. (248)

It is not Home and Mother he is escaping to, but Home and Mother that allows him to escape; they are the sole English words Marheyo comprehends, and they save Tommo's life. Far from eclipsing the sentimental work that Melville has done to this point, they solidify it by demonstrating the continuing existence of sentimental bonds even across the violent and tenuous space of the contact zone.

Interminable Oceans: *Typee*'s Wake

> In our more correct writing, we give to this generalization the name of Being, and thereby confess that we have arrived as far as we can go. Suffice it for the joy of the universe, that we have not arrived at a wall, but at interminable oceans.
>
> —Ralph Waldo Emerson, "Experience"[61]

This is not the entirety of the story. When measured against its own age, it becomes easier to see how Melville's early work left such controversy in its wake. Yet, when most contemporary critics compare the early narratives of the South Seas to *Moby-Dick*, they find a fuller expression of his vision, less trapped by the conventions in which *Typee* and *Omoo* remained enmeshed. When we make this critical move, we rely on an implicit argument about Melville's encounter with the religious community of the Marquesans. For him, the encounter with a religion based around ambiguous practices of taboo and tattooing, cannibalism and the collection of enemy heads is an encounter with both religion and community *tout court*. That is to say, it is only in this moment of radical contrast that the contingency of his own religion comes into focus, and it is only with the imminent prospect of his joining a radically other community—facial tattooing as conversion—that the values instilled by his own society become noticeably, even threateningly, contingent. What is often framed as Melville's metaphysical turn, with all its subsequent religious speculation and broadening philosophical engagements, has its condition of possibility in this encounter.

This trajectory is perhaps most strongly embodied in the figure of Kory-Kory. Despite all the attention to male friendship and homoeroticism in Melville's work, one of the great, undertheorized characters in his oeuvre is Kory-Kory. As Tommo begins to resolve himself to escape toward the end of the tale, he relates the following assessment of his mental state: "There was no one with whom I could freely converse; no one to whom I could communicate my thoughts; no one who could sympathise with my sufferings" (231). When taken in concert, this and many of Tommo's other actions begin to evoke a lingering sense of betrayal, of a friendship denigrated and ultimately abandoned. While Fayaway and Toby are often read as the central characters in Tommo's tale, Kory-Kory's presence looms largest throughout his sojourn in the Typee Valley. That his presence loomed largest in Melville's own mind is not hard to surmise; later, when wrestling with publishing issues and concerns about his tale's veracity, it is not to the figure of Fayaway that he appeals, but to Kory-Kory, "who I'll be bound is this blessed day taking his noon nap somewhere in the flowery vale of Typee."[62] But even more so, the connection between Kory-Kory and Queequeg, not just their obvious similarities but also the differences between the two, demonstrate that Tommo's Marquesan friend continued to insist upon a presence in the psychic life of Melville's writing: in the culmination of Melville's tales of the ocean, it is neither Toby nor the Long Doctor who reappears as Ishmael's archetypal male friend, but Kory-Kory.

A closer reading of the transformation of Kory-Kory into Queequeg might elucidate all the ways that he is something like an apology to the abandoned friend, an appeal to forgiveness through re-presentation. A psychoanalytic comparison of the two tales encounters no difficulties in seeing the resonance between Tommo's throbbing leg and Ahab's wounded appendage. As John Bryant notes, the pain in Tommo's leg seems to represent not a desire to leave the Typee, but a desire to stay among them as long as possible; it flares up in rhythm with the opportunities to prolong his stay in the Marquesas, and when presented with his best opportunity to escape, only then is his leg "made to throb at its greatest intensity."[63] The absence of that leg which throbs with desire for the other frames Ahab's monomania, a stark contrast to the relationship of Ishmael and Queequeg. While the scene of cannibalism—where Tommo's eyes "fell upon the disordered members of a human skeleton, the bones still fresh with moisture, and with particles of flesh clinging to them here and there!" (238)—crystallizes his resolve to escape, it does not set into motion this resolution. Instead, it is the earlier scene of tattooing that sends him into a virtual panic, when the tribe's tattooist Karky begins to enlist the community in his quest to mark Tommo's face:

> Horrified at the bare thought of being rendered hideous for life if the wretch were to execute his purpose upon me, I struggled to get away from him, while Kory-Kory, turning traitor, stood by, and besought me to comply with the outrageous request . . . At last, half wild with terror and indignation, I succeeded in breaking away from the three savages, and fled. . . .
>
> . . . I now felt convinced that in some luckless hour I should be disfigured in such a manner as never more to have the face to return to my countrymen. (218–19)

This terror only grows when Mehevi, whom Tommo styles a king, begins insisting on the process, an insistence that is eventually picked up by the rest of the community: "Hardly a day passed but I was subjected to their annoying requests, until at last my existence became a burden to me; the pleasures I had previously enjoyed no longer afforded me delight, and all my former desire to escape from the valley now revived with additional force" (220). For

Tommo, this is the ultimate horror. It evokes in him a moment of *aphanisis*, a sense of subjective annihilation. The circuit of enjoyment he has formed within the community of the Typee is interrupted, and he begins to feel as if he "is reduced to being only the instrument" of the other's desire, a relation which "dissolves the being of the subject."[64] This moment of aphanisis, "the *fading* of the subject," is one in which Tommo feels as if his very identity is disappearing—as if he will literally cease to be.[65] To be clear, this is not Tommo misreading the situation; facial tattooing would forever alter and proscribe his social status among his "countrymen," and among the Typee it would be redolent with religious significance. As the passage above indicates, this causes a whole series of cultural practices to begin to symbolically condense for Tommo. There is a metonymic slippage between tattoo and taboo, which in turn starts to draw in all the other fears he has about the savage nature of his captors into a paranoid vortex of resignification. As Geoffrey Sanborn convincingly argues, tattoo slips over into taboo, or the relation of the individual to the society as a whole—thus, a question of religion—which in turn encompasses the practice of taking human heads as trophies, including white ones, and from there it is just one short step to his final revelation in that cannibal encounter (*Sign of the Cannibal*, 103–9). Just as he links the heads with the reduction of people to property (108), Tommo sees facial tattooing as an eclipse of his own subjectivity and reduction to the status of mere object; as he exclaims of Karky: "What an object he would have made of me!" (219). Sanborn contends that "in each case, he fears that he will be made to enter the social economy of savagery, now understood as a mode of existence based on the continual display and recognition of 'face' " (*Sign of the Cannibal*, 109). However, it seems that it is not precisely entering into this new economy that he fears. Tommo seems to have little fear of otherness, but he does display an immense fear of the loss of his self. Instead, it seems that what galls him is not savagery per se, but the choice he is forced to make between civilization and savagery. He does not want to be a Christian missionary, but neither does he desire to convert to the beliefs of his Typee friends.

This moment of horror is tinged with a loss of religious and racial identity, but it is even more deeply tinged with a loss of identity per se. Here we also see the ambivalence of Melville's discourse, torn between a genuine attempt to understand others from within *their* own terms while simultaneously failing from within *his* own terms. Because, for all intents and purposes, he is correct: the process of bodily inscription is immanent to the religious practices of the Marquesans, just as it would be a repudiation of his own—a disfiguration of his (Christian) "face divine." Tommo has not escaped one civilization and its religious/moral strictures merely to be captured by another, no matter how valid and worthy of independent existence it may be. And it seems that ultimately there is no resolution to this metaphysical question of identity and social constraint that Tommo is grappling with; the tale ends in a riotous mess of violence and betrayal, as if the tossing of a few goods to Marheyo, Kory-Kory, and Fayaway could balance the accounts of friendship.

Archaeologically, Melville remains enmeshed within the concepts he has at hand, even as he transforms them in ways that make their old uses untenable. As historian Arnold I. Davidson has noted, "Automatisms of attitude have a durability, a slow temporality. . . . Such resistance [to conceptual shifts] can take place not only in a . . . community but even in the individual who is most responsible for the conceptual innovation."[66] At the end of *Typee*, Melville seems to be in just such a position, in the clearing of the concepts he is working with but not yet beyond, and without the new concepts that will emerge from his ethopoetic work and allow him to create a new form of community. Yet, it is to Melville's great credit that he begins that work almost immediately. Apropos of the problem of choice, we see the outlines of a new form of refusal that attempts to circumvent the either/or logic within which Tommo remains stuck. We see this in the figure of the rover, *omoo*, itself, but also in the politics of the mutiny of the *Julia*, where his compatriots "once more urged our plan of quietly refusing duty, and awaiting the result."[67] In this quiet refusal we can already hear the echoes of Bartleby and Ishmael, and in *Mardi* Melville begins to embrace the fact that the questions he is asking go deeper than the surface, presaging the metaphysical turn that would both alienate him from his contemporary readers and entrench him in the literary canon. But this transformation perhaps reaches its apex in Queequeg, where Melville reevaluates his representations of Kory-Kory and the Typee, occupies that conceptual space he has opened, and demonstrates that space's radical nature.

The shift from Kory-Kory to Queequeg is dramatic when compared directly. The subtending homoeroticism that peeks through in place names such as "Buggery Island" and the oft-analyzed masturbation scene—where Kory-Kory displays his jealousy at the attention Tommo receives from the young women and kindles a fire in an unquestionably erotic manner (23, 111)—becomes as overt as possible in the relationship of Queequeg and Ishmael. Crucially, the tattoo as an emblem of horror and disfiguration is completely transformed, and the process of reading the tattooed body is inverted. Whereas Kory-Kory "was, alas! a hideous object to look upon" despite being "robust and well-made" (83), Queequeg "for all his tattooing . . . was on the whole a clean, comely looking cannibal."[68] Moreover, although Tommo is cognizant that his aesthetic judgments are premised upon Kory-Kory's adornments being "a little curious to my unaccustomed sight," he proceeds with them anyway (83); Ishmael inverts this process by starting with the negative judgment—he first describes Queequeg's head as "a mildewed skull"[69]—before moving on to one that is positive in spite of his tattooed appearance being both curious and unaccustomed. Between the two judgments, Melville has taken his processual speculation into the new conceptual space he had opened beforehand, without stopping short and preventing the strange from entering the realm of the beautiful. Emphasizing the nature of this scene as a restaging of that previous encounter, Melville has the significant objects that framed his previous judgment reappear: this new cannibal also comes with both a "New Zealand head" and a "tomahawk."[70]

This encounter with Queequeg, Melville is telling us, remains positive not because it has failed to consider the three elements—cannibalism, trophy heads, and tomahawks—which had so destabilized Tommo's otherwise sympathetic representations of the Typee in that prior encounter, but because it has considered them differently. This juxtaposition culminates in the contrasting judgments of Ishmael and Ahab:

> Many spare hours he spent, in carving the lid with all manner of grotesque figures and drawings; and it seemed that hereby he was striving, in his rude way, to copy parts of the twisted tattooing on his body. And this tattooing, had been the work of a departed prophet and seer of his island, who, by those hieroglyphic marks, had written out on his body a complete theory of the heavens and the earth, and a mystical treatise on the art of attaining truth; so that Queequeg in his own proper person was a riddle to unfold; a wondrous work in one volume; but whose mysteries not even himself could read, though his own live heart beat against them; and these mysteries were therefore destined in the end to moulder away with the living parchment whereon they were inscribed, and so be unsolved to the last. And this thought it must have been which suggested to Ahab that wild exclamation of his, when one morning turning away from surveying poor Queequeg—"Oh, devilish tantalization of the gods!"[71]

Here, all these competing questions of God, otherness, and knowledge come together in a crucial nexus. Like Tantalus, the deeper meaning of Queequeg and his prophecy remains just out of Ahab's reach. His singular volume echoes the Bible, each a "wondrous work in one volume," one revealed religion and the other, at least to Ahab's eyes, concealed religion. Further, Queequeg here becomes another figure of the white whale, that impenetrable enigma which Ahab is driven to transcend/defeat. In this regard, Ahab's survey of Queequeg reproduces "the primary ethnological scene" of the nineteenth century.[72] While *Typee* seems almost unconcerned with race absent questions of religion and culture, *Moby-Dick* is fully engaged with the delineation of what Melville's contemporary Josiah Nott called "Types of Mankind."[73] As Samuel Otter notes, in ethnological thought "a scene is enacted: a scene of bodily and especially cranial contemplation, in which the observer stands before another and seeks access."[74] In Melville, this object is a somewhat strange one, as what is measured is not types of mankind, but whales: cetology as ethnology. Both the White Whale and Queequeg remain impervious to Ahab's gaze; both the other and the Leviathan, one of the biblical beasts of chaos subdued by God, subvert the standard ethnological script.

The subversive gesture of this ethnological substitution is only reinforced by an earlier passage where Ishmael relates some of his own tattoos to the readers, telling them that he is holding some space in reserve "for a poem I was then composing." Before, Tommo saw Kory-Kory's tattoos as reminiscent of prisoners "gazing out sentimentally from behind the grated bars of a prison window" (83); now, Ishmael perceives the tattoo no longer as a sort of wound, a cultural inscription bespeaking the pain of paralysis, but as a poem, and, more subtly though more profoundly, the body is no longer the space where the social codes of an identity are expressed, but a free space whose blankness signifies its mobility, its openness to future composition. The body becomes the space on which the poem of life is written, a writing that remains in progress. In the second passage, Queequeg's tattoos remain enigmatic, but their otherness takes on a deeper meaning. Newly perceived as precisely that which Ahab desires, access to metaphysical truth, but is denied; Ahab's desire to understand what Queequeg signifies is juxtaposed to Ishmael's friendship with Queequeg, no longer barred by the calcified concepts of civilization. Crucially, when Ishmael tells us he is saving room for a poem, he does so after relating an ethnological measurement of a whale's skeleton—one he has tattooed on his right arm.

Tommo's leg and Ahab's: Ahab desires to pierce through to the truth behind the veil of the Other, whereas Ishmael seems content in his love, his pleasure, his friendship with the other; ethnology is written on one arm, but the rest of his body remains open to the poetry of his encounter with the world. Ishmael reproduces Tommo's leg not as unconscious symptom, but as a conscious inscription on the body. Ahab is Tommo without his throbbing leg, that part of him that wants to remain with the Typee, which pulses with his desire to refuse the return to civilization. Ahab abjures the messy contradictions and unmeaning violence of the world; he wants to get through the phenomenal to the noumenal, a direct experience of the Real—the horror of cannibalism, of homosexuality, of home, of remaining with the Typee—but Melville wants to reject this forced choice as false, presenting instead an image of hybridity and connection across difference. And fundamentally, this conflict is once again framed as a question of religion, except that now Tommo's conversion anxiety is displaced onto Ahab, with Ishmael representing a new, third term. He does not want to rebel against the social and overthrow it in order to reach a purer state of being, but to transform it, to quietly refuse it; he prefers not to.

Notes

1. The epigraph is from Herman Melville, *Typee, A Peep at Polynesian Life*, ed. Harrison Hayford, Hershel Parker, and G. Thomas Tanselle (Evanston and Chicago: Northwestern University Press and the Newberry Library, 1968), 5. Subsequent citations given in the text.

2. Herman Melville, *Moby-Dick; or the Whale*, ed. Harrison Hayford, Hershel Parker, and G. Thomas Tanselle (Evanston and Chicago: Northwestern University Press and the Newberry Library, 1988), 23.

3. As the *Oxford English Dictionary* notes, the houri from this essay's epigraph is "a nymph of the Muslim paradise. Hence applied allusively to a voluptuously beautiful woman" ("houri, n.").

4. Carolyn Karcher, *Shadow over the Promised Land: Slavery Race and Violence in Melville's America* (Baton Rouge: Louisiana State University Press), 1.

5. Paul Lyons, "Global Melville," in *A Companion to Herman Melville*, ed. Wyn Kelley (Malden, Mass.: Blackwell, 2002), 65. While Karcher's text constitutes a "landmark study" in Melville scholarship, revitalizing as it does the previously ignored or marginalized question of race (Arnold Rampersad, "Melville and Race," in *Herman Melville: A Collection of Critical Essays*, ed. Myra Jehlen [Englewood Cliffs, N.J.: Prentice Hall, 1994], 160), it is certainly preceded by a number of important critics in this area, as she herself notes from the outset. Two of the most important of these are the antiracist readings of Melville undertaken by both C. L. R. James and Ralph Ellison (Rampersad, 164). For perspectives better described as falling in the Lyons camp, see Rasha al Disuqi, "Orientalism in *Moby-Dick*," *American Journal of Islamic Social Sciences* 4, no. 1 (September 1, 1987); Nicholas Birns, "Thickly Studded Oriental Archipelagoes" : Figuring the Indian and Pacific Oceans in *Moby-Dick*," *Leviathan: A Journal of Melville Studies* 14, no. 2 (2012): 4–24; Paul Lyons, *American Pacificism: Oceania in the US Imagination*, (New York: Routledge, 2006); William Cummings, "Orientalism's Corporeal Dimension: Tattooed Bodies and Eighteenth-Century Oceans," *Journal of Colonialism and Colonial History* 4, no. 2 (2003); Mary K. Bercaw Edwards, *Cannibal Old Me: Spoken Sources in Melville's Early Works* (Kent, Ohio: Kent State University Press, 2012); Mitchell Breitwieser, "False Sympathy in Melville's *Typee*," in Jehlen, *Herman Melville*, 15–26; Douglas Ivison, "I Saw Everything But Could Comprehend Nothing: Melville's *Typee*, Travel Narrative, and Colonial Discourse," *American Transcendental Quarterly* 16, no. 2 (June 2002): 115–30; Juniper Ellis, "Melville's Literary Cartographies of the South Seas," *The Massachusetts Review* 38, no. 1 (April 1, 1997): 9–29. For an overview of both sides of the issue, see G. R. Thompson, "Introduction: Being There, Melville and the Romance of Real Life Adventure," *ESQ: A Journal of the American Renaissance* 5, no. 1 (2005): 18–23.

6. Following the work of Michel Foucault, archaeological history, instead of assuming that concepts such as *race* or *racism* (or *cannibalism*, or even *literature*) are transhistorical objects, immutable over time, assumes that discourses are "practices that systematically form the objects of which they speak" and that such objects are constructed in discontinuous formations—layered historical strata that displace other strata while building upon them (Michel Foucault, *Archaeology of Knowledge; and, The Discourse on Language*, trans. A. M. Sheridan Smith [New York: Pantheon Books, 1972], 49). Implicit in this concept of discourse is that each discursive formation has a certain regularity, that is, a distribution of the statements in that discourse based on a certain internal logic governing the formation of truth concerning its objects, the concepts that govern those objects, its enunciative modalities (who speaks), and strategies/power relations (ibid., 38).

7. I. C. Campbell, *"Gone Native" in Polynesia: Captivity Narratives and Experiences from the South Pacific* (Westport, Conn.: Greenwood, 1998), 12.

8. Rod Edmond, *Representing the South Pacific: Colonial Discourse from Cook to Gauguin* (New York: Cambridge University Press, 1999), 9.

9. Quoted ibid., 108.

10. Ibid., 12.

11. Leon Howard, "Historical Note," in *Typee*, 294; see also Albert H. Tricomi, *Missionary Positions: Evangelicalism and Empire in American Fiction* (Gainesville: University Press of Florida, 2011), 73.

12. Tricomi, *Missionary Positions*, 76.

13. Thompson, "Introduction," 19.

14. Philip Joseph Deloria, *Playing Indian* (New Haven, Conn.: Yale University Press, 1998), 186.

15. Edmond, *Representing the South Pacific*, 14–15.

16. Herman Melville, *Omoo: A Narrative of Adventures in the South Seas*, ed. Harrison Hayford, Hershel Parker, and G. Thomas Tanselle (Evanston and Chicago: Northwestern University Press and the Newberry Library, 1968), 125.

17. Tricomi, *Missionary Positions*, 86.

18. Charles Roberts Anderson, *Melville in the South Seas* (New York: Columbia University Press, 1967), 132.

19. T. Walter Herbert, *Marquesan Encounters: Melville and the Meaning of Civilization* (Cambridge, Mass.: Harvard University Press, 1980), 102.

20. Michel Foucault, *The Order of Things: An Archaeology of the Human Sciences* (New York: Vintage, 1994), 226.

21. Michel Foucault, *Society Must Be Defended*, trans. David Macey (New York: Picador, 2003), 194–95.

22. Ibid., 60, 50.

23. Though race was certainly in the process of becoming biopolitical, Melville writes from the other side of a concept in transition. While elements of the new biologism can be detected in his time, they are not yet the dominant form of producing truth on the subject, or of instantiating regimes of domination. This can perhaps best be discerned in the practice of slavery in America, which still largely relied on an Enlightenment humanism to institute its benign, patriarchal vision of itself. While such authors as Samuel Cartwright were proposing florid new medical theories of the behavior of slaves such as *drapetomania* (running away; cause: cruelty) and *dysaesthesia aethiopica* (laziness; cause: freedom), they remain extremely rare in the slavery management literature of the period ("Diseases and Peculiarities of the Negro Race"). Instead, they point toward "a place yet unfilled, the locus in which" biological knowledge will take over from Enlightenment humanism (Michel Foucault, *Discipline & Punish: The Birth of the Prison*, trans. Alan Sheridan [New York: Vintage, 1995], 99; see also Richard A. Garner, "Aesthetics, Slavery, and Sentiment" [Ph.D. diss., State University of New York at Buffalo, 2012], 103). However, at this moment, race is still in the process of becoming "an anatomo-politics of the human body" and not yet a "bio-politics of the population" (Michel Foucault, *History of Sexuality:* vol. 1, *An Introduction*, trans. Robert Hurley [New York: Vintage, 1991], 139).

24. Robert C. Suggs, "Melville's Flight to Taipi," *ESQ: A Journal of the American Renaissance* 51, no. 1 (2005): 48–49.

25. Melville, *Omoo*, 99. A note on the narrator's name: while *Omoo* opens by claiming to be a continuation of *Typee*, the narrator does not go by the name of Tommo. No longer anonymous, Melville opens the book by referring to himself as Omoo, which he gives as a word "borrowed from the dialect of the Marquesas Islands, where, among other uses, the word signifies a rover" (ibid., xiv). However, the name does not make an appearance beyond the "Preface," though he is referred to as "Typee, my king of the cannibals" by one of his new shipmates toward the beginning of the text, which seemed to indicate that his tale was quickly notorious with his fellow crew, and that he was not just known for it, but known *by* it as well (ibid., 8). Consequently, some refer to the narrator as Tommo, some as Omoo, some as Typee, and some as simply Melville himself. The latter seems justified by the introduction to the text itself, though many scholars refrain from conflating the narrator and his fictionalizations with Melville, a practice which spills over from the criticism of *Typee*, and justifiably so.

26. Emmanuel J. Drechsel, "Sociolinguistic-Ethnohistorical Observations, on Maritime Polynesian Pidgin in Herman Melville's Two Major Semi-Autobiographical Novels of the Pacific," *Journal of Pidgin and Creole Languages* 22, no. 2 (2007): 234.

27. Bercaw Edwards, *Cannibal Old Me*, 145.

28. Drechsel, "Sociolinguistic-Ethnohistorical Observations," 249; Melville, *Typee*, 242.

29. Drechsel, "Sociolinguistic-Ethnohistorical Observations," 237, 253.

30. Claire Colebrook, "Questioning Representation," *SubStance* 29, no. 2 (2000): 59.

31. Herbert, *Marquesan Encounters*, 14.

32. Melville, *Omoo*, 183.

33. Foucault, *Society Must Be Defended*, 244.

34. Ibid., 257. While Samuel Otter notes the centrality of the skin in eighteenth-century ethnological discourses, his compilation of travel/discovery narratives' fascination with the skin of Polynesians and their tattooing could also lead us in a different direction. For a racial discourse which relies on the pigmentation of the skin to bear the weight of its argument about racial difference, and where, "most enthralling of all, 'white' skin became 'black'" (Samuel Otter, *Melville's Anatomies* [Berkeley: University of California Press, 1999], 27), tattooing radically calls into question that supposition. It is fascinating precisely because the transformation of the skin in tattooing destabilizes a foundational concept on which the pre-biopolitical concept of race is based. As noted later in this essay, while it seems clear that *Moby-Dick* deals more directly with an ethnological concept of race, it is unclear that the following statement applies to *Typee*: "The scene of tattooing . . . draws upon Euro-American representations of Marquesan encounter and is entwined with a scientific racialism on the American continent" (*Melville's Anatomies*, 41). It is not so much that Melville takes up the ethnological sources in *Typee*, but the ethnologists take up Melville's sources such as Stewart, Ellis, and Langsdorff in their treatises. While there is doubtless a resonance between these multiple, often contradictory discourses, which are in a state of rapid flux at the time, the causality seems much less clear than the resonance. Indeed, not only the abundance, but the explicit and overt references to savagery, civilization, and religion argue strongly against reading

ethnology as Melville's primary epistemic horizon when he "reads" Marquesan culture.

35. Breitwieser, "False Sympathy in Melville's *Typee*," 25.

36. Ivison, "I Saw Everything," 127.

37. Carol Colatrella, *Literature and Moral Reform: Melville and the Discipline of Reading* (Gainesville: University Press of Florida, 2002), 92.

38. On the question of whether or not *any* culture systematically practiced ritual/religious cannibalism, see, among other works by these authors, Gananath Obeyesekere and William Arens, "Cannibalism Reconsidered: Responses to Marshall Sahlins," *Anthropology Today* 19, no. 5 (October 1, 2003): 18–19; and Marshall Sahlins, "Artificially Maintained Controversies: Global Warming and Fijian Cannibalism," *Anthropology Today* 19, no. 3 (June 1, 2003): 3–5. Even if we agree with Obeyesekere and Arens, it can still be posited with little objection that the rituals at issue, even when directly (mis)witnessed, are of a religious nature and speak profoundly of the spiritual communion between the world of the living and the world of the dead.

39. Geoffrey Sanborn, *The Sign of the Cannibal* (Durham, N.C.: Duke University Press), 10, 23. For comparison, Bercaw Edwards highlights Georg Heinrich von Langsdorff's division of cannibalism into the categories of hunger, desire, mortuary/funerary, and hatred/revenge (*Cannibal Old Me*, 69).

40. Sanborn, *The Sign of the Cannibal*, 86–87.

41. Bercaw Edwards, *Cannibal Old Me*, 72–76.

42. David Porter, *Journal of a Cruise Journal of a Cruise Made to the Pacific Ocean by Captain David Porter in the United States Frigate Essex, in the Years 1812, 1813, and 1814*, 2 vols. (Philadelphia: Bradford and Inskeep, 1815), 2:45.

43. One can accept this fact even if one does not go so far as to accede to Bercaw Edwards's broader thesis, laid out in her chapter entitled "Questioning *Typee*," that Melville never visited the Typee Valley at all, but instead spent his time at another beach with a different tribe. Ironically enough, it seems that the combination of the opinions laid out by Robert C. Suggs and John Bryant in their fierce debate in a special issue of *ESQ* on *Typee* adequately call into question Bercaw Edwards's best arguments for her position. Suggs offers a compelling defense of Melville's linguistic choices (Robert C. Suggs, "Accuracy, Actuality, and Interpretation," *ESQ: A Journal of the American Renaissance* 51, no. 1 [2005]: 188–90), and while mutually exclusive on basic points, both Suggs's and Bryant's retracing of Melville's route into the Typee Valley seem to offer more compelling alternatives than Bercaw Edwards's (Robert C. Suggs, "Melville's Flight to Taipi: Topographic, Archeological, and Historical Considerations," *ESQ: A Journal of the American Renaissance* 51, no. 1 [2005]: 76; John Bryant, "Taipi, Tipii, Typee: Place, Memory, and Text: A Response to Robert C. Suggs," *ESQ: A Journal of the American Renaissance* 51, no. 1 [2005]: 154–55).

44. Martha B. Helfer, *Rereading Romanticism* (Atlanta, Ga.: Rodopi, 2009), 18.

45. Ralph Waldo Emerson, *Selected Writings of Emerson*, ed. Donald McQuade (New York: Modern Library College Editions, 1981), 6.

46. Henry Wadsworth Longfellow, *Hyperion: A Romance*, 2 vols. (New York: Samuel Colman, 1839), 144; H[enry] D[avid] T[horeau], "A Winter Walk," *The Dial* 4, no. 2 (October 1843): 213. For other critical reinterpretations of this

trope by Melville's contemporaries, see Nathaniel Hawthorne, "Earth's Holocaust," in *Tales and Sketches* (New York: Library of America College Edition, 1996), 902–3; Frederick Douglass, *Narrative of the Life of Frederick Douglass, an American Slave, Written by Himself* (Boston: Anti-Slavery Office, 1845), 85; Frederick Douglass, "The Heroic Slave," in *Autographs for Freedom*, ed. Rochester Ladies' Anti-Slavery Society (Boston: John P. Jewett, 1853), 181.

47. Jonathan A. Cook, "Typee and the Myth of Paradise," in *Herman Melville: Critical Insights*, ed. Eric Carl Link (Ipswich, Mass.: Salem, 2013), 181.

48. Melville, *Moby-Dick*, 327.

49. Bercaw Edwards, *Cannibal Old Me*, 79.

50. Ibid., 84.

51. Quoted in Sanborn, *The Sign of the Cannibal*, 36. On Atkins specifically and denialism generally, see ibid., 30–38.

52. D. H. Lawrence, *Studies in Classic American Literature* (New York: Penguin Books, 1977), 150.

53. Quoted in Sanborn, *Sign of the Cannibal*, 25.

54. Mary Davis Wallis, *Life in Feejee: or, Five Years among the Cannibals* (W. Heath, 1851), 47.

55. Quoted in Sanborn, *The Sign of the Cannibal*, 39–40.

56. See Gananath Obeyesekere, *Cannibal Talk: The Man-Eating Myth and Human Sacrifice in the South Seas* (Berkeley: University of California Press, 2005).

57. And while Tommo's Typee family may seem to deviate from the norm, this was, contrary to received wisdom, often par for the course for the sentimental novels of the day such as Susan Warner's *Wide, Wide World*, Maria Cummins's *The Lamplighter*, or E.D.E.N. Southworth's *The Mother-in-Law*, which all present odd, non-nuclear family structures.

58. Hershel Parker, *Melville Biography: An Inside Narrative* (Evanston, Ill.: Northwestern University Press, 2013), 326.

59. John Samson, "Dynamics of History and Fiction in Melville's *Typee*," *American Quarterly* 36, no. 2 (July 1, 1984): 276–90.

60. Emerson, *Selected Writings*, 341.

61. Herman Melville, *Correspondence*, ed. Lynn Horth (Evanston and Chicago: Northwestern University Press and the Newberry Library, 1993), 166.

62. John Bryant, *Melville Unfolding: Sexuality, Politics, and the Versions of "Typee": A Fluid-Text Analysis, with an Edition of the Typee Manuscript* (Ann Arbor: University of Michigan Press, 2008), 119.

63. Jacques Lacan, *Freud's Papers on Technique, 1953–1954*, ed. Jacques-Alain Miller, trans. John Forrester, book 1 of *The Seminar of Jacques Lacan* (New York: W. W. Norton, 1991), 222.

64. Jacques Lacan, *The Ego in Freud's Theory and in the Technique of Psychoanalysis, 1954–1955*, ed. Jacques-Alain Miller, trans. Sylvana Tomaselli, book 2 of *The Seminar of Jacques Lacan* (New York: W. W. Norton, 1991), 208.

65. Arnold I. Davidson, *The Emergence of Sexuality: Historical Epistemology and the Formation of Concepts* (Cambridge, Mass.: Harvard University Press, 2004), 91.

66. Melville, *Omoo*, 84.

67. Melville, *Moby-Dick*, 24.

68. Ibid., 21.
69. Ibid.
70. Ibid., 480–81.
71. Otter, *Melville's Anatomies*, 102.
72. Josiah C. Nott, "Introduction," in *Types of Mankind: or, Ethnological Researches*, by Josiah C. Nott, George R. Gliddon, and Samuel George Morton (Philadelphia: Lippincott, Grambo, 1855), 49.
73. Otter, *Melville's Anatomies*, 101–2.
74. Melville, *Moby-Dick*, 451.

Free Will and Determinism

Coleridge, Edwards, and the Peculiar Progress of Melville's Free Will Problem

Brad Bannon

Although he was not a theologian in the strict sense of the word, in his major works Herman Melville confronted the free will problem with nothing less than Puritan rigor. Equally persuaded by romantic affirmations of individual agency and Enlightenment conceptions of the universe as an ironclad network of cause and effect, he attempted to locate a rational model of the will that could somehow elude the grasp of both theological and natural determinism. Two of the most important influences on Melville as he struggled with this problem were Samuel Taylor Coleridge and Jonathan Edwards, both of whom were instrumental in awakening him to the larger philosophical stakes of the free will problem. In Coleridge, Melville found a powerful insistence on the supernatural quality of the will that was consistent with romantic conceptions of the individual, but in Edwards he found an appealing rationalism that resonated not only with theological determinism but also with a scientific view of the world that rejected the notion of a supernatural will. As I argue in this essay, the most vigorous confrontations with the implications of this dilemma appear in *Moby-Dick* and "Bartleby, the Scrivener" before Melville achieves the restless impasse of his final postulate in *Billy Budd*.

First, however, it will be useful to provide a brief outline of Edwards's influential argument for theological determinism and a synopsis of Coleridge's response.[1] Edwards set out his position in his 1754 treatise *Freedom of the Will*, in which he points out with an almost uncanny simplicity that the human will would have to be its own cause in order to be self-determining. If the power to will one thing or another does not create itself, he reasons, then the will itself has been shaped by the conditions that have preceded it, and its choices are determined in advance in the very same way that all natural occurrences proceed inevitably from the conditions that produce them. To dispute this, Edwards observes, would be to suggest "that the free acts of the will are existences of an exceeding different nature from other things; by reason of which they may come into existence without any previous ground or reason of it, though other things cannot."[2] In this way, Edwards is able to reduce the argument for a self-determining will to little more than wishful thinking as he marches relentlessly toward his vindication of Calvinist theology: "it infallibly follows from what has been proved, that God orders all events, and the volitions of moral agents amongst others, by such a decisive disposal, that the events are infallibly connected with his disposal" (435). For Edwards, the notion of a self-determining will is not only inconsistent with the laws of the physical universe but also with God's sovereignty—a point of particular importance that he takes care to highlight in his *Personal Narrative*: "The doctrine of God's sovereignty has very often appeared, an exceeding pleasant, bright and sweet doctrine to me: and absolute sovereignty is what I love to ascribe to God."[3]

The doctrine of God's sovereignty was also important to Coleridge, but what came to be of equal, if not greater, importance after he made the transition from radical politics and daemonic poetry to more conservative literary, theological, and philosophical prose works was the self-determined and self-determining will. As he writes in *The Friend*, which Melville borrowed from Richard Lathers in 1854,[4] "all true reality has both its ground and its evidence in the *will*, without which as its complement science itself is but an elaborate game of shadows . . . individuality, as individuality, is only conceivable as with and in the Universal and Infinite, neither before or after it."[5] Avowedly supernatural, Coleridge's conception of the will is a direct refutation of Edwards's argument in *Freedom of the Will*, a point that Coleridge himself makes clear in a notebook entry of 1823, in which he observes: "from Edwards' Book on Necessity it is certain (unless he had recanted and reversed his whole system of Theology) that his World is a *Machine*: and that his Convictions and mine can have no other than an apparent and accidental Resemblance."[6] Two years later, in *Aids to Reflection*, Coleridge even singled out Edwards's particular brand of Calvinism as a distortion of Calvin's system: "Now as the difference of a captive and enslaved Will, and *no* Will at all, such is the difference between the *Lutheranism* of Calvin and the Calvinism of Jonathan Edwards."[7]

Melville may have been unaware of the particulars of Coleridge's quarrel with Edwards, but as a reader of *The Friend* and *Biographia Literaria*, he could not have failed to notice Coleridge's opposition to Edwards's system. In the latter work, Coleridge had defined free will as "our only absolute self,"[8] and claimed that "the true system of natural philosophy places the sole reality of things in an ABSOLUTE, which is at once causa sui et effectus . . . and which in its highest power is nothing else but self-conscious will or intelligence."[9] Again, however, this definition of the will as a supernatural faculty to which the natural laws of the universe did not apply was the very idea that Edwards had denounced as inconsistent with itself in *Freedom of the Will*. It is unclear exactly how specific Melville's knowledge of Edwards's theology was, but his understanding of the argument for causal necessity and theological determinism, as well as of the important influence of the Puritan theologian, was certainly enough to compel him to cite *Freedom of the Will* as one of the works read by the narrator of "Bartleby, the Scrivener," and to return to thoughts of Edwards yet again during the composition of the unfinished *Billy Budd*, when, as Hayford and Sealts note, it seems that he "may have intended to work in an allusion to Jonathan Edwards in connection with 'the clergyman's announcement of his Calvinistic text.' "[10]

The influence of Coleridge in Melville's fiction is more visible than that of Edwards: Melville himself points the way in chapter 42 of *Moby-Dick* with Ishmael's famous digression on "The Whiteness of the Whale," in which he mentions Coleridge by name. "Bethink thee of the albatross," he muses, "whence come those clouds of spiritual wonderment and pale dread, in which that white phantom sails in all imaginations? Not Coleridge first threw that spell; but God's great, unflattering laureate, Nature."[11] Then, in the lengthy note appended to this passage, Ishmael goes on to explain why it is that his own thoughts on the holy significance of the bird are not indebted to *The Rime of the Ancient Mariner*:

> I remember the first albatross I ever saw . . . I saw a regal, feathery thing of unspotted whiteness, and with a hooked, Roman bill sublime. At intervals it arched forth its archangel wings, as if to embrace some holy ark . . . Through its inexpressible, strange eyes, methought I peeped to secrets which took hold of God. As Abraham before the angels, I bowed myself . . . Long I gazed at that prodigy of plumage. I cannot tell, can only hint, the things that darted through me then. But at last I awoke: and turning, asked a sailor what bird was this. A goney, he replied. Goney! I never had heard that name before; is it conceivable that this glorious thing is utterly unknown to men ashore! never! But some time after, I learned that goney was some seaman's name for albatross. So that by no possibility could Coleridge's wild Rhyme have had aught to do with those mystical impressions which were mine, when I saw that bird upon our deck. For neither had I then read the Rhyme, nor knew the bird to be an albatross. Yet, in saying this, I do but indirectly burnish a little brighter the noble merit of the poem and the poet. (190)

Here Melville pairs the divine inscrutability of the albatross with a reference to *The Rime of the Ancient Mariner*, allowing his narrator to both acknowledge and disavow Coleridge's influence. Ishmael's denial of any possible influence of *The Rime of the Ancient Mariner* also reverberates with Coleridge's rather suspicious acknowledgment of his own debt to Schelling in *Biographia Literaria*, and Melville is likely to have had this in mind. As Richard Gravil observes of Ishmael's evasions, "Melville as pasticheur must have noted with some glee that remarkable sentence in the ninth chapter of *Biographia*: 'all the main and fundamental ideas [of Schelling] were born and matured in my mind before I had ever seen a single page of the German philosopher,' a sentence that appropriates the leading ideas of one who is, after all, 'a great and original genius.' "[12]

Even the environment in which Ishmael encounters the albatross bears an obvious resemblance to Coleridge's poem. In *The Rime of the Ancient Mariner*, the albatross approaches the Mariner's ship after the ship has been "drawn by a storm toward the south pole,"[13] while Ishmael encounters the albatross "in waters hard upon the Antarctic seas" (190). But more importantly, like the mariners who hail the albatross "in God's name" and attribute to it the ontological status of "a Christian soul,"[14] Ishmael believes the bird to be not only of divine origin, but also possessed of an especial rank that allows it direct access to heaven and affords Ishmael himself with unutterable apprehensions of an otherwise unknowable God. Though he notes that the captain of the ship "made a postman" of the bird by "tying a lettered, leathern tally round its neck," he imagines that the collar, "meant for man, was taken off in Heaven, when the white fowl flew to join the wing-folding, the invoking, and adoring cherubim!" Ishmael and the Ancient Mariner are also guilty of extreme cruelty towards the animal: the Ancient Mariner shoots the albatross with a crossbow for no apparent reason, and Ishmael acknowledges himself as complicit in the capture of the bird "with a treacherous hook and line" (190) as well as in its subsequent confinement to the deck of the ship. In both instances, the albatross becomes an emissary of God, and a measure of human depravity—a vision of sublime terror that signifies an existential awareness of the divine as intractably present, albeit epistemologically impenetrable: the divinity of the albatross can be identified, but the secret of its being remains out of reach.

Yet another echo of Coleridge's poem can be found in chapter 51 as the *Pequod* pursues the Spirit-Spout that appears at irregular intervals in the middle of the night. Noting that the appearance of the Spirit-Spout nearly seems to be occasioned by the introduction of Ahab's devilish crew in the same way that the polar spirit is provoked by the Ancient Mariner's shooting of the albatross, and that a peculiar encounter with a ship called the *Albatross* follows in the next chapter, Jonathan A. Cook highlights the way in which these allusions serve to signal the dark consequences of Ahab's unyielding endeavor to strike at the very fabric of the universe: "Just as the mariner's killing of the albatross initiates his unholy ordeal, the silent encounter with the bleached-looking *Albatross* is a prophetic sign of Ahab's self-willed isolation and provocation of the divine powers of nemesis."[15]

It is the maddening inscrutability of the whale's whiteness, however, that most fully illustrates Melville's much deeper involvement with the same problem of free will and theological determinism that so troubled Coleridge. Much of this shared involvement also has to do with the appeal that pantheism had for both writers—an appeal that, as Leon Chai notes, also included the threat of a mechanistic universe that was wholly antithetical to its conscious inhabitants: "For Melville . . . pure being precludes all trace of either thought or consciousness. Ahab's evocation in *Moby-Dick* of the blind, unconscious force that pervades the world and manifests itself in the White Whale is but another expression of the same belief."[16] This darker side of pantheism was particularly distressing to Coleridge, to whom the thought of a "blind Nature ruled by a fatal Necessity"[17] was alarmingly convincing, as was the loveless God of Spinoza's *Ethics*, which exerted a powerful influence on his thinking. Following his reading of Coleridge's *Biographia Literaria* in 1848, Melville also turned to the problems presented by deterministic immanence.

But as Ahab's statement of purpose in "The Quarter-Deck" demonstrates, Melville's metaphysical consciousness was also inflected by Jonathan Edwards's system, which affirmed a loving, inscrutable, and omnipotent God who had established the order and connection of the universe from start to finish—nor is the appearance of this particular brand of determinism in *Moby-Dick* coincidental. As Hershel Parker observes, in the history of Berkshire County that Melville had purchased on a visit to the region in July 1850, he marked the passage that describes Jonathan Edwards's exile in Stockbridge as the time during which he "completed his greatest work, 'The Inquiry concerning the Freedom of the Will.'" Though it is surely impossible to know, perhaps this vision of Edwards producing his powerful statement of theological determinism following his dismissal from Northampton was, as Parker claims, "still fresh in his mind when Melville later wrote to Hawthorne that he had written a wicked book."[18]

The "wickedness" of the book seems rooted in Ahab's acceptance of theological determinism as a justification for his vengeance, though initially, the mad captain's statement of purpose is rooted in a brand of agnosticism that cannot countenance its own conclusions. "Sometimes I think there's naught beyond," Ahab muses, "But 'tis enough. He tasks me; he heaps me; I see in him outrageous strength, with an inscrutable malice sinewing it. That inscrutable thing is chiefly what I hate; and be the white whale agent, or be the white whale principal, I will wreak that hate upon him" (164). Here, confronting the two-pronged possibility of an impenetrable natural order and an unknowable God, Ahab decides that it is the inscrutability itself, regardless of origin, which warrants rebellion. What makes Ahab's pronouncement so blasphemous, however—so "wicked," as Melville has it—is his acknowledgment that the White Whale is possibly the representative of a larger intentionality whose full design cannot be known. Instrument of divine wrath though the whale may be, Ahab rebels anyway, effectively refusing to accept a God whose Providence does not accord with his own vision of justice.

The question of whether natural forces are manifestations of a greater agency or simply the necessary results of a mechanical universe is largely irrelevant here: to Ahab, the damage inflicted by the White Whale is unacceptable either way. In this respect, Sanford E. Marovitz's summation of Melville's use of the word "Being" in an oft-cited letter to Hawthorne provides a helpful gloss on Chai's reading: "Variously stimulated, frustrated, and disgusted by diverse and often conflicting viewpoints, Melville employed the word *Being* ambivalently, manifesting his confusion when the moral and religious Truths he longed to accept conflicted with the empirical truths that belied them."[19]

In other words, Melville struggled to decide what he believed, though it was not so much a matter of *not* knowing as it was one of knowing all too well what he could not know. Significantly, Melville seems to apprehend the fact that the argument for causal determinism, theological or natural, renders the difference between an intelligent creator and a mechanistic natural world somewhat beside the point. In both cases, he finds himself presented with the apparent fact that everything that is, and everything that will come to be, has been inevitable—and his use of the word "Being" tends to reflect this existential uneasiness. As he writes to Hawthorne in 1851,

> There is a certain tragic phase of humanity which, in our opinion, was never more powerfully embodied than by Hawthorne . . . We think that into no recorded mind has the intense feeling of the visable truth ever entered more deeply than into this man's. By visable truth, we mean the apprehension of the absolute condition of present things as they strike the eye of the man who fears them not, though they do their worst to him—the man who, like Russia or the British Empire, declares himself a sovereign nature (in himself) amid the powers of heaven, hell, and earth. He may perish; but so long as he exists he insists upon treating with all Powers upon an equal basis. If any of those other Powers choose to withhold certain secrets, let them; that does not impair my sovereignty in myself; that does not make me tributary. And perhaps, after all, there is *no* secret . . . We incline to think that God cannot explain His own secrets, and that He would like a little information upon certain points Himself. We mortals astonish Him as much as He us. But it is this *Being* of the matter; there lies the knot with which we choke ourselves. As soon as you say *Me*, a *God*, a *Nature*, so soon you jump from your stool and hang from the beam. Yes, that word is the hangman. Take God out of the dictionary, and you would have Him in the street.[20]

In this passage, as he vacillates between the possibility of there being no absolute truth or actuality to comprehend beyond what is perceptible—the "apprehension of the absolute condition of present things"—and the possibility that there may exist powers both immanent and inscrutable, Melville ultimately expresses his admiration for what he believes to be Hawthorne's refusal to say one way or the other. "There is the grand truth about Nathaniel Hawthorne," Melville pronounces, "He says NO! in thunder; but the Devil himself cannot make him say *yes*."[21] Put another way, Hawthorne's contentment with Being as it is without concern for how or in what way it actually *is*, including his steady evasion of the free will problem, seemed to have struck Melville as indicative of supernatural self-determination, or of what he deems a "sovereign nature"—as if Hawthorne had simply dissolved the secrets of the universe and thus had no need to explain them.

Given his own profound uncertainty, the ease with which Hawthorne affirmed Providence while passing over the threat of determinism must have seemed transcendent indeed. For his own part, Melville seems to have been troubled in the same fashion as Coleridge, who in *The Friend* had anticipated Melville's inquiry into Being: "The power, which evolved this idea of BEING, BEING in its essence, BEING limitless, comprehending its own limits in its dilatation, and condensing itself into its own apparent mounds—how shall we name it?"[22] Melville's increasing preoccupation with the free will problem is also evidenced in Ahab's progress from recalcitrant agnosticism to a vicious brand of determinism. As the pursuit of the White Whale reaches beyond the point of madness, and Starbuck pleads for a return to his wife and son in Nantucket, Ahab wonders at his own actions as he invokes the difficulty in conceiving of self-determination when all the processes of nature seem subject to omnipresent law, whether divine or natural:

> Is Ahab, Ahab? Is it I, God, or who, that lifts this arm? But if the great sun move not of himself; but is as an errand-boy in heaven, nor one single star can revolve, but by some invisible power; how then can this one small heart beat; this one small brain think thoughts; unless God does that beating, does that thinking, does that living, and not I. (545)

Again, although it is unclear exactly how much Melville knew of Edwards's *Freedom of the Will*, or whether he read it in full, it does seem that he was aware of the disturbing implications that followed from the prominent theologian's persuasive argument for causal necessity and theological determinism.

Like Coleridge, Melville seems to have been drawn to meditating on this problem to the point of excess, and he even makes a reference to Coleridge when, in a journal entry made during his voyage to London in 1849, he alludes to the same passage from *Paradise Lost* that Coleridge had quoted in *Biographia Literaria* to characterize his affinity for "the unwholesome quicksilver mines of metaphysic depths."[23] According to Robin Grey, Melville found "the inscrutable omniscience and omnipotence of Milton's God more compelling and more troublesome than the apparently hollow assertions of free will in *Paradise Lost*."[24] On his voyage at sea, however, Melville seems largely unaware of the frustration and anxiety that will result from his habit of attempting to think in teleological terms: "Last evening was very pleasant. Walked the deck with the German, Mr Adler till a late hour, talking of 'Fixed Fate, Free-will, foreknowledge absolute' &c. His philosophy is *Colredgian* [*sic*]: he accepts the Scriptures as divine, & yet leaves himself free to inquire into Nature."[25] Pleasant as this conversation may have been, by the time Melville began writing *Moby-Dick* in early 1850, his interest had turned into something of an obsession. As Richard Brodhead notes, "the demon of metaphysical speculation seized on Melville around 1850 . . . His letters, full of ease and generous enthusiasms before, become at this time grimly driven, unable to leave the question of the anchoring of our world or the quest for an independent position toward first things."[26]

Nor does the metaphysical exploration of *Moby-Dick* seem to have provided Melville with any clear answers. The closest he gets is Ishmael's mat-making allegory of chapter 47, where chance holds a limited sway over both free will and necessity:

> Aye, chance, free will, and necessity—no wise incompatible—all interweavingly working together. The straight warp of necessity, not to be swerved from its ultimate course—its every alternating vibration, indeed, only tending to that; free will still free to ply her shuttle between given threads; and chance, though restrained in its play within the right lines of necessity and sideways in its motions modified by free will, though thus prescribed to both, chance by turns rules either, and has the last featuring blow at events. (215)

This schema is compelling insofar as it provides the reader with a visual hypothesis, though as Walton R. Patrick points out, it is also "quite similar to the viewpoint that the necessitarian philosophers advocated and is in thorough accord with the position that both Edwards and Priestley took on the will in their treatises." Moreover, since free will is still circumscribed by causal necessity, "every volitional determination has a prior cause or motive just as the one before it had a cause or motive, and so on back and back in an endless chain, the first link of which rests in God's hand."[27] Chance, too, unless defined as a supernatural break in the natural order of things, would also have to be determined in these terms.

Maurice Lee has argued that Ishmael's meditation on chance should be taken far more seriously, suggesting that Melville "understood the etiological implications of the miracles controversy, as well as the fact that the argument from design . . . ultimately rested on probabilistic ground." Furthermore, he claims, "*Moby-Dick*'s refusal to affirm providence places Melville in a tradition of skepticism stretching from the classical Pyrrhonists and Cicero and Montaigne, Bayle, and Hume."[28] On balance, however, it is difficult to imagine that Melville would not have known that there was no more reason to believe in chance than in miracles, for both consist of a faith in the idea that the normal processes of the universe can be suspended in special circumstances. Put another way, if chance is not simply an occurrence of which the actual origin is unknowable, but rather an occurrence with no cause other than the intrusion of another agency altogether, then it would be no different than a miracle. Even Hume denied the existence of chance: "Though there be no such thing as *Chance* in the world; our ignorance of the real cause of any event has the same influence on the understanding, and begets a like species of belief or opinion."[29] In Melville's usage, then, chance seems to appear as an illustration of what cannot be known rather than as a viable third option between fate and free will.

Of course it is never clear whether the destiny of Ahab and the rest of the crew has been preordained or freely chosen. Ishmael, for instance, invokes "the Fates" to explain his own survival and preservation on the open sea, where, following his survival of the sinking of the *Pequod*, the sharks "glided by as if with padlocks on their mouths; [and] the savage sea-hawks sailed with sheathed beaks" (573). Likewise, AnnLouise Keating reads Ahab's quest in ambiguous terms, arguing that "Ahab freely acts on his will" while at the same time "he cannot choose what he wills,"[30] which is more a reiteration of Edwards's argument than it is a delineation of Melville's evolving position on the free will problem. Given the ultimate direction of Ahab's quest, it seems that Melville was intuitively opposed to the argument that he nevertheless found difficult, if not impossible, to refute on rational grounds, and that, like Coleridge, he found himself occupied with somehow finding a way around the impenetrable logic of causal necessity. Motivated by the impulse to self-determination at the same time as he understood the seriousness of the objections to the kind of thinking that would grant the godlike status of self-caused agency to the individual, Melville continued to pursue the possibility of a self-determined will that he seemed to know was impossible to affirm without contradiction. In this respect, the minute focus on the operations of the will that appears in "Bartleby, the Scrivener" is indicative of Melville's sustained attention to the problem.

Thus we find that although Bartleby's employer has "looked a little into 'Edwards on the Will,' and 'Priestley on Necessity,' " and that he is for a short time persuaded that "Bartleby was billeted upon me for some mysterious purpose of an all-wise Providence,"[31] the doctrines of theological determinism and causal necessity are ultimately of little use to him in his attempt to understand his employee's peculiar recalcitrance. But it is ultimately unclear whether Bartleby's refusals are a heroic exercise of the will, an "assertion of the will by the destruction of the will,"[32] as Kingsley Widmer puts it, or a painstaking demonstration of Edwards's point that self-determination cannot consist in a state of indifference: "for how ridiculous would it be for anybody to insist, that the soul chooses one thing before another, when at the very same instant it is perfectly indifferent with respect to each!" (*Freedom of the Will*, 207). On the contrary, Edwards argues, it is preference and inclination with which freedom is rightly associated, given that those who act with the strongest sense of inclination and purpose seem to do so "with the greatest freedom, according to common sense."[33] Though we cannot know for certain, it may be that Bartleby is unaware, or perhaps apathetic, to the objections of common sense, and since he is most fully inclined to "prefer" not to do anything (except to remain on the premises), could it be that he achieves some higher degree of freedom insofar as he seems to deny the inclinations that come to inform the choices that we make? But isn't he inclined to do this? In this way, Bartleby's refusal to prefer anything but Being (and in the end, even Being isn't good enough) may simply reduce the function of the will to a state of blind defiance—something like the child who has learned the word "no."

As Allan Moore Emery suggests, "the rebel can maintain his freedom only so long as he continues to reject as potentially 'determining' all behavioral motives . . . but ironically enough, having refused to obey the dictates of any particular motive, the rebel discovers to his chagrin that his will is now *less* free (by one alternative) than it was before."[34] That is, by rejecting out of hand all particularity and preference, Bartleby surrenders the option to prefer anything but negation. Yet the assumption here is that Bartleby's resistance is absolute, or that he has necessarily and immutably ruled out all positive preferences for all time—and it is not entirely clear that this is the case. For example, when the narrator asks if the former scrivener will leave the office building and come to stay at his home until "some convenient arrangement" can be established, Bartleby's response, though absolute in its refusal, is otherwise quite provisional: "'No: at present I would prefer not to make any change at all'" (41). For not only does this particular response feature the indeterminate subjunctive mood that Bartleby sporadically employs, but also the limited temporality implied by the phrase "at present."

Unfortunately, however, the actualities of the physical world cannot be dispensed with entirely. "'Now one of two things must take place," the attorney warns Bartleby, "Either you must do something, or something must be done to you'" (41). Apparently indifferent to this fact, or perhaps unwilling to contest it, Bartleby is forcibly removed from the building and then imprisoned until his refusal to eat deprives him of life altogether. Though his eviction and imprisonment are not strictly necessary consequences, the nature of Bartleby's death is a harsh illustration of the fact that acts of willing, or not willing, are always limited by the boundaries of the possible—and living without food simply cannot be done regardless of what one wills or "would prefer." It may be that Bartleby does not want to live, or that he simply wants to be excused from willing altogether, regardless of the consequences; ultimately, of course, we simply do not know, and there is a certain sense in which Lewis Mumford's early assessment of Bartleby, itself perhaps a kind of warning, remains instructive: "There is no getting behind his silence, his dead-wall reveries, his blank self-possession."[35]

Gilles Deleuze suggests that we think of Bartleby, along with Benito Cereno and Billy Budd, as "angels or saintly hypochondriacs . . . They can only survive by becoming stone, by denying the will and sanctifying themselves in the suspension. Such are Cereno, Billy Budd, and above all Bartleby."[36] That none of these characters actually survive, and only Bartleby seems to deny the will, seems of little concern to Deleuze, who concludes that "Bartleby is not the patient, but the doctor of a sick America, the Medicine-Man, the new Christ or the brother to us all."[37] But encomiums upon such a thoroughly abject, and eventually suicidal, state of being are less than convincing. Can we truly celebrate a character who starves himself to death for no apparent reason? Above all, Melville's triumph in the creation of Bartleby is that of having fashioned a character who is truly and overwhelmingly inexplicable, a point well-illustrated, as Dan McCall notes, by the sheer abundance of explanations: "The paradoxical achievement of the Bartleby Industry is that any of its single contributions in light of all its others, and the enormous weight of all of them together, can only convince us that there never could have been a 'key.' "[38] Indeed, Bartleby is a curiosity, and perhaps a metaphysical test case: an instance of Melville speculating on what a renunciation of the will might look like (if it could even exist), and then following the inquiry through to its natural conclusion—though he is surely conscious of the paradox implied in his character's steadfast determination to dispense with the will altogether.

At times, Bartleby even refuses to acknowledge the word itself. As Giorgio Agamben points out, when the narrator asks Bartleby to go to the post office and Bartleby responds by saying that he "would prefer not to," the attorney renders the phrase back to him in the altered form of willing: "You *will* not?" (25). "But Bartleby," Agamben notes, "with his soft but firm voice, specifies, 'I *prefer* not' ('I prefer not,' which appears three times, is the only variation of Bartleby's usual phrase; and if Bartleby then renounces the conditional, this is only because doing so allows him to eliminate all traces of the verb 'will,' even in its modal use)."[39] In fact, whenever his employer uses the word "will," Bartleby's response, if he gives one at all, substitutes the less definite "prefer," which, as Agamben observes, he sometimes modifies further with the subjunctive mood, as if to suggest an additional removal from actuality: Bartleby "would" prefer not to, if he had to prefer at all, which he does not. But then doesn't he prefer not to prefer? How could it be otherwise?

Frustrated with Bartleby's refusals to perform any work at all, the attorney ultimately attempts to make a personal connection with him. " 'Will you tell me, Bartleby, where you were born?' " he asks, to which Bartleby now predictably responds, " 'I would prefer not to.' " Sensing the familiar direction of things, he then asks if Bartleby will respond to personal inquiries at all: " 'Will you tell me *any thing* about yourself?' " Yet again, of course, the response is the same: " 'I would prefer not to' " (30). These refusals to even allow himself to be conceived of as one who wills or does not will reach their consummate expression after the attorney has offered Bartleby money and told him that he must leave the premises, only to find that the despondent scrivener has remained. " 'Will you, or will you not, quit me?" the attorney demands as he frames the matter finally as a plain case of choosing one option or another. That Bartleby's response again attempts to evade this oppositional framework by deploying the conditional modifier is by this point no surprise, though the emphasis on "not" is telling: "I would prefer *not* to quit you" (35). Why, for instance, does Bartleby not simply say that he would prefer not to decide, or that he would prefer neither?

Though Agamben would have us believe that Bartleby exists in some liminal state between Being and Nothingness, or that he has achieved a kind of indeterminate potential that defies Edwardsian logic, he seems to underestimate the extent of Melville's skepticism toward both determinism *and* indeterminism. For although Melville seems to have held a "contemptuous attitude toward purely rational analysis," as Merton Sealts notes,[40] he does not propound a theory of indeterminism: that is to say, he does not deny that effects appear to have causes, or that the physical world is governed by natural laws—he only proposes in various cases that final causes may be beyond our intellectual grasp. In the case of the will, this could only mean that individual actions or inactions are simply effects that follow from prior causes, whether those causes are known or not. To argue this point would be to claim that Bartleby becomes a prime mover, or that he somehow harnesses the power of causation. Melville knew from his explorations in *Moby-Dick* that these sorts of claims were too mystical to satisfy a rational mind, but in "Bartleby, the Scrivener" he seems to have been interested to see what a renunciation of the will could accomplish—or if it were possible to somehow elude the will by denying the motives that determine its acts. He stops short, however, of suggesting that such a denial could afford the individual access to a plane of indeterminism wherein the will would be free from restraint.

Or does he? Drawing upon the distinction made by medieval theologians between *potentia absoluta* and *potentia ordinata* (i.e., the infinite scope of divine omnipotence as opposed to the finite expression of the divine will), Agamben suggests that Bartleby is somehow endowed with the former, and therefore not subject to the limitations that are otherwise imposed on inhabitants of the natural world. "If God (at least *de potentia ordinata*) is truly capable only of what he wants," he speculates, "Bartleby is capable only without wanting; he is capable only *de potentia absoluta* . . . one could say of Bartleby that he succeeds in being able (and not being able) without wanting it."[41] But according to the dictates of the causal and theological determinism with which Melville was familiar, Bartleby's preference for preferring not to do anything is merely the execution of what, in retrospect, is the only potential that can, or will, come to be. In this view, what does not occur did not have the potential to occur. Or, as Edwards puts it, "when men act voluntarily, and do what they please, then they do what appears most agreeable to them; and to say otherwise, would be as much as to affirm, that men don't choose what appears to suit them best, or what seems most pleasing to them; or that they don't choose what they prefer" (*Freedom of the Will*, 217). Simply stated, it makes little sense to claim that individuals could ever possess the potential to perform actions that they do not, and will not, perform.

Following in the tradition of Agamben and Deleuze, Branka Arsić takes a slightly different tack, arguing that Bartleby's preference is involuntary, and hence impervious to causality. In Arsić's reading of Agamben, Bartleby's rejection of the language of willing reveals that his preference is "involuntary and indeterminate," which demonstrates "that something can be devoid of reason, that something may or may not be, or even that something may and may not be at the same time—an indeterminate and reasonless existence."[42] Perhaps not surprisingly, the foundation for this line of thinking is grounded in an affirmation of the supernatural: "accidents" and "events," as Arsić claims, may simply occur at random, since "the event is what is without any connection with causes or antecedents, what is therefore without history, origin, or future . . . It is loose existence, the unaccountable, the interruption of the course of the world."[43] But even if this were the case, neither indeterminacy nor randomness would address the problem of how it is that an unaccountable event could be summoned or controlled by an act of will. For if it is simply the case that wholly unforeseeable events occur at random—that is, without reason, cause, or intent—then Bartleby would be subject to the same unknowable indeterminacy as anyone else. Such a radical uncoupling would suggest that we live in a world where events and actions only appear to have come about as a result of the causes and motives that have preceded them, when in fact there is no power of consequence or causality that forms a necessary link between the past and the future. The possibility of such a state of affairs may very well have been familiar to Melville by way of Hume, who had famously shown that the commonly held belief in cause and effect was based on contiguity rather than reason; but there is no evidence that this is the case in the story. Indeed, the typical contiguities of cause and effect appear to be firmly in place throughout the tale; for example, when Bartleby eventually stops eating, he dies.

To pursue the notion that Bartleby's actions are somehow uncaused also overlooks the serious consideration that Melville gave the threat of determinism of one kind or another. In fact, if we look closely at Bartleby's behavior, it appears that in the act of increasingly preferring not to do or change anything, he actually illustrates the seeming inevitability of demonstrating inclination and motive by action. As Edwards observes,

> If the will or mind, in willing and choosing after the manner that it does, is excited to do so by no motive or inducement, then it has no end which it proposes to itself, or pursues in so doing; it aims at nothing, and seeks nothing. And if it seeks nothing, then it don't go after anything, or exert any inclination or preference towards anything. Which brings the matter to a contradiction; because for the mind to will something and for it to go after something by an act of preference and inclination, are the same thing. (*Freedom of the Will*, 225)

Of course Bartleby *does* seem to exert his inclination and preference. An especially clear example of this occurs when Turkey enters into the space behind Bartleby's screen, which is already occupied by both Bartleby and the narrator, causing the latter to "jostle" the scrivener, who subsequently states his preference unambiguously: "'I would prefer to be left alone here'" (31).

Likewise, on the following day, the narrator tells us that when he asks Bartleby why he is not writing, the scrivener declares that he has "decided upon doing no more writing." Upon further questioning from the narrator, who poses the affirmation in the form of a question—"'do no more writing?'"—Bartleby rather tersely reaffirms his decision: "'No more'" (31). It is true that the vast majority of Bartleby's expressions of preference and inclination are articulated in negative terms, but to prefer not to copy documents, or go to the post office, or eat, and then to actually not do these things, also illustrates the paradox of attempting to renounce all positive action. Consequently, if we view Bartleby as having sought to deny the will, the result is something of a tragicomic failure, and perhaps a grim reminder that the preferences, dispositions, and motives that inform the actions of the will are as inexorable as the physical laws that may very well determine them. Though Melville was ultimately unsure if he could accept this conclusion, "Bartleby, the Scrivener" does seem to demonstrate that he was fairly convinced of, or at least frustrated with, Edwards's logic concerning the nature of preference and inclination. Moreover, since Bartleby continues to exist, and continues to perform actions such as remaining in the lawyer's building, sitting on the banister, and staring silently at a dead wall, there can be little doubt that he has chosen, or preferred, to do these things rather than others.

The remaining question for Melville, then, was whether or not the inevitable facticity of the will could ever exert a power not entirely subject to natural law. He had certainly encountered a conception of this type in *Biographia Literaria*, where Coleridge exalts what he believes to be the only way in which self-consciousness as we know it, or are aware of it, is possible:

> It has been shown, that a spirit is that, which is its own object, yet not originally an object, but an absolute subject for which all, itself included, may become an object. It must therefore be an ACT; for every object is, as an *object*, dead, fixed, incapable in itself of any action and necessarily finite. Again, the spirit (originally the identity of object and subject) must in some sense dissolve this identity, in order to be conscious of it: fit alter et idem. But this implies an act, and it follows therefore that intelligence or self-consciousness is impossible, except by and in a will. The self-conscious spirit therefore is a will; and freedom must be assumed as a *ground* of philosophy, and can never be deduced from it.[44]

Also significant to Melville would have been Coleridge's assertion of the will as exclusive to spirit, and of freedom of the will as a necessary ground rather than an empirically discoverable fact. Nevertheless, Melville was caught somewhere between Coleridge and Edwards as he attempted to resist the view of human existence as a complex, predetermined mechanism. Coleridge, for example, was free to declare that Edwards's "World is a *Machine*"[45] and to openly defy the argument for theological determinism with avowals of free will as the ground of human experience, but Melville was too cautious to explicitly affirm a self-determining will.

Though F. O. Matthiessen is in some sense correct to argue that Ahab "is an embodiment of his author's most profound response to the problem of free individual will *in extremis*,"[46] he does underestimate the significance of the eponymous character's hanging in *Billy Budd*, where the possibility of a self-determining will, rather than the spectre of theological or causal determinism, is brought to the fore. The oversight is somewhat strange given that Matthiessen does note that in the margin of the manuscript of chapter 23 of *Billy Budd*, Melville writes the name of Jonathan Edwards just at the point where Captain Vere's announcement of Billy's sentence is "listened to by the throng of standing sailors in a dumbness like that of a seated congregation of believers in hell listening to the clergyman's announcement of his Calvinistic text."[47] Moreover, given that Melville mentions Edwards by name in "Bartleby, the Scrivener," and then again in the manuscript of *Billy Budd* over thirty years later, it is apparent that he continued to meditate seriously on the challenges posed by the Puritan theologian. Matthiessen himself speculates that the "rectitude of Vere" perhaps reminded Melville of "the inexorable logic, the tremendous force of mind in the greatest of our theologians."[48] That both mentions of Edwards are critical (the implication of the marginalia in *Billy Budd* a bit more so than the narrator's passing allusion in "Bartleby, the Scrivener") tends to indicate that, over time, what may have been intellectual frustration had evolved into an aspiration to actually provide an alternative.

Much of the criticism of *Billy Budd* has been split between those who argue that the tale expresses a kind of political resistance, and those who view Melville's final work as an intricate defense of the inevitability of accepting the rule of law. "The issues in this plot are momentous," observes Hershel Parker, "and seem designed to take one of two mutually incompatible positions."[49] Spearheading a more aggressive element of recent resistance criticism, however, William V. Spanos claims that although Parker seems to take a nonpartisan stance, his "real criticism is directed against critical perspectives, emerging in the context of the protest movement during the Vietnam War—and theoretically emanating from Europe (the 'Old World')—that was politicizing Melville's text, indeed, reading it (and his earlier fiction) as a radical political critique of a conservative society of law and order."[50] Spanos may overstate his case, however, when he makes the larger claim that Melville "was ferociously critical of both the emergent optimism inherent in metaphysical ontologies and the hegemonic worldly practices they justified, particularly, the providential Puritan Calvinism that gave rise to the nationalist/capitalist/imperialist policies of American exceptionalism."[51] For it is no doubt the Calvinist doctrine of original sin and of an innate evil that Melville's narrator traces back to Plato which plays so large a role in Billy's undoing, and which Captain Vere dismisses as irrelevant to what he believes to be the larger context of the case.

Although he is pressed by both the first lieutenant and the officer of marines to look further into Claggart's inexplicable malice towards Billy, Vere concludes that it is, in fact, "a mystery; but to use a scriptural phrase, it is a 'mystery of iniquity,' a matter for psychologic theologians to discuss. But what has a military court to do with it?" (108). It is precisely an awareness of Claggart's malevolence, however, described by the narrator as "born with him and innate, in short 'a depravity according to nature'" (76), that would presumably mitigate Billy's sentence. It is also important to note that the doctrine of original sin is softened by the narrator so that "it by no means involves Calvin's dogma as to total mankind" (75), though as Gail Coffler points out, Melville's interest in Calvinistic ways of thinking was, to say the very least, complex. For "even though [he] repudiated Calvinism, its strong effect on him is seen in his lifelong attacks, overt and covert, on church dogma, religiosity and hypocrisy. It is evident too in his fascination with Hawthorne's themes of secret guilt, sin, and heresy."[52] In this sense, Calvinism seems to have functioned as a vital intellectual sparring partner for Melville, as it contained much that he disagreed with, and yet enough that he found convincing, or otherwise influential. In the case of *Billy Budd*, Coffler makes a convincing case that the opposition between Billy and Claggart is both representative of Melville's interest in Matthew Arnold's vision of the Western world as divided between Hellenism and Hebraism as well as of warring factions within Melville himself: "Claggart is a complex representation of Melville's sense of evil, guilt, Calvinistic sin, 'blackness' . . . John Claggart is both the wicked sinner and also the man-of-sorrows upon whom iniquity is unfairly laid; he is both Melville and not-Melville."[53] The vision in *Billy Budd*, then, is perhaps more heterogeneous than Spanos is willing to grant.

It also seems that a kind of deadlock occurs wherein Melville salvages those aspects of Edwardsian Calvinism that he values—rationalism within limits and an acknowledgment of natural, if not universal, depravity—while discarding the less desirable elements; and as a means of responding to Edwards without abandoning reason, he attacks causal and theological determinism by way of ambiguity and suggestion before introducing the possibility of Billy exercising an inexplicable act of will. The first instance of this occurs in chapter 24 when Melville describes Billy "as nipped in the vice of fate" (119) when he is lying between two guns on the *Bellipotent*'s upper-gun deck. Here, using the word "as" in the sense of "as if he had been," Melville's narrator suggests that, although the appearance of Billy "lying prone in irons"

(118) between the two guns certainly makes available the impression that the present circumstance is also representative of a metaphysical state of affairs (i.e., that fate actually has ensnared the handsome sailor), this may not be the case. Moreover, the inclusion of the word "as" here makes it clear that Melville's invocation of fate in *Billy Budd* is both a guarded and skeptical affair. It *could* be that Billy is no more caught in the vice of fate at this point than he is at any other, and that his ultimate direction is simply clearer now than it had formerly been. It may also be that Melville is suggesting a more dynamic state of affairs in which individuals exercise their wills without restriction unless they happen to stumble, as Billy has, into the ineluctable machinery of fate. But are they destined to do so? Has God (or the physical laws of nature) foreseen, permitted, and therefore underwritten all the circumstances of Billy's life? Melville seems to have raised these questions here in order to suggest what the alternatives might be in the chapters that follow.

For instance, when Billy's unexpected blessing of Captain Vere is reiterated by the entire crew, Melville uses a strangely paradoxical simile to evoke a deterministic, albeit pantheistic, state of affairs: "Without volition, as it were, as if indeed the ship's populace were but the vehicles of some vocal current electric, with one voice from alow and aloft came a resonant sympathetic echo: 'God bless Captain Vere!' " (123). In his readings of *Moby-Dick* and *Pierre*, Paul Gilmore suggests that Melville conceives of electrical currents between humans as both destructive and alluring,[54] though here the "vocal current electric" seems to indicate a feeling of collective compassion and acquiescence. The similarities between this shared blessing and the more pantheistic sentiments of Coleridge's "The Eolian Harp" are also striking. The "one life" passage that was added to the poem in 1817, for example, bears a suggestive resemblance to the notion of the *Bellipotent*'s crew speaking and feeling as one, but it is the question that earns Coleridge the reproof of his young wife that may have been in the back of Melville's mind as he wrote of the sailors as "but the vehicles of some vocal current electric":

> And what if all of animated nature
> Be but organic harps diversely framed,
> That tremble into thought, as o'er them sweeps
> Plastic and vast, one intellectual breeze,
> At once the Soul of each, and God of All?[55]

The difference in *Billy Budd*, of course, is that the individual crew members appear to be the vehicles not of some omnipresent divinity, but rather of Billy and his benediction. For though it is Captain Vere whom they are compelled to bless, "at that instant Billy alone must have been in their hearts, even as in their eyes" (123)—the implication being that if in fact the sailors are the "vehicles of some vocal current," then it is Billy's act of blessing that has somehow initiated the current's spontaneous flow.

Following this, the chapter closes with the remarkable moment when Billy is hanged, and "to the wonder of all no motion was apparent, none save that created by the slow roll of the hull in moderate weather, so majestic in a great ship ponderously cannoned" (124). Thus it is that the inexplicable absence of muscular spasm in Billy's body seems to punctuate the explicit attention that Melville has suddenly turned to the question of free will and determinism, and the following chapter is devoted entirely to the metaphysical stalemate that he appears to have reached on the matter. From the information that Melville does provide concerning the two disputants in the chapter that follows Billy's hanging—describing the purser as "a rather ruddy, rotund person more accurate as an accountant than as a philosopher," and the surgeon as "saturnine, spare, and tall, one in whom a discreet causticity went along with a manner less genial than polite" (124)—it is nevertheless clear that while he did not believe the argument for free will to be particularly strong in the philosophical sense, he simultaneously found the cold logic of determinism nearly inhuman.

"'What testimony to the force lodged in will power,'" the purser remarks of Billy's death, to which the surgeon responds by affirming that the peculiar absence of muscular spasm can be "no more attributable to will power, as you call it, than to horsepower—begging your pardon" (124). Simply put, so far as the surgeon is concerned, it makes no sense to affirm any concept that cannot be substantiated in scientific terms; and will power, as he states, is "a term not yet included in the lexicon of science" (125). For even though he admits that there is no explanation for why Billy's body did not exhibit any sign of the muscular spasm that, as the purser points out, is "more or less invariable" (124) in the event of a hanging, his response to the purser's subsequently asking if such an absence may be deemed "phenomenal" is merely to observe that the case is only "'phenomenal . . . in the sense that it was an appearance the cause of which is not immediately to be assigned'" (125).

When considered alongside Melville's caricature of Edwards, as well as his skeptical invocations of determinism and his suggestion of pantheism, the purser's argument is not so easily dismissed. In this sense, Melville does seem to have sympathized to some extent with the purser's point of view, but he was unwilling to cast his lot with Coleridge and affirm the supernatural power of will that he could not prove. In Eric Goldman's view, it is actually the presentation of the problem itself—the fog of uncertainty surrounding the contest between our intuitive sense of a self-determining will and our more rational apprehension of a universe of effects following upon causes ad infinitum—that is of greater importance than the fact that Melville "introduces the possibility of a transcendent residuum that eludes postbellum science and preserves a place for 'psychologic theologians' in the new, naturalistic worldview that the story otherwise unflinchingly renders."[56] However, in highlighting the inexplicable nature of Billy's death in the dialogue between the surgeon and the purser that follows, it seems that

Melville is directly acknowledging both the indemonstrability of the self-determining will and the irrefutability of theological determinism in a way that he had been unable or unwilling to do in either *Moby-Dick* or "Bartleby, the Scrivener."

Making note of the fact that *Billy Budd* was written while Melville was reading Schopenhauer's *The World as Will and Representation*, among other works, Olive L. Fite suggests that Melville's narrative seems to function in accordance with Schopenhauer's conception of freedom, in which "only by an involuntary instreaming of knowledge of the will could an individual free himself from [the] chain of necessity and deny or suppress the very will to live. This Billy seems to have achieved."[57] Yet to presume that Billy has achieved a transcendent state whereby his actions become supernatural is to exaggerate the matter somewhat. Although Billy *appears* to transcend the boundaries of what is physically possible, I would suggest that Melville finally arrives at the precipice of the epistemological limits that had vexed him over the years—an impasse whereby both rationalism and an intuitive belief in free will can continue to coexist only by virtue of the fact that both arguments fail to provide an adequate account of the world.

The larger trajectory of Melville's position from *Moby-Dick*, to "Bartleby, the Scrivener," and then to *Billy Budd*, thus illustrates a perceptible shift: from a frustrated hostility toward causal and theological determinism to an acknowledgment of motive, disposition, and the exercise of the will as inevitable, and ultimately to an unresolved meditation on the possibility of a self-determining will. Melville does not provide an answer to the question that he poses in his final work of fiction, and yet it is surely significant to note that in the forty years between the composition of *Moby-Dick* and *Billy Budd*, his thinking moves from an obsession with the impossibility of rejecting determinism to an acknowledgment of the possibility that there may in fact be instances in which the will becomes its own cause.

Such a progression not only illustrates the intensity and duration of Melville's pursuit of the free will problem, but also the direction of that pursuit. In *Billy Budd*, Melville finally constructs a narrative in which the Coleridgean possibility of supernatural self-determination is put into an open, albeit irreconcilable, dialogue with Edwardsian determinism. The effect of this juxtaposition, however, is one that tends to underscore the practical use and value of self-determination as a principle of human belief, as well as Melville's own sense that the argument for causal necessity was deeply disappointing when applied to the actions of the individual and the course of human events. So then we might say that Melville is antagonistic enough toward Edwards's argument for causal and theological determinism to wish that he could endorse Coleridge's supernatural conception of free will as the ground of human experience, but that he is unable to do so without reservation. Influenced both by the legacy of Edwards's rationalist theology and Coleridge's self-determining romanticism, this final refusal to believe wholly in one or the other is among the most powerful of the American literary responses to the free will problem in the nineteenth century.

Notes

1. For a fuller discussion of the relationship between these two figures and its importance to the American Romantics, see my essay, "President Edwards and the Sage of Highgate: Determinism, Depravity, and the Supernatural Will," *Journal of the History of Ideas* 77, no. 1 (2016): 27–47.

2. Jonathan Edwards, *Freedom of the Will*, ed. Paul Ramsey, vol. 1 of *The Works of Jonathan Edwards*, ed. Perry Miller and Harry Stout, 26 vols. (New Haven. Conn.: Yale University Press, 1957–2008), 184–5. Subsequent references to this volume will be cited parenthetically in the text.

3. Jonathan Edwards, *Letters and Personal Writings*, ed. George S. Claghorn, vol. 16, *Works*, 792.

4. See Herman Melville, *Correspondence*, ed. Lynn Horth (Evanston, Ill.: Northwestern University Press and the Newberry Library, 1993), 260.

5. Samuel Taylor Coleridge, *The Friend*, ed. Barbara E. Rooke, 2 vols.; vol. 4 of *The Collected Works of Samuel Taylor Coleridge*, 16 vols., gen. ed. Kathleen Coburn (Princeton, N.J.: Bollingen, 1969–2002), vol. 1: 519–20.

6. Samuel Taylor Coleridge, *The Notebooks of Samuel Taylor Coleridge*, ed. Kathleen Coburn, Merton Christensen, and Anthony John Harding, 5 vols. (Princeton, N.J.: Bollingen, 1957–2002), vol. 4, entry 5077.

7. Samuel Taylor Coleridge, *Aids to Reflection*, ed. John Beer, vol. 9, *Collected Works*, 160.

8. Samuel Taylor Coleridge, *Biographia Literaria*, ed. James Engell and Walter Jackson Bate, 2 vols, vol. 7, *Collected Works*, vol. 1: 114.

9. Ibid., 285.

10. Herman Melville, *Billy Budd, Sailor (An Inside Narrative), Reading Text and Genetic Text,* ed. Harrison Hayford and Merton M. Sealts Jr. (Chicago: University of Chicago Press, 1962), 264.

11. Herman Melville, *Moby-Dick, or, The Whale*, ed. Harrison Hayford, Hershel Parker, and G. Thomas Tanselle (Evanston and Chicago: Northwestern University and the Newberry Library, 1988), 189–90. Subsequent references will be cited parenthetically in the text.

12. Richard Gravil, *Romantic Dialogues: Anglo-American Continuities, 1776–1820* (Basingstoke, Eng.: Macmillan, 2000), 150.

13. Samuel Taylor Coleridge, *The Rime of the Ancient Mariner* (1834), in *Poetical Works*, ed. J. C. C. Mays, 3 vols,, vol. 16, *Works*, vol. 1.1: 375.

14. Coleridge, *Rime of the Ancient Mariner*, 377.

15. Jonathan A. Cook, *Inscrutable Malice: Theodicy, Eschatology, and the Biblical Sources of "Moby-Dick"* (DeKalb: Northern Illinois University Press, 2012), 107.

16. Leon Chai, *The Romantic Foundations of the American Renaissance* (Ithaca, N.Y.: Cornell University Press, 1987), 296. See also Richard Hardack, *"Not Altogether Human": Pantheism and the Dark Nature of the American Renaissance* (Amherst: University of Massachusetts Press, 2012).

17. Coleridge, *Notebooks*, vol. 1, entry 174.

18. Hershel Parker, *Melville: A Biography*, vol. 1, *1819–1851* (Baltimore: Johns Hopkins University Press, 1996), 796.

19. Sanford E. Marovitz, "Melville's Problematic 'Being,'" *ESQ: A Journal of the American Renaissance* 28 (1982): 11.

20. Melville, *Correspondence*, 186.

21. Ibid.

22. Coleridge, *The Friend*, vol. 1: 514.

23. Coleridge, *Biographia*, vol. 1: 17.

24. Robin Grey, *The Complicity of Imagination: The American Renaissance, Contests of Authority, and Seventeenth-Century English Culture* (New York: Cambridge University Press), 225.

25. Herman Melville, *Journals*, ed. Howard Horsford and Lynn Horth (Evanston and Chicago: Northwestern University Press and the Newberry Library, 1989), 4.

26. Richard Brodhead, "Trying All Things: An Introduction to *Moby-Dick*," in *New Essays on Moby-Dick*, ed. Richard Brodhead (New York: Cambridge University Press, 1986), 14–15.

27. Walton R. Patrick, "Melville's 'Bartleby' and the Doctrine of Necessity," *American Literature* 41 (1969): 40.

28. Maurice S. Lee, *Uncertain Chances: Science, Skepticism, and Belief in Nineteenth-Century American Literature* (New York: Oxford University Press, 2012), 63, 69.

29. David Hume, *An Enquiry concerning Human Understanding: A Critical Edition*, ed. Tom L. Beauchamp (New York: Oxford University Press, 2000), 46.

30. AnnLouise Keating, "The Implications of Edwards' Theory of the Will on Ahab's Pursuit of Moby Dick," *English Language Notes* 28 (1991): 35.

31. Herman Melville, "Bartleby, the Scrivener," in *Piazza Tales and Other Prose Pieces, 1839–1860*, ed. Harrison Hayford, Alma A. MacDougall, and G. Thomas Tanselle (Evanston and Chicago: Northwestern University Press and the Newberry Library, 1987), 37. Subsequent references will be cited parenthetically in the text.

32. Kingsley Widmer, *The Ways of Nihilism; A Study of Melville's Short Novels* (Los Angeles: California State Colleges, 1970), 120.

33. Ibid., 359.

34. Allan Moore Emery, "The Alternatives of Melville's 'Bartleby,'" *Nineteenth-Century Fiction* 31 (1976): 178–79.

35. Lewis Mumford, *Herman Melville* (New York: Harcourt Brace, 1929), 237.

36. Gilles Deleuze, "Bartleby; or the Formula," in *Essays Critical and Clinical*, trans. Daniel W. Smith and Michael A. Greco (Minneapolis: University of Minnesota Press, 1997), 80.

37. Ibid., 90.

38. Dan McCall, *The Silence of Bartleby* (Ithaca, N.Y.: Cornell University Press, 1989), 30.

39. Giorgio Agamben, "Bartleby, or On Contingency," in *Potentialities: Collected Essays in Philosophy*, ed. and trans. Daniel Heller-Roazen (Stanford, Calif.: Stanford University Press, 1999), 254.

40. Merton M. Sealts Jr., *Pursuing Melville, 1940–1980: Chapters and Essays* (Madison: University of Wisconsin Press, 1982), 7.

41. Agamben, "Bartleby," 254–55.

42. Branka Arsić, *Passive Consitutions, or 7½ Times Bartleby* (Stanford, Calif.: Stanford University Press, 2007), 30.

43. Ibid., 27.

44. Coleridge, *Biographia*, vol. 1: 278–80.

45. Coleridge, *Notebooks*, vol. 4, entry 5077.

46. F. O. Matthiessen, *American Renaissance: Art and Expression in the Age of Emerson and Whitman* (New York: Oxford University Press, 1941), 447.

47. Herman Melville, *Billy Budd, Sailor (An Inside Narrative): Reading Text and Genetic Text* (Chicago: University of Chicago Press, 1962), 117. Subsequent references will be cited parenthetically in the text.

48. Matthiessen, *American Renaissance*, 513.

49. Hershel Parker, *Reading Billy Budd* (Evanston, Ill.: Northwestern University Press, 1990), 97.

50. William V. Spanos, *The Exceptionalist State and the State of Exception: Herman Melville's Billy Budd, Sailor* (Baltimore: Johns Hopkins University Press, 2011), 60.

51. Ibid., 70.

52. Gail Coffler, "Religion, Myth and Meaning in the Art of Billy Budd, Sailor," in *New Essays on Billy Budd*, ed. Donald Yannella (New York: Cambridge University Press, 2002), 62.

53. Ibid., 75.

54. See Paul Gilmore, *Aesthetic Materialism: Electricity and American Romanticism* (Stanford, Calif.: Stanford University Press, 2009), 77–78, 87, 107, 124–25.

55. Coleridge, "The Eolian Harp," in *Poetical Works*, vol. 1.1: 234.

56. Eric Goldman, "Bringing out the Beast in Melville's *Billy Budd*: The Dialogue of Darwinian and 'Holy' Lexicons on Board the *Bellipotent*," *Studies in the Novel* 37 (2005): 438.

57. Olive L. Fite, "Billy Budd, Claggart, and Schopenhauer," *Nineteenth Century Fiction* 23 (1968): 342.

"The Apocalypse of Pain"

Suffering, Theodicy, and Religious Identity in *Moby-Dick*

Haein Park

> Epicurus's old questions are yet unanswered. Is [God] willing to prevent evil, but not able? then is he impotent. Is he able, but not willing? then is he malevolent. Is he both able and willing? whence then is evil?
>
> —David Hume, *Dialogues concerning Natural Religion*

> If I could by any means comprehend how this God can be merciful and just there would be no need of faith.
>
> —Martin Luther, *The Bondage of the Will*

In *A Secular Age*, Charles Taylor identifies a growing interest in theodicy within Western culture as the shift from a theocentric to anthropocentric understanding of the world that transpired in the eighteenth century. Whereas in the premodern world, suffering was viewed as a mystery—individuals were inclined to accept it as something "quite beyond" them—in the eighteenth century, with the rise of disengaged rationality that accompanied what Taylor calls "exclusive humanism," the purpose and meaning behind suffering became increasingly questioned. As Taylor notes, "The idea of blaming God gets a clearer sense and becomes much more salient where people begin to think they know just what God was purposing in creating the world."[1] This concern with theodicy intensified as individuals began to conceive of human flourishing in purely immanent terms. When tragedy struck, it was legitimate to question God, to blame him for his ethical failures to attend to the welfare of human beings, because the anthropocentric turn "allows us to imagine a world shorn of violence and suffering" and to ask God "why they are there in the first place." As Taylor goes on to show, "Our hyper-Augustinian ancestors were part of a religious culture in which it was normal to find divine meaning to suffering and destruction. All previous human cultures had done so." However, "the break of modernity means that this kind of reading can no longer be taken for granted." In Melville's *Moby-Dick*, Captain Ahab rebels against what Taylor describes as the "hyper-Augustinian" and "juridical-penal" reading of suffering—suffering as punishment or pedagogy or divine plan.[2] In doing so, he conveys the protest of those who evaluated the doctrine of predestination by an ethics of benevolence and love, exposing God's apparent moral failures to display the requisite traits of generosity and kindness in his ordination of suffering on human beings.

Contrary to scholars who argue that the religious controversy in Melville's text unfolds within a background of a collapsing theocentric system, I propose that the debate over theodicy in nineteenth-century America was especially acute precisely because of the forceful "cross-pressures" exerted by both predestinarian theology and exclusive humanism.[3] On the one hand, Calvinists accepted suffering as part of the divine will; on the other, a growing number of Americans rebelled against this position as an affront to the idea of the good life conceived largely in immanent terms. The tension between these two ways of understanding the world—that of "human flourishing and the demands of God"[4]—clash powerfully in *Moby-Dick*. The novel's preoccupation with theodicy, in turn, expresses a larger cultural quest for an adequate theological understanding of suffering, a quest that becomes all the more urgent because the legacies of Calvinism and the ideals of exclusive humanism existed in close proximity to each other in the nineteenth-century United Sates.

By the mid-nineteenth century, the preoccupation with theodicy among orthodox Protestants had reached a critical turning point. Leo Hirrel describes the pressure American Calvinists faced to modify "the highly theocentric orientation of traditional Calvinism."[5] This pressure was generated in part by their effort to articulate the ethical standards of God in terms that would be more acceptable to human beings. "Despite their professions of orthodoxy," explains Hirrel, a growing number of Calvinists "wanted a religion that would agree with their standards of justice." Whereas Calvinists of an earlier era such as Jonathan Edwards "might have consistently argued that humans were incapable of judging the divine plan," New Divinity theologians Samuel Hopkins and Joseph Bellamy and their nineteenth-century disciples "implicitly conceded that God's ways might be evaluated by human standards."[6] The historical shift occurring within Calvinism, however, connects to a larger cultural trend in which Americans attempted to find comfort in a humanitarian God who showed deep concern for the social welfare of human beings. "Victorians," notes historian James Turner, "typically expected God to be kind, generous, and fair."[7] They also witnessed new ways of grieving and mourning with "a shift in focus from the dead to the mourner,"[8] a change that underscored the subjective experience of loss and trauma. Medical advances heightened the sense of uneasiness associated with suffering. In particular, the development of anesthesia in 1846 contributed to an epistemological shift in view toward suffering as doctors began to see pain "as a treatable pathology rather than as divine punishment."[9] This shift in perspective deepened the existential dilemma located in tragic circumstances as individuals, equipped with an increasingly rational, individualistic, and moralistic faith, challenged the notion that a God who is both just and loving would allow his creatures to undergo horrific pain in order to fulfill a set of predetermined course of events.

Simultaneously, however, many Americans in the nineteenth century still remained haunted by the legacy of Calvinism. Despite the well-known rebellion by Unitarians and later by transcendentalists, Calvinism had a stronghold on the American imagination outside the intellectual circles of Boston. Religious historian Douglas Sweeney acknowledges that Calvinists in the nineteenth century "did not enjoy the legally sanctioned cultural power [they] had in colonial New England." He shows, however, that the fierce debate being waged between conservative and progressive theologians of this era indicates Calvinism's "clear and abundant signs of life—signs that also abounded among the millions of other American Calvinists to survive the nineteenth century."[10] These signs point to the ways in which a vibrant theocentric framework of Calvinism existed side by side with an increasingly robust anthropocentric understanding of the world, a coexistence that fueled the era's interest in theodicy.

Calvinism in Nineteenth-Century America

Historians have traditionally argued that Calvinism declined after the death of Jonathan Edwards, a gradual waning that continued into the nineteenth century and that could not fully withstand the increasingly dominant ideological forces of Unitarianism and transcendentalism.[11] Likewise, many Melville scholars have discounted the vibrancy of Calvinism in nineteenth-century America. T. Walter Herbert, for example, argues that *Moby-Dick* was written in a historical moment in which "the great central issues of providence and original sin were losing their power over the religious imagination of Americans."[12] Melville's spiritual explorations thus allegedly occurred within a setting "anticipating the imminent collapse of the theocentric world."[13] Robert Milder interprets Melville's writing in a similar context: he sees the exploration of theodicy within Western culture culminating in *Moby-Dick* and maintains that the author's concern with theodicy is occasioned by the growth of "rational, anthropocentric thought."[14] Richard Forrer also asserts that Melville saw the inadequacies of traditional Puritan and secular theodicies—particularly their failure to accommodate to new philosophical ideas—and argues that Melville was looking for an unorthodox theodicy that would replace outdated beliefs. Forrer views Melville's approach to theodicy as one that responded to "a pluralistic vision of the universe."[15]

While it is important to attend to Melville's innovative and daring philosophical explorations in the novel, and while it is equally crucial to heed Emory Elliot's caution that recognizing "the ties between Calvinism and *Moby-Dick* accounts for only one of the multiple ways that religious forms and ideas circulate" in the novel, it is also vital to place Melville's work within a robust theocentric framework.[16] In doing so, one recognizes that Melville's interest in Calvinism and, in particular, the Calvinist response to theodicy, conveys not an anachronistic preoccupation with an outdated theology or even a dying faith but, on the contrary, reveals the extent to which he was deeply immersed in the theological debates of his time.[17] As Sweeney carefully documents, the Calvinist tradition of Edwards "did not die out in the early nineteenth century" but "grew by leaps and bounds until at least the 1840s."[18] Joseph Conforti also shows the dominance of the Edwardsian tradition in the nineteenth century. As he remarks, "Edwards' works were first canonized and widely published in the nineteenth, not the eighteenth, century. The history of the creation of New England theology stands as a case study in the persistence of dynamic Edwardsian and Calvinist traditions in American culture at least down to the Civil War."[19]

Calvinism was a rich topic of discussion not only among theologians but also among laymen of this period, for "theology belonged not merely to ministerial elites, but was internalized and appropriated by all levels of society."[20] Harriet Beecher Stowe attests to this reality in her 1859 novel, *The Minister's Wooing*, which explores the legacies of Calvinism in New England. The narrator describes how sermons were "discussed by every farmer, in intervals of plough and hoe, and by every woman and girl, at loom, spinning-wheel, or wash tub":

> New England was one vast sea surging from depths to heights with thought and discussion on the most insoluble of mysteries. And it is to be added that no man or woman accepted any theory or speculation simply as theory or speculation: all was profoundly real and vital—a foundation on which actual life was based with intensest earnestness.[21]

In an 1858 essay published in the *Atlantic Monthly*, Stowe reiterated theology's influence on the daily lives of New Englanders: "nowhere in the world," she writes, "unless perhaps in Scotland, have merely speculative questions excited the strong and engrossing interest among the common people that they have in New England. Every man, woman, and child was more or less a theologian."[22]

Like many nineteenth-century Americans, Melville evinced a strong interest in religion. What has not been adequately examined is the degree to which the theological concerns articulated by Calvinists of his time reverberate throughout *Moby-Dick*. Like many of his contemporaries, Melville did not accept theological ideas "simply as theory and speculation" but "all was profoundly real and vital." In 1856, when he stopped to visit Nathaniel Hawthorne in Liverpool, England, the latter noted the intensity and persistence with which Melville grappled with metaphysical ideas, remarking that his younger friend would "never rest until he gets hold of a definite belief. It is strange how he persists—and has persisted ever since I knew him. He can neither believe, nor be comfortable in in his unbelief."[23] In particular, nineteenth-century Calvinists were intensely preoccupied with the question of how much volitional capacity sinners had within a providential system in which God had foreordained the events of human history. This inquiry, explored at length in Jonathan Edwards's 1754 treatise, *Freedom of the Will*, became all the more relevant within a post-Revolutionary context in which Americans looked for "a divine moral governor whose rule encouraged moral effort and upward mobility, not an arbitrary monarch."[24] Melville dramatizes the existential predicament raised by Edwards in *Freedom of the Will*, one that continued to preoccupy nineteenth-century Americans. While the connection between Edwards's *Freedom of the Will* and Ahab's quest for Moby Dick has been explored,[25] the link between Melville's novel and the theological discussions taking place among contemporary Edwardsians, who redefined Edwards's theory of the will in significant ways, needs to be more carefully investigated. This essay will demonstrate the extent to which Melville remained acutely conscious of the Edwardsian discourse on natural and moral ability articulated by Calvinists of his time.

New England Theology: From Jonathan Edwards to Nineteenth-Century Edwardsians

Calvinism was not in its death throes in the nineteenth century but was a powerful intellectual current. Evangelical Calvinists who had inherited the Edwardsian tradition bitterly fought over how to maintain an ideological balance between human responsibility and divine sovereignty. Throughout the early part of the nineteenth century, they carefully negotiated this balance, debating the precise nature of what Edwards had meant when he argued in *Freedom of the Will* that human beings possessed a natural capacity to repent but were morally disabled from doing so. He had maintained this distinction in order to encourage immediate repentance while reinforcing the Calvinist belief in humanity's absolute dependence on divine grace. As Conforti points out, "*Freedom of the Will* bequeathed to the New Divinity both a Calvinist definition of liberty and an evocative, manipulable vocabulary that supported the evangelical work of the pulpit."[26] The text provided a powerful conceptual framework that enabled Calvinists to maintain the integrity of human freedom without compromising on the absolute nature of divine sovereignty.

One of the ways Edwards accomplished this task was by making the crucial distinction between natural ability and moral inability inherent in each person. He provided an example to illustrate this point: a compassionate prince grants liberty to a prisoner and opens the prison doors; the prisoner, however, refuses to accept his freedom and remains in bondage, "his rooted strong pride and malice hav[ing] perfect power over him."[27] Edwards explained that the rebellious prisoner has the *natural* ability to experience freedom "if he pleases; though by reason of his vile temper of heart which is fixed and rooted, 'tis impossible that it should please him." Because human beings are morally incapable of reorienting their wills, their condition mirrors the prisoner who, though he has been physically set free, cannot taste his freedom. Thus, "to talk of liberty," according to Edwards, "as belonging to the very will itself, is not to speak good sense. For the will itself is not an agent that has a will: the power of choosing, itself, has not a power of choosing."[28]

The theological debates begun by Edwards had a profound influence on New England culture. As Archibald Alexander noted in 1831, "Edwards has done more to give complexion to the theological system of Calvinists in America, than all other persons together."[29] Disciples of Edwards continued his legacy in the second half of the eighteenth century. "But Edwardsian advances in the eighteenth century," notes Sweeney, "would not begin to compare with the movement's tremendous growth in the nineteenth century."[30] Nineteenth-century Calvinists responded to Edwards's critical distinction between natural ability and moral inability, continuously debating, distinguishing, and redefining these terms. During a period when American lawyers revived the legal concept of *mens rea*, "declaring the mentally ill not culpable for their crimes insofar as their insanity had deranged their natural volitional capacities," many Edwardsians renewed the emphasis on human guilt and responsibility.[31] They qualified and even rejected Edwards's arguments on moral inability. This emphasis on the natural and, ultimately, moral ability of sinners to repent and turn toward God gave the impression, as their conservative opponents charged, that they were treading dangerously on Arminian territory.

In 1812 Nathanael Emmons stressed natural ability over moral inability, articulating the role sinners played in effecting both their conversion and regeneration. The title of his work, *The Duty of Sinners to Make Themselves a New Heart*, encapsulated his theology of moral uplift. While reinforcing the Calvinist belief in utter dependence on God—human beings were "not sufficient of themselves but their sufficiency is of God"—Emmons also asserted that "sinners are free and voluntary in making them a new heart" and that "regeneration is not a miraculous or supernatural work."[32] Another Edwardsian, Nathaniel Taylor, remained within the Calvinist tradition; but he, too, moved away from Edwards's idea of moral inability. In his controversial 1828 work *Concio ad Clerum* he acknowledged: "Unless there be some [divine] interposition, . . . unless something be done which is above nature, the case is hopeless."[33] However, like increasing number of Calvinists, he put the emphasis on the freedom of the will, asking "what is this moral depravity for *which* man deserves the wrath of God?" Taylor answered, "*it is man's own act, consisting in a free choice of some object rather than God, as his chief good; or a free preference of the world and worldly good, to the will and glory of God.*" Taylor enjoined others to exonerate God by "throw[ing] all the guilt of sin with its desert of wrath upon the sinner's single self. Let us make him see and feel that he can go to hell only as a self-destroyer." He concluded the *Concio* by stressing human ability to reorient the will and obey God. The sinner "yields himself by his own free act, by his own choice, to those propensities of his nature . . . He is going to his wretched eternity, the self-made victim of its woes."[34]

This emphasis on the moral agency of human beings would culminate in Charles G. Finney's lectures on regeneration. As Finney declared in his *Lectures on Systematic Theology* (1846–47), "passive holiness is impossible. Sinners are required to make to themselves a new heart, which they could not do, if they were not active in this change."[35] Using "regeneration and conversion as synonymous terms," the revivalist argued that the moment of conversion occurs when God and sinner both act together to enact change: "God is said to turn him and he is said to turn himself. God draws him, and he follows. In both alike God and man are both active and their activity is simultaneous." Finney thus urged his audience to take responsibility for their salvation by reorienting their "object of life" from self-glorification to "a state of entire consecration to God." The evangelist made it unequivocally clear that "sinners must not wait for and expect physical omnipotence to regenerate them"; ultimately, "God cannot do the sinner's duty and regenerate him without the right exercise of the sinner's own agency." Rejecting Jonathan Edwards's distinction between natural ability and moral inability, he asserted: "To talk of a man's being free to will, or having liberty to will, when he has not the power or ability, is to talk nonsense." Finney explained his view more succinctly: "Edwards I revere; his blunders I deplore."[36]

Nathanael Emmons redefined moral depravity in 1842, challenging the belief that depravity was innate and inherited. In *Man's Activity and Dependence Illustrated and Reconciled*, he rejected moral inability altogether and attempted to forestall any excuse one might offer in refusing to convert. Like his contemporaries, Emmons was careful to note that viewing human beings as "morally free agents" does not mean that "we are not dependent on the Supreme Being for all our moral exercises."[37] Nevertheless, as he explained, "action always implies choice and choice always implies motive . . . And in thus acting voluntarily in the view of the motives presented to us, we exercise the most perfect liberty or moral freedom."[38]

In *Moby-Dick*, Melville evinces a profound interest in the discussion revolving around the Edwardsian distinction between natural and moral inability, a distinction that had been first articulated in *Freedom of the Will* and that was gradually being redefined by the inheritors of the Edwardsian tradition in the nineteenth century. That Melville knew of Edwards's treatise on the will is clear. Hershel Parker notes that as Melville read through an account of Berkshire County history, he marked passages related to Edwards's *Freedom of the Will.*[39] Furthermore, Melville makes a brief yet significant reference to *Freedom of the Will* in "Bartleby, the Scrivener." The narrator, in a frustrating moment, reads Edwards's essay as the tension with Bartleby escalates in his law office. Just as "Bartleby" is concerned with the question of volition (the eponymous character insists on his preferences, an insistence that leads to his tragic death), so *Moby-Dick* explores the distinction between natural ability and moral inability as the author investigates theodicy through the voice of his central characters. In the novel, Ahab questions the logic of Edwards's claim that one possesses the natural ability to obey God but is simultaneously incapable of doing so. The crux of Ahab's quarrel with theodicy resides in this paradox, the flawed logic that remains at the heart of a theological system that makes him responsible for his disordered will and that, at the same time, incapacitates him from reorienting this will toward obedience to God. Rather than submitting himself to this paradox, he stages a violent, tragic revolt against it. Simultaneously, however, he remains equally suspicious of the claims offered by nineteenth-century Calvinists who emphasized the moral ability of human beings.

Suffering and Providential Theology in *Moby-Dick*

Herman Melville's experience with tragedy early in life had a profound effect on the ways he would address theodicy in *Moby-Dick*. At the age of twelve, Melville witnessed the mental derangement of his once-prosperous father, Allan Melvill, who had tried desperately but unsuccessfully to avert a sudden financial ruin brought on by risky business investments. During his last days, Allan Melvill railed against his misfortune, a protest that "at times," noted his older brother Thomas, "was fierce, even *maniacal*."[40] After the death of his father and the economic decline of the family, Melville then witnessed his mother turning to her inherited Dutch Calvinist faith to come to terms with her loss.[41]

The tragic events in the author's early life would intensify his search for meaning before the specter of human suffering. Melville reveals how the Calvinist effort to uphold the justice of God in the face of harrowing affliction remains ultimately inadequate. Captain Ahab rebels against his predestined lot to be a carrier of divine will: to suffer the physical mutilation inflicted by Moby Dick. When Ahab's leg is brutally torn off by the whale, the captain lies recovering for many days: "for months and days and weeks, Ahab and anguish lay stretched together in one hammock."[42] The intense physical and psychic pain that the captain endures during this time would eventually fuel his "audacious, immitigable, and supernatural revenge" (186) against Moby Dick. Within the stark Calvinist world that elevates the sovereignty and transcendence of God, and without the sacramental imagination that would enable him to recognize the face of divine empathy, Ahab's only recourse is to assert his power over the seemingly arbitrary power of God who consigns him to suffer. Beneath the captain's maniacal search for Moby Dick lies a profound cry against the injustice generated by the theological fatalism of traditional Calvinism.

Ahab stages a violent revolt against his fate and in so doing defies a metaphysical system that endangers his freedom and that leads him to accept suffering as a predetermined will of God. Theologian David Bentley Hart, in response to the double predestination articulated in book 3 of Calvin's *Institutes*—"that God predestined the fall of man so as to show forth his greatness in both the salvation and the damnation of those he has eternally preordained"[43]—exposes the potential pitfalls in Calvin's theology. As Hart writes, "if indeed there were a God whose true nature—whose justice and sovereignty—were revealed in the death of a child or the dereliction of a soul or a predestined hell, then it would be no great transgression to think of this as a kind of malevolent or contemptible demiurge, to hate him, and to deny him worship."[44] Hart explains that this is because within the predestinarian scheme, "everything is merely a fragment of divine volition, and God is simply the totality of all that is and all that happens; there is no creation, but only an oddly pantheistic expression of God's unadulterated power."[45] This is the logic that drives Ahab to perceive God as a malevolent agent, for within the providential arrangement, the horrific wound he receives from Moby Dick bears the stamp of divine volition.

Unlike Starbuck, who simply interprets the wound inflicted by the whale as a natural, albeit unfortunate, occurrence—a "dumb brute" has smote the captain "out of blind instinct" (145)—Ahab perceives a malevolent, spiritual motive behind the event. Just as nineteenth-century Calvinists reaffirmed predestinarian theology even as they began to emphasize the moral agency of human beings, so *Moby-Dick* betrays the extent to which this doctrine still haunted the cultural imagination. Nathaniel Taylor, for example, asserted the freedom of individuals to bring about their spiritual transformation, while he also declared that "God has from eternity purposed that every event which takes place shall take place," and that "no event whose actual existence he has purposed will fail to take place."[46] Ahab echoes the schizophrenic tension evident in the Edwardsian struggle to maintain human freedom within a predestinarian system.

When Starbuck seeks to reason with Ahab, crying—"Vengeance on a dumb brute. To be enraged with a dumb thing seems blasphemous" (163–64)—Ahab responds with a telling rebuttal: "All visible objects, man, are but as pasteboard masks. But in each event some unknown but still reasoning thing puts forth the mouldings of its features behind the unreasoning mask" (164). For Ahab, the very enactment of Moby Dick's violent assault on his body bears an unmistakable mark of a supernatural orchestration: "an unknown but still reasoning" agent has condemned him to suffer mutilation through the actions of the White Whale. Thus Ahab is driven to seek revenge not only against Moby Dick; his immitigable hatred is directed more precisely toward the transcendent agent who is behind the act. Ahab passionately declares, "I see in him outrageous strength, with an inscrutable malice sinewing it. That inscrutable thing is chiefly what I hate" (164). The captain seeks to deploy a violent retaliation against the arbitrary, if unfathomable, power who has ordained him to a cruel mutilated fate. Asserting his moral agency, he chooses to rebel against the system that reduces him to a mere vehicle of transcendent will.

Ahab only confronts "the howling infinite" as he suffers, an infinite whose nothingness resembles the seemingly indifferent God of the universe. This experience of dereliction connects powerfully to the afflictions of his early years. Near the beginning of the novel, we learn from Captain Peleg that "Captain Ahab did not name himself. 'Twas a foolish, ignorant whim of his crazy, widowed mother, who died when he was only a twelvemonth old" (79). Ahab's quest for answers concerning his tormenting wound is both poignant and urgent precisely because it hearkens back to a psychic disfiguration sustained in childhood and youth: the death of his father, the mental instability and death of his mother, the loss, bereavement, and pain of orphaned existence, and the arbitrary assignment of the name "Ahab" that casts him outside salvation history.[47] As if to acknowledge the bitter irony of his fate, the captain while brooding in his cabin sees the choice to rebel against his lot as a foregone conclusion: "The path to my fixed purpose is laid with iron rails, whereon my soul is grooved to run" (168). At the heart of Ahab's rebellion lies his tragic assertion of freedom "within the closed continuum of his wounded world."[48] He is denied the knowledge that God is not the architect of his misery, and with the denial of this knowledge, he rebels against the sublime agent who has condemned him to suffer an unimaginably cruel fate.

Ahab simultaneously ratifies and protests against his predestined lot, understanding his suffering and articulating his rebellion through the language of Calvinism. In the *Institutes*, Calvin had affirmed: "No one can deny that God foreknew what end man was to have before he created him, and consequently foreknew because he so ordained by his decree."[49] Ahab questions this doctrine even as he ironically echoes its language and reinforces its logic. Late in the novel, when Starbuck attempts to dissuade Ahab from pursuing Moby Dick, the captain replies, "Ahab is for ever Ahab, man. The whole act's immutably decreed. 'Twas rehearsed by thee and me a billion years before this ocean rolled. Fool! I am the Fates' lieutenant" (561). In *Moby-Dick*, the language of divine fiat joins with an epic assertion of human will, a convergence that discloses the metaphysical tension of inhabiting a system that simultaneously affirms the moral agency of human beings and upholds the inexorable decrees of a sovereign God. Ahab's dream of destroying Moby Dick belies an absolute helplessness that manifests itself as a violent protest of one who remains deeply entrenched in this predetermined world.

Freedom of the Will in *Moby-Dick*

In *Moby-Dick*, Ahab's anxiety points to the ontological instability generated by the Edwardsian debates on natural ability and moral inability. This tension is dramatized vividly toward the end of the novel as the captain prepares his combat against the White Whale. When Starbuck attempts to dissuade Ahab from continuing on his mad pursuit, entreating him to think of those who await their safe return, the captain remains momentarily touched by Starbuck's words. At a crucial moment, however, Ahab turns away from Starbucks's pleading eyes: "Ahab's glance was averted; like a blighted fruit tree he shook and cast his last, cindered apple to the soil" (545). The turning point occurs when Ahab contemplates his inability to avert the impending disaster: "What cozening, hidden lord and master, and cruel, remorseless emperor commands me, that against all natural lovings and longings, I so keep pushing, and crowding, and jamming myself on all the time; recklessly making me ready to do what in my proper, natural heart, I durst not so much as dare? Is Ahab, Ahab? Is it I, God, or who, that lifts this arm?" (545). Ahab's "natural heart" possesses the capacity to discern that what he is about to enact—his revenge against Moby Dick—will result in a certain destruction of his ship and crew. He is, however, morally incapable of stopping himself; he cannot choose the good—the preservation of himself and others—even though he has the capacity to see the abhorrent nature of his quest.

Ahab is horrified by the vision of his nihilistic pursuit, crying out against the force within himself that compels him "to do what in [his] proper, natural heart, [he] durst not so much as dare" (545). Fully conscious that he is hurling himself and others toward annihilation, he shudders at the scale of ruin before him. The captain recognizes that what he is about to undertake can be conceptualized only at the limits of thought itself, so horrifying is the act; nonetheless, he remains morally incapacitated, unable to overpower his impulse toward certain ruin. He can only utter the desperate, poignant words, "Is Ahab, Ahab? Is it I, God, or who, that lifts this arm?" (545).

Ahab, in fact, possesses "natural lovings and longings" for the domestic world of a young wife and child who faithfully await his homecoming, a world for which he, like Starbuck, yearns and knows to be a good far superior to his absurd quest—a good he might choose but is simultaneously unable to enact. Starbuck pleads with Ahab to end his pursuit of Moby Dick, and return to "the wife and child of thy loving, longing, paternal old age" (544). In response, Ahab declaims with passionate intensity against his forty solitary years of whaling:

> Away, whole oceans away, from that young girl-wife I wedded past fifty, and sailed for Cape Horn the next day, leaving but one dent in my marriage pillow—wife? wife?—rather a widow with her husband alive! Aye, I widowed that poor girl when I married her, Starbuck; and then, madness, the frenzy, the boiling blood and the smoking brow, with which, for a thousand lowerings old Ahab has furiously, foamingly chased his prey—more a demon than a man! (544).

Ahab recognizes the spectacular folly of leaving the domestic happiness that is within his grasp, and acknowledges the moral dereliction of abandoning his family. He is, however, disabled from making the profitable choice that can bring him the joy for which he longs: "aye, aye! what forty years' fool—fool—old fool, has old Ahab been! Why this strife of the chase? Why weary, and palsy the arm at the oar, and the iron and the lance? how the richer or better is Ahab now? (544). These words expose the absolute moral helplessness of Ahab: he understands the futility of his quest and yearns to escape the approaching disaster but simply cannot ratify that choice.

The tension dramatized in this scene also points to Starbuck's increasingly desperate efforts to sustain his belief in Ahab's moral agency. At the end of the second day of chase, when Starbuck sees that the captain still will not abandon his senseless plan, he tells Ahab, "Great God! But for one single instant show thyself" (561). Starbuck fervently clings to the possibility that Ahab will choose to forgo his irrational scheme: "In Jesus' name, no more of this, that's worse than devil's madness. Two days chased; twice stove to splinters; thy very leg once more snatched from under thee; thy evil shadow gone—all good angels mobbing thee with warnings:—what more wouldst thou have?" (561). Starbuck, like the Edwardsians who emphasized the self's capacity to turn away from morally disastrous choices, believes in Ahab's ability to choose: Ahab is able to recognize the senselessness of the chase and forgo his pursuit of Moby Dick.

Implicit in Starbuck's urging is the distant but still extant faith in the moral agency of his captain: the first mate believes that with the demise of Ahab's "evil shadow," after two days of chasing the White Whale and narrowly escaping death, the captain's truer, better self would show itself. Starbuck utters the plea in the passionate hope that the revelations of the past two days would finally come to restore sanity in his commander. Even until the very last moment, on the third day of the chase, just before the final annihilation, Starbuck attempts to persuade Ahab to abandon his reckless pursuit. "O, my captain, my captain!—noble heart—go not—go not!" he implores, "see, it's a brave man that weeps; how great the agony of the persuasion then!" (66). Ahab is unreachable, however, and responds only with the peremptory order to "lower away" the boats. Starbuck is left to face the inconceivable scale of the tragedy resulting from this fateful command.

Ishmael's Calvinist Anthropology: A Vision of Moral Cannibalism

The story of the self and its consuming shadow appears in Ishmael's allusion to the fate of Narcissus in the beginning of the novel and in Ahab's battle with Moby Dick toward the end; we also witness this story in Ishmael, who implicitly acknowledges the moral cost of Ahab's violent, irrational schemes but is nonetheless moved by a force within and beyond himself to join in the chorus of shouts crying out for revenge against the object of Ahab's revenge: "I, Ishmael, was one of that crew; my shout had gone up with the rest; my oath had been welded with theirs; and stronger I shouted and more did I hammer and clinch my oath, because of the dread in my soul. A wild, mystical, sympathetical feeling was in me; Ahab's quenchless feud seemed mine" (179).

Later on, perhaps in recognition of his moral failures—his inability to listen to the promptings of his more principled self—Ishmael draws a frightening topography of the human soul in which the territory of the rational self remains surrounded by another terrain, one inhabited by a cannibalistic self that attempts to gratify its voracious, insatiable appetites. "Consider the universal cannibalism of the sea," he notes in the chapter on "Brit," "all whose creatures prey upon each other, carrying on eternal war since the world began. Consider all this; and then turn to this green, gentle and most docile earth" (274). The shark-infested "cannibalism of the sea" that encircles the peaceful land becomes a metaphor for the amoral force that threatens the very boundaries of a rational self:

> Consider them both, the sea and the land; and do you not find a strange analogy to something in yourself? For as this appalling ocean surrounds the verdant land, so in the soul of man there lies one insular Tahiti, full of peace and joy, but encompassed by all the horrors of the half known life. God keep thee! Push not off from that isle, thou canst never return! (274).

Ishmael sees two selves at work: the more powerful of the two is the ungovernable self that can potentially devour reason and obliterate any sense of principled judgment, a self that lies behind the self and that exists by the terms of its own amoral logic. The rational self, then, remains helplessly at the mercy of this engulfing, cannibalistic force warring within the human psyche.[50]

Ishmael narrates Ahab's self-engulfment by his own destructive alter ego, but this vision of the self's powerlessness against itself, the novel tells us, is universal. It is a vision of human personality that has precise correspondences to Jonathan Edwards's Calvinist anthropology, which accepts moral inability as an irrefutable fact of human condition. Even Starbuck, who sees through the machinations of his captain and desperately wishes to stop the impending disaster, ultimately remains helpless, lacking the moral strength to resist Ahab's malevolent schemes. The first mate, in the language of Edwards, possesses the natural ability to avert the tragic ruin looming before him, but is morally disabled from doing so; he thereby complicates and overturns his own belief in human freedom. Even Starbuck, the best of the crew, cannot perform the good that he so urgently desires to execute. He confronts his own moral incapacity to confront his captain following the scene on the quarterdeck: "I see his impious end; but feel that I must help him to it. Will I, nill I, the ineffable thing has tied me to him. Oh! I plainly see my miserable office—to obey, rebelling" (169). Toward the end of the novel, as Ahab takes the *Pequod* headlong into the destructive path of the White Whale, Starbuck once again grasps the moral helplessness of his condition vis-à-vis Ahab: "Against the wind he now steers for the open jaw" (564). But he is unable to do what is required to save the ship and recognizes the horrifying moral predicament before him. Moments before plunging into the final catastrophe, he utters the last, tormented cry: "I disobey my God in obeying him!" (564). While Starbuck represents the voice of the nineteenth-century Edwardsians who stressed human agency, attempting to do away with the language of both natural and moral inability, he recognizes the impossibility of carrying out the necessary act that would salvage his life and that of his crew.[51]

Ishmael confirms the fatalism that pervades the novel, reinforcing a vision of an inexorable decree unfolding within the domain of human history, one that cannot be thwarted by even the grandest, most ambitious of human will. As Ishmael describes Ahab's frenetic effort to kill Moby Dick, he notes that "in that wild simultaneousness of a thousand concreted perils—Ahab's yet unstriken boat seemed drawn towards Heaven by invisible wires" (559). T. Walter Herbert reminds us that Ishmael and Ahab "never exchange a word in the long course of the voyage, yet they are linked as figures of a spiritual crisis."[52] Ishmael, like Ahab, repudiates the idea of free will, acknowledging instead a sublime force that controls his life, an agent who deceives him into thinking he acts freely when in reality he, like his captain, is the fates' lieutenant. In the beginning of the novel, as the narrator surveys his voyage retrospectively, he reflects:

> Though I cannot tell why it was exactly that those stage managers, the Fates, put me down for this shabby part of a whaling voyage, I think I can see a little into the springs and motives which being

> cunningly presented to me under various disguises, induced me to set about performing the part I did, besides cajoling me into the delusion that it was a choice, resulting from my own unbiased freewill and discriminating judgment. (7)

The self-deprecating irony Ishmael deploys in this passage cannot hide the unsettling belief in a transcendent force that directs and controls human life. Ishmael alludes to the eternal decree that had been ordained from the beginning of time, one that leads to Ahab's tragic ruin. In this allusion, Ishmael complicates and casts doubt on the very idea of human agency.

Fading Incarnation and Domestication of Transcendence

Nineteenth-century Edwardsians attempted to define, categorize, and explain the precise nature of divine will and human freedom in terms of natural and moral ability. This attempt at doctrinal clarification with the tools of rationality had an important corollary: the gradual fading of divine mystery and increasing concern with theodicy as one tried to grasp God's intended meaning behind human suffering. William Placher shows how this trend paralleled a diminishing influence of Trinitarian theology as a more unitary vision of God as creator, sustainer, and universal judge replaced a sacramental theology that upheld a Christocentric vision, at the heart of which stood the image of the Man of Sorrows.[53] By the end of the seventeenth century, explains Placher, "the authority of the scripture, and decrees and covenants, were replacing the Trinity at the center of theological debates" among Protestants.[54] The waning influence of Trinitarian theology also paralleled a growing emphasis on human responsibility in effecting one's spiritual regeneration, as the Edwardsian concern over the sinner's natural and moral ability demonstrates.[55] Sweeney notes, for example, that Nathaniel Taylor's "concern with human nature and its potential yielded a rather innovative theology of human moral agency," a theology that was especially conscious of the need to adapt to the ideals of a new democracy.[56]

These trends, argues Placher, contributed to the "domestication of transcendence":

> Before the seventeenth century, most Christian theologians were struck by the mystery, the wholly otherness of God, and the inadequacy of any human categories as applied to God. . . . In the seventeenth century, philosophers and theologians increasingly thought they could talk clearly about God. Rather than explaining how all categories break down when applied to God, they set the stage for talking about transcendence as one of the definable properties God possesses—a quality we can understand.

For the premoderns, a sense of divine mystery tended to dominate their understanding of God. Even the systematic Calvin, in affirming the coexistence of God's providence and human freedom, qualified one's ability to grasp fully the doctrine of predestination. As Calvin wrote, "If anyone object that this [doctrine] is beyond comprehension, I confess it. But what wonder if the immense and incomprehensible majesty of God exceed the limits of our intellect?"[57]

In *Moby-Dick*, Melville not only explores the theological debates taking place among Calvinists of his time, but he also betrays an anxiety toward the fading of sacramental theology. He displays an intense preoccupation with the absence of Christ: without the sacramental vision of a suffering God identifying with suffering humanity, Ahab is left to confront a stark, indifferent world, protesting against the injustice of his tragic circumstance without the consolation of divine empathy.[58] William Braswell notes that "whereas in *White Jacket*, published the year before [*Moby-Dick*], Christ is held up as a model for all men to imitate, in *Moby-Dick* Christ is barely mentioned."[59] Moreover, "One might expect the good Father Mapple to represent the Deity as kind, but his God is the stern, severe God of the Old Testament, known to man chiefly by his chastising."[60] The absence of Christ in the novel is intentional, for the author is staging a theological experiment, investigating a world that remains bereft of divine pathos. During a period when "the authority of the scripture, and decrees and covenants, were replacing the Trinity at the center of theological debates" among Protestants, Melville explores the implication of this historical drift, displaying for his readers the haunting, secularized space of a disenchanted world.[61]

Ahab attempts to grasp the inscrutable, sublime force joined to Moby Dick and thereby to decode the transcendent language inscribed in the White Whale, a language that can shadow forth some glimmer of meaning behind his suffering. By the sheer force of his logic, he strives to overpower the mystery of evil that is encapsulated in his tragic circumstance, to read the meaning of God's behavior within the chaotic domain of his pain. "Gnawed within and scorched without, with the infixed, unrelenting fangs of some incurable idea," Ahab "piled upon the whale's white hump the sum of all the general rage and hate felt by his whole race from Adam down" (184). Ahab expresses humanity's perennial struggle to understand the problem of evil and suffering: Moby Dick swims tantalizingly before him "as the monomaniac incarnation of all those malicious agencies which some deep men feel eating in them" (184). Jonathan A. Cook points out that "Ahab 'plays God' in his attempt to vanquish the evil he imputes to Moby Dick, in imitation of God's final conquest of Leviathan," as evoked in the book of Isaiah.[62] While Ahab's premodern ancestors would have accepted the mystery of evil and suffering, the captain himself is driven by a theological question he never utters but one that unmistakably governs his relentless quest: why evil and suffering exist; and, more specifically, why he himself was selected to undergo an unimaginable physical and psychological anguish through the actions of the White Whale.

These are questions that Ahab proposes to a deity who remains impassive and indifferent, for he cannot glimpse the face of a suffering God who suffers with him and who can offer the consolations of divine compassion. While Ahab stands on deck for the first time with a "crucifixion in his face" (124), he is unable to perceive this expression of pain in the face of his God. In this world of fading incarnation, without the image of God as the Man of Sorrows, Ahab is left to solve the mystery of evil by the sheer force of his will and intellect. "There's a riddle now might baffle all the lawyers backed by the ghosts of the whole line of judges:—like a hawk's beak it pecks my brain. *I'll, I'll* solve it, though!" (562; emphasis original). This triumphant declaration of reason's ability to decode the mystery of suffering also connects to its tragic corollary: Ahab's descent into madness. In the chapter outlining Ahab's moral derangement, Ishmael notes that after "deliriously" transferring the idea of evil "to the abhorred white whale, he pitted himself, all mutilated, against it" (184). In his study of biblical theodicy in *Moby-Dick*, Cook examines the influence of the book of Job in Melville's dramatization of Ahab's monomaniacal quest. In effect, the captain's "demonization of the White Whale and his elevation of its pursuit to an apocalyptic mission" is the result of his transforming the albino whale "into a mythological embodiment of evil closely related to the marine chaos monster Leviathan found most prominently in the book of Job."[63] Ahab is unable to see God as a self-revealing subject and understands the deity only as an abstraction, an overpowering force that can be subdued by his will, or an object whose mystery he means to crack with the tools of his intellect. Through Ahab's tragedy, Melville perceptively explores the spiritual predicament of those inhabiting a modern world bereft of revelation and grace. Within this world one can intuit that "the gods themselves are not for ever glad. The ineffaceable, sad birth-mark in the brow of man, is but the stamp of sorrow in the signer" (464). The abstract language Melville employs to describe God, however, conveys an ever-diminishing presence of a deity whose particular features are eclipsed by an imprecise articulation. In this world void of incarnational God, Melville leaves us at best with an "ineffaceable" but barely visible trace of divine sorrow.

In *Moby-Dick*, Ahab refuses the eschatological hope that would enable him to traverse the threshold of meaningless suffering. Instead, he stages a fierce protest against "the heartless voids and immensities of the universe" (175). His struggle with theodicy captures the tension of negotiating predestinarian belief in light of exclusive humanism, one that elevates the goal of human flourishing shorn of suffering as an ultimate good. *Moby-Dick* thus foreshadows a crisis of belief that would dominate the modern imagination, a crisis that Fyodor Dostoevsky, for example, would explore twenty years later in his epic novel, *The Brothers Karamazov*, in the voice of Ivan Karamazov.[64] In *Moby-Dick*, Melville presciently captures the metaphysical questions raised by the experience of tragic loss, exploring what it means to confront the problem of evil and suffering head-on within the spiritual realm of an emerging secular world.

Notes

1. Charles Taylor, *A Secular Age* (Cambridge, Mass.: Harvard University Press, 2007), 388.

2. Ibid., 650–51, 653, 654.

3. The concept of "cross-pressures" appears in Charles Taylor's *A Secular Age*. It refers to the conflicting and competing ideas of the good individuals experience within a secular age. See pp. 594–617. In particular, I will be responding to arguments in T. Walter Herbert, *"Moby-Dick" and Calvinism: A World Dismantled* (New Brunswick, N.J.: Rutgers University Press, 1977), and Herbert, "Calvinist Earthquake: *Moby-Dick* and Religious Tradition" in *New Essays on Moby-Dick*, ed. Richard Brodhead (New York: Cambridge University Press, 1986); Robert Milder, "Herman Melville: 1819–1891: A Brief Biography," in *A Historical Guide to Herman Melville*, ed. Giles Gunn (New York: Oxford University Press, 2005); Richard Forrer, *Theodicies in Conflict: A Dilemma of Puritan Ethics and Nineteenth-Century American Literature* (New York: Greenwood, 1986); Emory Elliot, "Wandering To-and-Fro: Melville and Religion" in *Historical Guide to Herman Melville*, ed. Gunn; and Jonathan A. Cook, *Inscrutable Malice: Theodicy, Eschatology, and the Biblical Source of "Moby-Dick"* (DeKalb: Northern Illinois University Press, 2012).

4. Taylor, *A Secular Age*, 656.

5. Leo Hirrel, *Children of Wrath: New School Calvinism and Antebellum Reform* (Lexington: University of Kentucky Press, 1998), 25.

6. Ibid., 25, 22. To be sure, there were orthodox Calvinists, most notably Charles Hodge from Princeton, who warned against the dangers of "justify[ing] God's ways to men," arguing that such an attempt would dismantle "the entire structure of Calvinism" (Hirrel, *Children of Wrath*, 43).

7. James Turner, *Without God, Without Creed: The Origins of Unbelief in America* (Baltimore: Johns Hopkins University Press, 1985), 142.

8. Peter Balaam, *Misery's Mathematics: Mourning, Compensation, and Reality in Antebellum American Literature* (New York: Routledge, 2009), 4.

9. Elizabeth Clark, "'The Sacred Right of the Weak': Pain, Sympathy, and the Culture of Individual Rights in Antebellum America," *Journal of American History* 82, no. 2 (1995): 473. Clark's essay addresses how the dissociation of suffering from moral growth generated a cultural discomfort with religious suffering at large.

10. Douglas Sweeney, "'Falling Away from the General Faith of the Reformation'? The Contest over Calvinism in Nineteenth-Century America," in *John*

Calvin's American Legacy, ed. Thomas Davis (New York: Oxford University Press, 2010), 131, 113.

11. See, for example, Turner, *Without God, without Creed*; and Mark Noll, *America's God: From Jonathan Edwards to Abraham Lincoln* (New York: Oxford University Press, 2002). Noll argues that one of the most important forces contributing to the collapse of Puritanism was its accommodation to culture. He explains, for example, that the inheritors of Calvinism increasingly adopted commonsense theism and shifted the focus of theology from divine revelation to rationalist epistemology. See in particular "The Collapse of the Puritan Canopy" (31–50) and "Theistic Common Sense" (93–113). Douglas Sweeney provides a counterargument to this declension narrative in *Nathaniel Taylor, New Haven Theology, and the Legacy of Jonathan Edwards* (New York: Oxford University Press, 2003). Sweeney explains that "when interpreted only in thin, doctrinal terms, or in terms of 'religion and' historiography, the Edwardsian tradition remains susceptible to the power of the declension model of religious history . . . When defined in thicker, 'culture of' terms, however, it becomes clear that the Edwardsian tradition actually gained momentum during the Second Great Awakening" (10).

12. Herbert, "Calvinist Earthquake," 109.

13. Herbert, *"Moby-Dick" and Calvinism*, 18.

14. Milder, "Herman Melville," 34.

15. Forrer, *Theodicies in Conflict*, 220. Balaam similarly notes that Melville, along with other antebellum writers, "strove to evade the self-deception of facile solutions to the affective crisis of grief"; instead, Melville "envision[s] new theodicies, new forms of sovereignty and order with which to illuminate the continuity behind even the most wrenching particular losses" (*Misery's Mathematics*, 9). See also Jenny Franchot, "Melville's Traveling God," in *The Cambridge Companion to Herman Melville*, ed. Robert Levine (New York: Cambridge University Press, 1998); Franchot situates Melville's religious views in relation to an "ailing theology and resplendent anthropology" (171).

16. Elliott, "Wandering To-and-Fro," 188.

17. See also Cook, *Inscrutable Malice*. Cook examines Melville's theodicy in relation to the book of Job and the problem of evil in the biblical tradition. In *Melville's Bibles* (Berkeley: University of California Press, 2008), Illana Pardes traces the influence of the European exegetical tradition on *Moby-Dick*. She suggests that probing Melville's interest in biblical exegesis will enrich the reader's understanding of the author's spiritual journey (13).

18. Sweeney, *Nathaniel Taylor*, 5.

19. Joseph Conforti, *Jonathan Edwards, Religious Tradition, and American Culture* (Chapel Hill: University of North Carolina Press, 1995), 4. Conforti defines Edwardsianism in the following way: "'Edwardsians' refers to Congregationalist and Presbyterian leaders who either helped create or who accepted and attempted to come to terms with Edwards's new authority on personal piety, revivalism, and theology during the Second Great Awakening" (5).

20. Sweeney, *Nathaniel Taylor*, 44.

21. Harriet Beecher Stowe, *The Minister's Wooing* (New York: Penguin Books, 1999), 194.

22. Harriet Beecher Stowe, "New England Ministers," *Atlantic Monthly* 1 (February 1858): 486–87.

23. Herman Melville, *Journals*, ed. Howard C. Horsford and Lynn Horth (Evanston and Chicago: Northwestern University Press and the Newberry Library, 1989), 628.

24. Sweeney, *Nathaniel Taylor*, 99. Nathan O. Hatch, *The Democratization of American Christianity* (New Haven, Conn.: Yale University Press, 1989), provides an account of how the American Revolution created a more democratic religious culture. Hatch writes that an increasing number of Americans "called for a revolution within the church to place laity and clergy on an equal footing and to exalt the conscience of the individual over the collective will of any congregation or church organization" (71).

25. See AnnLouise Keating's "The Implications of Edwards' Theory of the Will on Ahab's Pursuit of Moby Dick," *English Language Notes* 28, no. 3 (March 1991): 28–37.

26. Conforti, *Jonathan Edwards*, 121.

27. Jonathan Edwards, *The Freedom of the Will*, in *The New England Theology: From Jonathan Edwards to Edwards Amasa Park*, ed. Allen Guelzo and Douglas Sweeney (Grand Rapids, Mich.: Baker Academic, 2006), 67.

28. Ibid., 68, 63.

29. Archibald Alexander, "An Inquiry into the Inability under Which Sinners Labour, and Whether It Furnishes Any Excuse for the Neglect of His Duty," *Biblical Repertory and Theological Review* 3, no. 3 (July 1831): 362.

30. Sweeney, *Nathaniel Taylor*, 40.

31. Ibid., 77.

32. Nathanael Emmons, *The Duty of Sinners to Make Themselves a New Heart,* in *The New England Theology*, ed. Guelzo and Sweeney, 121.

33. Nathaniel Taylor, *Concio ad Clerum,* in *The New England Theology*, ed. Guelzo and Sweeney, 201.

34. Ibid., 197, emphasis in original; 203, 204, emphasis in original. See Sweeney's extended discussion of Calvinism in nineteenth-century America in *Nathaniel Taylor*.

35. Charles G. Finney, *Lectures on Systematic Theology*, in *The New England Theology*, ed. Guelzo and Sweeney, 238.

36. Ibid., 238, 239, 241, 242, 242.

37. Emmons, *The Duty of Sinners to Make Themselves a New Heart*, in *The New England Theology*, ed. Guelzo and Sweeney, 175.

38. Ibid., 176–77.

39. Hershel Parker, *Herman Melville: A Biography*, vol. 1 (Baltimore: Johns Hopkins University Press, 1996), 795–96.

40. Quoted in Herbert, *"Moby-Dick" and Calvinism*, 53; emphasis in original. Herbert suggests, "Melville came to recognize that the perplexity of his quest for religious truth resulted somehow from the impact of his father's example upon his own life" (*"Moby-Dick" and Calvinism*, 55).

41. Ibid., 57. Emory Elliott notes that Melville "was born into a family that was steeped in Calvinist religious tradition. His great-great grandfather was a Congregationalist clergyman in Scotland for fifty years, and his grandfather

Thomas Melville studied divinity at Princeton with the intention of entering the ministry" ("Wandering To-and-Fro," 173).

42. Herman Melville, *Moby-Dick; or The Whale*, ed. Harrison Hayford, Hershel Parker, and G. Thomas Tanselle (Evanston and Chicago: Northwestern University Press and the Newberry Library, 1988), 184–85. Citations to this edition will hereinafter be noted in the text.

43. David Bentley Hart, *The Doors of the Sea: Where Was God in the Tsunami?* (Grand Rapids, Mich.: Eerdmans, 2005), 90.

44. Ibid., 91.

45. Ibid.

46. Nathaniel Taylor, *Lectures on the Moral Government of God* (New York: Clark, Austin and Smith, 1859), 304, 306.

47. Melville's sense of abandonment after the death of his father can be echoed in the dereliction Ahab experiences. Robert Milder in "Herman Melville" points out that "the mature Melville's feeling of God the Father's indifference, abdication, or nonexistence was rooted in the boy's sense of paternal desertion" (20).

48. Hart, *The Doors of the Sea*, 102.

49. John Calvin, *Institutes of the Christian Religion*, ed. John T. McNeill, trans. Ford Lewis Battles, 2 vols. (Louisville, Ky.: Westminster John Knox, 1960), 2:955.

50. In "A Psychoanalytic Look at Herman Melville from His Use of Source Materials for *Moby-Dick*," *Psychoanalytic Review* 96, no. 5 (October 2009): 743–67, Thomas Allen examines Melville's interest in the 1819 shipwreck of the *Essex*, whose survivors had resorted to cannibalism before they were rescued. Melville confesses that the story had "a surprising effect upon me" (quoted in Allen, 744). Allen provides a psychoanalytic reading of Melville's interest in the *Essex* narrative, suggesting that "at an unconscious level, a wish for a more adequate father with which to identify played a part in his fascination with cannibalism" (757). I would argue that Melville's fascination with cannibalism accords more with his pessimistic vision of human nature, one that finds its correspondence in Edwards's Calvinist anthropology. See also Hershel Parker's discussion of Melville's interest in the *Essex* narrative in *Herman Melville*, 1:194–98.

51. On Starbuck's Quaker identity and ethical code of nonviolence, see Wynn M. Goering, "'To Obey, Rebelling': The Quaker Dilemma in *Moby-Dick*," in *New England Quarterly* 54, no. 4 (December 1981): 519–38. Goering describes how "some [Quaker] writers suggested that the world was providentially designed to make peace; others believed that God would personally defend those who followed the way of peace" (530). According to these writers, the use of violence to stop violence signals a lack of faith in God's protection over those who choose a path of nonviolent resistance against evil (530). The world that Ishmael describes, however, is an indifferent one, devoid of providential care; thus the tragedy of the narrative resides in Starbuck's adherence to a code of nonviolence demanded by his Quaker faith, one that requires him to submit to Ahab's "impious ends" without the benefit of divine protection. For Goering, "the conflict aboard the *Pequod* is between Starbuck's 'mere unaided virtue' and the 'potency' of Ahab's monomania" (532).

52. Herbert, "Calvinist Earthquake," 114.

53. See William Placher's *The Domestication of Transcendence: How Modern Thinking about God Went Wrong* (Louisville, Ky.: Westminster John Knox, 1996). As Placher writes, "By the end of the seventeenth century, . . . arguments to God as the creator and sustainer of the universe and debates about the role of God in the accomplishment of salvation tended to simply talk about 'God'—the Trinitarian Persons did not play much role in the analysis" (168).

54. Placher, *Domestication of Transcendence*, 172.

55. Placher claims that the "marginalization of the Trinity went hand in hand with greater optimism about . . . the capacity of human moral efforts to cooperate in accomplishing salvation" (*Domestication of Transcendence*, 172).

56. Sweeney, *Nathaniel Taylor*, 102–3.

57. Placher, *Domestication of Transcendence*, 6–7; quoted in Placher, 123.

58. Placher articulates what is vitally at stake in the Crucifixion and in Trinitarian theology at large: "In light of the cross, we may still not know how to tell the story of the world in which we live, but we cannot tell it as a story of God's indifference to our suffering" (209).

59. William Braswell, *Melville's Religious Thought: An Essay in Interpretation* (New York: Pageant Books, 1959), 68.

60. Ibid., 70. See also Lawrence Buell, "*Moby-Dick* as Sacred Text," in *New Essays on Moby Dick*, ed. Richard Brodhead (New York: Cambridge University Press, 1986). Buell similarly points out that while the language of *Moby-Dick* "is drenched in sacramentalism," Emerson's transcendentalist work, "Divinity School Address," "remains more Christocentric" (54, 58).

61. Placher, *Domestication of Transcendence*, 172.

62. Cook, *Inscrutable Malice*, 11.

63. Cook, *Inscrutable Malice*, 21.

64. See Hart's discussion of theodicy in relation to Dostoevsky's *The Brothers Karamazov* in *The Doors of the Sea*, 36–44.

CONTRIBUTORS

Brad Bannon is a lecturer in the Department of English at the University of Tennessee, Knoxville. His work has appeared in *James Joyce Quarterly*, *Journal of the History of Ideas*, and *The Cormac McCarthy Journal*. He is the author of *Coleridge, Edwards, and the American Religion*, forthcoming from Routledge, and coeditor of *Determinism and Fatalism in the Works of Cormac McCarthy*, which will be published by the University of Tennessee Press.

Dawn Coleman is an associate professor and the director of graduate studies in the English Department at the University of Tennessee, Knoxville. She is the author of *Preaching and the Rise of the American Novel* (2013) and of numerous essays on nineteenth-century literature and religion. She serves as the book review editor for *Leviathan: A Journal of Melville Studies*, as a research associate for the Melville Electronic Library, and as a contributing scholar for *Melville's Marginalia Online*, for which she has written the critical introduction to the Melvilles' copy of William Ellery Channing's six-volume *Works*.

Jonathan A. Cook is chair of the English Department at Middleburg Academy in Middleburg, Virginia. He is the author of *Satirical Apocalypse: An Anatomy of Melville's "The Confidence-Man"* (1996) and *Inscrutable Malice: Theodicy, Eschatology, and the Biblical Sources of "Moby-Dick"* (2012). He has written the introduction and annotations to Melville's copy of Hawthorne's *Mosses from an Old Manse* for the website *Melville's Marginalia Online*. His essay on "*Typee* and the Myth of Paradise" appeared in the collection *Critical Insights: Herman Melville* (2013), and "*Moby-Dick* and Nineteenth-Century Natural History" in *Critical Insights: Moby-Dick* (2014). His articles on Melville and other nineteenth-century American writers have been published in *ESQ*, *Texas Studies in Literature and Language*, *Nineteenth-Century Literature*, *Leviathan*, *Prospects*, *ATQ*, *The Nathaniel Hawthorne Review*, *Papers on Language and Literature*, *Christianity and Literature*, and *New England Quarterly*.

Richard A. Garner is a lecturer in the Honors College at the University of Houston. His academic research focuses on eighteenth- and nineteenth-century American literature, particularly the relationship between aesthetics and regimes of slavery and sentiment in early America.

Zachary McLeod Hutchins is an assistant professor of English at Colorado State University, where he teaches courses in early American literature and culture. He is the author of *Inventing Eden: Primitivism, Millennialism, and the Making of New England* (2014) and the editor of *Community without Consent: New*

Perspectives on the Stamp Act (2016). His essays on religion in the writings of Herman Melville and other works of nineteenth-century literature have appeared in *ELH*, *Leviathan*, *Early American Studies*, and *Nineteenth-Century Literature*.

Martin Kevorkian is a professor and associate chair of English at the University of Texas at Austin. He is the author of *Writing beyond Prophecy: Emerson, Hawthorne, and Melville after the American Renaissance* (2013) and *Color Monitors: The Black Face of Technology in America* (2006), as well as of essays on John Ashbery, Samuel Beckett, Alfred Hitchcock, and Washington Irving.

Eileen McGinnis is an adjunct professor in English Writing and Rhetoric at St. Edward's University. Her 2014 dissertation looks at how Whitman's and Melville's engagements with pre-Darwinian evolution motivated their literary experiments. She has published on gender and reading technologies in Neal Stephenson's *The Diamond Age* for *Science Fiction Studies*, and is currently researching a book about Victorian computer programmer Ada Lovelace and her contemporary representations in literature, computing, and geek culture at large.

Haein Park is an associate professor of English at Biola University in La Mirada, California. Her research focuses on religion and American literature, particularly how literary texts reflect shifting conceptions of suffering. She is currently working on a manuscript titled "The Apocalypse of Pain: Suffering, Theodicy, and Religious Identity in American Literature."

Brian Yothers is the Frances Spatz Leighton Endowed Distinguished Professor of English at the University of Texas at El Paso. He is the author of *Sacred Uncertainty: Religious Difference and the Shape of Melville's Career* (2015), *Melville's Mirrors: Literary Criticism and America's Most Elusive Author* (2011), and *The Romance of the Holy Land in American Travel Writing, 1790–1876* (2007). He is also associate editor of *Leviathan: A Journal of Melville Studies*, an associate editor and contributing scholar at *Melville's Marginalia Online*, coeditor of the travel section of the *Melville Electronic Library*, and coeditor of the interdisciplinary journal *Journeys*. He has published numerous essays on such topics as Melville, Edgar Allan Poe, Mark Twain, travel, and religion in nineteenth-century America.

INDEX

Aaron, Daniel, 196, 197
Adams, Henry, 22, 55
Adventism, 3
Agamben, Giorgio, 253–54
Alexander, Archibald, 270
Alexander, Michael Solomon, 24
Algers, William Rounseville, 9
Allen, Gay Wilson, 83
Allen, Thomas, 285n50
All Souls' Church, 15, 118, 130, 133, 135–37, 141, 146, 151n5
Alter, Robert, 13
Anderson, Charles Robert, 199, 216, 218
Andrew, Edward, 138, 139, 149
Anglicanism, 24, 28, 31, 35. *See also* Broad Church movement
apocalypse genre, 13
Arnold, Edwin, 9
Arnold, Matthew, 6, 9, 15, 21, 23, 27, 28, 31, 33–34, 36, 42–44, 46, 48, 51, 104; Hellenism vs. Hebraism in, 67n34, 258
Arnold, Thomas, 34–35
Arsić, Branka, 255
Atkins, John, 224

Baird, James, 12
Balaam, Peter, 283n15
Baptist Church, 3, 24
Barrow, John, 224–25
Bartlett, William H., 9
Bate, Walter Jackson, 189
Battle Pieces and Aspects of the War, 8, 145; "Lee in the Capitol," 194
Bayle, Pierre, 5–6, 12, 130, 141, 250
Beecher, Henry Ward, 49
Bell, Millicent, 12
Bellamy, Joseph, 266
Bellows, Henry Whitney, 130, 131, 133–37, 139–40, 150, 154n49
Bentley, Nancy, 168–69
Bernard, 113, 115
Berthold, Dennis, 99
Bezanson, Walter, 71, 88, 95n63, 189
Bible: higher criticism of, 8, 25; Melville's use of, 3, 12, 13–14, 204, 283n17; versions of, 3, 4, 12, 204
BOOKS:
Old Testament: Genesis, 54, 92n24, 173, 175, 181n40; 2 Samuel, 53; Nehemiah, 191; Job, 14, 17, 45, 52, 281, 283n17; Ecclesiastes, 41, 45, 203; Song of Songs, 41, 112; Isaiah, 280; Daniel, 14, 39; Hosea, 44
New Testament: Matthew, 44, 144, 169, 188 (Sermon on the Mount, 168, 198, 201); Luke, 55, 187–88; John, 40; Acts, 32; 1 Corinthians, 42, 59; James, 202; Revelation, 14
Bierce, Ambrose, 22
Billy Budd, 9, 10, 16, 156n67, 252–53, 257–62; conscience in, 129, 146–50; critical reception, 11, 118n8; free will in, 245, 257–62
Blake, William, 166
Bligh, William, 215
Bolingbroke, Henry, 226
Book of Mormon. *See* Mormonism
Bowen, Francis, 72
Bowen, Merlin, 118n8
Bowler, Peter J., 91n8
Braswell, William, 11–12, 133, 280
Broad Church movement, 23–24, 25, 34–35, 49–50, 52
Brodhead, Richard, 250
Brontë, Anne, 25–26, 36
Browne, Thomas, 5
Browning, Robert, 186
Bryant, John, 15, 97, 104, 113, 119n10, 121n45, 122n71, 230
Buddhism, 9, 12, 105, 176, 187, 202–5

Buell, Lawrence, 78, 83, 136
Bunyan, John, 4, 156n61
Burke, Edmund, 149, 191
Burton, Robert, 6
Butler, Joseph, 6

Calvin, John, 244, 258, 273, 274, 280
Calvinism, 3–4, 7, 10, 16–18, 47, 135, 139, 244, 257, 258, 266–74, 282n6, 283n11
Camões, Luis de, 6
Cardano, Gerolamo, 167
Carey, Jonathan, 135
Carlyle, Thomas, 6–7, 15, 21, 23, 28–29, 30, 34, 53–58
Carruth, W. H., 84
Cary, Henry Francis, 99, 105, 107, 110–14, 116n2, 121n45, 122n73, 123n74
Cassels, Walter Richard, 31
Catholicism, 3, 12, 24, 50, 62, 176, 187, 202
Chai, Leon, 246–48
Chambers, Robert, 5, 25, 26, 72, 75
Channing, William Ellery, 6, 129–33, 139–41, 142, 146, 150
Charvat, William, 224
Chaucer, Geoffrey, 49
Church of Jesus Christ of Latter-day Saints. *See* Mormonism
Cicero, Marcus Tullius, 7, 45, 250
Clarel, 9, 14–15, 17, 21–23, 34–62, 71–73, 81–90, 99, 100, 102–5, 120n23, 145; art defined in, 83; conclusion of, 102, 104–5; critical reception, 13, 14, 71, 73–74, 95n63; Darwin in, 72–73, 83, 84, 88, 89–90; faith in, 118n10; geology in, 73, 75, 82, 85–86, 89; Hawthorne in, 22, 40, 49, 101, 102, 116n3; "heavenly love" in, 113–14; immortality in, 37, 43, 58–59, 61, 118n10, 177, 189; "implicit theism" in, 59, 69n59; meter and diction in, 88–89; missionaries in, 16, 17, 185–97, 200, 202, 207–8; Mormonism in, 16, 159, 174–75; sources for, 23, 34–35, 91n11; travel imagery in, 74. *See also* Victorian Crisis of Faith
Clarke, James Freeman, 8, 151n4
Clifford, William Kingdon, 31–32, 36
Clough, Arthur Hugh, 21, 23, 27–28, 36, 41–42, 59–60
Coan, Titus and Titus Munson, 186, 196, 206–7
Coffler, Gail, 258
Colacurcio, Michael, 99–100
Colatrella, Carol, 219
Cole, Thomas, 109
Colebrook, Claire, 218
Coleman, Dawn, 14
Coleridge, Samuel Taylor, 6, 44, 180n32; philosophical and theological views, 16, 35, 44, 243–47, 249, 251, 256–57, 260, 261; poetry of, 245–56, 259
colonialism (and anticolonialism), 211–15, 217, 219–21
comparative religion, 9, 11, 13, 44–45, 187
Comte, Auguste, 29–30, 32, 33, 44
Condorcet, Nicolas de, 167
Confidence-Man, The, 80, 94n50, 145, 168; critical reception, 13; Mormonism in, 171–72; religious doubts in, 7–8
Conforti, Joseph, 268, 269
Congregationalism, 3, 24, 132, 136, 283n19
conscience, 138–41, 148–51; in Melville's fiction: see *Billy Budd*; *Moby-Dick*; *Pierre*
Cook, Jonathan A., 13–14, 17, 106–7, 122n64, 223, 246, 280–81, 283n17
Corey, James, 71
Cornish, Allison, 114
Cotton, Elizabeth, 175
Coviello, Peter, 183n59
Cowan, Bainard, 13
Crane, Stephen, 22

Dante Alighieri, 6, 15, 97–99, 101, 102, 104–15, 116n2, 119n10, 121n45, 121n52, 166; Emerson on, 123n74; Milton and, 122n73
Darley, Felix, 8
Darwin, Charles: on cannibalism, 226–27; in *Clarel*, 72–73, 83, 84, 88, 89; Coan family and, 206; *Journal of Researches* (*The Voyage of the Beagle*), 5, 15, 71, 72, 75–81, 82–83, 88, 92n25, 93n33; in Melville's "The

New Ancient of Days," 93n47; *Origin of Species*, 4, 9, 25, 71, 74, 75–76, 84, 90. *See also* evolution
Darwin, Erasmus, 73, 135
Davidson, Arnold I., 232
Davis, Clark, 97
Davis, Merrell, 180n32
Delbanco, Andrew, 83, 89, 131–33, 156n67
Deleuze, Gilles, 252–53
Democritus, 7
determinism. *See* free will and determinism
Detlaff, Shirley M., 67n34
Dewey, Orville, 133–34, 143, 155n57
Dickens, Charles, 29
Dickinson, Emily, 61
Dickson, Walter, and family, 192, 195
Dillingham, William B., 15, 98, 117n6
Disraeli, Benjamin, 25, 29, 36
Donoghue, Denis, 83
Dostoevsky, Fyodor, 282
Drechsel, Emanuel J., 218
Dryden, Edgar, 12
Duban, James, 13, 105, 142
Dutch Reformed Church, 3, 130
Duyckinck, Evert, 6, 10, 85, 162, 165, 178; review of *Moby-Dick*, 11; review of *Pierre*, 168

Edmond, Rod, 215
Edwards, Jonathan, 6, 16, 243–45, 247, 249–51, 254–58, 260–61, 266, 268–72, 278; Edwardsianism defined, 283n19
Edwards, Mary K. Bercaw, 196, 218, 222, 224, 238n43
Eliot, George, 21, 25, 29–30
Elliott, Emory, 74, 268, 284n41
Ellis, William J., 5, 199
Emerson, Ralph Waldo, 6, 85, 89, 123n74, 132, 136, 223, 229; Mormonism and, 162; transcendentalism and, 43, 135, 154n49, 286n60; Unitarianism and, 134, 135
Emery, Allan Moore, 252
Emmons, Nathanael, 270, 271
Epictetus, 7, 167
Epicurus and Epicureanism, 7, 10, 265
Episcopalianism, 3
eschatology, 14
evangelicalism, 3–4, 23–24, 29, 198
evil, problem of, 4, 6, 10, 265, 283n17; in *Billy Budd*, 258; in *Clarel*, 41, 45; in *Moby-Dick*, 280–82. *See also* theodicy
evolution, 5, 15, 25–26, 71–72, 74–76, 83–84, 89–90, 91n8, 176

Feuerbach, Ludwig, 25, 29
Field, Maunsell B., 8
Finkelstein, Dorothee Metkitsky, 12
Finney, Charles G., 271
Fite, Olive L., 261
Fitzgerald, Edward, 10
Flaubert, Gustave, 155n55
Folques of Marseilles, 113–14, 124n98
Forrer, Richard, 267
Foucault, Michel, 213–14, 235n6; on biopolitical racism, 216, 220, 236n23
Franchot, Jenny, 74, 81, 90, 94n52
Franklin, H. Bruce, 12, 75, 200
Frazer, James G., 45
Freccero, John, 105
Frederick the Great, 57, 58
free will and determinism, 16, 243–62, 271–80
Frothingham, Octavius Brooks, 146
Froude, James Anthony, 21, 29, 32, 36
Fuller, Thomas, 6

Galápagos Islands, 5, 72, 75–78, 93n33; in *Clarel*, 81–82, 87; in *Mardi*, 93n41
Gansevoort, Maria, 3, 130, 183n68, 272
geology, 25–26, 45, 72; Ruskin on, 30–31. See also *Clarel*: geology in
German idealism, 6
Gibbon, Edward, 8
Gilmore, Paul, 259
Giordano, Matthew, 98–99
Giovanni, G., 109, 123n74
Givens, Terryl, 165–66
Gnosticism, 5–6, 47
Goering, Wynn M., 285n51
Goethe, Johann Wolfgang von, 6, 28, 29, 223
Goldman, Eric, 260
Goldman, Stan, 13, 71, 73, 75, 76, 87, 90, 91n11, 92n24, 95n63, 118n8

Gravil, Richard, 245
Gray, Asa, 72
Great Awakenings, 3, 136, 196, 283n11
Greek drama, 7
Grey, Robin, 249
Griswold, Rufus Wilmot, 190–91, 208
Grow, Matthew, 162

Hafiz, 10
Harper Brothers, 3
Hart, David Bentley, 273
Hatch, Nathan O., 284n24
Hawthorne, Nathaniel, 4, 7, 99–104, 115, 124n105, 156n61, 258; on Being, 248–49; *The Blithedale Romance*, 170; in *Clarel*, 22, 40, 49, 101, 102; *Dolliver Romance*, 115; on immortality, 62n4; *The Marble Faun*, 99; Melville's letters to, 91n10, 101, 116n3, 124n108, 189, 247–48; on Melville's religious beliefs, 15, 21–22, 49, 61, 74, 87, 98, 100, 103–4, 118n8, 119n12, 124n108, 269; Melville's review of *Mosses from an Old Manse*, 6, 7, 97
Hawthorne, Sophia, 103, 227
Hazewell, Charles, 170
Hazlitt, William, 7
Herbert, T. Walter, 13, 16, 152n20, 197, 216, 267, 278, 284n40
Higgins, Brian, 145
Hinduism, 8, 9, 12, 187, 200, 205
Hirrel, Leo, 266
Hoadley, John, 174
Hobbes, Thomas, 138, 148–49
Hodge, Charles, 282n6
Hole, Samuel Reynolds, 117n6
Hollander, Robert and Jean, 111
Holmes, Oliver Wendell, 8, 32
Holy Land: Melville's tour of, 8, 9, 21, 34, 98, 192, 195; Victorian interest in, 24–25, 29
Homer, 6
Hopkins, Samuel, 266
Howard, Leon, 160
Howe, Daniel Walker, 139
Howe, Julia Ward, 84
Howells, William Dean, 89
Hume, David, 6, 138, 250–51, 255, 265
Hurst, John Fletcher, 137
Hutchinson, Anne, 138, 149
Huxley, Thomas H., 31–32, 46

Islam, 10, 11, 12, 176, 181n41, 187

Jacoff, Rachel, 110–11
James, Clive, 113, 115, 116n2
Jerome, 138
Jesus Christ, 5, 7, 9, 25, 46, 60–61, 168, 188, 193, 204, 279; absence from *Moby-Dick*, 280–81
John Marr and Other Sailors, 10, 99
Jowett, Benjamin, 25, 31, 34
Judaism, 12, 13, 24, 67n34, 187–88, 194, 203, 205
Judd, Gerrit P., 198

Kane, Thomas, 162, 169
Kant, Immanuel, 6, 32
Karcher, Carolyn, 211
Keating, AnnLouise, 251
Keats, John, 104, 189–90, 192, 208
Kelley, Wyn, 113
Kenny, Vincent, 13, 91n11
Kevorkian, Martin, 14
Khayyam, Omar, 10, 117n6, 119n10
Kierkegaard, Søren, 13
Kitto, John, 4
Knapp, Joseph, 13
Knowles, James, 32
Kring, Walter D., 15, 118n8, 130, 135, 137, 151n7
Kulkarni, H. B., 200

Lamarck, Jean-Baptiste, 25, 72, 75
Lamartine, Alphonse de, 9
Lang, Andrew, 45
Larson, Edward, 76–77
Lawrence, D. H., 11, 226
Lee, Maurice, 250
Lewes, George Henry, 29–30
Locke, John, 138, 139, 224
Longfellow, Henry Wadsworth, 223
Lorentzen, Jamie, 13
Lowell, James Russell, 22, 32
Lucian, 7
Lucretius, 7
Luther, Martin, 84, 138, 139, 149, 265
Lyell, Charles, 25, 26

Macgregor, John, 9
Mallock, W. H., 31
Mansel, Henry, 32
Marcus Aurelius, 7
Mardi, 5, 93n41, 95n65, 180n33, 232; composition of, 180n32; critical reception, 162; Dante and, 99, 166; Monboddo in, 85; Mormonism and, 16, 159, 163–67, 170, 176; nature in, 89; Petrarch and, 121n45
Marivitz, Sanford E., 247–48
Marlowe, Christopher, 6
Marnon, Dennis C., 4
Martineau, Harriet, 25
Mason, Ronald, 12
Mather, Cotton, 6
Matthiessen, F. O., 118n8, 257
Maurice, Thomas, 8
McCall, Dan, 253
Melvill, Allan, 130, 152n20, 272, 285n47
Melville, Alexander, 177–78, 184nn75–76
Melville, Elizabeth Shaw, 8, 10, 97, 118n8, 123n86, 130, 133–35
Melville, Herman: critical reception, 11–12, 189; domestic behavior, 135; early religious exposure, 3–5, 7, 130, 159–60, 258, 284n41; education, 4; intellectual development and reading, 5–10, 180n32; pessimism, 98–99; poetry turn, 10, 83, 99; religious doubts and skepticism, 4, 5–8, 10, 15, 17, 21–22, 49, 61, 74, 87, 98, 117n8, 176, 247–50; religious pluralism, 12, 13–14, 119n12, 186, 205, 267; renewed interest in religion, 8–10, 99, 146, 205; on "visible truth," 91n10, 248
BOOKS: *See individual titles*
MISCELLANEOUS WORKS: "Hawthorne and His Mosses," 6, 7, 81, 97, 116n3; "Mr. Parkman's Tour," 161–62, 167, 170; "The New Ancient of Days," 93n47, 176; "Rammon," 202–5; "The South Seas," 172–73, 183n60; "The Tartarus of Maids," 109
Melville, Malcolm, 8, 130
Melville's Marginalia Online, 4, 105, 123n81
Menippean satire, 13
Metaphysical Society, 32, 34
Metcalf, Eleanor, 124n105, 133
Methodism, 3, 24, 198
Meyer, Joseph, 181n40
Milder, Robert, 13, 15, 73, 91n11, 117n4, 118n10, 267, 285n47
Mill, John Stuart, 23, 31, 32, 33, 44, 45–46, 61, 68n43, 68n48
Miller, William, 181n33
Milton, John, 6, 57, 109, 122n73, 141, 249; Channing on, 131, 132
missionaries, 5, 16, 185–208, 214–16; hostility toward Melville's novels, 11, 196, 197, 206; sympathetic views of, 190–91, 208
Mithraism, 69n49
Moby-Dick, 163, 181n34, 205, 207, 218, 224, 266–69, 271–82; Ahab in, 6, 122n64, 129, 141–42, 147–48, 230, 233–34, 246–47, 249, 251, 257, 266, 269, 272–81, 285n47, 285n51; Asian elements in, 200; Bayle and, 12; Calvinism in, 16–17, 268–69, 272–73, 278, 280; cannibalism imagery in, 277, 285n50; Coleridge in, 245–47; conscience in, 129, 141–42, 145, 147, 148; critical reception, 11; Dante and, 123n76; doubt in, 17; empyreal love in, 106–7; Extracts section, 92, 100, 101–2; form in, 88; free will (chance, determinism, predestination) in, 246–51, 257, 266, 269, 271–79; Hinduism in, 8, 200; influences on, 4–6, 7, 245; Ishmael in, 17, 82, 142, 152n20, 163, 201, 207, 213, 218, 230, 232–34, 245–46, 250–51, 277–79, 281; missionaries in, 16, 200–201; Queequeg in, 142, 200–210, 205, 207, 211, 217–18, 230, 232–34; racial representation in, 211, 213, 217–18, 233; sacramentalism in, 286n60; sermons in, 14, 155n51; theodicy in, 266–68, 272, 281
Monboddo, James Burnett, Lord, 85
Montaigne, Michel de, 5, 6, 180n32, 250
Moore, Maxine, 180n25

Morley, John, 31, 36
Mormonism, 3, 15–16, 159–78, 182n53; Book of Mormon, 16, 159–60, 163, 167, 180n32; Melville's posthumous baptism, 176–78, 184nn74–75
Muhammad, 130, 176, 181n41
Müller, Max, 45
Mumford, Lewis, 252
myths, 3, 12; Egyptian, 44

naturalism, 12
natural theology, 4, 5, 33
nebular hypothesis, 84, 94n57
Nelson, Frederick O., 195–96
Newman, Francis, 29, 36
Newman, John Henry, 29
Newman, Lea, 105, 109, 121n45, 123n81
Nichol, John W., 160
Niebuhr, Barthold Georg, 8
Noll, Mark, 283n11
Norberg, Peter, 4
Norton, Andrews, 6
Norton, Charles Eliot, 22, 32, 55
Nott, Josiah, 233
Numbers, Ronald, 75

Obenzinger, Hilton, 13, 73, 93n43, 159, 174
Olsen-Smith, Steven, 4, 116n2, 208n7
Olson, Charles, 95n61
Omoo: influences on 3, 5, 199–200; missionaries in, 16, 185–86, 197, 199–200, 207, 216, 219–20; narrator's name, 232, 237n25; religion and race in, 214, 219–21
Orientalism, 211, 225
Otter, Samuel, 233, 237n34
Ovid, 109–10, 114, 123n83

Paine, Thomas, 149, 179n14
Paley, William, 4, 152n20
Palmer, Edward H., 9
pantheism, 6, 246–47, 259–60, 273
Pardes, Ilana, 13–14, 17, 283n17
Parker, Hershel, 99, 134–35, 247, 272; on *Billy Budd*, 257; on *Pierre*, 143, 145, 156n61, 170
Parker, Theodore, 140, 142
Parkman, Francis, 161–63
Pater, Walter, 31
Patrick, Walter R., 250
Paul, 32, 42, 59, 204
Petrarch, 121n45
Piazza Tales, The: "Bartleby, the Scrivener," 16, 81, 145, 232, 245, 251–57, 272; "Benito Cereno," 81, 145, 157n72, 252–53; "The Encantadas," 15, 72, 75–83, 86, 87, 89–90, 109, 207; "The Piazza," 123n76
Pierre, 7, 122n64, 201; conscience in, 129, 139–40, 142–45, 148, 154n49; critical reception, 170; Dante and, 109; empyreal love in, 106; free indirect discourse in, 142, 155n55; incest and polygamy in, 167, 168–71, 181n40; Mormonism in, 16, 159, 167–71; religious doubts in, 7, 170–71, 173; Unitarianism in, 152n20
Placher, William, 279, 286n53, 286n55, 286n58
Plato, 5, 43, 46, 147, 258
Plutarch, 7
Polynesia, 211–34; cannibalism, 221–27; Mormons and, 163, 172–73, 179n17; myths, 3; pidgin vocabulary, 199, 218; religion and race representations, 105, 211–14, 217, 220, 237n34; tattooing, 211–13, 229–34, 237n34. *See also* missionaries
Porter, David, 222, 227
Potter, William, 13, 92n19, 94n55, 105, 187n
Pratt, Orson, 170
Presbyterianism, 3, 24, 201, 283n19
Price, Richard, 139
Priestley, Joseph, 6, 250, 251
Promey, Sally, 137
Protestantism. *See individual denominations*
Proudhon, Pierre-Joseph, 39
Pusey, Edward Bouverie, 31
Pyrrhonism, 250

Quakerism, 3, 24, 285n51

Reade, Winwood, 31
Reardon, Bernard, 69n56
Rebhorn, Matthew, 157n72

Redburn, 124n108, 167
Rees, Robert, 159, 163
Reid, Thomas, 139
Renan, Ernest, 39, 189
Renker, Elizabeth, 135, 153n25
Reynolds, David, 76
Robillard, Douglas, 15
Robinson, David, 139
Romanes, George L., 31, 36
Rosenstock, Bruce, 168
"Rose Poems." See *Weeds and Wildings*
Rossetti, Dante Gabriel, 104
Rousseau, Jean-Jacques, 224–25
Ruskin, John, 15, 21, 30–32, 34
Rust, Richard, 159
Ryan, Robert Charles, 108

Sa'di, 10, 117n6
Said, Edward, 74–75
Samson, John, 76, 197
Sanborn, Geoffrey, 221, 224–26, 231
Schelling, Friedrich Wilhelm Joseph, 245–46
Schleiermacher, Friedrich, 6, 44
Schmidt, Leigh Eric, 137
Schopenhauer, Arthur, 9, 98, 261
Sealts, Merton M., Jr., 4, 254
Sedgwick, William Ellery, 12
Seelye, John, 152n20
Seneca, Lucius Annaeus, 7
Servetus, Michael, 149
Shaker theology, 3, 7
Shakespeare, William, 6, 104, 141, 180n32
Shaw, Lemuel, 133, 151n4
Shelley, Percy Bysshe, 71, 88
Sherrill, Rowland, 13, 180n33
Shurr, William, 13, 73, 82
Singleton, Charles, 106
Sivarandam, Sujit, 197
slavery, 236n23; Christianity and, 210n36; *The Confidence-Man* and, 172; *Pierre* and, 141, 156n59
Smith, Adam, 138
Smith, Joseph, 159–61, 163, 165–67, 170, 171, 176, 179n14, 181nn33–34
Smith, W. Robertson, 45
Somerset, Edward Seymour, Duke of, 31, 66n24, 68n44, 69nn49–50
Sordello da Goito, 113
South Seas in Melville. *See* Polynesia
Spanos, William V., 257–58
Spencer, Herbert, 45
Spinoza, Baruch, 6, 247
Stanley, Arthur P., 9, 25, 32, 34–35, 51
Stein, William Bysshe, 13
Sten, Christopher, 13, 123n76
Stephen, Leslie, 23, 31, 32–33, 36, 44–48, 52, 69n50
Stephens, John Lloyd, 9
Stern, Milton R., 12
Stewart, Charles S., 5, 199, 219
Stoicism, 7
Stone, Geoffrey, 12
Stowe, Harriet Beecher, 207, 210n36, 268
Strang, James, 171–72
Strauss, David, 8, 25, 29, 39
Sweeney, Douglas, 267, 268, 270, 283n11
Sweet, Nancy, 156n59
Swinburne, Algernon, 31, 34, 37–38, 104

Tasso, Torquato, 6
Taylor, Charles, 17, 205, 265–66
Taylor, Nathaniel, 270–71, 273, 279
Tennyson, Alfred, Lord, 21, 23, 26–27, 32, 34, 36, 41, 60–61, 104
Thackeray, William, 25
theodicy, 4, 14, 17, 265–68, 272, 279
Thompson, Lawrance, 12, 73, 91n11
Thomson, James, 98–99
Thomson, William McClure, 9
Thoreau, Henry David, 140, 223
Tillich, Paul, 118n10
Timoleon, 10, 99; "Buddha," 202
transcendentalism, 135, 140, 165, 267; in *The Confidence-Man*, 168; in *Pierre*, 142
"traveling theory," 74–75, 77, 89
Tricomi, Albert, 197
Trinitarianism, 139, 279, 286n58
Tucker, Abraham, 167
Turner, James, 266
Twain, Mark, 22, 195, 207, 210n36
Tylor, Edward B., 45
Tyndall, John, 31–32
Typee: cannibalism in, 221–26, 228, 230; critical reception, 196, 207; homoeroticism in, 227, 229–30, 232;

Typee, continued
Kory-Kory in, 218, 227–32, 234; missionaries in, 16, 185–86, 197–200, 207, 213, 215–17, 223, 228; racial representation in, 211–13, 217–21, 227; sensuality in, 105, 227; sentiment in, 223, 226–29, 239n57; sources for, 3, 5, 199–200, 219, 222, 237n34

Unitarianism, 3, 7, 15, 24, 47, 129–51, 267; Melville scholarship on, 152n20
Universalist Church, 3

Verduin, Kathleen, 123n74
Victorian Crisis of Faith, 21–22, 25–36, 48; *Clarel* and, 15, 34, 36, 45, 51, 59, 61–62
Virgil, 6, 88, 137
Volney, Constantine de, 9
Voltaire, 56

Walker, William, 173
Wallis, Mary, 226
Warburton, Eliot, 9
Watson, E. L. Grant, 11
Weaver, Raymond, 11
Weeds and Wildings, 10, 15, 124n105; "Rose Poems," 97, 100, 102, 104, 106–15, 119n10, 122n65, 122n71, 123n86, 175
Weinauer, Ellen, 169
Wenke, John, 13
White-Jacket, 125n108, 167, 280
Whitman, Walt, 57
Whittier, John Greenleaf, 162, 169
Widmer, Kingsley, 251
Willey, Basil, 69n56
Williams, Roger, 138
Williams, William Chickering, 133, 134, 137
Wilson, A. N., 31
Wood, Leonard, 190
Wordsworth, William, 33, 35, 61, 104
Wright, Conrad, 135
Wright, Frances, 7
Wright, Jean Melvill, 4
Wright, Nathalia, 12

Yannella, Donald, 135
Yeats, William B., 48
Yoneyama, Masafumi, 152n20
Yothers, Brian, 13, 14, 73, 86, 119n12
Young, Brigham, 159, 162–63, 169, 171–74

Zend-Avesta, 167
Zoroastrianism, 5, 12, 47, 69n49